Labor in Cross-Cultural Perspective

SOCIETY FOR ECONOMIC
ANTHROPOLOGY (SEA) MONOGRAPHS

Deborah Winslow, University of New Hampshire
General Editor, Society for Economic Anthropology

Monographs for the Society for Economic Anthropology contain original essays that explore the connections between economics and social life. Each year's volume focuses on a different theme in economic anthropology. Earlier volumes were published with the University Press of America, Inc. (#1–15, 17), Rowman & Littlefield, Inc. (#16). The monographs are now published jointly by AltaMira Press and the Society for Economic Anthropology (http://nautarch.tamu.edu/anth/SEA/).

Labor in Cross-Cultural Perspective

E. PAUL DURRENBERGER AND
JUDITH E. MARTÍ, EDITORS

Published in cooperation with the
Society for Economic Anthropology

A Division of
ROWMAN & LITTLEFIELD PUBLISHERS, INC.
Lanham • New York • Toronto • Oxford

AltaMira Press
A Division of Rowman & Littlefield Publishers, Inc.
A wholly owned subsidiary of The Rowman & Littlefield Publishing Group, Inc.
4501 Forbes Boulevard, Suite 200
Lanham, MD 20706
www.altamirapress.com

PO Box 317, Oxford, OX2 9RU, UK

British Library Cataloguing in Publication Information Available

Library of Congress Cataloguing-in-Publication Data

Society for Economic Anthropology (U.S.). Meeting (2001 : Milwaukee (Wis.))
    Labor in cross-cultural perspective / edited By E. Paul Durrenberger and Judith Marti.
        p. cm. — (Society for Economic Anthropology (SEA) monographs ; no. 23)
    Papers originally presented at the 2001 Annual Meeting of the Society for Economic Anthropology held in Milwaukee.
    Includes bibliographical references and index.
    ISBN 0-7591-0582-0 (cloth : alk. paper) — ISBN 0-7591-0583-9 (pbk. : alk. paper)
    1. Economic anthropology—Congresses. 2. Labor—Cross-cultural studies—Congresses.
I. Durrenberger, E. Paul, 1943– II. Marti, Judith. III. Title. IV. Series: Society for Economic Anthropology monographs ; v. 23.

GN448.2.S63 2006
306.3—dc22   2005009749

Printed in the United States of America

∞™ The paper used in this publication meets the minimum requirements of American National Standard for Information Sciences—Permanence of Paper for Printed Library Materials, ANSI/NISO Z39.48-1992.

Contents

Preface

All useful products are the creation of human labor, but there are many ways to organize and reward labor. This is a book about the anthropology of labor. We have collected ethnographic work from around the world from a variety of economic anthropologists all focused on the topic of labor. A number of overlapping issues surface when we begin to try to understand the role and place of labor in processes of production and in social orders. These we discuss in the introduction.

This is how the book came into being: Judith Martí's students' work on topics that involved organized labor or the organizing of labor in one way or another aroused her interest in the topic as a question for anthropological treatment. Meanwhile, E. Paul Durrenberger's work took him in a similar direction with his studies of labor unions in Chicago. We asked ourselves, how do we bring the insights that have served anthropology so well in the past to bear on these phenomena? What are the relevant questions? How do we answer them? We corresponded with each other and others, and we began to organize sessions at professional meetings to compare notes and exchange ideas.

As we sought to bring the comparative perspective of anthropology to bear on the ethnographic details we were finding, we decided that we would cast our net wider and proposed to the executive board of the Society for Economic Anthropology that the topic of the annual meeting of 2001 should be "labor." We worked with the board to develop a call for papers, which we circulated widely. In response, we received some forty-eight responses, of which we could only accommodate fifteen in our program. We expanded the program by organizing another session for the American Anthropological Association meetings later the same year and by a well-attended poster session.

For those who are interested in the peer review process and the status of the work we present here, this book is a result of a multistage review process. First, we screened the abstracts for their contribution to the topic and the call for papers. Second, we submitted a tentative program to the executive board for their review. Then contributors presented their papers at the meeting in Milwaukee and we invited them to submit complete papers for us to consider for the volume. We scheduled ample time for discussion at the Milwaukee meeting and, as is the custom of the Society for Economic Anthropology, there was lively and challenging discussion. We then reviewed the complete papers and invited the contributions that we present in this book. We edited the completed papers and, finally, three readers selected by the Society for Economic Anthropology's editor, Deborah Winslow, read the whole manuscript and offered suggestions.

So, this book has also been a collaborative process from its inception to the crafting of the call for papers to the review process and finally in its publication. We thank all of our colleagues for their participation in the process, whether they submitted abstracts, presented papers, helped with the reviews, or contributed discussion and comments at the meeting.

E. Paul Durrenberger
Pennsylvania State University

Introduction

E. Paul Durrenberger and Judith Martí

Every social order has to recruit labor—whether by wages, slavery, households, or lineages—and organize, direct, or channel labor to determine who does what, when. Labor is what humans do, across time and across space. Labor is fundamental, crucial for satisfying our most basic needs (Malinowski [1944] is often cited). Labor thus provides a window for understanding all of human behavior, thought, and organization from the most macro-level of a global political economy to the most micro-level of the individual worker in a household. It is what we do and who we are. It shapes, and is shaped by, how we see ourselves as individuals or components of larger groups. Labor is embedded in all relationships from kinship and household relationships to non-kin social networks, to market based employee/employer relationships, to political relationships such as ruler and ruled that direct the recruitment and uses of labor. Labor divides and links—it defines class and crosses class lines and it may link or divide gender and age categories.

Because labor is at the core of what a society is all about, its conceptualization has been central to the writings of the founders of the social sciences. Weber's Protestant Ethic thesis saw modern capitalism as a melding of capitalistic business ethic and Protestant religious ethic; Durkheim's social solidarity rests on his distinction between differences in division of labor between mechanical and organic integration. The role of labor is foundational to Marx's thinking.

Some—for example, Paul Ransome (1996)—take a very narrow perspective on what labor is. Ransome distinguishes between work, "defined as activities which are performed in return for direct financial remuneration" (10) and labor, obligatory toil such as housework—reproductive work. He further distinguishes craft, job, occupation, and employment as separate categories. As the chapters in this book will show, we take a much broader view of labor. These differences do not distinguish between labor and anything else but different means of recruiting and organizing human effort for productive and reproductive work. If we confine our category of work to wage or contract work, we eliminate a wide range of effort in social orders not organized by capitalism, as well as rendering large segments of labor in capitalist social orders invisible.

John Calagione and colleagues (1992) look at festival work, music, and artistic creations as labor: "We argue for looking at the rich material on leisure, popular entertainments and ostensibly nonwork activities certainly not connected to a restricted notion of 'economic' action to gain insight into the labor processes" (2). In *High Art Down Home: An Economic Ethnography of a Local Art Market*, Stuart Plattner (1996) takes us into this realm of labor to gain insight into the labor processes. Nor would we consider nurturance, which embraces a variety of models of exchange from nonreciprocal to reciprocal to pooling to market. Penny Van Esterik (1996) shows how the Thai term for providing food or eating together, *liang*, "provides the most widely understood arena for negotiating and displaying power and hierarchy, yet it is also a metaphor for intimacy and closeness" (23) and how it is basic to understanding the construction of gender and power in Thailand. Nurturance is explained by several theories of exchange. But at base, nurturance is the provision and sharing of food. It rests on work.

Economists are known for their qualification "all other things being equal," while anthropologists have made a discipline of the fact that things are never equal. Economic anthropology today is not best thought of as economics in non-Western settings, but rather as anthropological approaches to economics in any setting. To meet their material needs, people produce, distribute, and consume goods. Economic anthropology explains how these systems are organized, how they operate, how they got that way, how they relate to other systems, how people behave and make decisions in terms of such systems, and the consequences of people's actions for the systems. Another goal of economic anthropology is to describe these systems in locally meaningful terms that are universally relevant and useful for understanding any economic system at any time and any place (Durrenberger 1996).

Eric R. Wolf (1999) visualized a complex dynamic of the interworkings of ideology, organization of labor, and disposition of products, such as Katherine A. Bowie and Stephen A. Kowalewski describe in this volume. In his 1997 preface to *Europe and the People without History*, Wolf understood political economy as the study of "societies, states, and markets as historically evolving phenomena" (ix) and questioned whether there is a universally valid analysis of capitalism. He wanted to understand how unstable systems of power to control labor develop, change, and expand their reach through time and space over the structures that determine and circumscribe peoples' lives.

Social configurations have always been parts of larger contradictory connections. Since the rise and expansion of capitalism to all parts of the planet, the connections and contradictions have intensified until the system is so complex that it is quasi random. That doesn't mean we cannot understand it, but it does mean we cannot predict with any degree of accuracy.

Wolf (1997) argued that the main causes of this expansion and its effects are the processes by which a social order mobilizes labor. To understand that, he focused on the institutional structures that guide relations of people with each other and with natural environments. The combination of ownership and management of resources with the use of hired labor in factory production enabled capitalism to undo other arrangements. There have been changes in the distribution of factories, markets, the recruitment of workers, technology, and organization to produce differing mixes of products. In early times, the capital of traders financed these arrangements. In recent times, computer-based information and control technologies with new means of transportation are decentralizing production and increasing production in households and workshops that are more flexible than factories.

As anthropologists and others committed to the ground-truth testing of ethnography encounter the reverberations of globalization in the locales where we work, we can either retreat into a romantic localism or contend with the realities as they present themselves to us and the people we are trying to understand. In this book we are concerned with the ways different social orders recruit and allocate labor, whether to the limited ends of households, the unlimited ends of firms or corporations, or the more diffuse ends of nations or states. The contributors illustrate the strong point of anthropology, the examination of great issues in terms of the minute observations of everyday life, ethnography. We rely more on observation than assumption. Setting their studies in the complexities of evolving global systems, the contributors bring our attention to a number of related issues—global structures, family size, the organization and use of household labor in different circumstances and locales, and consequences of different uses of labor as people struggle with gender and age identity, with prestige and status. Some of these dimensions are the hard surfaces of political and economic structures that control labor, while others are the internal mindscapes of ideological construction and culture. The examination of everyday life shows us the importance of networks of relationships to support migrants, to organize production, and to harness volunteer labor. At virtually every turn, we see that economic relations are embedded in broader social relations.

STRUCTURES OF DOMINATION

Denizens of industrial lands are accustomed to the logic and organization of factories and how these have spread to all fields of endeavor from scholarship to medicine and other professional fields to redefine work and workplaces. In highly stratified social orders defined by differential access to productive resources (Fried 1967)—the kinds of societies in which factories can come to exist—agency and structure may have different positions in different classes because access to resources—hence, class position—rests on differential power, a structural dimension given by position in the social order. The chief goal of the union movement in industrial social orders is to redress the structural imbalance and give some sense of agency to those who provide labor but do not necessarily control the conditions for its use. It does this by attempting to develop collective power based on structural principles other than wealth. The intentions of the powerful are more consequential than those of the unpowerful. Actions of the powerful create structures that shape the cognition of the powerless. Cognition and agency may determine structure for some classes while for others structure may determine cognition; the causal arrows may be functions of class position or power rather than being constant across the whole social order. Even the question of causal relations between structure and cognition is not a constant but varies by class. As Bowie shows in her chapter, decisions of ruling elites in Thailand had much more scope and established structures to contain and limit the agency of their slaves and mute their resistance. We don't think twice about the separation of the value a person produces from the person who produces it in a factory system based on wages. But it seems odd to us to do the same thing under the rubric of the ownership of persons—slavery—via kinship relations or gender relations or ethnic relations. One way or another, different social orders recruit labor and focus it to the purposes of those with the power to do so. Ethnography shows us the various means by which products are separated from those who produce them—various ways of organizing class structures and economic systems.

Those who listen to or read about current events also detect a change, a weakening of the grip of the factory on production as firms contract out various functions and as households once again take up the slack. Flexibility becomes a byword for the corporation and that affects the people who provide its labor no less than households that must deal with the exigencies of ever-changing realities of policy and fast-paced economic change. Christian Zlolniski documents flexible migrant household labor in the Silicon Valley. With globalization and the new economy comes an increase in subcontracting that utilizes flexible, unskilled, and semiskilled labor and taps into their social networks for labor recruitment and control. Paid workers draw on unpaid, invisible household labor, as entire families perform one janitorial job

People make decisions in terms of what they know from experience and what they can learn, on information that may be in short supply, misleading, or wrong. Other things being equal, as our economist colleagues would say, the feedback loop is the experience that allows us to evaluate information and our techniques for gaining it. Its purest form defines the realm of science, and thus of anthropology. In its everyday form, people have to make do with what they can get. Our contributors discuss how they do that in various circumstances of risk and uncertainty of markets, governments, and the quality of materials and workers.

The observations of the anthropologists whose work we have brought together in this book challenge a number of comfortable models and assumptions—from the ideology that markets are as natural as weather to the more academic models of public versus private domains and the scholarly speculations on the function of remittances in households of migrant workers.

Throughout we see the importance of social relations and of that principle of all social relations, reciprocity.

We anthropologists have just recently acknowledged that nations and states are important. Much of our understanding and conceptualization of the fundamental operation of states comes from the work of archaeologists who, though they may lack the detailed economic and political data of ethnography, are not blinded by the same kinds of ideological factors that limit ethnographic treatment of classes and states. We can agree on the complexities of despotism and class relationships of long ago and far away if not in the here and now. Kowalewski and his colleagues argue that military violence, not technological change, was a factor in the reorientation of labor and urban transformation in pre-Columbian Oaxaca, and that rather than hierarchical and centralized control of labor, intensive community-level labor built the fortified, terraced hilltowns that were a response to military threat. John M. Steinberg argues that in Viking Age Iceland, Icelandic chiefly social organization maintained its power by differential control over labor, rather than land. For both Kowalewski and Steinberg, control of labor figures as an explanation for political/economic change.

Bowie shows how ideological blinders distort our view of slavery in Thailand, where it was a major means for control of labor through the early decades of the twentieth century. She uses documentary evidence and ethnohistorical methods to show that peasants did not organize resistance or revolt because the principalities controlled labor by a number of different but mutually reinforcing means, such as geographic diversity, economic specialization, social diversity, internal village heterogeneity, and the manipulation of ethnic identities—all of which inhibited slaves from making common cause with one another. Reading Bowie reminds us that there is nothing especially new in the tactics of labor fragmentation to strengthen the political and economic power of the ruling elites and weaken peasantry (Griffith 1993; Stull, Broadway, and Griffith 1995).

Susan D. Russell documents how the flexibility of household labor in kin-based commercial fisheries can adjust to fluctuations in income and output. She shows the relationships of ecological factors (such as the populations of various commercially valuable species of fish), technologies of fishing, policies, households, and gender ideologies in her understanding of this fishery. In contrast to the Philippines where, because of official corruption and lack of enforcement, policy plays a relatively minor role in fisheries, in Canada, policy caused fisheries to bifurcate (Apostle et al. 1998) into an inshore fishery that became more or less dependent on household welfare payments while an offshore fishery followed the industrial-factory model of production with trawlers and vertical integration and was supported by corporate welfare payments. In Norway, where state policy supported fisher organizations and their influence in policymaking, household production persisted.

So while the logic of capitalism may be the same, its variability in operation produces heterogeneity of forms. As it expands, it sets up new entrepreneurial scenarios that attract new workers, middle classes, and entrepreneurs that face the problem of how to fit their cultural understandings to the requirements of this ever-changing political economy. "How these adaptations unfold is not predictable a priori" (Wolf 1997, xiii).

VERSATILITY, MOBILITY, ADAPTABILITY

The point of the ethnographic work we bring together in this book is to show that there are many ways that these adaptations develop in a complex and quasi-random global system of economic, political, and social relationships. Sutti Ortiz's contrasts between the Argentine lemon and coffee industries show that seasonal migrant labor brings flexibility but also hidden transaction costs for both citrus and coffee growers, including the risk of not knowing how unfamiliar laborers will treat delicate crops.

Tamar Diana Wilson discusses the relationships between networks, transnational migration, modernization, and capitalism. Like many others in this volume, Wilson sees networks as social capital because they allow greater access to information and thus diminish risk, increase flexibility, and play a role in employment clustering and the expansion of opportunity. One of the themes of the recent ethnography of labor represented in this book is that while the social networks are responsive to policy and opportunity, they are not phenomena of the market, and do not appear as transactions in any national or neoclassical bookkeeping.

Some scholars of global processes have lamented increased homogeneity. Like Wolf (1997), Ulf Hannerz (1996) challenges the assumption that increased interconnectedness threatens diversity. As cultural forms vanish, new diversity results from incessant creolization processes in the innovations that interconnectedness fosters in four organizational frames: everyday life, the deliberate and asymmetrical forms of the state, the market, and purposeful movements for change. People continuously create cultural knowledge in practice. Like Wolf, Hannerz has a strong sense of the power bases of cultural processes that he understands in terms of everyday life, states, and the market.

Wolf (1997) argued that the production and trading of commodities incorporates the producers in various ways. One way or another, they sell their labor and thus "align and realign their understandings to respond to the opportunities and exigencies of their new conditions" (xii). We cannot predict on theoretical grounds alone how people will do this. Thus, "more ethnography is urgently required" (xii) to understand the variety of processes and responses.

The contributors to this volume provide just that—more ethnography on just these topics. Martha Woodson Rees challenges the orthodoxy that male migration supports Zapotec households in Mexico through remittances and shows that it is women's work that makes men's migration possible. Putting aside Western terms that impose inapplicable concepts, and taking gender and ethnicity into account, she overthrows a view of household labor as unpaid, invisible, and devalued.

Dolores Koenig challenges another common model of households. Scholars of globalization have argued that with modernization there is a shift from other forms of households to nuclear families that are sufficiently flexible to respond quickly to economic change. Koenig's ethnographic work in Africa shows, however, that traditional kinship patterns of extended families are an economic strategy in a changing environment of risk, uncertainty, and unpredictability, and of infrastructure failure.

VALUES, POLICIES, AND WORKER RESPONSES

Wolf (1997) contended that people do not freely reinvent themselves, choose their own cultural constructions, or resist their constraints because strongly determinate circumstances may inhibit or encourage creativity, induce resistance, or stifle it. "Only empirical inquiry can tell us how different peoples, in their particular varied circumstances, shape, adapt, or jettison their cultural understandings" or are inhibited from doing so (xiii).

This is played out in rural Iowa. In her chapter in this book, Barbara J. Dilly argues that the cultural value of volunteer labor production is the reproduction of a viable rural culture in a deteriorating economic environment. While neoclassical economic discussions center on the demand for public goods and maximization of personal benefits, and sociological approaches see volunteer labor as a function of social networks organized for social good, Dilly's ethnographic and anthropological approach offers a fuller account and explains that because volunteer labor is not offered as a market commodity but produces value, it is part of an informal economy characterized by reciprocity within social networks.

When we look at labor as the production of value rather than as a market commodity, we see the role of gender and gender ideologies in making women's labor invisible either because it is centered in households or because it is directed at the reproduction of labor rather than the creation of commodities. Mary Beth Mills (1999) shows how infrastructure improvements in the northeast of Thailand allowed rural people to develop new economic relations with distant markets and shifted peasants more decisively toward commodity production. Women from prosperous landed families do not go to work for wages in factories in Bangkok as part of a farm household's economic strategy but in response to images of modernity from elite-controlled markets. If working in Bangkok challenges one gender ideal of restraint and virginal purity, the women are still dutiful daughters supporting their families at home to pay expenses of farming, educating younger siblings, constructing houses, Buddhist generosity to indicate morality, and televisions and refrigerators to proclaim modernity. Robert C. Marshall, in this volume, also argues that Japanese women who form worker cooperatives do not do so as a challenge to gender ideology. They control their work schedules in order to continue to meet standards they hold sacred, the care of their families. In contrast, nineteenth-century Mexican women street vendors riddled their letters of protest to city hall with rhetoric of the vulnerable and submissive female to turn patriarchal ideology into a tool of resistance to challenge government regulation of labor. Their actions clearly reflected a take-charge manner that frequently accomplished their goals (Martí 1993, 2001).

Images of modernity, Mills argues, contrast with lived experiences of wage labor. Wages go mainly for food and crowded living quarters. Running water, electricity, transportation, markets, and entertainment come with pollution, noise, congestion, crowding, isolation and insecurity, and unhealthful and oppressive working conditions. Workers do not accept employers' image of traditional patron-client relationships, but any protest is disciplined. Schools teach people how to bow but do not "impart a critical awareness of one's rights under the law" (Mills 1999, 124). The labor movement is weak and "one cannot ignore the historical willingness of the Thai state to mobilize forces of repression or coercion against open expressions of discontent" (170). Translation: they shoot demonstrators. The women in Karaleah S. Reichart's study of West Virginian mine workers are also disciplined by corporate elites and yes, they also shot workers who organized in the mines.

ECONOMIC GLOBALIZATION AND NEOLIBERAL PARADIGMS

Just as ground-truth checking is a safeguard against abstract fantasies of the logical but invalid, we must transcend the local to understand the global processes and structures that contain and constrain local activities and systems.

In the second edition to their book *The Evolution of Human Society*, Johnson and Earle (2000) consider "the emerging world order of global economic integration, which liberal economists hope will encourage the democratic, middle-class structures of the liberal state" to be a continuation of evolutionary processes of intensification, integration, and stratification that have always characterized social evolution. Expanding market involvement integrates wider areas and processes. With great commercial wealth, elites fund elections to defend their special interests and increase stratification.

> So-called imperfections in the market persist, both because the market itself exacerbates problems such as pollution that must be controlled by government and because the expanding market creates opportunities for control that lead to monopolies, corruption, wars over resources and other self-activities that the emerging world order strives—with heroic, if often unsuccessful, efforts—to overcome. (389–90)

If one wonders why concentrations of wealth do not achieve the same function as its wider distribution, it is a matter of economic theory, or from our more anthropological perspective, theology. The conditions may restrict government expenditures for social and welfare programs. Many in developing countries may regard increasing wages and government expenditure on public infrastructure and social programs to be progressive and may be suspicious of such constraints.

Even economists such as Debraj Ray (1998, 705) recognize this. "Just because the [World] Bank or [International Monetary] Fund imposes certain conditions for financing, as economists, we need not accept these conditions as appropriate. It is important, often, to look at these conditions from the point of view of the country itself, and not just from the point of view of international lenders or funding agencies."

Such programs are components of the policy of development from above with its roots in neoclassical economic theory based on the notion of dynamic sectors or areas of development that spread and trickle down to the rest of the system. This approach tends to be urban, industrial, capital intensive, dominated by high technology. An alternative view is development from below, which focuses on the satisfaction of basic needs of the inhabitants of an area and concentrates on small-scale, regional, rural (labor-intensive) use of appropriate rather than high technology. Structural adjustment programs originate at national levels and require substantial financing from the top down (Hackenberg 1997).

Governments may retain a sense of sovereignty, but international policymaking bodies often determine their economic policies. The philosophy, "nattily attired in scientific robes" (Finan 1997, 79), that guides these policies is neoliberalism, whose tenets include the assumptions that markets distribute goods and services most efficiently, that free trade increases the wealth for all partners, that increased consumption is the measure of well-being and national wealth, and that the role of government is limited to providing institutions that facilitate free markets. Anthropologists have both shown that structural adjustment programs have imposed negative burdens on the disadvantaged and underprivileged and critiqued the theory as fallacious (Finan 1997). James Greenberg (1996) shows how these programs do not have uniform consequences but depend on local endowments, as well as how the policies are implemented and mediated at different levels between the global and the local, and points out the dearth of valid data upon which to judge effects.

Whatever the possibilities, whatever the contribution anthropologists might make to correcting fallacious theory or pointing out misguided practice, the devastating effects of the Structural Adjustment Programs (SAPS) are real and continue to be real. Cunningham and Reed (1995) conclude that conditions mandated by the World Bank and IMF include increased export industry and cuts in government spending that increase poverty, especially for women and children. Most women work on small-scale agriculture. SAPS favor export industries that increase the prices of agricultural equipment for export so women farmers with few resources can no longer afford such equipment. As several of the chapters in this book indicate, women then are forced into export industry where they work long hours for low wages. SAPS require reduction in government spending and the first to go are social services, including child care. Middle-class women are the most likely to work in these areas and are the first to get fired. SAPS have failed to reduce poverty and debt, but are seen as successful because they have increased export-oriented industry. They have attracted multinational corporations, who move their factories from first-world locales to the third world where there is cheap labor and little labor organizing. Women are the preferred laborers, cheaper by 40 percent, seen as a docile, flexible supply of labor that can be hired when economy grows, and fired when it slows.

Here, one frequently heard argument in defense of such programs of third-world industrialization is to wonder where else uneducated men or women would get jobs that pay any wage at all. The conclusion of such arguments seems to be that the factories are doing their workers a favor by hiring them. The reality is that these people have been deprived of alternatives such as farming or working in their own households for their own programs of local improvement. Factory work and capitalism are not natural phenomena like a hurricane or a tornado or an earthquake. They are creatures of policies enacted by those with the power to implement them. These policies make markets paramount and create pools of "free labor," people with no alternative but to sell their labor. In the face of such policies as the Enclosure Acts in Britain, farmers had no choices. Historically household economies always win the competition for labor if all other things are equal. But such policies as Enclosure Acts, development programs, structural adjustment programs, and work laws make sure that all things are not equal and provide the pool of willing labor, if people with no alternatives can be called willing.

Consider some statistics: from 1970 to 1999, incomes in the poorest 20 percent of the world decreased by up to 23 percent, while incomes of the richest 20 percent increased by 15 percent; the 358 billionaires of the world own assets that exceed the combined annual incomes of countries with 45 percent of the population of our planet (Mills 1999); the economic crashes in Asia, Russia, and Brazil are correlated with the high interest rates commanded by IMF (for example, Russia at 150 percent) (Weisbrot, Naiman, and Kim 2000). In the front of the developed world, in the United States (where 1 percent of the people control 48 percent of the wealth, the next 19 percent control 46 percent of the wealth, and the bottom 80 percent of the people control 6 percent of the wealth), the real median wage of workers has not changed for the past twenty-seven years (Weisbrot, Naiman, and Kim 2000). If this is so for the most powerful land of the first world, what hope of trickle down or spreading effects of equality of any kind in the third?

Pierre Bourdieu (1998) observed that globalization is "the extension of the hold of a small number of dominant nations over the whole set of national financial markets" (38). Just as some think corporations are doing women a favor to allow them to work for minimum wages in their third-world factories, some see outsourcing of tasks and labor as a benefit to workers. But such strategies of labor recruitment arouse fear and insecurity among the workers because they might not be able to discern or live up to the standards of their contractor or the person to whom they are contracted.

Bourdieu's larger perspective suggests that corporations put workers in perpetual and habitual danger of losing their jobs to reduce their costs and increase workers' compliance. Corporations that can link distant facilities, flexible labor supplies, training, communications, and technological knowledge in global networks avoid any connection with places. Boeing doesn't have to be linked to Seattle or Chicago, General Motors to Detroit or the United States. The neoliberal ideology of the market creates institutional structures through which such corporations can seek the lowest wages and increase competition rather than cooperation among workers in different locations. Across the first world, labor unions have lost power and influence. Bourdieu (1998) observes that these developments are the creations of policies, not natural or inevitable developments. Zlolniski documents how undocumented immigrant laborers who constitute the flexible labor pool in the Silicon Valley call on intrahousehold-kin networks to resist corporate control over their labor.

POLITICAL ECONOMY, LOCALIZED CULTURAL REPRESENTATIONS

On the theoretical side, Wolf (1997) argued, all the social sciences face two kinds of realities—of the natural world and what people do in it and how people understand that world and what they do. We can disregard one or the other, but Wolf argued for mediating them by attending to the relations of power that mediate between "the mobilization of social labor in society and the mental schemata that define who does what in the division of that labor" (xiv). This requires us to understand that both social tasks and mental representations are distributed variably among gender, age, and other categories, which directs us to understanding the processes that bring these variable repertories of understandings into some kind of concordance—how knowledge is accumulated, communicated, and withheld, and how cosmological orders are built up and invoked to construct and accumulate some forms of power and to disarticulate others, and how some conceptual structures come to dominate others in forming genders, classes, ethnicities, and alternative schemata that contest the hegemonic ones. These processes define the units we want to understand by joining history, political economy, and ethnography. There are no arbitrarily or a priori delimited societal or cultural entities. They are dependent, not independent, variables. Hannerz (1996) suggests the central questions are how to identify the component relationships of emergent social structures that may cover great distances and cross national boundaries and understand how these relationships are related to one another.

On this there is a widespread consensus among anthropologists of different theoretical leanings. Today, Arjun Appadurai (1996) argues, global flows of meanings challenge the idea of culture as a set of organic relationships among populations, areas, political organizations, languages, and coherent assemblages of meanings—a notion that derives from nationalism. Cultures are not integrated wholes with edges. As media and states treat identities as primordial, people therefore act as though identities are. States create ethnicities that drive others to construct opposing ethnicities, nationalities in search of their own states. The technicalities of censuses and welfare legislation with cynical electoral politics can produce ethnic identities and fears. Nation-states provide the imaginative and ideological materials of ethnic mobilization to which global flows of sounds, images, and finances contribute to energize local issues to propel violent responses. Thus global finance, labor recruitment, and communication organize complex social formations—some for violence, some to keep peace, and some to relieve famine.

Since Anthony Wallace (1961) suggested that sharing of ideas is problematical in complex societies, anthropologists have faced the challenge of understanding just what ideas are shared among whom and to what extent. Now that we have some methods of answering these questions (Moore et al. 2001), such ethnographic situations as these present ripe grounds for the development of theories of culture as well as descriptions of cultures and the extent to which they are shared across such divides as those of the conqueror and conquered, genders, and management and workers.

In this book, Marshall shows how women in Japan have developed networks of women's cooperatives to resist wage-labor employment and hierarchic control and in the process have changed the marketplace and the context in which goods are produced and distributed, and thus challenged the structure of power. Resistance takes another form as workplace networks transfer into political activism. Here, flexibility and temporary status of labor is not a function of control by management, but built in as a benefit by workers, in opposition to the power structure. The transfer of household skills to the marketplace may be understood as an extension of women's traditional household labor—food preparation, provisioning—which blurs the private/public domains framework. This example shows the intricate mutual relations among structural and cultural dimensions of labor and power, and shows how tax policy places a limit on the women's alternative economic structures. Again, the structures that policies create determine the latitude for thought and action.

EMPIRICAL ENFORCEMENT OF CONCEPTUAL DUALITIES

In questioning the necessity of power and prestige accruing to the public domain, Judith Martí (1993) surmounts the distinction between public and private domains. The borders between the two spheres blurred when women applied interpersonal skills and interpersonal relations honed in the private domain to organize a union in the public sphere of the Duke University Medical Center (Sacks 1988), or use networks formed in the private sphere to agitate for better working conditions in the Santa Clara canneries (Zavella 1987), or as Zlolniski discusses in this volume, to informally organize the actual work people do in the formal sector.

Reichart's chapter in this book explores the relations among capitalism, waged labor, and unequal gender relations in the mines of West Virginia. Industrial capitalism in the form of the coal industry effected social change when it sought to relegate women to the private domain by means of draconian regulations that governed life in the company towns where coal companies could set the rules of inhabitation of their housing, purchases in their stores, and even what foods women prepared and enforce them through constant surveillance and armed force. Because their effective strategies of resistance during union strikes and their presence in the public domain—sometimes on the side of the union and sometimes not—have gone unrecorded, women were made invisible to history as well as to the market. In this example, we see again the importance of social networks in support of political and economic relationships as women organized strategies of reciprocal support under conditions of uncertainty, and passive as well as active resistance.

In a more contemporary context, Katherine Newman (1999) mobilized a remarkable group of anthropology students to crisscross lines of color and class to learn about people who lived near Columbia University in New York. From the inside, Newman's research team shows us not only exotic cultural constructs but also the structures of opportunity and failure that determine levels of health, child-rearing practices, marriage, reproductive decisions, employment, and achievement. To understand, we must first see them in their own terms, as the realities that determine peoples' life courses, not as a set of assumptions from the economic or sociological theory.

The working poor whose lives Newman documents believe as much as the great American middle class that we are all responsible for our destinies and masters of our fates. In this ideology, the forces of economic destiny and structural inequality and government policy "pale beside the assumption of individual autonomy, control, and mastery" (Newman 1999, 216). For the working poor, people who have struggled against the structural odds, "no one is entitled to a free ride" (216). Family values must stretch "to accommodate the special demands that living in a poor neighborhood imposes" (217) and even such laudable values cannot "turn back the damage done by arsonists, the failures of the city to invest in the schools in their neighborhoods, the disappearing job base, and the infection of drugs" (229).

If values could get people through school, the working poor of Harlem would have no worry. But education is not a right in our land and the working poor were anxious because they "could not see how they were going to pay for their return to school" (Newman 1999, 159).

Newman does not suggest that the poor cause their own poverty. She is clear that the working poor "do not need their values reengineered or lessons about the dignity of work" (1999, 297). Newman's ethnography shows graphically and in detail that hard work does not in fact pay off. The market will not solve the problem of poverty. Employment, even full employment, will not solve the problem of poverty if wages are as low as they now are. And that level of wages is not a consequence of markets but of the subsidization of low wages by public policy, a policy of corporate welfare payments, often disguised as individual welfare, aimed at maintaining a ready supply of cheap labor.

In this volume, at the other end of the status and wage scale of labor, John R. Pulskamp also looks at the relations among capitalism, waged labor, and ideology. He discusses the transformation of the workplace as the traditional autonomy of professional workers is eroded by increasing management through increasingly bureaucratized companies or public agencies, as new categories of professionals enter into waged-labor employment. This results in transferring power to the employer and the proletarianization of professional workers as the procedures of factory production—Taylorism—gain ascendancy. In the process, professionals lose prestige and their identities merge with those of workers. Professionals may resist these moves by forming organizations, some of which take the step to become bargaining agents for their members and thus unions rather than professional organizations. Here, professionals who are in the structural position of workers but maintain the ideology of identity as professionals rather than workers can be an obstacle to attaining their goals. We see in this example the dynamic interplay of structural and ideological factors. Again, they sell their labor—as Wolf said—the only question is whether they set the conditions, as the Japanese women's cooperatives do (Marshall, this volume), or whether the employers set the conditions as the aristocrats of Thailand did for their slaves (Bowie, this volume).

With globalization and the new economy, Zlolniski shows in this book, firms increasingly slough off functions to subcontractors to utilize flexible, unskilled, and semiskilled immigrant labor, especially for janitorial functions. He shows how this allows informal means to operate through the social networks of immigrants to recruit and control labor. One paid worker may organize a whole household to help accomplish his task, so invisible household labor not only sustains and reproduces labor, it also amplifies the formal on-the-books labor. The networks that immigrants have formed for their own subsistence in the new land also offer a means for unions to organize and mobilize collective labor resistance. This provides another example of adaptation to structural features as people develop networks of support, as contractors use them to replenish their labor supply to serve corporations, and as unions use the same networks to organize workers for resistance.

IDEATION, IDEOLOGY, AND SOCIAL PRACTICE

Wolf (1999) explored the ways cultural configurations articulate with power to arrange the settings and domains of social and economic life, especially the allocation and use of labor. He wanted to understand and analyze the ways relations that organize economic and political interactions shape ideation to make the world intelligible. He said that the "specification of ideologies in cultural terms can only be a part of our task. We must also know how these cultural forms engage with the material resources and organizational arrangements of the world they try to affect or transform" (Wolf 1999, 289).

Wolf (1999) argued that people use their ideas as guides to act upon the world and change it, and thus affect their ability to act in the future and, in the process, work and understand the world and cope with the power that directs their work and shapes their understandings. When activity changes the world and social relations, people reappraise their relations of power and their cultural constructs.

Marshall Sahlins (2000) has long discussed the relationship between events and ideas, between agency and social order. What is determined? What do we decide? His intent is to show that the West did not simply dominate the Rest with the onslaught of capitalism, but that each locale, each people, responded according to their own lights. The Europeans provided the means to achieve locally meaningful cultural goals.

For a long time, Western social scientists did not recognize the new synthetic formations peasant and tribal people were creating as they surfed the global economy in service of their own cultural aspirations. Western researchers saw urbanization, migration, remittance, dependency, labor recruitment, and ethnic formation and not the translocal cultural whole. Others have written whole books to say what Sahlins manages in a sentence, "Symbolically focused on the homeland, whence its members derive their identity and their destiny, the translocal community is strategically dependent on its urban outliers for material wherewithal" (Sahlins 2000, 523). Sahlins leaves no doubt that patterns of culture determine events—how people think determines what they do. Fair enough, but that leaves unanalyzed the whole question of how they got into those situations in the first place. Where did the Europeans come from and why did they go to those places? What processes established the conditions to which people in different locales understood and responded in their own terms?

Jean Lave's practice theory (e.g., 1988) offers a more theoretical treatment of the relationships among thought, culture, and action than Sahlins or Wolf did, but Wolf conceptualizes the relationships of power and labor more clearly. Wolf poses significant questions, Lave provides a theoretical means of answering them, and Romney and others provide the means.

Practice theory suggests that actions shape thought. As Lave and Wenger (1991, 33) put it, "agent, activity, and the world mutually constitute each other." Practice theory suggests that "priority, perspective and value are continuously and inescapably generated in activity" (Lave 1988, 181). Hannerz (1992, 1996) reviews a wide-ranging literature on culture theory to arrive at a similar notion of the continual creation of culture. To control activity, then, is to shape thought.

If we can specify the relations among structural, organizational or tactical, and interpersonal power—how the exercise of power organizes settings, controls settings, and shapes interpersonal action—we can show how power shapes activity and thus those patterns of thought we call culture. Thus we can move from the assertion that there is cultural hegemony to an understanding of how it operates by shaping daily activity and through it, thought.

Lave and Wenger (1991) argue that while abstractions do not change people's actions, changing the nature of concrete everyday life to involve them continuously in action does. This raises the question of the relationship between thought and action. E. Paul Durrenberger (1997) showed that union members' awareness of their union is related to the structures of their worksites. Durrenberger and Erem further showed (1999b) that when the structures of everyday action change, members' patterns of thought change. These findings support D'Andrade's (1999, 89) conclusion that patterns of thought are "strongly influenced by the structure of the world as normally perceived." Or, "Cultural reality is more often reality-shaped than culturally constituted" and corroborate Barrett's observation (1999, 251) that "social structure (or material culture) shapes people's lives at least partly independent of their consciousness."

TOWARD AN AWARENESS OF SOCIAL CLASS

It is true, as Wolf argued (1999, 281) that the brain receives inputs from nature, but "grinds out and permutes distinctions that are not found in nature but are cultural." In his musings on the nature of religion, Wolf is correct to suggest that the firing of neurons might account for imaginary beings—the work of Michael Persinger (1987) shows it clearly. Wolf is also right to suggest that belief is a consequence of power, as others who have discussed the relationship between belief and thought have shown before.

Through this whole body of writing, as Sahlins collected in his latest book, *Culture in Practice* (2000), is an echo, a faint suggestion that surfaces now and then, as though it is waiting to break through, but never does. What's the difference between the politics of personality in Melanesia and the politics of position in Polynesia? Polynesian chieftains could control household economies and Melanesian leaders could not. That's the difference between being able and not being able to appropriate other people's labor. In short, that's the difference between systems built on class and those that are not. The Brits were amazed to find social orders without "heads"—acephalous, they called them—headless. How can a society maintain order without a place for everyone and everyone in his place? A society without a state is inconceivable, as Sahlins points out (549, 552). It took American anthropologists of Sahlins' own, at least early, cultural ecological persuasion to systematically describe these structural differences as egalitarian, rank, and stratified social orders and the dynamics of each. Consider another pithy Sahlins summary sentence: "The amount of work (per capita) increases with the evolution of culture, and the amount of leisure decreases" (130). Work for whom? Again, the suspicion of class; and on the next page, "One third to one half of humanity are said to go to bed hungry every night" (131). Or the next, "This is the era of hunger unprecedented. Now, in the time of the greatest technical power, is starvation an institution" (132). He observes that the evolution of economy enriches as it impoverishes, but this insight, so well put, never breaks through to become an organizing concept. It stays buried under layers of cultural determination. So it is culture that organizes production, not power (194) and the differences of dress are only symbolic. The differences between the dungarees and chambray of prisoners, sailors, and college kids. The difference between any of these and the suits and ties of the military-industrial ruling class? Why symbolize these differences? Whence the differences to symbolize if not class? Whence class? In Sahlins (2000, 223), we find a subheading, "The Ruling Class." But this is about the elite in South Vietnam, an elite that American policy kept in power. Never do these insights about Vietnam extend to the United States or generalize to become a concept of his anthropology.

In the mid-1960s, during the American war in Vietnam, Sahlins visited Vietnam and observed (229) that the peasants he encountered were excluded from the West's historical processes. Maybe. But in the highland village in Thailand where Durrenberger was living not long after, a shaman reported seeing many more Americans in the land of the dead and wondered why that might be. "It is difficult to see," Sahlins reported (2000, 232), "how the peasant can be 'on' the side—'for' the cause—of a world from which he has been structurally excluded." Right. Class. Power. And so for the Americans who fought in Vietnam, and so for the Americans who do not vote in our elections. Consider this observation about Vietnam: "Hijacked American dollars in the cities capitalize a whole social system, and one in which just this unequal distribution of wealth is proper, a constituted condition." And so for the widening economic gap in the United States, recently engraved in 2001 even more strongly in our policies and realities by an asymmetric tax cut to favor the rich. In Vietnam it was not a question of personalities, of "who is the matter" (Sahlins 2000, 238), but of "a political structure of economic interest . . . a constituted relation to the national economy and the underlying population." Just so—as the difference between Polynesia and Melanesia. Is this because of differences of general cultural perceptions between peasants and rulers? No, not here. Not where Sahlins sees the undeniable in front of his eyes—where class and power were palpable. This was a thing of here and now and not a thing of long ago and far away.

And, yes, surfers of the global economy do focus on their home communities (Sahlins 2000, 523), but this only raises the question of the means—how do capital, ideas, and people move around the planet to make this possible? This system transcends the local—and again Sahlins raises the question, but then leaves it in the background. Time to bring anthropology home.

Class is our most important ethnographic and theoretical problem. All of the other things we discuss and debate—from gender to literary stylings, from ritual to choice of mates, from conceptualization to commerce—are derivative. No longer is there refuge for people outside a global system of information, culture, commerce, capital, labor, and affect, all of which mutually affect the others, all of which class determines.

Our theoretical stylings must start and end with the stark observations of the radically unequal distribution of wealth and power. Postmodern fashionability demands nuance, shading, shadows, moving from the clear light of day into the recesses of the less visible. We need fewer distinctions, not more, so we can see the phenomenon more clearly rather than obscure it. We need a less nuanced approach to class. What happened to the working class that was so clearly visible to the Industrial Workers of the World that they could unambiguously state in the preamble to their constitution that there are but two classes—the employing class and the working class—and they have nothing in common?

What Scott observed of Southeast Asian peasants in *Weapons of the Weak* (1985) is true of other stratified societies—not only are people not fooled by ruling class symbolic or ritual proclamations but they also know from hard-won experience that head-on resistance only results in tragedy. It may be that every generation in every land must pay a price in blood to learn that lesson, but what the peasants taught the Yale scholar remains true.

The safer alternative is to remain within the law and try to organize for common purposes. Some countries, such as those of Scandinavia, demand it. But even this element of corporatist states is weakening under the hammer of global economics as manufacturing moves its well-paying jobs to the cheap labor markets of the third world to achieve greater profits for shareholders, save on their tax bill, undercut the tax base, and threaten the social contract that has underwritten class cooperation on mutually agreed terms. Other lands, such as the United States, incorporate into law charters for the employing class to systematically prevent such cooperation and destroy whatever gains the working class may threaten to make through organization. The Taft-Hartley amendments to the Wagner Act are examples. Local and national administrative interpretation of the law is another avenue. The third avenue is the inevitable and tragically predictable internal collapse of organized labor under the weight of its own political necessities and personal proclivities (Durrenberger 2001).

In this volume, Frank Zeidler analyzes the national trend of Democrats and Republicans joining together to thwart any threat from a successful third party—one that enjoys any electoral success—and shows the reason we have a two-party system nationally. He shows, from his long and wide experience, the co-optation of dissident politics. He shows historic relations among utopian groups and settlements, American political parties, Marxist thought, and conditions of labor and labor unions.

Anthropology is one component in the training of the managerial middle class in the United States. Universities reassure the middle class of the essential rightness, humanness, and universality of its outlook and ratifies its right to control (Ehrenreich 1990). If anthropology ceases to challenge cultural constructions or to provide scientific evidence on the human condition and ratifies the outlook of one class of one economic system, it becomes an ideological tool of that class. In this it becomes like the medieval church ratifying the concept of divine right to justify the kings and their aristocracies. This is the consequence of the capitulation of science to the dictates of the middle class.

Eric Wolf discusses the distance in the Marxian tradition between Promethean Marxism and Systems Marxism—the one given to utopian imaginings and the other to pedestrian understandings, the one to the poetics and politics of liberation and the other to scholarship and science (1997, xii). Here, we bridge that distance by including in the book not only the writings of our colleagues, other anthropologists, scholars, and observers of the human condition but also of Mayor Zeidler, four-term Socialist mayor of Milwaukee who, under the auspices of Alice Kehoe (who ably took care of all the local arrangements for our meeting), took time to address the Society for Economic Anthropology at our meeting in his town. He shows us that what we learn can be useful, useful not just for bandying ideologies about and framing slogans but for getting sewers and streets and schools and making life better for people.

REFERENCES

Apostle, Richard, Gene Barrett, Petter Holm, Svein Jentoft, Leigh Mazany, Bonnie McCay, and Knut Mikalsen. 1998. *Community, State, and Market on the North Atlantic Rim: Challenges to Modernity in the Fisheries.* Toronto, ON: University of Toronto Press.

Appadurai, Arjun. 1996. *Modernity at Large: Cultural Dimensions of Globalization.* Minneapolis: University of Minnesota Press.

Barrett, Stanley R. 1999. "Forecasting Theory: Problems and Exemplars in the Twenty-First Century." In *Anthropological Theory in North America*, ed. E. L. Cerroni-Long, 235–54. Westport, CN: Bergin and Garvey.

Bourdieu, Pierre. 1998. *Acts of Resistance: Against the Tyranny of the Market*, trans. Richard Nice. New York: New Press.

Calagione, John, Doris Francis, and Daniel Nugent, eds. 1992. *Workers Expressions: Beyond Accommodation and Resistance.* Anthropology of Work Series, ed. June Nash. Albany: State University of New York Press.

Cunningham, Shea, and Betsy Reed. 1995. "Balancing Budgets on Women's Backs: The World Bank and the 104th US Congress." *Dollars and Sense* 202 (November 1): 2–25.

D'Andrade, Roy. 1999. "Culture Is Not Everything." In *Anthropological Theory in North America*, ed. E. L. Cerroni-Long, 85–104. Westport, CT: Bergin and Garvey.

Durrenberger, E. Paul. 1996. "Economic Anthropology." In *Encyclopedia of Cultural Anthropology*, vol. 2, ed. David Levinson and Melvin Ember, 365–71. New York: Henry Holt.

———. 1997. "That'll Teach You: Cognition and Practice in a Union Local." *Human Organization* 56(4):388–92.

———. 2001. "Explorations of Class and Consciousness in the U.S." *Journal of Anthropological Research* 57(1):41–60.

Durrenberger, E. Paul, and Suzan Erem. 1999a. "The Abstract, the Concrete, the Political, and the Academic: Anthropology and a Labor Union in the United States." *Human Organization* 58(3):305–12.

———. 1999b. "The Weak Suffer What They Must: A Natural Experiment in Thought and Structure." *American Anthropologist* 101(4):783–93.

Ehrenreich, Barbara. 1990. *Fear of Falling: The Inner Life of the Middle Class.* New York: HarperCollins.

Finan, Timothy J. 1997. "Changing Roles of Agriculture in Global Development Policy: Is Anthropology (Out)Standing in Its Field?" *Culture and Agriculture* 19(3):79–84

Fried, Morton. 1967. *The Evolution of Political Society: An Essay in Political Anthropology.* New York: Random House.

Greenberg, James B. 1996. "Political Ecology of Structural-Adjustment Policies: The Case of the Dominican Republic." *Culture and Agriculture* 19(3):85–93.

Griffith, David. 1993. *Jones's Minimal: Low-Wage Labor in the United States.* Albany: State University of New York Press.

Hackenberg, Robert A. 1997. "Rural Development in the Global Village: An Oppositional Political Ecology?" *Culture and Agriculture* 19(3):71–78.

Hannerz, Ulf. 1992. *Cultural Complexity.* New York: Columbia University Press.

———. 1996. *Transnational Connections: Culture, People, Places.* New York: Routledge.

Johnson, Allen W., and Timothy Earle. 2000. *From Foraging Group to Agrarian State.* 2nd ed. Stanford, CA: Stanford University Press.

Lave, Jean. 1988. *Cognition in Practice: Mathematics and Culture in Everyday Life.* Cambridge: Cambridge University Press.

———. 1996. "The Practice of Learning." In *Understanding Practice: Perspectives on Activity and Context,* ed. Seth Chaiklin and Jean Lave, 3–32. Cambridge: Cambridge University Press.

Lave, Jean, and Etienne Wenger. 1991. "Situated Learning: Legitimate Peripheral Participation." In *Learning in Doing: Social, Cognitive and Computational Perspectives.* Cambridge: Cambridge University Press.

Malinowski, Bronislaw. 1944. "A Scientific Theory of Culture and Other Essays. Basic Needs and Cultural Responses." In *A Scientific Theory of Culture and Other Essays*, ed. B. Malinowski, 91. Chapel Hill: University of North Carolina Press.

Martí, Judith E. 1993. "Economics, Power and Gender, Introduction." In *The Other Fifty Percent: Multi-Cultural Perspectives on Gender*, ed. Mari Womack and Judith Martí. Prospect Heights, IL: Waveland Press.

———. 2001. "Nineteenth-Century Views of Women's Participation in Mexico's Markets." In *Mediating Identities, Marketing Wares: Culture, Economy and Gender among Market Women*, ed. Linda Seligmann. Stanford, CA: Stanford University Press.

Mills, Mary Beth. 1999. *Thai Women in the Global labor Force: Consuming Desires, Contested Selves.* New Brunswick, NJ: Rutgers University Press.

Moore, Carmella C., A. Kimball Romney, Ti-Lien Hsia, and Graig D. Rusch. 2001. "Universality of the Semantic Structure of Emotion Terms: Methods for the Study of Inter- and Intra-Cultural Variability." *American Anthropologist* 101(3):529–46.

Newman, Katherine. 1999. *No Shame in My Game: The Working Poor in the Inner City.* New York: Alfred Knopf/Russell Sage Foundation.

Persinger, Michael A. 1987. *Neuropsychological Bases of God Beliefs.* New York: Praeger.

Plattner, Stuart. 1996. *High Art Down Home: An Economic Ethnography of a Local Art Market.* Chicago: Chicago University Press.

Ransome, Paul. 1996. *The Work Paradigm.* Avebury, UK: University of Nottingham, School of Social Sciences.

Ray, Debraj. 1998. *Development Economics.* Princeton, NJ: Princeton University Press.

Sacks, Karen. 1988. *Caring by the Hour: Women, Work and Organizing at the Duke Medical Center.* Urbana: University of Illinois Press.

Sahlins, Marshall. 2000. *Culture in Practice.* New York: Zone Books

Scott, James C. 1985. *Weapons of the Weak: Everyday Forms of Peasant Resistance.* New Haven, CT: Yale University Press.

Stull, Donald D., Michael J. Broadway, and David Griffith, eds. 1995. *Any Way You Cut It: Meat Processing and Small-Town America.* Lawrence: University of Kansas Press.

Van Esterik, Penny. 1996. "Nurturance and Reciprocity in Thai Studies." In *State Power and Culture in Thailand*, ed. E. Paul Durrenberger, 22–46. Southeast Asia Studies Monograph, 44. New Haven, CT: Yale University Press.

Wallace, Anthony F. C. 1961. *Culture and Personality*. New York: Random House.

Weisbrot, Mark, Robert Naiman, and Joyce Kim. 2000. *The Emperor Has No Growth: Declining Economic Growth Rates in the Era of Globalization*. Washington, DC: Center for Economic and Policy Research.

Wolf, Eric R. 1997. *Europe and the People without History*. Rev. ed. Berkeley: University of California Press.

———. 1999. *Envisioning Power: Ideologies of Dominance and Crisis*. Berkeley: University of California Press.

Zavella, Patricia. 1987. *Women's Work and Chicano Families: Cannery Workers of the Santa Clara Valley*. Ithaca, NY: Cornell University Press.

Sewer Socialism and Labor: The Pragmatics of Running a Good City

Frank P. Zeidler

The city of Milwaukee has had a reputation of being a "clean city," that is, a city with a good and honest government. This reputation has largely been derived from the presence of a Socialist movement in the city since about 1850. In the twentieth century it had three Socialist mayors who held office in total for thirty-eight years—however, not continuously. In 1982 a two-volume publication by Elmer A. Beck appeared, describing this movement from 1897 to 1940. Beck entitled this book *The Sewer Socialists.*

This appellation of the Socialist movement came as a result of a heated exchange in a 1932 convention of the Socialist Party of America in Milwaukee. At that time, the Socialist Party of America was sharply divided between a group known as the "Old Guard" and a group known as the "Militants," who were allied with other groups.

Attorney Morris Hillquit of New York, who had long been the party chairman, led the Old Guard. It represented an older Jewish and Yankee constituency in the party. The Militants included younger Jewish members who favored closer ties with the Communists. Other groups did not support Hillquit, but did not support the Communists either. They included pacifists like Norman Thomas and the Milwaukee Socialists who at one time were also considered a part of the Socialist Party's "Right Wing."

In the 1932 convention the Old Guard candidate for chairman of the Socialist Party of America was Hillquit. The candidate supported by the Militants and other groups was Daniel W. Hoan, who then had been mayor of Milwaukee for sixteen years. Hillquit, in accepting the nomination for chairperson, said of his opposition that they were "an unholy alliance of so-called Militants, extreme opportunists and 'practical' Socialists who are first concerned with getting into office." He also said, "I do not belong to the Daniel Hoan group to whom Socialism consists of merely providing clean sewers of Milwaukee." Hillquit said of himself, "I am above all else a Marxian socialist."

It was this description of Milwaukee Socialists by Hillquit that Elmer Beck selected to title his comprehensive work on the history of the Socialist Party of Milwaukee as "The Sewer Socialists." This label has since spread so that people now speak of "the Sewer Socialists" and not just of "the Socialists." This name inspires a curiosity as to who were the Sewer Socialists, what they believed, and how they carried out their beliefs in practical city administration.

In a forward to Beck's book I said,

> The title "Sewer Socialism" is not to be considered a derogation by the author. Rather it reflects a time when the practical Socialists of Wisconsin were held in some derogation by Socialist theoreticians, especially in the eastern states, who said the Milwaukee Socialists were incapable of great theoretical thinking and were content to see that rubbish was collected and sewers installed. The Milwaukee Socialists readily accepted the label as an answer to their detractors whom they considered impossibilists who could not win any elections.

However, it must be said that people committed to the market economy now apply the term "Sewer Socialists" as a kind of a sneer to all Socialists. Socialism itself is now considered a very wrong philosophy on which to base public administration, especially because "look at what has happened in 'socialist' Russia."

To understand the concepts upon which Socialists acted pragmatically in government requires reciting history. The term "socialism" now has many interpretations and definitions according to the views of people who call themselves "Socialist." In Milwaukee its basic concept was the public ownership and democratic management of the basic means of production and distribution. Except for the opinions of a few people, it did not mean a fully collectivized society. Milwaukee Socialists were not interested in owning the corner grocery store. Socialists held the idea that there is a general public good that must be served, and this idea of a public good implied especially the protection of the working class and the poor. This, in turn, had major implications for pacifism, nature protection, education, social support systems, and cultural advancement.

In practical terms this resulted, among other things, in Socialists' demands for clean air and clean water. The latter demand resulted in a world famous sewerage system and two water purification plants. The term "Sewer Socialism" tends to obscure emphasis on land use planning, good housing codes, clean streets, park and playground development, good fire protection, and honest policing.

The Socialists were especially active and successful in promoting labor and social legislation. The Milwaukee Socialist movement in the first decade of the twentieth century, together with Progressive Republicans (a now vanished group), had a potent influence on the establishment of Social Security and social support systems by the 1930s, systems unfortunately now being systematically destroyed through adverse legislation.

To understand the pragmatic actions of Socialists in local government, then, one has to look to historical development. It should be noted that the Milwaukee Socialist movement started about 1850 with persons who left the German states as a result of the failure of the Liberal Revolution of 1848. August Willich of Ohio, a refugee of the revolution and later an American Civil War colonel, helped found the Socialer Turnverein in Milwaukee in 1853, now the Milwaukee Turners. The original American Turnvereine (gymnastic societies) fostered ideas of social liberalism but especially of the right of free speech and clean government. This tradition still exists in Milwaukee and some Milwaukee mayors have been members of the Milwaukee Turners.

The people who left the German states after 1848 were called "the '48ers." They had a great influence on improving the ethics in American governments. With the '48ers were persons who were Freethinkers—*Freidenker*—persons who also held Socialist ideas. An organized Freethinker movement of German tradition no longer exists in Milwaukee. Numerous Freethinkers also were in the Socialist movement.

The German immigrants who brought Socialist ideas to Milwaukee as well as to much of the United States were influenced by two different concepts of German Socialist thought. For Milwaukee the most important influence over time was that of Ferdinand Lassalle (1825–1864), a lawyer who founded the General German Workers Association, whose descendant political party is the Social Democratic Party of Germany. Lassalle's concept was that the condition of the working class could be improved through legislation and participation in political organizing as well as in labor organizing. Some of Lassalle's proposals to improve the condition of the working class were incorporated later by Bismarck in an attempt to suppress the growing Socialist and labor movements in Germany. These Bismarckian laws later found their way to Milwaukee and were a factor in the Milwaukee Socialists making proposals for a shorter workday, vacations for workers, and injured worker protection.

Another and more spectacular influence was that of Marx (1818–1883) and Engels (1820–1895), who offered a militant kind of socialism, based on the idea that the exploiters of the working class—the bourgeoisie, the nobility, and the clergy—would not give up their deleterious control over human progress except by force. This concept was later embodied in the communist movements of the world.

Marxism, of course, is more than this idea. It also included the set of ideas that is called "dialectical materialism." This concept, crudely expressed here, is that relationships in the material world determine all other relationships of society, including law and thought; and that changes in material relationships take place following the Hegelian concept of thesis, antithesis, and synthesis. Thus a feudal society has produced a capitalist society and a capitalist society, because of its internal contradictions, must by laws of nature produce a socialist society. A socialist society will then at some time wither away to a truly communist society. This concept is called "scientific socialism." Lassalle's idea of improving the working-class condition is thought of as utopian socialism.

The concept of Marx and Engels also was that there were only two classes to society—the bourgeoisie and the proletariat (the owner and the workers)—and that there must be class warfare. The Leninist and Stalinist interpretations of Marx and Engels were quite strong in Milwaukee in the 1930s and 1940s and made it difficult for practical Socialist administrations to advocate step-by-step legislative improvement of working-class conditions.

Milwaukee Socialists accepted parts of both Lassalle's and Marx's theories. For many, "socialism" amounted to a religious conviction. While many held that there were two classes, capitalists and workers, they also believed that changes could be made by labor organizing and getting favorable legislation. Class war, if at all, was to be conducted at the ballot box.

In 1864 Marx organized an International Workingmen's Association. There was a chapter of Marx's First International in Milwaukee in 1876, of which a fiery orator named Joseph Brucker was a member. What happened to this chapter is not recorded. There were also anarchists and people influenced by Mikhail Bakunin (1814–1876), the Russian anarchist and bitter foe of Marx, though the anarchists did not play as significant a role here as they did in other American cities in the 1880s and 1890s, particularly in Chicago.

Concurrently with these German Socialist ideas, there were communal societies of various types in the United States, like the Oneida community, the Rappites, and the Owenites of New Harmony, Indiana. In Wisconsin, people of Yankee stock in the 1840s formed a socialist type of communal society in Kenosha, Wisconsin. This was a "Phalanx" of the type of community advocated by Charles Fourier (1772–1837) of France. This group moved to near Ripon, Wisconsin, where their communal society was known as Ceresco. People of this group became Free Soilers and as Free Soilers they helped form one of the first two sections of the Republican Party. It can be said that the Republican Party has its anchor roots in a truly communalist society.

As the industrial revolution spread throughout the United States in the period after the Civil War and conditions of hardships were exacerbated for workers, labor movements spontaneously organized, mostly in the skilled trades. This was true in the Milwaukee area. The Socialist movement until recently was closely tied to the unions.

The conditions of industrial labor resulted in the formation of the Knights of Labor in 1869. The Knights of Labor had many members in Milwaukee in the 1880s. Membership included small business as well as labor, and under Terence V. Powderly (1849–1924) emphasized negotiation rather than strikes to obtain better working conditions. There was also a Populist movement in Milwaukee in the 1890s. From both of these movements came principles and goals for society that influenced Milwaukee Socialist governments.

At the same time, there was in Milwaukee a Socialist movement led by a fiery German, Paul Grottkau (1846–1898). The hostility of Socialists against the trusts and railroads and corporations was much stronger than that found in the Knights of Labor. In 1875 Grottkau and others published a newspaper with the German title *Der Sozialist*. By the 1880s there was a Socialist Labor Party in Milwaukee, which advocated many reforms like the eight-hour working day.

There were great national strikes that affected the coal, railroad, and iron industries in the 1870s and 1880s. They had their effect in the twentieth century on Milwaukee Socialists and still do today. May 1, 1886, was the day set for a national demonstration by the Knights of Labor and others for the eight-hour workday. Demonstrations in various parts of the nation brought strife between police and workers. Of particularly worldwide importance were the events in Chicago known as the Haymarket Riot of May 4, 1886, in which policemen and workers were killed and later five men were sentenced to hang and three others later pardoned. One day later, in Milwaukee, on May 5, 1886, six or seven workers were shot to death by the Wisconsin militia in the Bay View area of Milwaukee for demonstrating for the eight-hour workday. Events like these across the nation shattered the Knights of Labor but made way for a new union development in the formation of the American Federation of Labor in 1886 and the Wisconsin State Federation of Labor about 1893. Thereafter the Socialist movement considered the Socialist Party as its right hand for improving the conditions of labor and the labor movement as its left hand. Much of the later progress of the Socialist city administrations was made only through the support of organized labor.

In Milwaukee a Union Labor Party appeared to contest city elections in 1888. This party might have been successful except for the fact that Paul Grottkau's Socialists did not support it. Nevertheless, there was a *Socialisticher Vereinigung* in this city in the 1880s and 1890s. This movement included mostly German workers, like Emil Seidel (1864–1947), a woodcarver who later became Milwaukee's first Socialist mayor. It also included Polish workers and increasingly a number of American stock people thought of as Yankees—that is, New Englanders and New Yorkers.

The Socialist movement at this time was helped by the emergence of the Methodist Social Gospel, which brought people of ethnic groups other than Germans into the movement. The Socialist movement's greatest opposition was found in the Roman Catholic Church. Pope Pius IX in the Syllabus of Errors of 1864 and Pope Leo XIII in the 1890 encyclical "Rerum Novarum" severely denounced the Socialist movements of Europe as godless, though in "Rerum Novarum" there was expressed concern for the working class. Indeed, many Socialist leaders saw churches with official ties to governments as the persecutors of the working class. There was thus a long conflict between some Milwaukee Socialists and some Roman Catholics over public policy. In the development of the trade union movement in Milwaukee by the 1950s, the Catholic trade union leaders had displaced the Socialists who had been dominant forty years earlier.

The major person who built the Milwaukee Socialist movement so that it became nationally and internationally known was Victor L. Berger (1860–1929). Berger, from the Austrian Hungarian empire, came to Milwaukee about 1880. Some time thereafter through his activity in the South Side

Turnverein he became a Socialist. Berger became editor of labor and Socialist papers, including one called the *Vorwaerts*. Later he edited the *Social Democratic Herald*, a weekly. Although he spoke with an accent, he had a remarkable ability to express his thoughts and his editorials could be devastating. He pounded away at the corruption in local, state, and national governments and fought the trusts. It is said Berger in 1894 went to see Eugene V. Debs (1855–1926), the great railroad union leader who was under house arrest in Woodstock, Illinois, for a strike in 1893. Berger converted Debs, a Democrat, to Socialism. This was a great development for the American Socialist movement. Debs thereafter from 1900 to 1920 was the Socialist Party's candidate for president. He obtained nearly a million votes in 1912 and again in 1920.

At this point it must be said that one aspect of the Socialist movement that emerged early was an antiwar sentiment. Wars were said to be fought between capitalist states; workers would be killing each other for the enrichment of the bourgeoisie who controlled those states. The Socialist movement developed a strong streak of national pacifism in international matters while maintaining a militant position in labor internally.

Under Berger's leadership, the Social Democratic Party, as it was then called, fielded candidates for city offices in 1898, obtaining a small number of votes, but each two years thereafter they obtained more votes. In 1904 they obtained the first seats as Socialists in the city and county governments. At that time, the city and the county of Milwaukee were burdened with corrupt officials. During the decade, many officials were indicted and sentenced for various forms of corrupt practices. The Socialist political victories reflected a public reaction against bad government, especially against corrupt contracting.

Socialist platforms in the first part of the twentieth century were replete with demands for better municipal housekeeping—including, incidentally, a demand for a public abattoir. Socialists also called for protective labor laws. Honest contracting of public services was demanded and workers' protection after injury was sought. Old age pensions were advocated as early as 1908. Much of what was then advocated became embodied in New Deal legislation of the 1930s.

When Emil Seidel was elected mayor in 1912 he sought the help of University of Wisconsin professors to improve the practices of government. One of these was the famous professor John R. Commons (1862–1945). Seidel formed a Bureau of Economy and Efficiency staffed by academics to clean up what Beck has described as an Augean stable of corruption and graft in Milwaukee city government left over from the previous Democratic administration. Thus began the activities in local government, which under a later Socialist mayor, Daniel W. Hoan (1881–1961), earned Milwaukee the reputation as the "cleanest city government" in the United States. Hoan wrote a book, *City Government* (1936), in which he described his fight against the banks and how a city budget and honest elections were set up.

In 1910 Berger was first elected an alderman and in the same year a member of the House of Representatives. The Socialists felt themselves as a nearly irresistible movement toward state and national political power. Their opponents, Democrats and Republicans, however, had the Wisconsin legislature enact a law in 1911 that ended party representation on the ballot in local government, supplanting it with a nonpartisan type of ballot. The new ballot was a fusion type of ballot permitting Democrats and Republicans to vote for the same person. Within two years, Seidel and Berger were both defeated by the fusion ticket, but not before much of the city administration had been improved for the better and when the red-light district in the downtown had been nearly shut down by a Socialist district attorney, Winfred Zabel. In the succeeding four years of fusion government, the work of the Socialists in bringing order and responsibility in government was not undone.

In the 1910 election, Socialist city attorney Daniel Webster Hoan, a Lincolnesque person, was elected. Hoan obtained popular support for his attack on what was thought to be a corrupt electric street car company that used the city streets but did not pave between the rails and often struck people fatally. Hoan was reelected in 1912 and 1914 despite the failure of the rest of the Socialist ticket. In 1916 Hoan ran for mayor and was elected. Thereafter he was mayor for twenty-four years, until 1940, when he was defeated by my older brother, Carl F. Zeidler (1908–1942), who was not a Socialist.

In Hoan's administration, the standards of honest and frugal government were upheld rigorously. The city services were improved, attention was paid to stricter housing and fire codes, playgrounds and school support expanded, and Socialists served on the school board.

Though things looked promising for the Socialist movement in 1916, the ominous development of the war in Europe affected the Socialist movement. In Milwaukee most Socialists were opposed to the United States' entrance into the fighting on the side of the Allies in the First World War. Some of this was due to the fact that many Socialists were of Germanic extraction, but even more the resistance was due to the feeling that wars were fought for capitalists and that working-class people should not fight them. The war split the Socialist Party nationally and locally. Generally persons with ancestry from the British Isles left the party, leaving it to German, Polish, and Jewish persons.

About 1911 Berger changed his *Social Democratic Herald*, a weekly, to the *Milwaukee Leader*, a daily, without a Sunday edition. This paper carried on a vigorous and polemic discussion of Socialist policies at home and abroad, and was therefore antiwar. When the United States declared war on Germany in 1917, the Socialist Party nationally in a meeting in St. Louis expressed opposition to the war. Berger accepted this policy, though perhaps not fully. Hoan, however, felt that in his position of mayor he could not too openly resist the effort to provide support for the troops. This led to a division between Hoan and Berger, but it strengthened Berger's support among the German working class.

Unfortunately, Berger's paper had its second-class mailing rights taken away by the Woodrow Wilson administration. The *Milwaukee Leader*, which looked like a prosperous venture, suffered such a blow with this denial of mailing privileges that it never fully recovered and staggered on until its extinction during the Depression in 1938.

Berger himself, while running for Congress, was indicted under the Espionage Act and ultimately sentenced to twenty years in federal prison, even though he had won the election for Congress. The Supreme Court threw out the case, but Congress refused to seat Berger in 1918 and again in 1920 when he was reelected. It finally seated him in 1922 and he served until 1928. Berger died in 1929 in a streetcar accident and thousands of people came to pay him tribute in the city hall. The Socialist party was his lengthened shadow.

Hoan, because of his clean government, was reelected in 1920, 1924, and 1928, but usually narrowly. Milwaukee was now considered among the best-governed cities in America. However, there never was a majority of Socialists elected to the Milwaukee Common Council so Hoan was limited in his ability to get through Socialist measures, and he was under continual adverse scrutiny of the major Milwaukee newspapers.

From the beginning in the 1890s, Berger had worked closely with the unions and many members of the trade union leadership were Socialists. There were few industrial unions as compared to unions of skilled trades. The Socialist movement in the 1920s, nationally as well as among the Milwaukee Socialists, encountered a militant type of union activity fostered by the growing national

Communist Party supported by funds from the Soviet Union, which also set policies. From about 1919 to the 1950s, the Milwaukee Socialist movement was internally occupied with efforts by the Communists to infiltrate and take over the movement and unions.

Also during the 1900s the Milwaukee and Wisconsin Socialists had cool relationships to the LaFollette Progressive Republicans, who often supported the same measures locally and in the Wisconsin legislature as did the Socialists. For example, in the 1911 legislature the Progressive Republicans and the Socialists enacted laws for workmen's compensation, factory safety legislation, and shortened hours of work for women and children. An Industrial Commission was created. This social protection type of legislation was developed and improved in successive sessions of the Wisconsin legislature thereafter, with Socialists and trade unionists playing an active role, and it is said to have been the foundation of the national legislation in the 1930s described as the New Deal.

Milwaukee Socialists in the 1920 elections had supported Eugene V. Debs, the railroad and union leader, for president even though Debs was in prison in the Atlanta penitentiary for speeches he made criticizing U.S. participation in the First World War. In the 1924 elections, however, the Socialists along with trade unions supported Senator Robert M. LaFollette Sr. for president. LaFollette carried only Wisconsin.

When Debs died in 1926 he was succeeded in national leadership of the Socialist Party of America by Norman M. Thomas (1884–1968), a former Presbyterian minister, Princeton graduate, and New York social worker. Thomas was close to being an absolute pacifist. He was a wonderful orator and was especially attractive to university students up until the time of his death in 1968. He was also probably the best platform speaker among American political leaders. His leadership greatly influenced the Milwaukee Socialist movement, which accepted him as the main Socialist leader after the death of Berger in 1928. Thomas then was the presidential candidate of the Socialist Party for every presidential election through 1948.

The Milwaukee Socialist movement during the 1920s and 1930s continued to maintain some electoral strength in the German North Side and the Polish South Side of Milwaukee. It had some Irish adherents, but most of the people of English stock had left the party. Through the *Milwaukee Leader*, it was the voice of the trade union leadership. In public life it advocated better working conditions, clean streets, a new sewage plant and later a water treatment plant, the building of schools and libraries, and the support of cooperatives, including a cooperative housing project known as Garden Homes. It also was the party that favored development of public parks, especially through the leadership of a one-time member, Charles B. Whitnall (ca. 1860–1949). It advocated public ownership of the lakeshore within Milwaukee city limits. It advocated public ownership of the streetcar company and its parent, the electric power company. This later advocacy was to prove the nemesis of the movement in the 1936 municipal election.

The Great Depression beginning in 1929 saw many people out of work. Some turned to the Socialist Party and the Socialists were hard put to find public works for such people but did begin a limited program of such works. At one time when the city government was having severe trouble collecting property taxes, it issued "Baby Bonds." These were bonds of very small denominations from five dollars up as payment to its employees, and ultimately merchants accepted these bonds. It is said that the city made a million dollars on bonds not cashed later. Socialists on the Milwaukee County Board of Supervisors helped in the expansion of "outdoor relief" to cash relief and expanded public health services.

The Depression also brought a rise in militancy of the Communist Party, which attacked Socialists as well as the Democrats and Republicans, and which led to many street demonstrations of the unemployed. Strikes and labor disturbances challenged the Socialist city administration when policing was required. In a streetcar strike of 1934, Hoan stopped strikebreakers from entering the city.

In the mid-1930s the heads of the Wisconsin State Federation of Labor, who were at one time identified with the Socialist movement, determined that the Socialist Party should get off the ballot in Wisconsin and join with forces in the Progressive Party. After much anguished discussion, the major Socialist figures led the vote to take the Socialist Party off the ballot in Wisconsin and to join the Progressive Party, which, having separated from the Republican Party, had at this time its own ballot column. Socialists were to join the Farmer Labor Progressive Federation. This action delivered another severe blow to the Socialist Party, which never fully recovered.

Although nearly one-half of the Milwaukee Council in 1932 was Socialist and there was a Socialist city attorney, in 1936 the Socialists ran as members of the Farmer Labor Progressive Federation. Their numbers were sharply reduced in losses to nonpartisan candidates, a fusion of Republicans and Democrats.

Hoan, as mayor, survived with a handful of aldermen. The Farmer Labor Progressive Federation had called for public ownership of the electric power company and for support of the Boncel ordinance, an ordinance that allowed the city to close down a business that was not abiding by the federal labor relations law. The business forces administered the federation a drastic defeat.

In 1940 Hoan was defeated by the same nonpartisan forces, whose candidate was Assistant City Attorney Carl F. Zeidler, a moderate conservative. Carl Zeidler was killed in the Second World War in 1942.

While this minor political drama was going on in Milwaukee, during the Great Depression, nationally Franklin Roosevelt, succeeding President Hoover, had to deal with business failures, bank closings, and huge unemployment. Roosevelt and the Congress adopted measures to address the problems, measures that had been advocated by Socialists. The Wagner Labor Relations Act favored union organizing. Public works programs of many types were set up and housing projects began, including a federally planned new city near Milwaukee, the city of Greendale, Wisconsin. This project was begun here probably because Hoan was the mayor in Milwaukee.

The success of the Roosevelt program led the top trade union leaders of the nation to move into the Democratic Party and to have subordinate leaders do so also. The top AFL leadership in Wisconsin went from being Socialists to being Progressives to being Democrats. The Socialist movement lost its close ties to the labor movement and has never regained them. Democrats controlled federal patronage including temporary project work.

Another factor militated against the Milwaukee Socialists. This was the growth of the industrial union movement under John L. Lewis in the Committee of Industrial Organizations, later the Congress of Industrial Organizations. When the Socialists locally and nationally supported the organization of industrial unions, the trade union leadership took offense and broke ties.

In the industrial union movement, Lewis employed many Communist Party members, albeit not as such, as organizers, and they led a number of industrial unions in Milwaukee. Their policy was to be unfriendly to the Hoan administration.

When Daniel W. Hoan and the major top leadership of the Socialist Party left it in 1940 to become Democrats, the remaining Socialists reformed the party in 1941. A Socialist city ticket was conducted in 1944. Three of the persons on it were nominated but none were elected. In 1947 Socialists, Progressives, some

Liberal Democrats, and labor people formed a committee, the Municipal Enterprise Committee. The committee had a platform calling for an emphasis on land use planning, public housing for low-income people, improved transportation, and refurbishing municipal equipment, among other things. The committee was able to nominate only one candidate. Other political leaders had flocked to the Democrats. Socialism was now thought to be the same as Communism, the kind found in the Soviet Union. I was nominated as a last resort as the candidate for mayor in the 1948 primary election. By a series of events, which can only be described as a series of flukes, I was elected. No other Socialists were elected in the city or county at that time and none have been since.

In my term of office of twelve years I followed what can be described as Democratic Socialist policies. I always campaigned on a platform that spelled out those policies. In my administration there was a major refurbishing of municipal equipment, including fire apparatus, sanitation equipment, and police cars. About 3,200 public housing units were built, including the first housing for the elderly. Major blighted areas were cleared and in some instances rebuilt by private developers. I helped begin the building of the first freeways here and in the nation. New harbor lands were purchased and docks and port facilities were built. I had a small role in bringing about the expansion of the St. Lawrence Seaway. Streets were improved and many new bridges were built. Grade separations took place. Through annexation and consolidation, the city went from forty-six square miles to ninety-six square miles, thus bringing in both residential and industrial lands.

In the cultural area, support was given to the Milwaukee public school system, as it too had to expand. Funding was provided for the Milwaukee vocational and adult schools for new buildings. I formed a committee in 1951 that brought into existence the first educational television station in the state, and this after severe opposition from Hearst radio. A new museum was built, a large addition was built to the central library, several large branch libraries were built, and playgrounds and parklands were expanded. I worked with Dr. George Parkinson in getting the University of Wisconsin-Milwaukee established about 1954. A new large water purification plant was built. I helped form the Milwaukee Council on Adult Education.

These actions occurred at a time when the business community was quite hostile, when one newspaper was chilly toward my administration, and one newspaper considered me a Khrushchev-type Communist. A major failure in my own opinion was the failure to save a defunct electric interurban railway line to the western suburbs.

Primary support for my sponsoring these programs came from the Federated Trades Council and its secretary, Jacob F. Friedrick, and from the members of the Socialist Party and the Municipal Enterprise Committee. This committee is now the Public Enterprise Committee and acts as a municipal watchdog.

The Socialist Party in my time, though not so earlier, had a policy of accepting every individual on equal terms, whatever race, origin, or religion. I made many public appearances before the scores of ethnic and racial groups of the city, speaking of social and political equality. I adopted this stance toward the increasing number of African Americans who were coming into the city. In the municipal election of 1952 a rumor suddenly appeared that the presence of new African American peoples in Milwaukee was due to the fact that Frank Zeidler advertised for them in the U.S. South. The great movement of African Americans from southern states after the Second World War was interpreted in Milwaukee to be the work of one man, myself. The rumor spread, in part due to real estate people engaged in block-busting in the old German and Socialist districts.

In the 1956 municipal election, the race issue became the central theme of the election, but I survived it. The rumor still occasionally surfaced but this time in the form that the reason African Americans are in Milwaukee is that the Socialists brought them. The race issue in my estimation has been the main issue in every Milwaukee municipal election since 1952. Public projects that might encourage people of color are discouraged, as for example after 1952 it was almost impossible to get any public housing except that for the elderly, who presumably were white.

In 1960, when I was succeeded by a former Republican who had turned Democratic for purposes of election, municipal policy was then to shut down public housing and slow down blight clearance. Municipal enterprise was now to give way to contracting out public services and to suffocate social policies leading to equality. Both Socialist Party and now the Public Enterprise Committee still function but with greatly lessened influence of public policy. The Public Enterprise Committee endorsed candidates for local office, but the issue of racial change determined the winners in every local election since.

The Socialist Party in the 1970s was again under an attempt of a takeover by Leninists. Also in the 1970s the Socialist Party of the United States was taken over by the followers of Max Shactman, a charismatic figure who had been a Communist, then a Trotskyist, and then a member of the Socialist Party. This group sought to abolish the Socialist Party and did form the Social Democrats of America. The members of the Social Democrats became key advisers in foreign policy to the Reagan administration.

The Milwaukee movement reformed the Socialist Party U.S.A. in Milwaukee in 1973. In the 1980s the national movement was taken over for a time by radical feminists, but not the Milwaukee Socialist movement, which focused on city, school board, county, and state matters. In 1997 the Milwaukee movement celebrated its 100th anniversary. Since the 1980s it has been increasingly known as the Sewer Socialist movement because of Elmer Beck's book. It describes itself as a Democratic Socialist party.

In 1976 I ran as the candidate of the Socialist Party for president. My running mate was J. Quinn Brisben, a Chicago schoolteacher. Our slate got on the ballot in eight states and we received a tiny vote, since Socialist write-in votes are generally not counted. In 2000, the Milwaukee Socialists ran an African American man for mayor and a male college teacher for county executive. Each received about 18 percent of the vote. Recent policies of the party call for opposition to the privatization of the Milwaukee waterworks. We may be calling ourselves the "Cleanwater Socialists." We call for reestablishing direct public assistance for the poor, especially mothers with children. We strongly support the public schools. We call for an expansion of the bus and transportation systems to get the inner-city poor to suburban jobs. We stand for civil rights and are opposed to prison expansion and harsh sentencing. The party also calls for fair trade instead of free trade. The party is concerned about a new arms race.

The population of Milwaukee, with about seventy-five or more ethnic stocks in a city of 600,000 people, is not composed of people with a Socialist tradition. The benefits of good government and social advancement that the Sewer Socialists brought as a working-class movement are little recognized or appreciated now and may be less so in the future—unless, of course, there is a severe depression again.

The new social activism is spreading among peace advocates, women, religious groups, and people focused on single issues such as the environment. Socialism itself has become too closely identified with Lenin's and Stalin's Communism and the Sewer Socialist movement labors mightily to overcome that handicap.

Currently, the nation is under the influence of libertarian principles and a market ideology that appears to be rapidly undoing the social safety net and privatizing public services. The Democratic Socialist movement in the United States finds this hard to deal with. Democratic Socialists are in governments in France, Germany, Great Britain, and the Scandinavian countries. Currently, in a time in the United States when elections are determined in great part by negative television advertising, the Democratic Socialists have a hard time to get a positive message to the public.

The long-time charge made against Socialists is that people are not capable of acting cooperatively and are by nature selfish, so socialism is impractical. Whether this is the case is yet to be determined. Perhaps economic anthropologists will answer this question.

From this recitation the reader might not have learned the key to new successful pragmatics on how to control or influence government, but might have gained some insights as to how some of the people in the Milwaukee Sewer Socialist movement functioned and under what motivations.

I

HOUSEHOLDS

The chapters in this volume present a broad picture of the similarities and differences in the processes of labor mobilization in widely disparate times, places, and circumstances. Taken as a whole, these chapters show how labor changes with social, political, and economic conditions, in a wide range of contexts, in both Western and non-Western societies. One of the major contributions the book makes is to present innovative research that brings into question the basic assumptions that underlie much of globalization scholarship and economic theory. In this section on household labor, the authors look at the flexible management of household resources.

Koenig challenges globalization scholars who assert that with modernization there is a shift to nuclear families, which have the flexibility to respond quickly to economic change. Rather, it is extended households, not the nuclear family, that is a flexible means for organizing economic activity. For rural Mali, persistence of the traditional kinship patterns of extended families are an economic strategy in a changing environment of risk, uncertainty, and unpredictability, and of infrastructure failure. Networks are one important aspect of this strategy, young male migration another. But while migration may add to household income, the household loses their labor during the agricultural season. Migration and patterns of partial sharing (not pooling) lead to intrahousehold negotiation and contestation.

Russell, too, questions conventional economic theory. She critiques the neoclassical wage/profit model by showing how kin-based commercial fisheries press more, not fewer, members into work. And where Koenig shows us that extended households are a flexible means for organizing economic activity, Russell documents how flexibility of kinship labor can adjust to fluctuations in income and output. In addition, there is a reproduction of household labor, as younger kin replace elders as skippers. Fishing in the Philippines presents the same problem of recruiting labor that Ortiz discusses, but with different solutions. Here, the solution is the formation of coalitions to recruit labor. This means of recruiting labor, in turn, influences the fishing effort. Russell, like Rees and Koenig, shows that household strategies meet the needs of members for sustenance in the face of uncertainty and risk.

Rees challenges conventional theory on four fronts. If the model of neoclassical economics is imposed, much of the economic behavior studied by economic anthropologists would be rendered irrational. Rees, like Russell, gives us another example of the misapplication of this model. What appears to be labor performed for a loss under neoclassical economics, here is understood more clearly as a transfer of control of resources within the household from male to female. And Rees, like Koenig, challenges conventional economic views on household composition. Large families, she argues, rather than a drain on scarce resources, can be explained as production of labor for export. Also like Koenig, she challenges how data on transnational migration and gender have been hitherto interpreted. Rather than a model of male migration supporting households through remittances, she shows that it is women's work that makes men's migration possible. Her final challenge is to linguistic misinterpretation. Zapotec women are working under the Zapotec concept of reciprocal labor that views women's labor as a substantial contribution to the household, not undervalued, a misconception based in linguistic error. Economic strategies for combating uncertainty and risk link all three chapters, and will be a reoccurring theme in this book.

2

Political-Economic Change, Cultural Traditions, and Household Organization in Rural Mali

Dolores Koenig

The relationship of household organization to economic conditions is a basic question of anthropological research. While one approach has looked at how households adapt to larger economic circumstances, the major alternative has been to see how cultural traditions of kinship and family determine action (Creed 2000). This chapter integrates these two approaches by looking at household forms that rural Malians use to cope with changing economic circumstances. It focuses on household size and structure.

Some have argued that recent economic changes, especially globalization, have led to smaller, more flexible households because they can respond quickly to economic change. This chapter, however, analyzes a contrasting case, the rural hinterlands of Kita, Mali, where extended households have proven to be quite tenacious. Here, household size appears to have increased from the late 1970s to the late 1990s, despite rather dramatic economic change and growth in both rural and urban Mali. The ideal household has not changed in form; large extended families did and do offer economies of scale that help cope with economic and ecological uncertainty. However, it has changed in internal organization; it has shown flexibility in its capacity to deploy labor in new ways. The ability to combine a stable form with multiple internal structures has allowed the extended household to retain its importance in the contemporary world.

This chapter begins with a short discussion of study methodology. It then looks at theories about the relationship of household size to economic constraints and some of the changes in political-economic context in Mali. Then, it turns to specific aspects of African households and a few cultural traditions particular to this zone. Finally, it looks at the size and organization of households in contemporary Kita.

METHODOLOGY

This chapter is based on a 1999 study of sixty rural households in two village clusters in the zone of Kita, Mali. Kita is a market and railway center of about 40,000 inhabitants some 200 kilometers northwest of Mali's capital, Bamako. Since households do not pool all resources (discussed below), individuals were the main unit of research. Within each household, up to five people were sampled, one from each of the following categories: the head, one married man, one unmarried man, one older married woman, and one younger married woman; the entire sample included 229 individuals.[1] At periodic intervals throughout the 1999 agricultural season, Malian research assistants gathered data from these individuals on work times in agricultural and nonagricultural activities, incomes, and expenses. Supplementary information was collected on livestock and consumer goods ownership, migration histories, consumption practices, demography, and other related topics. Approximately one-third of the sample was targeted for complementary qualitative interviews designed to elucidate varied economic strategies. A team of Malian social scientists and I interviewed eighty-two individuals; a Malian historian collected oral histories in the nine study villages. This chapter is based on some of these data.[2]

These two village clusters in Kita were chosen specifically to duplicate an earlier study done by Purdue University in the late 1970s. The quantitative part of the 1999 study was designed to collect data comparable to that collected during the 1978 agricultural season. Contextual information about national political and economic change in Mali comes not only from documentary sources but also from my participation in other projects in the interim.

THE POLITICAL-ECONOMIC CONTEXT

The Impact of Economic Changes

One hypothesis about the ways that larger economic structures affect household size is the notion that contemporary economic conditions have encouraged smaller, nuclear households; this idea has considerable time depth and has been advanced by analysts with diverse theoretical perspectives (Creed 2000). In the 1960s and 1970s, theorists working within the functionalist paradigm of modernization theory suggested that economic structures, household forms, and values systems were congruent. In particular, they suggested that the industrial values of universalistic achievement, individualism, and social mobility were consistent with nuclear family structures and urban bureaucratic technology (Goode 1963). While later theorists questioned the tenets underlying modernization theory, many approaches to the household still stressed growing nuclearization. For example, Gewertz and Errington (1999) argued that the establishment of nuclear families was crucial in creating a middle class in contemporary Papua New Guinea because these households could accumulate at the expense of duties to their less-well-off kin.

As anthropological perspectives on development have become more concerned with the international inequalities brought about by globalizing capitalism, some have suggested that the division of an extended household into smaller, nuclear units in different places is one means that kin can use to take advantage of global opportunities and better meet local constraints. For example, Congolese in Paris and their kin in the two Congos continued to be part of a single social field when economic activities depended upon different family segments in the two places (MacGaffey and Bazenguissa-Ganga 2000). Rural Thai families made use of the earnings of daughters working in Bangkok factories, who in turn gained status once married precisely because of the skills they learned while working outside the village (Mills 1999). While families may remain important as they integrate different households over considerable distances, the household group residing and working together becomes smaller. The larger family units do not appear as a census category and may remain invisible in rural and international statistics.

Economic Change in the Zone of Kita

Like most of Africa, Kita has faced a changing political-economic context. In the late 1970s, Mali was a single-party state with a centrally planned economy. Since then, it has undergone a series of structural adjustment initiatives. Market privatization was arguably the most important aspect of economic liberalization in rural areas. In 1981, Mali removed price controls from the basic grains: millet, sorghum, and maize (Dembélé and Staatz 2000). Parastatal agricultural extension agencies that relied on extensive international subsidies and had no possibility of self-sufficiency lost resources; some eventually disappeared.

In Kita, farmers in the 1970s grew peanuts as a cash crop alongside basic food grains. A parastatal rural development organization, the Opération Arachide et Cultures Vivrières (OACV), stressed peanut cultivation, provided extension advice, inputs, and equipment on credit, and commercialized peanuts. The many farmers who grew peanuts had relatively good incomes (Koenig 1986). In the 1970s postdrought years, complementary OACV programs in literacy and health promised to transform rural society. Yet the system began to fall apart in 1981 when the world price of peanuts fell precipitously, donors decreased funding, and the OACV lost financial viability.[3] Through the mid-1980s, the OACV moved in and out of peanut commercialization somewhat arbitrarily and ceased to provide credit. Farmers began to believe that commercial peanut farming was no longer viable, yet they appear to have made few attempts to look for new crops or markets. They continued to cultivate peanuts and complained loudly about the poor prices offered by the few private merchants buying, but appear to have continued their existing farming strategies. Meanwhile, a small local nongovernmental organization (NGO) began to explore the potential for cotton cultivation in the zone and to encourage another organization active elsewhere in Mali, the Compagnie Malienne de Développement des Textiles (CMDT) to come to Kita. By 1999, the CMDT had been in Kita for several years and was encouraging farmers to adopt cotton as a major cash crop. Farmers were attracted in part because the CMDT continued to function much like a 1970s parastatal organization, offering input, credit, and assured markets.[4]

Economic changes were accompanied by political ones; a coup d'état in 1991 removed from power Moussa Traoré, head of state since 1968. The leader of the coup, Amadou Toumany Touré, stepped down voluntarily a year later when national elections chose Alpha Oumar Konaré as president. National elections were followed by plans for decentralization, which finally occurred in 1999, when the first municipal rural elections established popularly elected communal governments.

Alongside a political-economic context shared by other rural Malians, Kita faced a particular constraint: isolation. Mali's First Region encompasses Kita and most of western Mali; its main transport link has been the railroad between Bamako and Dakar, Senegal. Until recently, in part to encourage use of the rails, there has been no major alternative road transportation. Yet the rails have proved less flexible than roads and have been subject every rainy season to disruption from washouts and derailments. Development activities in the First Region have until recently lagged behind other more accessible areas. Although Kita was integrated into the Malian state and served by various government organizations, its rural hinterland was less touched by the Malian administration than many areas to the southeast of Bamako not far from major roads to Côte d'Ivoire and Burkina Faso. NGO activity has also been less and later in these zones.[5] The situation began to change with construction of a major hydroelectric dam in the early 1980s at Manantali, 120 kilometers west of Kita. Substantial growth from the 1970s to the 1990s created new urban markets for rural produce and rendered more important Kita's role as a bulking center for goods headed to Bamako.

Kita was not really much more accessible to Bamako and its markets until late 1999 when an all-weather road was finally built. Nevertheless, people believed that it would be when traffic increased to Manantali; this belief only grew when plans for new roads became known. Counting on increased accessibility, NGOs finally began programs in Kita. Plan International has been particularly active, carrying out health and education programs. Other programs created village-level savings banks and facilitated the construction of small dams for vegetable gardening. While people maintained their basic rainy season agricultural strategies as the economy changed, they rapidly took up dry season vegetable gardening and many new nonagricultural activities.

While the impact of structural adjustment activities has been extremely problematic, one effect in Mali has been widespread economic growth through unleashing entrepreneurial activities previously stifled by the centrally controlled economy. In some cases, grassroots economic activity has benefited smaller entrepreneurs who had found previous barriers to access too formidable. In the coarse grain trade, the numbers of smaller traders grew and they were more innovative than larger ones (Dembélé and Staatz 2000); at Manantali, the growth in small traders broke the monopolies held by a few large ones (Diarra et al. 1995).

Although many Kita residents considered the economic changes to have constrained their ability to earn good incomes from farming, they were relatively positive about other economic and political changes. For many people in Kita and the study villages, the standard of living had increased quite dramatically from 1978 to 1999. For example, villages were less isolated because collective bus and truck transport had increased, bicycles were widespread, and some villagers had motorcycles. Health projects provided vaccinations and encouraged new clinics, wells, and cement latrines. In the 1970s, there were few options for buying goods other than local periodic markets. By the 1990s, these markets had grown significantly and virtually every village had several small stores. Several villages had local bakers, and children could buy chewing gum, candy, and cookies, all unimaginable in the 1970s. Malian television reached a few households in rural areas, when villagers used car batteries to run their sets. Education levels had increased, although they were still low. To be sure, people had to pay for new goods, but they were much more available than in the 1970s.

Poststructural adjustment Bamako has seen the growth of a two-tiered system: private organizations open to the privileged versus public agencies, with significantly lower resources, upon which the poor must rely. This has been particularly evident in the rapid growth of private health clinics and schools. However, because of Mali's poverty, the public system has rarely, if ever, had sufficient resources. People, both urban and rural, tended to talk positively of the increased availability of resources after privatization, although they were aware of inequality in access. Many noted the difficulty of paying for medications. In the villages, private entrepreneurs often accepted alternative forms of payment because they were aware that their markets were constricted by their potential clientele's lack of cash.

Nevertheless, unequal access was not the primary concern of our study sample. Their major concerns were risk and unpredictability. Both the physical and political-economic environments were considered to be essentially hazardous and uncertain, with limited means available to rural residents to change this unpredictability. For example, they believed the larger economic and political changes were outside their control. They did not see themselves as people who could either make markets or formulate policies. Although they could (and did) respond to opportunities, they perceived these as contingent. Many adults had experienced other forms of government and economic systems in their lifetime; they saw no evidence that recent changes were irreversible. This created a certain emphasis on making use of new opportunities and using social linkages to generate resources as quickly as possible.

Given the unpredictability of the larger context, people approached basic changes to the local system with caution. They continued to use generations-old and proven sociocultural traditions to cope with contemporary risk. This included sending certain household members on migration to profit from new resources, as the globalization theorists suggest, but this too was an old strategy. Migration has not meant the formation of smaller units at home, however, where elders, in particular, have tried to keep the extended household functioning, while adapting it to take advantage of new opportunities.

The Importance of Cultural Traditions

For those interested in the ways that cultural and social factors influence household and family structure, African households have raised a particular theoretical concern: the stresses created by households that are not unitary centers for pooling and resource sharing (Guyer 1981). In virtually all of Mali, as in many other parts of Africa as well, a few household resources are shared but many are not. Rather, responsibilities are divided, and individuals need to have their own resources to meet them. For example, in many cases, agricultural land can be considered "owned" and shared by a household, yet it is divided into many different parcels with different owners, each of whom must find the labor to cultivate that parcel and in turn owns its produce. In this region, staple grains produced on fields managed by the household head are considered to be family patrimony and hence shared, but the ingredients for complementary foods are typically owned by individual cooks. People do live together in one compound and identify themselves as part of a named unit with an acknowledged head, usually the senior male. Key tasks may be divided among all adult members; most notably one woman cooks for the entire extended household on any one day. Yet households do not have common budgets. Individuals fulfill household responsibilities from personal budgets. Husbands rarely know all the economic activities of their wives or what they earn and vice versa. The same is true for parents and children.

This pattern of partial sharing suggests a tension between individual interests and the requirements of household membership. The divergent interests of male and female household members as well as those of younger and older men may lead to the departure of individual members when they feel that the costs of household membership outweigh its benefits (Meillassoux 1975; Roberts 1987). In West African savanna households, considered gerontocratic and patriarchal, the relationship between the male head of household and his younger brothers and sons has been particularly problematic. Although younger men could leave and create their own households, it was clearly in the political interests of elders to keep healthy young men in the household to provide most of the labor on the household's staple grain fields. Many young men stayed because of the benefits they received: wives, food, and a sense of security. Yet it was at the cost of obeying their fathers, uncles, or older brothers, and many chafed under this control. Local people as well as external theoreticians recognized this tension; segmentation was considered a serious problem that dispersed the household's labor power.

When households in the Kita zone confronted national political-economic changes, they used the semi-pooling extended household with all of its tensions. As the larger environment changed, the ability of one or another group to obtain resources could change, suggesting different results for old contests. To cope, households could and did change the internal allocation of labor, produce, or power to encourage individual members to stay.

LABOR USE AND HOUSEHOLD ORGANIZATION IN KITA

The Kita cultural traditions that governed household form and function developed in an area of relatively sparse population density, impacted by precolonial, colonial, and postindependence state activity, but rarely at the center of any state. Precolonially, states involved in warfare recruited soldiers and raided for slaves. Postindependence states carried out programs of economic development, collected taxes, and offered some new services. This section looks at traditions of economic activity, settlement patterns, and migration.

Those in the study saw farming as their major economic activity, and each household contained many fields divided among collective and individual fields. Collective fields were under the control of the household head. People said that all household members were required to work on these fields; in fact, although women performed important harvest and postharvest activities, men did most of the work until then. So it was all men, rather than all members, who were expected to work regularly. The produce of these fields became the patrimony of the household. In this zone, there were usually several collective fields in a single household, primarily staple grain fields to feed the household; they sometimes also included cotton and peanut fields, cash crops that provided money for household needs.

Alongside these fields were individual fields, where household members controlled labor and the disposition of produce. In theory, individual fields could be owned by any household member capable of getting access to land (relatively easy in this area of low population density) and organizing the labor to work it. Small fields were often cultivated almost exclusively with the labor of the field owner. Yet the ability to have individual fields varied substantially between women and men, linked to their role in the household.

Virtually all married women had several individual fields; widows and divorcees as well continued to cultivate unless their health prevented it. Women were expected to have fields because their household responsibilities included providing ingredients for the sauce; either they had to grow the ingredients directly or grow something to sell so they could buy what they needed. Although women have sometimes found it difficult to get sufficient land in other areas of Mali (Koenig, Diarra, and Sow 1998), this was not the case in Kita, where virtually all women in the sample had individual fields.

The situation was much more complicated among men since they were responsible for most of the work on collective fields. Many household heads believed that if they allowed younger men to have individual fields, this would lead to household segmentation and lower total production. Some households would not permit young men to have individual fields; others posed restrictions. For example, some let married men have individual fields but forbade the practice among unmarried men. Others said that men's individual fields should only contain certain crops; while peanuts or cotton might be acceptable, basic food grains were not: these ought to be grown in the collective fields. In our sample, thirty-nine of the sixty households had other married men present; of these, six had no individual fields because they managed the collective fields (the household head having retired from active work). Four others simply did not have individual fields; overall 75 percent of married men in the sample had individual fields. Among the twenty-eight unmarried men in the sample, only seventeen (61 percent) had individual fields.

Alongside farming, people undertook a number of "complementary" activities, which have varied with the possibilities offered by the larger political-economic context. Recently, there has been growth in the variety of nonagricultural activities as well as non-field-crop agriculture, particularly fruit and vegetable cultivation. Activities undertaken by men included "traditional" ones such as hunting, blacksmithing, trade, fishing, gathering, cord, basket and mat making, shoemaking, weaving, and traditional and Islamic healing. There were also Koranic schoolteachers and musicians. Among "modern" activities were construction; carpentry; tailoring; modern medicine and the sale of pharmaceuticals; bakeries; motorcycle, bicycle, and radio repair; activities on small development projects; and small stores. Women undertook a more restricted range of activities, based in "traditional" female activities, such as cotton spinning, hairdressing, pottery, provision of cooked foods, and trade. Virtually none of these practitioners were full-time specialists and almost all continued to cultivate either their own fields or the household's collective fields. They maintained a vision of themselves as farmers or peasants even though these complementary activities brought in substantial earnings and became a major factor in changing internal household organization.

Tradition suggested physical movement as one way to deal with economic, environmental, and political risk and uncertainty. This could occur when entire households moved, being integrated as "strangers" into existing villages or forming entirely new villages in sparsely populated areas.[6] Both village clusters in the study were relatively recent immigrants into their locations. In one cluster, some forty-five kilometers to the north of Kita town, people of the Malinke ethnic group founded six villages between 1916 and 1940. Most Malinke traced their ancestors to the ancient medieval empire of Mali; people in the study villages said they had migrated from the southern Mande heartland north to the area around Kita town. They then moved further north in at least two different phases, finally arriving at their present site. The main village in this cluster was founded within living memory by the great-uncle of the present village chief. The villages of the other cluster, about thirty-five kilometers south of Kita town, were founded between the mid-1880s and the early 1900s by Fulbe moving northward from a fortified citadel conquered by the nineteenth-century Toucouleur state. These Fulbe presumably came originally from southern Mali, having migrated there from both the Fouta Djallon in Guinea and Macina in eastern Mali. Like the Fulbe who remained in the south, these Fulbe are sedentary and speak only Malinke. Called Birgo Fulbe, they retained a distinctive ethnic identity (mostly evident in patronyms), but followed customs virtually identical to their Malinke neighbors. Although there were some important differences between the two village clusters in the study, they were not linked in any obvious way to ethnic differences. Moreover, there was also little correlation between traditional social distinctions (caste or former slave status) and contemporary economic opportunity. In light of this, the study participants can be considered a single cultural tradition.

Movement by individuals was also a cultural tradition of some depth. It provided a way to take advantage of transient economic opportunities as well as to learn new skills that could be useful at home. Migration was considered particularly appropriate for young unmarried men; when they married, they were expected to return to participate in the extended household. Precolonial armies were staffed in part by mercenaries and other men who joined up, drawn by the promise of booty (Izard and Ki-Zerbo 1992). Some rulers encouraged migration and settlement to key areas of conquest (Robinson 1985). Economic activities such as trade, herding, fishing, transport, and Islamic teaching were itinerant, requiring practitioners to move over large areas. With colonial domination, the economic context changed. When colonial authorities abolished local slavery, large farm owners turned to their own male kin to replace the slave labor that had once worked the farms; many young men evidently responded to what they viewed as increased exploitation by leaving their villages to take up other kinds of work. As early as 1910, young Malian men were going to Guinea to work in mines, to Côte d'Ivoire to enter cocoa farming or work on the railroad, and to Ghana for cocoa farming (Roberts 1987; Manning 1988; Berry 1993). Some of this movement was a response to French labor requisitions, but much was a local response to changing economic opportunities.

Contemporary globalization has changed the places people go and the kinds of work they do, but unmarried men still migrate. For some men, working away from the village was seasonal. Others found year-round work; jobs could last several years or become permanent, in which case the young man might marry a local woman and become lost to the family. Since independence, the potential places for migration have proliferated. Young men may work relatively close by, in areas far away but within Mali, or internationally. Some worked in rural zones; others went to urban areas. At the time of the study, the sample had family members living in Bamako and other areas in Mali, Guinea, Côte d'Ivoire, Mauritania, Gabon, Libya, and Spain. A few of the family members living elsewhere were educated and had urban jobs (e.g., civil servants, teachers, accountant, electrician, photographer); it was not expected that they would return to live in the village before their retirement. Others were working in jobs not that different from what could be done in the village: agriculture, trade, tailoring. These families often expected that they might return.

The tradition of migration for young unmarried men would appear to have both economic and human development aspects. While earning money was clearly an important goal, locals referred to migration as leaving on adventure.

This appears to symbolize the riskiness of the venture; while a few found this time away quite remunerative, others returned with nothing, sometimes even in debt. However, by taking the individual away from his family, labor migration required a young man to learn to fend for himself to a much greater degree than if he had remained in the village; in this sense, it accentuated resourcefulness. When a man returned, he had hopefully gained an economic advantage for his family as well as skills and knowledge for himself. Contemporary labor migration equips some young men with the capacity and interest to undertake nonagricultural activities within their villages; men in our sample used knowledge gained to begin activities such as bakeries, advanced fruit and vegetable gardening, and trade. In part, labor migration by young men can be seen as an investment in the household, fulfilled when the young man gets a job away that allows him to send regular remittances, or, more commonly, by allowing him to exercise new capacities when he returns to the village, ideally coincident with his marriage.

Yet there were costs to the migration of young men. Grosz-Ngaté (2000) documents the growing tensions between elders and juniors. The most immediate problem, however, was that their labor was not available to work on the household fields during the agricultural season. Even more than whether they had individual fields or not, access to the labor of young men on the collective fields depended on whether they were there. While thirty-nine of the sixty study households had married men present, only twenty-eight had unmarried men. Indeed, several unmarried men included at the beginning of the study left soon after it began to work in other villages during the agricultural season. Many worked for other farmers using a practice called the *navetanat* (Perry 2001). Young men were recruited to work on collective fields for the entire agricultural season alongside the receiving family's sons. Unlike male household members, they virtually always cultivated individual fields whose produce belonged to them. While the young man would gain some economic advantages from this practice, the *navetanat* cannot be understood in solely economic terms. Working for someone other than one's own household head allowed a greater degree of independence and avoided some of the tensions of the elder-junior relationship.

HOUSEHOLD STABILITY AND CHANGE IN CONTEMPORARY KITA

Malians believed that extended families were disappearing. In the workshops connected to this study, urban intellectuals claimed that extended households were subject to increasing segmentation and fragmentation. Rural inhabitants, who were particularly concerned about youth who left on migration in the middle of the agricultural season or "disappeared" while on long-term labor migration, echoed this concern.

Yet the effective household size in the study area had actually increased from the 1970s. Although most household heads included some people who did not live at home, when asked to enumerate members, the figure most of interest here is the people residing together, those who regularly interacted and shared responsibilities. In the Malinke village cluster, the average household size in 1978 was 16.9 persons; in 1999, it had increased to 18.4 persons. The smallest household in the sample had three persons, the largest fifty. In the Fulbe village cluster, the average household size in 1978 was 14.9; by 1999 it had increased to 18.2. Here the smallest household had two people, the largest forty-eight.[7] Although some segmentation did occur, nuclear households did not become the norm. The continued importance of large extended households was not an isolated circumstance and many rural areas of southern Mali have continued to have large extended households (Koenig, Diarra, and Sow 1998). This chapter suggests that the extended household continues to be important because it continues to meet local needs to cope with risk and uncertainty. It is not rigidly structured, but is a flexible institution that can be changed to benefit from new economic opportunities and adapt to new constraints.

The new opportunities that have come in recent years have been disproportionately offered to and taken up by young men, who also provide the major farm labor. While some might have been tempted to start nuclear families elsewhere, away from the extended family, senior men have worked hard to keep this from happening. The reasons for this appear to include their desire to retain the power they hold as household heads, access to sufficient labor for the collective fields, and access to at least some of the income earned by young men. The need to keep young men from leaving permanently is linked to cultural notions of household patrimony that emphasize the continuity of the kin group. Many young men indeed recounted returning from remunerative jobs on migration when family members needed them to return; one even claimed to have been ready to leave for the United States, with a visa procured by his employer, when his mother called for him.[8] Yet residents realized that cultural ideologies needed to be supported by action, and elders tried to create conditions that would persuade young men to contribute to the rural household.

First, they encouraged young men to marry. In this zone, most young men and women still entered arranged marriages requiring substantial bridewealth. When young men had to earn bridewealth on their own, marriage was often delayed; but if elders provided it, they could marry sooner. This reinforced the sense of debt that youth had toward elders. Once married, men were usually expected to farm in the village; it did appear that married men were more likely to remain at home, unless they had exceptionally well-paid outside work. The young men in our sample mostly married quite young; a substantial number were married before they were twenty-five. This was in contrast to many urban educated men who did not marry until they found stable work, often in their late twenties or thirties. My own interviewing staff, mostly single, educated young men, were frankly amazed at the number of village men their age who were already married. Once a man married, children tended to come quickly, and it was easier to support a family in the village than in the city.

Second, household heads invested in agricultural equipment as a way to lessen the difficulty of fieldwork. As they put it, young people these days were unwilling or unable to work as hard as they did when they were young; they could not or would not work exclusively with a hand hoe (*daba*). Elders also recognized that young people wanted to be "modern" and the use of agricultural equipment (mainly ox-drawn plows) had become one indicator of modernity. Of the sixty households, thirty-nine used agricultural equipment on their fields during the study season. The growth of equipment use since the late 1970s was substantial.

Third, household heads allowed significant autonomy to young men in regard to the disposal of income earned from nonagricultural activities. Younger men always had the option of keeping any income they earned from the sale of produce from their individual fields. Earnings were limited since the time that they could spend on these individual fields was strictly circumscribed by the priority given to collective fields. These restrictions were less clear in regard to nonagricultural activities, especially those carried on outside of the main agricultural season (Cf. Grosz-Ngaté 2000). What has changed, however, was the willingness of some household heads to let their income-earning sons and younger brothers carry out nonagricultural activities during the agricultural season, especially when the activity was remunerative and the young man would contribute to the household in some way (e.g., the store owner who gave his household rice). In the past, this was not possible because the standard of living was so low that few village residents had money to purchase the goods and services offered by local entrepreneurs. Even in 1999, few could make a full-time living from nonagricultural activities, but substantial numbers of people earned cash from activities that they carried out within their own villages. Thus a young man did not need to leave the village to earn money. Because most of these jobs were not full time, a father often had access to a young man's agricultural labor at critical periods, while making do without at other times. The young man in turn could not keep all his earnings, but neither was he required to turn all money over to the head.

Fourth, the outside political economy supported this system. Most of these village residents were poorly educated in national terms; they usually had relatively unstable employment when they left the village. Rarely did they find themselves within the national middle class or above; rather most became part of an incipient working class. Despite urban growth, many believed that city opportunities were less than they once were. For those who went abroad, the situation was even worse. Migrants were often stigmatized for being foreigners, and the undocumented were subject to deportation. In contrast, at home, they often found themselves among the most experienced and knowledgeable. They had the security of family and knew that their families and children would be taken care of.

From the local point of view, the problem with these strategies was that they were open only to the wealthier segments of the population. Not all families could afford to pay their young men's bridewealth; many young men had to leave to earn that money. Not all families could afford agricultural equipment; some poor household heads talked eloquently of their inability to purchase equipment and make agriculture more attractive to their youth. Even fewer families could underwrite their young men's activities. Wealthier heads gave loans to young entrepreneurs as they started businesses (e.g., one of the bakers), and one man brought his younger brother back from a disastrous migration experience and gave him capital to start a small trading business. These options simply were not open to poorer heads, who saw their youth leave sooner and stay away longer. This was reflected in a clear correlation between family size and wealth. Virtually all large families were considered to be among the wealthier in the rural zone, while small families usually were quite poor.

This raises the question of whether the differential ability of wealthier households to keep functional extended households will lead to greater stratification.

This remains to be seen. Access to the basic agricultural resource, land, was not restricted and is not likely to be so in the near future. In contrast, access to labor did differentiate wealthier and poorer; in particular wealthy households often hired in labor while poorer households hired themselves out. This may change patterns of labor exchange between households. The extent to which the opportunity to learn more remunerative skills on labor migration or in school is linked to village-level wealth also is unclear.

Nevertheless, it was already evident that poorer households were more likely to use the income from nonagricultural activities to meet immediate subsistence needs, while more affluent households used it to invest in other activities. Moreover, the more affluent households appear to have been able to gear themselves toward particularly remunerative niches, while many poorer households were stuck in activities with only minimal return. Diversifying the activities of the extended household could also allow individuals to attempt some risky activities that promised higher returns; a certain level of failure could be absorbed because of the economies of scale available to them. Smaller households, with less labor, were obliged to put their effort into activities in which return was surer, even if lower.

While the "traditional" form of the household has been retained, the mix of activities done by individuals has changed with the increase in cash-earning, nonagricultural activities. In a desire to keep the labor of young men as well as to increase the benefits from the cash returns of these activities, household heads let some young men decrease their involvement in agricultural work and increase their autonomy in regard to use of income. Extended households benefited differentially because of their greater access to labor. But flexibility did not mean that the tensions inherent in extended family households disappeared. Particular personalities as well as economic factors played into the willingness of young men to remain in extended households. Some young men despaired of ne'er-do-well older brothers or autocratic fathers. Yet as long as the larger economic system remains unpredictable, leaving the extended household brings risk and uncertainty. As long as elders make some accommodation, the extended household continues to provide a context that can provide security yet accept innovation. This has contributed to its tenacity.

NOTES

This chapter is based on research funded by Fulbright Hays PO19A80001, NSF SBR-9870628, and USAID LAG-A-00-96-90016-00. Research in 1970s Kita was funded by

USAID AFR-C-1257 and 1258. Many Malian and U.S. agencies in Bamako facilitated this research; most important was the collaboration of Malian colleagues from the Institut des Sciences Humaines, especially Tiéman Diarra, Mama Kamaté, and Seydou Camara. I bear sole responsibility for the views presented here.

1. See Camara et al. (2000) for further information.

2. Preliminary results can be found in Camara et al. (2000) and Diarra et al. (2000).

3. The OACV's name changed several times since the 1970s; for simplicity, the text refers simply to the OACV.

4. The history of the CMDT in Kita, although only a few years old, has been quite complicated. First, certain activities, although offered through the CMDT, were privatized; most notable was credit, which put the risk of crop failure directly on farmers. This caused problems for the 1999 study sample when extremely heavy rains flooded fields at crucial moments, destroying crops. Second, although the CMDT has had many successful years in Mali, bringing in both significant foreign exchange and increasing farmer incomes (Koenig, Diarra, and Sow 1998), world cotton prices fell in the late 1990s. Charges of corruption within the CMDT also caused problems, and Kita farmers faced falling producer prices in the first years of production. Local feelings about the CMDT were very strong, but varied. While some farmers thought the opportunities offered by the CMDT were positive, others claimed that it had destroyed farming in their zone.

5. Because of the difficulty of access, the First Region has also been less studied.

6. Koenig, Diarra, and Sow (1998) discuss contemporary rural-to-rural migration in Mali.

7. Some small part of the increase in family size may be an artifact of study strategy, where we returned to the same households in the original study. Those household heads from the original study were by definition twenty years older, yet they formed fewer than half of the household heads (twenty-five out of sixty). The other heads were younger heirs, usually sons or younger brothers.

8. Note, however, that by interviewing in the village, we met only those who did return when family members requested it. People rarely told us about those who refused to return, although many did mention children with whom they had lost contact.

REFERENCES

Berry, Sara. 1993. *No Condition Is Permanent: The Social Dynamics of Agrarian Change in Sub-Saharan Africa.* Madison: University of Wisconsin.

Camara, Seydou, Tiéman Diarra, Mama Kamaté, Dolores Koenig, Fatimata Maiga, Amadou Tembely, and Sira Traoré. 2000. *L'économie rurale à Kita: Etude dans une perspective d'anthropologie appliqué.* Rapport interimaire. Bamako: Institut des Sciences Humaines.

Creed, Gerald. 2000. "'Family Values' and Domestic Economies." *Annual Review of Anthropology* 29:329–55.

Dembélé, Niama Nango, and John M. Staatz. 2000. "The Response of Cereals Traders to Agricultural Market Reform in Mali." In *Democracy and Development in Mali,* ed. R. J. Bingen, D. Robinson, and J. M. Staatz, 145–65. East Lansing: Michigan State University Press.

Diarra, Tiéman, Dolores Koenig, Yaouaga Félix Koné, and Fatimata Maiga. 1995. *Reinstallation et développement dans la zone du barrage de Manantali.* Bamako: Institut des Sciences Humaines.

Diarra, Tiéman, Ladji Siaka Doumbia, Mama Kamaté, Dolores Koenig, and Amadou Tembely. 2000. *L'économie rurale à Kita: Resultats de la première étape.* Bamako: Institut des Sciences Humaines.

Gewertz, Deborah, and Frederick Errington. 1999. *Emerging Class in Papua New Guinea: The Telling of Difference.* New York: Cambridge University Press.

Goode, W. J. 1963. *World Revolution and Family Patterns.* Glencoe, IL: Free Press.

Grosz-Ngaté, Maria. 2000. "Labor Migration, Gender, and Social Transformation in Rural Mali." In *Democracy and Development in Mali,* ed. R. J. Bingen, D. Robinson, and J. M. Staatz, 87–101. East Lansing: Michigan State University Press.

Guyer, Jane. 1981. "Household and Community in African Studies." *African Studies Review* 24:87–137.

Izard, M., and J. Ki-Zerbo. 1992. "From the Niger to the Volta." In *Africa from the Sixteenth to the Eighteenth Century.* Vol. 5 of *UNESCO General History of Africa,* ed. B. A. Ogot, 327–67. Berkeley: University of California Press.

Koenig, Dolores. 1986. "Research for Rural Development: Experiences of an Anthropologist in Rural Mali." In *Anthropology and Rural Development in West Africa,* ed. M. Horowitz and T. Painter, 29–60. Boulder, CO: Westview Press.

Koenig, Dolores, Tiéman Diarra, and Moussa Sow. 1998. *Innovation and Individuality in African Development: Changing Production Strategies in Rural Mali.* Ann Arbor: University of Michigan Press.

MacGaffey, Janet, and Rémy Bazenguissa-Ganga. 2000. *Congo-Paris: Transnational Traders on the Margins of the Law.* Bloomington: International African Institute with James Currey and Indiana University Press.

Manning, Patrick. 1988. *Francophone Sub-Saharan Africa: 1880–1985.* Cambridge: Cambridge University Press.

Meillassoux, Claude. 1975. *Femmes, greniers et capitaux.* Paris: Maspero.

Mills, Mary Beth. 1999. *Thai Women in the Global Labor Force: Consuming Desires, Contested Selves.* New Brunswick, NJ: Rutgers University Press.

Perry, Donna. 2001. Strangers and Sons: Trends in Senegalese Time-share Labor. Paper presented at the annual meeting of the Society for Economic Anthropology. Milwaukee, April 26–28.

Roberts, Richard. 1987. *Warriors, Merchants, and Slaves: The State and the Economy in the Middle Niger Valley, 1700–1914.* Stanford, CA: Stanford University Press.

Robinson, David. 1985. *The Holy War of Umar Tal: The Western Sudan in the Mid-nineteenth Century.* Oxford: Clarendon Press.

Labor Discipline, Debt, and Effort in a Philippine Fishing Community

Susan D. Russell

Relatively little anthropological research has been conducted on the factors that influence the nature of fishing labor and strategies pursued by commercialized household fishers, despite the importance of understanding the organization and variation within this group. Worldwide fisheries data collected by the Food and Agriculture Organization (FAO) show an increase in the number of fishers in developing countries, and fisheries management models assume that profit seeking is the principal motivation for this increase. Furthermore, some fisheries management models assume that the best way to reduce overharvesting of ocean resources is to reduce fishing effort through quotas, licenses, and other restrictions on entry. By neoclassical economic predictions, reduced catches per boat will, depending on price factors, logically lead to reduced fishing pressure on maritime resources as more boats find fishing unprofitable. Specifically, as fishing effort increases, the stock is reduced and the catch per boat decreases. As economic returns for effort fall below a predicted equilibrium, then fishing effort should decline enough for biological stocks to recover (Townsend and Wilson 1987).

A number of criticisms of this general model exist. First, some anthropologists (e.g., Russell and Poopetch 1990; Durrenberger 1997) have argued that neoclassical economic assumptions predict behavior based on categories of wages and profits more appropriate to capitalist firms, and that these assumptions do not fit the reality of commercial household fisheries. Kin-based or commercial household fishers retain an ability to respond to lower income from fishing by intensifying effort, by drawing on other household members' sources of income, and/or by reducing consumption costs (e.g., Jorion 1984; Doeringer, Moss, and Terkla 1986; Dyer and Moberg 1992; Durrenberger 1997). Second, it has been argued that fishermen operate according to a worldview that sees maritime conditions as complex and unpredictable—conditions that are not reducible to notions of equilibrium but instead are closer to models of chaos theory (Smith 1990; Wilson and Kleban 1992; Acheson and Wilson 1996). Third, it also has been argued that there is far more variation within the commercial fishing sector than economic models capture, and that policies designed to reduce fishing effort may not be successful if differential skill or technology cause patterns wherein a few boats capture most of the fish (Hilborn 1985; Durrenberger 1993; Russell and Alexander 1998).

These various studies speak to the fact that many commercial fishing enterprises defy policy predictions that they will exit the fishery when catches and/or prices drop below a level of profitability. This "peculiar" behavior, or the "stickiness" of commercial fisheries, sometimes seems irrational to economists while all too familiar to economic anthropologists. Generally, anthropologists note that household and/or owner-operated fishing outfits work harder and can survive lower returns than capitalist fishing firms, owing to the logic of Chayanovian-based household economic theory.

Other anthropologists recently have noted that state policies and high personal debts among fishers have a significant impact on fishing effort. Davis (1991), for example, blames national policies in Canada for creating conditions that have led to high debts and higher effort expended by fishers despite declining stocks. Durrenberger (1994, 1997) also has argued that shrimp processors in Mississippi fund the purchase of expensive fishing boats and fuel, and so fishers work even harder in the event of stable or declining incomes in order to pay off debts and protect a way of life. This relationship wherein high debts lead to increased effort despite reduced catches may be especially true where there are quotas. In Nova Scotia, for example, Maurstad (1992) argues that since quotas go with boat size, people incur high debts in order to buy large boats, which facilitate the capacity and motives for increased fishing effort. Because quotas are allocated to boat owners, the fleet itself has increased and there are now more boats fishing than prior to the quota system (also see Durrenberger 1997).

Since these studies have been conducted in industrialized, Western nations where bureaucratic infrastructure, policies, and plans have long been focused on the modernization of coastal fisheries, they are usefully contrasted with the Philippines, where forms of fishing enterprises and the design and enforcement of fishing policies are significantly different, but where the declining production of coastal fisheries is very pronounced since 1989. This chapter explores these issues by discussing the form of labor organization and discipline among coalitions of crew on baby purse seiners in a Tagalog region of the Philippines. I then discuss three cultural institutions that influence debt relationships, labor recruitment, and discipline in this fleet. Finally, I review some statistical data on the effects of boat owners' wealth, debt to fishing merchants, and fishing effort to show the degree to which high debts account for increased effort.

THE STATE OF PHILIPPINE FISHERIES TODAY

The Philippines is an important producer of fish on a global scale, ranking thirteenth among the fifty-one top fish-producing countries in 1996, with a total production of 1.8 million tons (FAO 1996). Over 90 percent of the catch in the Philippines is sold and consumed fresh.

There are three types of fisheries production subsectors, including coastal fishers, commercial fishers, and aquaculture. Municipal fisheries, the kind I am concerned with in this chapter, encompass vessels that fish within fifteen kilometers of the coastline and that weigh three metric tons or less; they provide 32 percent of total fish production in the country. They also employ 68 percent of the total fishing labor force in the country.[1] Commercial fisheries encompass all larger vessels, and primarily consist of purse seine and ring net fishers, who encircle schools of fish swimming freely or attracted to fish aggregating devices (*payao*) placed in the sea; they provide 34 percent of total fish production. In reality, these two categories overlap, so that many fishers with larger vessels that fall within the commercial fisheries category actually are often informally classified by local officials as municipal fishers. Because such vessels fish offshore within the fifteen-kilometer range of the coastline, they are an indeterminate category by fisheries code definitions, and yet usually comprise an enormous sector of the coastal fisheries population (FAO 2000). The ambiguity of the classification of these vessels as municipal fishers enables boat owners to avoid navigational training requirements for captains, minimum age employment requirements for crew, and the provision of safety equipment on board.

Municipal fisheries in the Philippines show a declining trend of fish production from 1992 to the present owing to overfishing in an open access system and environmental degradation. Municipal fisheries production has declined steadily, from 237,000 tons in 1990, to 186,674 tons in 1995, to 146,471 tons in 1998. Since 1989, municipal fisheries overall have declined by 2.3 percent. In addition, 70 percent of coral reefs have been destroyed by rampant dynamite fishing and the accumulation of silt from the watershed areas (FAO 2000).

LABOR ORGANIZATION IN PURSE SEINING AND RING NET FISHING
In contrast to gill net or other fishing activities popular in coastal areas of the Philippines, purse seining and ring net fishing—two of the most common forms of coastal municipal and commercial fisheries—employ larger crews and use larger boats. Crew size ranges from six to seven individuals on smaller ring net and drive-in net operations to ten to twenty-five individuals on baby purse seine boats, with variability depending on whether it is a peak period for fishing. Powered by sails and oars in the past, all of these outriggered boats today are powered by diesel fuel engines; otherwise, the fishing gear is labor intensive. The nets are large, and must be set and hauled by human labor. No fish-finding gear, radio communication systems, safety equipment, or formal training of skippers characterize the baby purse seine fishing sector.

Baby purse seine and ring net fishing enterprises are generally household owned and operated. However, they are diverse in the degree to which the owner of the boat is also the skipper, the degree to which male kin of the owner or nonrelated males compose the crew, the degree of fishing effort throughout a season, and the degree to which loans from middlewomen helped finance the purchase of a boat and gear.

In San Andres, Batangas, a Tagalog fishing community, there were 4,341 inhabitants in 1990. In 1991–1992, there were sixty-two seining boats owned by residents in the community, twenty smaller ring net fishing boats, and fifty to sixty canoe fishers who practiced hook and line or gill net fishing. There were also 500 to 800 crewmembers who worked seasonally on the purse seiners. Seining is a multispecies tropical fishing venture, with mackerel, small tunas, and round scads comprising a large percentage of the catch. Fishing and fish vending are the primary sources of income for two-thirds of the households; however, about one-third of the households receive remittances from relatives working abroad or in Manila.

The organization of labor on board the fishing boats of baby purse seiners reflects what I have elsewhere described as a petty commodity form of production that adjusts flexibly to declines in income or fluctuations in output through its central reliance on kinship labor (Smith 1986; Russell and Poopetch 1990). Boat owners operate their own boats until they grow too old, when they no longer have the strength to go to sea and prefer to hire their own sons or other close relatives as skippers to keep the money within the family. On fifty-nine of the sixty-two active purse seining boats in the community, twenty-four are skippered by the boat owner, ten by sons of the boat owner, thirteen by other close relatives (cousin, nephew, brother), and only twelve by individuals unrelated to the boat owner. However, owing to the necessity of having a large crew that expands during the peak period, boat owners rely on recruiting other kin and community members. The average number of crew midway through the 1991–1992 season was 13.5, of which an average of 42 percent (5.74 individuals, or less than half) were relatives of the boat owner. An additional 21 percent (2.84) are individuals recruited from elsewhere in the Philippines, primarily Bikol, where the language is similar to Tagalog. Hence, boat owners are required to recruit more than half of their crew from outside their extended bilateral kin groups.

Owing to overfishing and pollution from industries located along the shores of Batangas Bay, the overall catch has declined in this community, although prices for fish have continued to rise. The season for seining, or *pukot*, is fairly erratic and has become unpredictable, with several seasons of poor fishing often followed by a good season. Several factors explain the ability of fishers to stay in operation. First, fishing boat owners rely on their ability to recruit laborers from within their kin groups and the wider community at somewhat unpredictable times throughout the fishing season. Because payment for work is in shares, rather than wages, and because the timing and number of trips depends on the variability in catch throughout a season, owners engage in a constantly shifting form of either attracting or discouraging the number of crew by manipulating formal and informal share payments. If the boat is not successful at catching fish, then owners must support their core crew in other ways until fishing improves. Usually, core crew are relatives or neighbors of the owner. For more casual labor on the fishing boat, however, the number of crew varies with fishing success. If the boat has been unsuccessful in recent trips, casual crewmembers seek temporary piecework or wage employment elsewhere, participate in canoe fishing, or simply remain unemployed. Boat owners and skippers maintain a network of social relations with casual crew, however, which enable them to call on them when fishing activity intensifies.

Labor recruitment in this fishing community has much to do with the nature of interpersonal relationships that underlie the informal work contracts in the fishery. Because these contracts operate between males in the Philippines and extend far beyond family membership to encompass friends and neighbors, as well as strangers recruited from distant areas, they are more properly understood as "coalitions" (Tilly and Tilly 1998). Coalitions are based on exchange contracts, not wage contracts, and link members of a work community with a household; they fall somewhere in between "firms" (characterized by markets and hierarchies) and "households" (characterized by kinship labor). As Tilly and Tilly note (1998, 71–72), "Coalitions sprawl across the boundary of work and non-work, whereas kinship, friendship, and neighborhood concatenate social ties in different ways outside of the world of work." The configuration of any work contract at any time is not a determinate outcome of short-run demands for quality, power, and efficiency but an outcome of a historically contingent bargaining process set within a cultural framework. In short, the nature of labor mechanisms is itself a result of past history and social relations that affect bargaining power between groups (Tilly and Tilly 1998, 73).

Elsewhere I have described the transaction costs in seining that pertain to crew relations with skippers and the set of informal claims among different categories of individuals that govern the highly variable way that shares are distributed in San Andres (Russell 1994; Russell and Alexander 2000). I argued that the maritime share systems on seining boats appear to have even higher transaction costs than agricultural sharecropping systems owing to the greater risk and uncertainty surrounding the timing and amount of the "harvest" and because of the much greater frequency with which shares are divided throughout a fishing season (Russell 1994, 89). In areas where marine resources have diminished, crew sizes are larger, and fishing is the principal form of income, share systems must often be renegotiated during a fishing season or perhaps balanced over several seasons through complicated bargaining between crewmembers and boat owners. The low, uneven, and unpredictable nature of the catch also encourages opportunism among the casual crew and relatively high monitoring and enforcement costs (Russell 1994, 104; also see Szanton 1971). The informal bargaining, flexibility, and variability that mark share systems in Batangas are cultural and historical, but have become accentuated in recent years because of the low returns from fishing and because many boat owners are short of operating expenses. This situation is not unique to Batangas and is common in other parts of Southeast and South Asia (Firth 1966; Szanton 1971; Alexander 1982; Villafuerte and Bailey 1982; Bailey 1983; Barnes 1996).

Boat owners in Batangas are obliged to balance the costs and returns of their fishing boat with the demands of their crew. While most boat owners or their sons are the skippers, in charge of making decisions at sea, when it comes to the share system they are more akin to "managing directors" (Barnes 1996, 180) and must reconcile conflicting opinions and disputes among relatively autonomous crewmembers in order to get them to cooperate. Because they could not attract a minimal crew, three of the sixty-two seining boats studied were inoperative in 1991–1992. The autonomy of crew in these forms of fishing has historical roots (Firth 1966), but is exacerbated by a shortage of labor within the community, which enables young, casual crew to transfer to other boats (Russell 1994), leave the community, or join the canoe fishery.

Owing to this degree of autonomy and mobility, boat owners rely heavily on the incentives of *commitment* (including appeals to solidarity) and, in a minority of cases, *coercion* (unequal bargaining power). Whereas *compensation* would be an ideally efficient way to attract and maintain a disciplined crew, the uncertainty and low returns from fishing largely preclude this as a reliable transaction for most boat owners since income (based on the catch) is so unstable. To a large degree, then, boat owners succeed in attracting and compensating crew by negotiating through the nonproduction networks that intersect most rural labor relations of production. In other words, rather than comprising an impersonal labor market, labor in fishing industries in much of the Philippines is shaped by the forces of nepotism, gossip, patronage, friendship, and *utang ng loob* (debts of the inside), in addition to kinship. Three cultural institutions or patterns enable this type of labor coalition to function: Tagalog understanding of debts, male friendship groups, and the fact that fish dealers (who loan money to boat owners) are almost always women.

CULTURAL INSTITUTIONS AND THE FISHING EFFORT

Debt and Interpersonal Relations Historically

In pre-Hispanic Philippine chiefdoms, as was true elsewhere in Southeast Asia, low population densities relative to land area created political structures where power resided in *datu,* or leaders of shifting personal alliances, rather than territorial political units. *Datu* ruled through a personalized set of political ties that needed constant material and ideological reinforcement, usually cemented through debt sponsorship, intermarriage, elaborate ceremonialism and ritual feasting, coercion and co-optation (such as military raids for captives and slaves or supernatural threats), and the acquisition of foreign trade goods as gifts to be redistributed to followers. While most of the population in one settlement or region was ranked and bound through precisely graded forms of debt bondage to a *datu*, the inherent competition for followers engendered political cycling and the instability of political leadership (Reid 1988; Scott 1980, 1983; Junker 1999). Hierarchy, then, was unstable, and gift exchange was a bond between individuals that gave both donors and debtors power; to participate in social relationships was to participate in the offering and acceptance of debt (Rafael 1988, 122–27, 131).

This type of exchange cemented not only superordinate-subordinate relationships but also relationships between equals. In modern Bikol in the southern Tagalog region, Cannell notes that "despite the relaxed tenor of daily life, encounters with other people are often represented as the mutual, though not always conscious or intentional, testing of power and influence. Social life leads to the discovery of who can 'manage' whom, who will be overwhelmed by whom, or will succumb to another person's powers of seduction" (Cannell 1999, 230).

Kerkvliet (1990, 14) similarly notes in Central Luzon that everyday politics consists of "people trying to make claims on each other and on a range of resources according to their relationships to those superordinate or subordinate to themselves and in terms of their interests and values." Both class and status hierarchies coexist with egalitarianism and all social relationships are marked by strong values of mutual support and aid. Social respect is accorded to those who exhibit and can manage these values in their personal relationships.

Political scientists more recently have argued that the reciprocity and status rank, which once may have characterized patron-client relations, has been eroded, and instead political leaders or "bosses" rule the country. Such bosses may operate as patrons, but essentially are warlords (small-town mayors, provincial governors, congressmen, etc.) whose power rests on inducements, threats, and sanctions, as well as their access to state resources, rather than affection or status (Sidel 1999, 19).

At more local village levels, however, "ordinary" individuals have far less wealth than a mayor. Hence people who vie for local-level informal or formal positions of political influence (such as *barangay* captains) need to attract followers through their social, not material, capital. The most important form of social capital is a mixture of personality and family reputation, as well as the networks provided by a large, extended kindred and their clients and allies (Fegan 1993). Among these allies are one's *barkada* (see below).

As noted earlier, fishing boat owners in San Andres cannot compensate crewmembers or followers through substantial offers of either monetary inducements or lucrative jobs. While they are respected members of their communities, they have little wealth relative to urban elites (Russell 1997). Instead, they rely heavily on their reputations as successful skippers and their wide social networks to recruit crew.[2] While a few boat owners rely on coercion (e.g., by recruiting laborers from the southern tip of Luzon, and by providing them food and housing in barracks but no monetary payments until the end of the season), most boat owners stress their reputation as fair, hardworking captains who share the same plight as their crew. They support an average of one to two crewmembers in their homes, providing them with food, cigarettes, and lodging. In many cases, such crew also share food with the family of the boat owner, thus comprising a household-like unit. In Southeast Asia, the act of eating meals with rice with other individuals is highly symbolic of intimate social relations. In Malaysia, such acts are equivalent to the process of transforming strangers or acquaintances into kin, since the sharing of rice is the sharing of personal substance (Carsten 1997). Tagalog boat owners also commonly make small loans to crewmembers to incur loyalty, and give larger loans (e.g., to purchase a refrigerator or a stove, for example) to the *mamumutot* (or core, specialized crew, usually composed of relatives or very close friends). Such gifts of money, food, and loans are an essential part of masculine behavior and expected of individuals who employ others in the Philippines, and the top skippers in the fleet tend to attract the largest number of crew. In the 1991–1992 seining season, the four most successful skippers caught 25.6 percent of the total catch of the fleet; their average crew size was seventeen, compared to fourteen for the rest of the fleet.

Masculine Gender and the Fishery

Family ties and kinship loyalty, as well as the provision of food and shelter, can account for only a portion of crew recruitment and retention. While the issue is multifaceted, the importance of male friendship groups in Philippine fishing communities accounts for a significant amount of this explanation. A *barkada* refers to an informal gendered group of males, usually of a similar socioeconomic status or class, who have been friends since a young age. Dumont (1993, 402–3), who worked in a fishing village in Siquijor Island, commented specifically on the "seeming omnipresence of the barkada, the informality of its pervasiveness, its obviousness, its matter-of-fact quality." These groups of male intimates spend much of their time together. As a noun, the *barkada* refers to (1) a group of people forming a sort of social gang; (2) a group of people going together on a trip; or (3) a shipload of passengers.[3] Originally a Tagalog word, it has spread throughout the Philippines, although Dumont (1993, 404–5) argues it stems from the Spanish word for boat (*barco)* or boatload, and originally referred to the Filipino prisoners that were brought on Spanish boats to the National Penitentiary in Manila. The association with criminal activity was a message translated first through word of mouth, and later transformed through films and other media into an image of urban and rural male youth subculture. The famous Filipino writer Nick Joaquin wrote,

> The Spanish word for gang is pandilla; but when we preferred to adapt barkada, which means boatload, were we consciously moved by the memory of a time when being together in a boat made people not simply co-passengers but near-kinsmen, almost brothers, pledged to live and work together, to fight and die for each other? That was the Spanish word, an ancient Malay concept. The revival is not merely nominal. Are we not shocked by the fanatic devotion of our boys to their barkada? Have we not heard them say that the barkada is more important than parents or sweetheart or family, and that to fail it is the unpardonable crime? (Quijano de Manila 1980, 13, quoted in Dumont 1993, 405)

The image of male solidarity expressed in the institution of *barkada* is accompanied by the Tagalog concept of *sama,* (to go with, to accompany, to go along). It is at once a notion of identification and loyalty, as well as social support and unity. Dumont also notes that in the fishing village of Siquijor that the most important activity of males was fishing.

> It represented, in their own eyes as well as in everyone else's in the barangay, their main thrust, their constant preoccupation, their key to self-esteem, their claim to desirability, in short, the very justification of their lives. And fishing constantly pulled them away from home and brought them to sea together in a predatory

game in which they, at once and endlessly, collaborated and competed for the same morsels of common property resources. Fish was food and discourse. High-stake gambling of a different order, it determines their access to cash and to power and to women. Not only was caught fish emblematic of men's virility, but fishing was the defining feature of an all-male activity. (Dumont 1993, 423)

The house, in contrast, is the predominant locus of Tagalog women's activities, which in this community primarily include caring for children, preparing food, or engaging in piecework sewing. Married women of good reputation are expected to be in charge of the house, while men talk, repair fishing nets, or quietly drink or play cards and mah jong (a Chinese gambling game) on the verandah of their homes or by the beach (Russell 1997). Men in San Andres spend very little time indoors when they are not sleeping, and are usually present inside the house only during meals.[4] In the fishing village of San Andres, young men who spend much other time inside the home become the target of scandal or rumors about their masculinity. Dumont (1993) similarly notes that in Siquijor, men's time spent at home represents a "break" from time spent with their male friends and a threat to a man's reputation for virility and hardworking character.

In short, the nature of masculine gender is intimately tied to fishing in this community, and to spend time in the house elicits gossip and disdain. If a man has gainful wage employment, then he is working outside of the home and bringing in a regular cash income. For fishermen, however, staying in the home implies laziness or effeminate behavior, and spending time with male friends, fellow crewmembers, or skippers is a highly desirable alternative even though fishing does not ensure a regular or guaranteed income. This unique aspect, itself a function of underemployment in the community and the close intimacy common to groups of Tagalog males, enables boat owners to tap into a wide range of networks when they periodically need additional crewmembers.

Chinese Filipinos, Feminine Gender, and Fish Dealing

While masculine generosity and intimacy place constraints on relationships marked by debts, both Chinese Filipinos and Filipino women occupy a distinct position in regard to commercial transactions. The Chinese have dominated commercial wholesaling and retailing in urban areas, including fish marketing in the Philippines. Recently, Szanton (1998) observed that in the fishing town of Iloilo, Chinese merchants over the last four or five decades

have remained the primary suppliers of loans for fishing boats and equipment, but have steadfastly refused to operate such boats themselves. He attributes this to the social perception of Chinese as "outsiders," and to
consequent Filipino views that associate Chinese with narrow contractual relations of credit and debt. He also observes that groups of Filipino males re-
ject any direct management from Chinese employers.

> It was beyond the physical, social, and political capacity of a male Chinese to
> deal with large groups of Filipino men, precisely the kinds of workers needed to
> operate any sizable form of fishing outfit or other large-scale, labor-intensive
> enterprises. Filipino males, even the most unskilled, found it an affront to their
> dignity, to their definition of what it meant to be a man, to be ordered about by
> a Chinese boss, especially in front of their companions. (Szanton 1998, 257)

Filipino men, however, especially those knowledgeable and skilled at playing the role of patron, can readily organize and discipline the large number of
crew found on seining boats. The process is complex, and morally charged
with mutual expectations of reciprocity, masculine generosity, and the ability
to constantly negotiate and distribute shares from fishing in ways that enable
a boat owner to keep the bulk of profits for himself. The most successful and
popular boat owners in San Andres are considered legitimate "managers"
whose accumulated wealth supports the social and economic exchanges required for a coalition of crew to be sustained over time and in the midst of
daunting challenges. As Szanton similarly notes (1998, 259), the local discourse of patronage is cast in moral terms of reciprocity, mutuality, sharing,
generosity, and redistribution. Inequality is glossed by a "we are all in this together" rhetoric that diffuses the reality of egalitarian, communal, and hierarchical relations. Each catch is ultimately viewed as communal property of the
crew; they allow skippers to take their shares after they receive fish for consumption or to sell on their own. The economic and moral balance that boat
owners/skippers strive for is to reduce the amount of crew demands on the
catch while not manipulating the share system so rigorously that crew are
driven away. Szanton (1998, 260) also notes that outfit operators regularly got
publicly drunk with their crew once a month—whenever shares were distributed—to demonstrate "they were really just 'one of the boys.'"

The kinds of masculine constraints that underlie social interactions also inhibit Filipino boat owners from demanding that crew pay back loans (e.g., 80

percent of boat owners in San Andres had given out loans to crew that were over one year old). Asking someone of a lesser socioeconomic status to repay a loan is an insult (i.e., an insinuation that the debtor lacks the honor to repay). Similarly, captains do not ask crewmembers to return "extra" fish they may have pocketed during a catch, lest they be considered stingy and ungenerous (Russell 1994). Filipino women, however, are under very different gender constraints. It is expected that women will be concerned about money and financing first and social generosity or appropriate status behavior second. In San Andres, women typically handle the marketing of their husbands' catch and often calculate shares for crew. Men are given money for spending purposes by their wives or mothers, but otherwise women are expected to control these finances and keep an eye on expenses. When women are the ones who actually calculate the cash shares to crew after a catch is sold, men can always blame their wives for any objections by crewmembers regarding their payments. Male crewmembers, rather than confront a boat owner's wife, often grudgingly accept his helplessness at his wife's more astute accounting (Szanton 1998, 261).

In part for these reasons, fish dealing, at both the local level and the regional wholesale level in Batangas, is the provenience of Tagalog women. Chinese control the upper-level wholesaling of fish in Manila, but Tagalog women have become increasingly active in the regional commercial trade. In the early 1980s, one woman fish dealer helped finance the purchase of most of the boats in San Andres. The boats were also financed in part from the personal savings or loans from relatives of the boat owners. While this fish dealer capitalized much of the fleet, she did not loan money for fuel or minor expenses of the boat. Smaller loans of this nature are the provenience of local women fish wholesalers, and so most boat owners are in debt to both the large fish dealer and a smaller fish wholesaler. They are expected to sell any significant *kapital*, or fish catches left over after deducting the expenses of the boat and fish for consumption for crew, to the principal fish dealer at reduced rates 10–20 percent below market rates. However, since the principal fish dealer lives in a city some distance from the village, boat owners deliver fish to her irregularly. Any unusual catches of a significant size are reported to her, however, through a system of spies along the coast and in smaller retail markets (Russell 1994).

The role of external financing by this principal fish dealer resembles that described by Durrenberger (1997) in Mississippi, where loans from fish processors fueled an expansion in the fleet and increased the overall fishing effort. Where this case differs, however, is in the extent to which such financing results in higher effort *per boat*. The reality in San Andres is that despite several years of poor catches, only one boat has been confiscated for a failure to repay debts to this fish merchant. In this case, the boat owner refused to go fishing at all, claiming he simply could not attract enough crew. The fish dealer then eventually confiscated the boat owner's fishing net as final payment on the loan, leaving him with the boat but no fishing gear.

This pattern is interesting, in that it follows what I have described elsewhere among Chinese vegetable wholesalers, who dominate the country's fresh produce system. The emphasis is on funding a large number of suppliers, relying on Filipino intermediaries as regional wholesalers and creditors, and buying produce cheap against credit advances. Chinese merchants are competitive owing to their better control of sales and supply outlets, their access to nonformal systems of credit from Filipino-Chinese lending associations, and hence their ability to undercut prices offered by less well-positioned and less well-endowed Tagalog wholesalers who attempt to compete with them (Russell 1987). However, despite high debts to vegetable wholesalers, indebted landowners also very rarely will lose land for a failure to repay loans as long as they are making some attempt to work the land for commercial production (and otherwise not unduly cheating a creditor). Similarly, Tagalog wholesalers rarely will confiscate a boat and equipment if the owner fails to make reasonable repayments as long as he is going out fishing at least some of the time and selling some part of the catch to the dealer.

The reasons why large, external fish dealers do not confiscate boats for debts have much to do with an overall effort to retain steady suppliers of fish, but also relate to a wide range of transaction costs that inhibit repossession of capital assets that would imperil a household's survival. First, the transaction costs of dispossessing a major family in a rural area are high for an outsider, even of the same ethnic group. Resentment or even violent retaliation is likely to ensue and damage a wholesaler's reputation. Furthermore, few external fish dealers know how to operate fishing boats, and in any event lack the local connections necessary to recruit and discipline crewmembers. In contrast, local Tagalog boat owners are closely tied to the community and have the social connections with other males that are required in this kind of setting and coalition style of labor management.

Second, external fish dealers lack the knowledge necessary for determining an accurate amount of effort on the part of boat owners, which inhibits the already difficult process they face in monitoring effort. There are four different fishing strategies within this fleet that involve varying degrees of fishing effort. Some fishing strategies involve extended fishing trips during the peak periods, and other strategies involve more regularized hunting and "scouting" trips throughout the season (Russell and Alexander 1998). All of these strategies yield fish, but involve a wide range in the number of trips, and so fish dealers are forced simply to accept a minimal level of effort as a "good faith" effort on the part of indebted boat owners.

Third, while a major fish dealer helped finance the purchase of fishing boats and gear in this fleet, she does not advance loans for fuel and minor repairs. Local fish wholesalers do so, in return for more immediate repayment of smaller parts of the fish catch. Boat owners who are already heavily in debt to local fish wholesalers can explain that they have been forced to limit the number of trips for lack of financing.

In an earlier paper (Russell and Alexander 1998) that discusses fishing strategies within the San Andres baby purse seining fleet, I noted that debts to fish merchants and the relative wealth of a boat owner are correlated. Wealth also is a significant factor in explaining the number of trips that a boat makes in this fleet (Russell and Alexander 1996). If wealth determines fishing effort, then wealth should be correlated with the number of trips and periods throughout the season when the boat fished. Our data showed that the wealth of a boat owner is moderately correlated with both of these variables, indicating that the ability to afford fishing trips strongly affects the number of trips and length of the fishing season, especially since major fish merchants do not lend money to boat owners for fuel.

We also hypothesized that if a boat owner's debts to fish merchants are significant in determining fishing effort, then debts should be related to the number of trips and periods fished. These were not significantly correlated in our data. This finding suggests that skippers who are heavily in debt fish more intensely during periods when fish are most likely to be caught, but otherwise avoid the beginning and end of the seasons or when there are lulls in the overall fleet's catch record. These findings mirror the comments of Tagalog skippers (Russell and Alexander 1998).

CONCLUSION

Conventional views of fishing labor tend to contrast the organization and motivations of commercial household and industrial fishers in a dichotomous
fashion, while paying relatively less attention to contemporary cultural and
institutional factors that blur our conceptual boundaries among household-
based fishing enterprises, capitalist owner-operated fisheries, and industrial
firm-operated fisheries. Coalitions, a form of enterprise that best captures the
reality of seining operations in Batangas, are best understood as hybrid, albeit
enduring forms of enterprise that are household-owned and operated and
that can form under either capitalist or noncapitalist economies. They are a
hybrid form in that they rely extensively on non-kinship labor, even if the core
operating and ownership unit is based on a core of kinship labor. This conceptualization has the value of implicitly recognizing that workers and employers do not act as isolated individuals, but instead participate, manipulate,
and draw on wide networks of work and social relationships. The degree to
which those who act as employers or managers of coalition enterprises rely on
commitment, coercion, and compensation to motivate their labor force is
variable and likely to reflect and be shaped by strong cultural influences. Tilly
and Tilly (1998, 125) argue that industrial unions and university departments
also can be considered coalitions owing to the types of networks formed
through repeated interactions among workers. To characterize these alternative forms of enterprise as either firms or household enterprises obscures what
is most interesting and unique about the way in which they recruit and manage labor. These kinds of coalition enterprises are commonly found among
fishing enterprises in the rural Philippines and elsewhere, and have undoubtedly been in place for many decades (e.g., Firth 1966; Szanton 1971).

The fishermen I describe here are employed in family-owned and usually
family-operated enterprises, and owners of boats and equipment go fishing
for both subsistence (e.g., they consume their fish as a very significant part of
their family's daily food) and commerce (e.g., they hire both kin and non-kin
labor, seek out new markets for labor, borrow money from fish merchants for
investment in boats and fishing gear and even gasoline, and sell the bulk of
their fish in domestic Philippine fresh markets in order to buy rice—the staple food of the family). They seek profits as well as a minimum subsistence,
but whether they acquire profits or not very much depends on how successful
they are at fishing each season.

At the same time, the nature of economic relations between merchant cred-itors and boat owners, and between boat owners and their crew, are generally not impersonal, and boat owners calculate neither profits nor losses accord-ing to the strict logic of neoclassical economic theory. To explain why these Filipino fishers do not exit the fishery as quickly during "losing years" as econ-omists might expect, to explain why fishing is sticky in this regard, I argue that these fishers implicitly understand what some have called "chaos theory" in fisheries stock fluctuations. They know that the number of fish available to be caught in any particular fishing season is not predictable from year to year; and they take a much longer time framework to calculate their understand-ings of success. Furthermore, merchant creditors are satisfied with some kind of payment on loans during the fishing season, and rarely attempt to confis-cate boats during poor years for fishing.

The framework that I use in this chapter is a "loose" institutional economics theory that encapsulates the social and historical bases of this economy and rec-ognizes the role of transaction costs and bounded rationality in explaining eco-nomic phenomena. Wealthier boat owners tend to rely on compensation, commitment, and, in a few cases, coercion to maintain a crew. Wealth also pro-vides the ability to afford additional fishing trips, depending on a boat owner's fishing strategy. It also means that merchant creditors are likely to make loans for boats and equipment to them, since creditors do not wish to advance loans for diesel fuel and instead prefer to pass these costs on to boat owners. Poorer boat owners tend to rely more heavily on commitment to recruit crewmembers, and their crewmembers tend to have other sources of income in their households and own more material possessions than crewmembers of wealthier boats.

Similar to what Durrenberger (1994, 1997) has argued in Mississippi, the capitalization of this fishing fleet by merchant creditors led to the expansion of motorized fishing boats and increased pressure on maritime resources. For individual boats, however, there is little evidence to indicate that high-debt fishers necessarily pursue high-effort strategies in order to pay off debts. In-stead, they use a variety of fishing strategies; a boat owner's wealth, a skipper's skill, and the ability to attract adequate crew all account for effort. The nature of the labor market itself in this type of fishery also influences effort, as high underemployment enables many boat owners with strong social networks among local males to still go to sea. Debts are very common in rural Filipino farming and fishing life, and low-income populations have long depended on loans and long-term relationships with creditors to enable them to pursue commercial ventures. Assets, whether boats or farmland, are rarely repossessed owing to cultural and institutional barriers that influence market forces. Fishers, however, are not employees; they retain autonomous decision making in the fishery and fish in order to make a living. Their persistence in the fishery despite low catches has much to do with (1) the flexibility of the share system as a method of payment; (2) the differential use wealthy and poorer boat owners make of the local institutions of patronage and male solidarity in crew recruitment and compensation; and (3) the institutional barriers that inhibit fish dealers from repossessing boats.

NOTES

Field research for this project was supported by the National Science Foundation (Grant Nos. 9009745 and 9107136) and a Senior Research Fellowship from the Fulbright-Hays Foundation during 1990 and 1991–1992.

1. This fishing industry employs about one million individuals (5 percent) of the national labor force, of which 675,677 (68 percent) are in municipal fisheries, 258,480 (26 percent) are in aquaculture, and 56,715 (6 percent) are in commercial fisheries (FAO 2000).

2. See Russell (1997) for case studies of the styles of crew recruitment in this community.

3. *Tagalog-English Dictionary*, 160.

4. The exception to this generalization is if the family owns a television. Tagalog television shows are very popular among both men and women.

REFERENCES

Acheson, James M., and James A. Wilson. 1996. "Order Out of Chaos: The Case for Parametric Fisheries Management." *American Anthropologist* 98(3):579–94.

Alexander, Paul. 1982. *Sri Lankan Fishermen: Rural Capitalism and Peasant Society.* Canberra: Australian National University.

Bailey, Conner. 1983. *The Sociology of Production in Rural Malay Society.* Kuala Lumpur: Oxford University Press.

Barnes, R. H. 1996. *Sea Hunters of Indonesia: Fishers and Weavers of Lamalera.* Oxford: Clarendon Press.

Cannell, Fenella. 1999. *Power and Intimacy in the Christian Philippines.* Cambridge: Cambridge University Press.

Carsten, Janet. 1997. *The Heat of the Hearth: The Process of Kinship in a Malay Fishing Community.* Oxford: Clarendon Press.

Davis, Anthony. 1991. "Insidious Rationalities: The Institutionalisation of Small Boat Fishing and the Rise of the Rapacious Fisher." *Maritime Anthropological Studies* 4(1):13–31.

Doeringer, Peter B., Philip I. Moss, and David G. Terkla. 1986. *The New England Fishing Economy: Jobs, Income and Kinship.* Amherst: University of Massachusetts Press.

Dumont, Jean-Paul. 1993. "The Visayan Male Barkada: Manly Behavior and Male Identity on a Philippine Island." *Philippine Studies* 41(4):401–36.

Durrenberger, E. Paul. 1993. "The Skipper Effect and Folk Models of the Skipper Effect among Mississippi Shrimpers." *Human Organization: Journal of Applied Anthropology* 52(2):194–202.

———. 1994. "Shrimpers, Processors, and Common Property in Mississippi." *Human Organization: Journal of Applied Anthropology* 53(1):74–82.

———. 1997. "Fisheries Management Models: Assumptions and Realities or, Why Shrimpers in Mississippi Are Not Firms." *Human Organization: Journal of Applied Anthropology* 56(2):158–66.

Dyer, Christopher L., and Mark Moberg. 1992. "The 'Moral Economy' of Resistance: Turtle Excluders Devices and Gulf of Mexico Shrimp Fishermen." *Maritime Anthropological Studies* 5(1):18–35.

English, Leo James. 1986. *Tagalog-English Dictionary.* Manila: Congregation of the Most Holy Redeemer.

Fegan, Brian. 1993. "Entrepreneurs in Votes and Violence: Three Generations of a Peasant Political Family." In *An Anarchy of Families: State and Family in the Philippines,* ed. Alfred W. McCoy, 33–107. Madison: Center for Southeast Asian Studies, University of Wisconsin.

Firth, Raymond. 1966. *Malay Fishermen: Their Peasant Economy.* 2nd ed. Hamden, CT: Archon Books.

Food and Agriculture Organization (FAO). 1996. *Fisheries Yearbook.* Rome: FAO.

———. "Philippine Fishery Country Profile." 2000. *Fisheries and Agricultural Organization,* Rome, at www.fao.org/fi/fcp/philippe.asp (accessed March 2001).

Hilborn, R. 1985. "Fleet Dynamics and Individual Variation: Why Some People Catch More Fish Than Others." *Canadian Journal of Fisheries and Aquatic Science* 42:2–13.

Jorion, Paul. 1984. "Chayanov Should Be Right: Testing Chayanov's Rule in a French Fishing Community." In *Chayanov, Peasants, and Economic Anthropology*, ed. E. Paul Durrenberger, 71–96. New York: Academic Press.

Junker, Laura Lee. 1999. *Raiding, Trading, and Feasting: The Political Economy of Philippine Chiefdoms.* Honolulu: University of Hawai'i Press.

Kerkvliet, Benedict T. J. 1990. *Everyday Politics in the Philippines.* Berkeley: University of California Press.

Maurstad, Anita. 1992. Closing the Commons—Opening the 'Tragedy': Regulating North-Norwegian Small-Scale Fishing. Paper presented at the annual meeting of the International Association for the Study of Common Property, Washington, DC, September.

Quijano de Manila [Nick Joaquin]. 1980. *Language of the Street, and Other Essays.* Manila: National Book Store.

Rafael, Vicente. 1988. *Contracting Colonialism: Translation and Christian Conversion in Tagalog Society under Early Spanish Rule.* Ithaca, NY: Cornell University Press.

Reid, Anthony. 1988. *The Land below the Winds.* Vol. 1 of *Southeast Asia in the Age of Commerce, 1450–1680.* New Haven, CT: Yale University Press.

Russell, Susan D. 1987. "Middlemen and Moneylending: Relations of Exchange in a Highland Philippine Economy." *Journal of Anthropological Research* 42:139–61.

———. 1994. "Institutionalizing Opportunism: Cheating on Baby Purse Seiners in Batangas Bay, Philippines." In *Anthropology and Institutional Economics*, ed. James M. Acheson, 87–108. Society for Economic Anthropology Monographs, 12. Lanham, MD: University Press of America.

———. 1997. "Class Identity, Leadership Style, and Political Culture in a Tagalog Coastal Community." *Pilipinas: Journal of Philippine Studies* 28:79–95.

Russell, Susan D., and Rani Alexander 1996. "The 'Skipper Effect' Debate: Views from a Philippine Fishery." *Journal of Anthropological Research* 52(4):433–60.

———. 1998. "Measuring Seining Strategies and Fishing Success in the Philippines." *Human Organization: Journal of Applied Anthropology* 57(2):145–58.

———. 2000. "Of Beggars and Thieves: Customary Sharing of the Catch and Informal Sanctions in an Open Access Fishery in the Philippines." In *State and Community in Fisheries Management: Power, Policy, and Practice*, ed. E. Paul Durrenberger and Thomas D. King, 19–40. Greenwood, CT: Greenwood Press.

Russell, Susan D., and Maritsa Poopetch. 1990. "Petty Commodity Fishermen in the Inner Gulf of Thailand." *Human Organization: Journal of Applied Anthropology* 49(2):174–87.

Scott, William H. 1980. "Filipino Class Structure in the Sixteenth Century." *Philippine Studies* 28:142–75.

———. 1983. "*Oripun* and *Alipin* in the Sixteenth-Century Philippines." In *Slavery, Bondage and Dependency in Southeast Asia*, ed. Anthony Reid, 138–55. New York: St. Martin's Press.

Sidel, John T. 1999. *Capital, Coercion, and Crime: Bossism in the Philippines.* Stanford, CA: Stanford University Press.

Smith, Carol A. 1986. "Reconstructing the Elements of Petty Commodity Production." *Social Analysis* 20:29–46.

Smith, M. Estellie. 1990. "Chaos in Fisheries Management." *Maritime Anthropological Studies* 2(2):1–13.

Szanton, David L. 1971. *Estancia in Transition: Economic Growth in a Rural Philippine Community.* Quezon City: Ateneo de Manila University.

———. 1998. "Contingent Moralities: Social and Economic Investment in a Philippine Fishing Town." In *Market Cultures: Society and Morality in the New Asian Capitalisms*, ed. Robert W. Hefner, 257–67. Boulder, CO: Westview Press.

Tilly, Chris, and Charles Tilly. 1987. "An Economic View of the Tragedy of the Commons." In *The Question of the Commons: The Culture and Ecology of Communal Resource*, ed. Bonnie J. McCay and James M. Acheson, 311–26. Tucson: University of Arizona Press.

———. 1998. *Work under Capitalism.* Boulder, CO: Westview Press.

Townsend, Ralph, and James A. Wilson. 1987. "An Economic View of the Tragedy of the Commons." In *The Question of the Commons: the Culture and Ecology of Communal Resource*, ed. Bonnie J. McCay and James M Acheson, 311–26. Tucson: University of Arizona Press.

Villafuerte, E. D., and Conner Bailey. 1982. "Systems of Sharing and Patterns of Ownership." In *Small-Scale Fisheries of San Miguel Bay, Philippines: Social Aspects of Production and Marketing*, ed. Conner Bailey, ICLARM Technical Reports, 9. Quezon City: University of the Philippines in the Visayas, International Center for Living Aquatic Resource Management, United Nations University.

Wilson, James A., and Peter Kleban. 1992. "Practical Implications of Chaos in Fisheries: Ecologically Adapted Management." *Maritime Anthropological Studies* 5(1):67–75.

4

¿Ayuda or Work? Labor History of Female Heads of Household from Oaxaca, Mexico

Martha Woodson Rees

THE QUESTION

Several years ago, Julio García, a Mexican migrant in Atlanta, told me, "*Gracias a Dios, mi esposa nunca ha tenido que trabajar.*" ("Thank heavens, my wife has never had to work.") This, even though I'd worked with him through his unemployment, disability, and other problems, during which time he was unable to send her money. How did she make it if she didn't have a source of income?

Throughout Mexico, male informants report that women don't work in the *campo* (fields), even though everywhere I go, I see women working in the fields. About that same time, I read in Lynn Stephen's 1991 book, *Zapotec Women*, that women took over the agricultural work during the *bracero* (literally, "arms," for imported labor) period in the 1950s, when men from Teetotal del Valle in Oaxaca migrated to the United States. (The men returned with enough money to buy the looms—the means of production for the "genuine American Indian rugs" so beloved by tourists—with designs by Picasso, Escher, and lately, the Navajo.) These two contradictory versions (that women don't work, and that women's work made male migration possible) led me to write the proposal this research reports on.[1] I asked how women manage, especially when their husband is a migrant (who may or may not remit faithfully). One of my ideas was to

invert the migration question from asking how does (male) migration support the household back home, to ask: How does female labor support male
migration? This study has two goals. One is to describe the historical and
current remunerated activities of women heads of household (*jefas*)[2] and
the other, to look at definitions of work and *ayuda* (help) in the central valleys of Oaxaca, Mexico (see table 4.2).

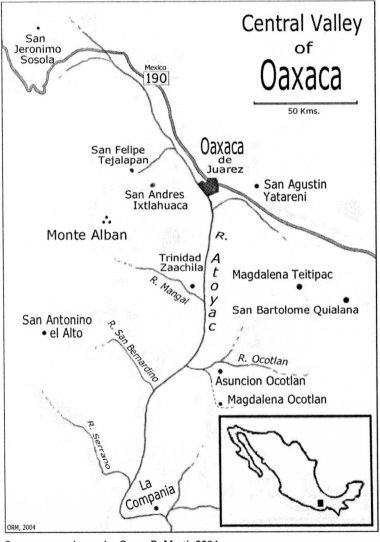

Source: map drawn by Oscar R. Marti, 2004.

THE STUDY

I designed the project to collect data from (a random sample of) female heads of household about their and other household members' activities. In 1998, we applied a survey to between thirty and forty female household heads (total 386) in eleven (out of 121) randomly selected municipal seats (see table 4.1).[3] The survey data describe household composition and structure, work histories of the male and female household heads, current activities of all household members, land and agriculture, migration, household resources, and community participation. In 1999, we carried out ethnographic interviews with selected informants from this sample.[4] These ethnographic interviews did not ask about informants' specific activities and income, but rather: "Tell us about the goat (basket, vegetable, etc.) business," "How much can a person earn?" "What are the costs, labor, and returns?" (see data collection sheet in table 4.2).

Aside from the fact that I've worked in the valleys for years (Rees 1993, 1996; DeWalt, Rees, and Murphy 1994; Murphy, Rees, French, Morris, and Winter 1990; Gijón-Cruz, Rees, and Reyes 2000; Rees, Murphy, Morris, and Winter 1991; Nahmad, González, and Rees 1988; MacNabb and Rees 1993), the valleys are an ideal spot to apply a comparative (synchronic and diachronic) design, since it is the site of a variety of ecological, ethnic, and economic adaptations. The design permits us to talk about regional systems, instead of sticking with the "one community" view so common in ethnographic studies. For example, forty-three of ninety-three studies in the Welte Institute for Oaxacan Studies (www.welte.org) are single-community studies. In addition, while the first studies that specifically deal with women in Oaxaca appeared in the 1980s, there is no survey research that focuses on rural Oaxacan women to date. This focus brings to the fore regional complexities and dynamics, allowing us to reach beyond the romantic story of "my pueblo." The focus on women broadens our knowledge about their role in the Mesoamerican community. Without studying the role of women, we cannot understand household demographics or social reproduction. An additional outcome of this research is better understanding of the dynamics of Mexican migration to the United States, an increasingly important social issue in communities in the United States as well.

VALLEYS OF OAXACA

The central valleys are an ideal site for comparative study because they contain a large number of communities in close proximity to the urban center, the city of Oaxaca. These communities are characterized by a wide variety of ecological conditions (soil, irrigation, and rainfall) (see de Avila 1992), accompanied by a wide variety of economic specializations (Cook and Binford 1990) in a dense market network (Beals 1975; Cook and Diskin 1976), as well as ethnic diversity (Zapotec and Spanish speakers). In the valleys (excluding the city of Oaxaca), 17 percent (122,349 of 735,334) of the population speaks an indigenous language, according to official census data (INEGI 1990), but most of the population of Oaxaca can be said to be of indigenous origin.[5] Because of ambiguity in the use of ethnicity and language, I define individuals, households, and communities by the language they speak (Zapotec or Spanish), without claiming that Spanish-speaking households are culturally distinct. The Zapotecs are a diverse language family, similar to the Romance language family, made up of numerous mutually unintelligible languages. In the central valleys there appear to be a number of separate languages (three in the Tlacolula wing of the valley alone) (Munro and Lopez 1999), although I suspect that "unintelligibility" has political connotations, in that allied communities may admit to mutual intelligibility and communities in conflict may deny it.

DEMOGRAPHIC CHARACTERISTICS

About half of the sample (five) communities have a significant number of Zapotec speakers, the other half have mainly Spanish speakers (six). Demographically, communities are similar—there is no significant difference in median household size (six), number of workers (three), number of female workers (two), or number of children (four) (table 4.1). Communities do differ significantly in terms of other characteristics, especially resources—hectares of land, weekly expenditures per capita, and months the (1997) maize harvest lasted (table 4.1). These differences result in different patterns of labor allocation, especially migration destination. This indicates that there is significant stratification in resources between households and communities in the sample, mainly along the language-use axis, and that this results in differential allocation of labor. Zapotec speakers generally have less education, less maize, more migrants, and spend less on food.

WOMEN'S WORK

How do women's activities fit into this picture? In order to describe women's activities, I look at *remunerated* labor, that is, activities that produce income

Table 4.1. Zapotec and Spanish Household Characteristics (Significant Differences between Communities) 8.5 Pesos = 1 USD in 1998

Community	Household	Female Workers	Workers	Children	Weekly Food Budget/ Capita	Jefa's Education	Service Weeks/ Year	Months Maize 1997	U.S. Migrants
Zapotec									
Asunción Ocotlán	6	2	3	4	28	2	6	5	1
Magdalena Ocotlán	6	1	3	4	37	2	0	5	1.5
Magdalena Teitipac	5	2	3	3	33	3	5	5	1
San Antonino el Alto	6	2	4	4	25	0	10	4	1
San Bartolomé Quialana	6	1	3	4	14	2	37	5	1.5
Spanish									
San Agustín Yatareni	6	2	4	4	25	3	24	9	1
San Andrés Ixtlahuaca	5	1.5	4	4	33	3	7	2	1
San Felipe Tejalapan	6	2	3	4	57	3	8	0	1.5
San Jerónimo Sosola	5	1	3	5.5	39	4	9.5	3	1
Trinidad Zaachila	5	1	3	3	35	4	13.5	1.5	0
La Compania	6.5	2	5	5	34	3	5	6	0
Median	6	2	3	4	30	2	7	4	0

Source: 1998 Survey

or food, not necessarily paid in cash (Berik and Bilginsoy [2000] speak of "not directly remunerative work"). The survey asked each *jefa* (self-designated female head of household) for a summary of her work history (first, second, etc. *trabajo*—roughly translated as work or job), as well as for all of her current activities (including *hogar*, or non-remunerated household work).[6]

Remunerated Labor

We asked each *jefa* to tell us about her (up to five) current activities in 1998. The average number of activities per *jefa* is 2.3 (median = 2). Only 16.3 percent of women report no remunerated activities (excluding *hogar*); these were often elderly women.

Table 4.2 indicates what percentage of women report each (major) activity. *Campo* is the most important activity in every community (66 percent overall), except Yatareni (a semi-urban community where women make and sell tortillas) and in Sosola (a mountain community where women make baskets). Other specializations include animals (26 percent) (mainly goats) in La Compañía as well as in Asunción Ocotlán, Magdalena Ocotlán, Magdalena Teitipac, Ixtlahuaca, and Sosola; commerce (24 percent) of various kinds in Yatareni, Quialana, and Zaachila; tortillas (22 percent) in Tejalapan and Yatareni; and *jornalera* (agricultural wage labor) in San Antonino. There isn't much specialization by language group. More Zapotec-speaking women work in agriculture and as peons, whereas more Spanish-speaking women migrate (mainly to urban areas to work as domestics).

Non-Remunerated Labor

Non-remunerated labor reproduces the household—preparation of food, cleaning, and so forth. *Hogar* refers to (theoretically unremunerated) labor that makes remunerated labor possible: food, fuel, clothing, cleaning, and so forth. In fact, the concept *hogar* needs refining, since 74 percent of respondents said that it was one of their current activities, even though we didn't elicit it, assuming that 100 percent of the women in our sample perform household labor.[7] *Hogar* is not necessarily just reproductive, unremunerated work, since many household activities include such difficult-to-measure but theoretically remunerated activities as raising animals (chickens and pigs) and managing the garden (fruits, herbs). Table 4.3 illustrates a case of pig production, supporting other studies that show that pigs are *not* a source of income. Small-scale animal production is at best a kind of savings (the original piggy

Table 4.2. Jefa's Activities (Jefa Is Self-Designated Female Head of Household) 1998 (%)

Community	Agriculture	Agriculture Day Labor	Tortilla	Crafts	Pasture	Animals	Education	Domestic Service	Vegetables	Commerce
Asunción Ocotlán	.85	.07	.25	.00	.03	.32	.00	.00	.00	.10
La Compania	.86	.04	.03	.07	.12	.45	.00	.00	.00	.01
Magdalena Ocotlán	.81	.00	.10	.00	.03	.42	.00	.00	.00	.19
Magdalena Teitipac	.72	.05	.54	.00	.00	.26	.00	.00	.00	.18
San Agustín Yatareni	.08	.00	.40	.00	.03	.05	.02	.07	.00	.40
San Andrés Ixtlahuaca	.73	.00	.00	.00	.03	.43	.07	.03	.00	.13
San Antonino el Alto	.84	.26	.00	.00	.13	.13	.00	.01	.00	.19
San Bartolomé Quialana	.67	.02	.19	.00	.00	.19	.00	.00	.00	.43
San Felipe Tejalapan	.54	.02	.49	.00	.00	.12	.02	.01	.05	.17
San Jerónimo Sosola	.67	.06	.11	.94	.06	.28	.00	.06	.00	.22
Trinidad Zaachila	.63	.03	.06	.00	.03	.31	.00	.03	.03	.56
Mean	.66	.05	.22	.05	.04	.26	.01	.03	.08	.24

Note: Since women can report up to five current activities, numbers don't add up to 100%.

bank) or transfer of resources within the household (e.g., from male to female) in which the return is, at best, equal to the cost of inputs (excluding labor), and at worst, a major loss.

The example in table 4.3 was generated in Trinidad Zaachila with Señora María,[8] a shopkeeper with a small child and several older children. She gasped with shock when we added up the numbers calculating her costs and returns, revealing that she'd just that morning sold her hog at an $p800 (Mexican peso) loss (June 27, 1999). I was as surprised as she was, thinking that at least she'd have made back her costs. Then she said, "What else can I do with my time?" (This said in spite of the fact that she runs the store and was taking care of a small child, in addition to her older children.)

Other livestock don't necessarily make more money. An analysis of cows in the same community led one informant to thank me for the interview—certainly a first for me—saying, she'd never done these calculations before. Doña Rosa said, "*Con razón no hacen nada. Ni el trabajo sacan*" (That's why they don't make anything, not even their work pays off) (Rosa, Trinidad Zaachila, Rees 27 June 1999). Now, this also surprised me, since I'd always figured that folks had a pretty good idea of what they were making (like a man in San Bartólo Coyotepec in 1985 who'd first explained to me, the dumb anthropologist, that pigs were a savings account, not a moneymaker). One theoretical explanation of the function of these losing propositions lies in the relation between domestic and commercial animal production. Domestic production operates at a loss in the market, but nevertheless raises prices to

Table 4.3. Pig Production

Inputs	Item	Time	Cost/Day/Animal
2 month male pig			250
Feed	1 sack @ $70	3.5 days/3animals	6.70
Maize	1 *almud* (4K) @ $8	1 day/3 animals	2.70
Alfalfa	A bale @ $8 dry season,	2 days/3 animals	1
	$4–5 rainy season	(150 days)	$1560
	(average = $6)		
TOTAL COST			$1810
Labor	Feeding 3 x day	.3	
	Clean pen, bathe pigs	.3	
	(1 hour every 3rd day)	90 hours	
INCOME	7 month pig (5 months		$1000
	of fattening)		
BALANCE			–$810
RETURN ON LABOR	90 hours/1000 pesos	$p10/hour	

the minimum acceptable to the domestic producer, thus permitting the commercial producer a higher rate of profit, a neat transfer from the domestic to the commercial sector (Margulis 1979). One explanation as to why anyone bothers with small-scale animal production suggests itself if we look at the return on labor, without including costs. For the pig in table 4.3, the return is over $p10 (over US$1) per hour, considerably more than the going wage rate. The (unprofitable) hog business might be a way of transferring cash from the store's till (controlled by her husband) to buy the alfalfa and so forth to her own control (in the form of that $p1,000 for the hog), even though it means a net loss to the household. In conclusion, pig production, like many other household activities, is a remunerated activity, even if often unprofitable. This case illustrates how questionable it is to classify *hogar* as unremunerated.

In conclusion, 74 percent of women report remunerated activity—almost all women work, although there are community specializations, affected by proximity to the market and other resources (tortilla production, for example, depends on being within an hour of Oaxaca City; goats need male children for herding). In addition, there may be significant remunerated, productive activity taking place under the rubric *hogar*. How important is this work in household maintenance?

There are a number of obstacles to finding the answer to this question. First, we felt it would be difficult to ask people to reveal their income to interviewers, *gringas* (North Americans) or Mexicanas, who show up at their door one day. Second, as shown above, folks don't always have an exact idea of the income they get from each activity (see table 4.3). But women do know, and aren't reluctant to divulge, often to the *centavo* (penny), how much they spend.[9] We asked women how much they'd spent the week before (or the month before in the case of utilities). In some cases, our interviews took place just after the end of the school year, a time that often involves extra expenditures for clothes and food, but otherwise we have no reason to think that spending was much different from normal during our interview period (summer 1998). People don't spend much on food (median $p800 per household per month, US$120 median per capita),[10] or on anything else, although the difference between communities is significant (table 4.1). Even the weekly per capita maximum, $p57 (US$7) in the peri-urban community of Yatareni, isn't a lot of money—totaling about $p280 per household of 5.8 per week (or $p1120/$US132 per household per month). Some communities are richer or have more cash (urban communities like Ixtlahuaca, Zaachila, and Yatareni). Poorer (or less cash-oriented) communities include San Antonino and Sosola (both located in the sierra).

So, we know how much households spend, but not how much is supplied by the *jefa*'s activities. In 1999, we returned to interview women who represented the range of activities in each community and who had been articulate and willing informants in 1998. Each of us interviewed about three women per community from our 1998 sample, for a total of about fifteen per community. From these interviews, we obtained a range of incomes for each major activity.

In order to estimate the income that a *jefa* could receive from each of her activities and, thus, her total potential income, I created a new variable (income per activity) and recoded each *jefa*'s activities with an income estimate derived from the ethnographic interviews. For example, women reported between $p200 and $p400 income from goats, so I recorded *cría de animales-chivos* (animal, or goat, husbandry) as $p300/month. For the activity *campo*, I calculated the amount of maize produced by the household and multiplied that by its market price of $p4 per kilo and calculated the monthly value of maize production. Admittedly, the *jefa* is not the only one responsible for household maize production, but the value of maize is low (median of $p62 per month). Generally I underestimated the income from different activities.

Women's estimated median monthly income is $p300 (US$35) and households spend $p835 (US$98) on monthly expenses, meaning that women supply 36 percent of household expenses, 75 percent of which is spent on food. If median monthly remittances ($p500/US$59) are calculated, migrants supply 60 percent of average household expenses.

What accounts for the importance of women's contribution to household maintenance? There is a significant negative relation between women's relative contribution and total female workers (p = -.200, sig. .001), and a positive relation with higher paying female occupations (teacher p = .201, sig. 001; domestic service p = .224, sig. .000). There is no significant relationship between monthly remittance, migrant *jefe* (male household head), total male migrants, or hectares of land and women's relative contribution. These data show that women are responsible for almost half of the household food bill.

History

Women's remunerated work is not a new thing, as *jefas*' work histories show. The main change we see since the 1950s[11] is an increase in commercial activities. Activities whose relative importance has not changed much include domestic service, crafts, and agriculture. Activities that increased during this time include agricultural day labor (peon), animals, and tortillas. Work remunerated in cash has increased overall, especially commerce and professional (teachers, nurses) activities.

¿AYUDA OR WORK?

How do these data compare with reports from elsewhere? Have I (re)discovered the wheel? Data from Africa indicate that women's participation in the labor force first declines and then rises with development;[12] that women move from work in family enterprises to work as employees as incomes grow; that fertility declines with income; and that gender gaps in education narrow with development (*Economist* 2001, 43–44; Mammen and Paxson 2000). This is also true for Zapotec-speaking women in the valleys, who have fewer (absolutely and relatively) years of education than their Spanish-speaking counterparts and than Zapotec- or Spanish-speaking males. For women born at the end of the 1960s, average years of education surpasses the average number of children. The relation between *jefas'* income, education, and number of children, however, controlling for her age, is not significant. Although the increase in female waged work is incipient at best, there doesn't seem to be a steady increase in waged (e.g., store employee) work over time; rather, numbers rose in the 1970s (the Mexican boom) and subsequently declined with the onset of the crisis in the 1980s (this is not inconsistent with data from the city of Oaxaca that show a shift into the informal sector over this same time period [Murphy et al. 1990]).

Like Stephen (1991), Coyle and Kwong (2000) report that male migration results in women taking over male agricultural and other duties (at the same time that this work is devalued). Women's strategies in taking on additional duties and the devaluation of their own contribution reinforce the patriarchal social system and bolster the subsistence family farm economy. While my ethnographic data support at least some devaluation of female work, I find no relation between male or *jefes'* migration and female agricultural activity or number of female remunerated workers in the household. Rather, my data seem to indicate that women have always worked, and mainly in the *campo*, regardless of whether or not their husbands and sons are migrants.

Seguino (2000) describes the relation between gender inequality in wages and women's role in the export sector. She suggests that women's relatively lower wages were a stimulus to growth by supporting export production between 1975 and 1995, and not a deterrent to growth as suggested by others. This supports my idea that women's work subsidizes male migration (labor export), although it is not relevant to agricultural work, which is generally not waged.

England, Hermsen, and Cotter (2000) argue that there is a wage penalty (a "general cultural devaluation of women's labor") in female occupations, refuting others who state that women concentrate in jobs that pay less (specialized human capital), especially if those occupations' demand for education is taken into account. This argument does not take women's work (including waged work) in agriculture into account, since there is no educational requirement and it is a field worked mainly by men. In Oaxaca, I can't really say that women concentrate in low-paying agricultural or craftwork, although they do get paid less for agricultural wage labor (as *jornaleras* [day agricultural laborers] they are often paid by the piece, which effectively lowers their daily remuneration).

Cerrutti (2000) finds that female participation in the labor market has increased as part of a strategy to reduce household economic uncertainty resulting from unemployment caused by structural adjustment policies. This contradicts my work histories that indicate that women have worked their whole lives, the crisis of the 1980s notwithstanding, although data from Oaxaca city indicates that more women entered the workforce (an average of one woman in every two households) during the period from 1977 to 1987, which spans the Mexican crisis (Murphy et al. 1990). The increase in numerically less important activities that are remunerated in money, including professional (teachers and nurses) work, responds to the ups and downs of larger economic systems.

Rothstein (2000) reports that the number of women in the workforce increased significantly in central Mexico as households increased the number of people earning a wage to cope with the decline in real wages. Data from the 1998 sample confirm that the number of women in the salaried workforce has increased, although the absolute numbers are small; nevertheless, the proportion of *jefas* working in agriculture has remained relatively stable.

Kramer and McMillan (1999) argue that modern technology reduced demands on women's labor time for preparing maize and, as a consequence, mothers have their first child at a younger age. In Oaxaca, marriage age has actually increased almost five years since the 1940s, and the number of children is not lower for younger women (married in the 1960s) than it is for older women (married in the 1940s); in order to eliminate the effect of ongoing births in younger women, I only look at women married before 1969, and I assume, perhaps in haste, that women married in the 1960s are mostly through having children. It is too early to say if there is a decrease in birth rate in rural areas (there is a decrease in Oaxaca City, see Murphy and Stepick 1991), but there, women married in the 1950s and 1960s certainly haven't reduced their family size. Considering the positive and significant relation between number of children and number of migrants (p = .421, sig. .000) and number of children and number of remitters (p = .164, sig. .001), it could be argued that migration encourages women to have more children, making women's number one remunerated activity the production of labor for export.

The data reported here show that commerce and professional jobs have increased in the central valleys of Oaxaca since 1950, but that there is remarkable stability in agricultural and other work. Unlike other sources, which report that "development" brings greater participation in the wage economy and fewer children, these data show that this participation isn't a linear process but is more attuned to economic cycles.

It turns out that the categories of work and *hogar* don't help us to understand the reality of women's labor in the central valleys of Oaxaca. In terms of the categories used by women in the valleys, other things than remunerated activities are included in their concept of work. Women manage by working, just as they always have. Poor women, landless women, and daughters-in-law earn less; independent women with migrant husbands and their daughters are more able to move into commercialization and earn a living.

Language and Ethnicity

Although over half of the communities don't speak Zapotec, I would argue that Zapotec concepts still pervade the culture of the valleys of Oaxaca. Maya Lin, the architect who designed the Vietnam Memorial, explains that all her life people asked her where she's from. From Akron, Ohio, she said. But, where are you really from? Akron, Ohio. It was only years later that she realized that, even though she did not speak Chinese and hadn't studied Chinese philosophy, she had absorbed (translated) Chinese concepts from her parents (Lin 2000; Krasny 2000). This is the same thing that I argue is going on with the Zapotec concept for reciprocal, unpaid labor, which may be glossed as *ayuda* (help) in Spanish.

I'm not arguing necessarily that there is a Zapotec *profundo* (deep) (Bonfil 1989), but that there is at least the possibility that Zapotec concepts continue to be relevant today, whether or not the people who use them speak Zapotec.

The prime example I want to use is the concept of *ayuda*, often used by men and women to categorize women's work, and often categorized as devaluation by anthropologists and others (England, Hermsen, and Cotter 2000; Coyle and Kwong 2000). Women and men often report that women don't work (*trabajar*), but merely help (*ayudar*) (see Cook and Binford 1990) even though this *ayuda* is often a major, material component of the household labor package. Women report different ideas about work: I help my husband; he doesn't want me to work; I work. These statements represent the variety of ideas about gender and the division of labor that run the gamut from a devaluation of women's work in a patriarchal setting to strong, independent women, conscious of supporting their households.

Not all men are unaware of the role of women's work. In other contexts, men have told me, "everyone knows that women work more than men" (Pedro, San Pedro Quiatoni, July 16, 1993). In San Juan la Jarcia, Juan said, "and this is something that we men have a hard time recognizing, but we're working on it" (July 8, 1989). These last two men were members of Christian-based communities (see MacNabb and Rees 1993). In my 1998 sample, some women (and some men) equate male and female work: "*Como trabaja el hombre, trabaja la mujer*" (Men and women work the same) (Luisa, San Antonino el Alto, 1998).

Other women devalue their work: "*No hice trabajo, nada mas cuidé 2–3 borregos. La mujer no trabaja en el campo hasta que los hijos tengan cuatro años*" (I didn't work, I just pastured a couple of sheep. Women don't work in the fields until their children are four years old) (Luisa, San Antonino el Alto, 1998). Some women categorize their work in the fields as *ayuda*: "*No mas ayudamos*" (We just help out) (Francisca, San Felipe Tejalapan, 1998).

Several women recognize that women's work is not visible: "*No se ve el trabajo de la mujer. Temprano hace tortillas, lleva el almuerzo al campo, trabaja el campo. No lo tomamos en cuenta. A veces da coraje, impotencia, de no poder hacer nada*" (A woman's work is invisible. She gets up early to make tortillas, she takes lunch to the campo, she works in the campo. We don't take it into account. Sometimes it makes you mad, impotent, that you can't do anything) (Juana, La Companía, July 1998).

Yet others report that they don't work because their husband won't let them: "*Mi marido no me deja. Si lo se hacer. Quiero trabajar para mi dinero—comprar la comida y con su dinero hagamos algo [construir]."* (My husband doesn't let me [work]. I know how. I want to earn my own money, to buy food and with his money we can do something [build] (Filomena, San Antonino el Alto, 1998).

A concept that is often said to include reciprocal labor is the word *gue-laguetza*,[13] used throughout Oaxaca to refer to a system of borrowed or loaned labor in Zapotec communities. People—kin, *compadres* (ritual co-godparents), and neighbors—help with agricultural activities with the understanding, often written down in a *libro de guelaguetza* (book), that they can "collect" on this debt when needed. Baptisms, marriage ceremonies, funerals, fiestas, and other social events are also paid for by this kind of loan in kind or money (Diskin 1979; Diskin and Cook 1975; Beals 1975); 33 percent of my sample have a *gue-laguetza* book. Reciprocal labor is also used to build houses (18 percent in the sample, although most people inherited an existing house). The fact that *gue-laguetza* reciprocity is found equally in Spanish- and Zapotec-speaking communities (Rees 2000a) reinforces my earlier points about the existence of translated concepts and the inadequacy of language as a definition of ethnicity. The existence and persistence of *guelaguetza* relations, even in the city, indicate that reciprocity is an important strategy for dealing with inflation, uncertainty, and lack of adequate savings or investment opportunities.

The word *guelaguetza* does not appear in Zapotec dictionaries except as a Spanish word (Munro and Lopez 1999). The core of the word, *guela*, is a transformation of *yela*, an abstract concept meaning, among other things, greatness, the "soul of the word" (Zanhe Xbab 1995). Most intriguing of all is the meaning *precioso* (beautiful), related to the Nahuatl term *quetzal* (the precious feathers of *quetzal-coatl*, the feathered serpent) and perhaps to a generalized Mesoamerican concept of value, or the precious value of reciprocity, the basis of community. *Getz* does not appear in the Zapotec dictionary compiled by Munro and Lopez (1999). The importance of this discussion of reciprocal exchange, called *guelaguetza* or translated as *dar la mano* (lend a hand), is that reciprocity is the basis of peasant communities[14] throughout Mesoamerica. And that reciprocity is often couched (in Spanish) in terms of *ayuda*.[15] *Ayuda*, then, can be redefined, not necessarily as devaluated, noncash work, but as reciprocal labor, labor that the giver expects will be returned one day.[16] Women don't just help out; they make a substantial contribution to the support of their families.

Women aren't the only ones who "help out." Elson (1992) notes that male bias means that female unpaid labor is often not taken into account, and that, especially in agriculture, women (and children) are an integral part of the work force (refer to table 4.1). Donahoe (2000) critiques work typologies in the developing world. Conventional labor force participation measures often ignore a substantial proportion of women's total productive activity, resulting in a limited understanding of the many processes that affect and are affected by women's work. Benería (2000) notes that bias leads to the underestimation of women's work in the labor force. The attempt to account for women's work has gradually evolved to include all unpaid work, including work done by men and children, illustrating how feminist issues have challenged traditional economic thinking. This is in agreement with my findings on work and *ayuda*.

Afshar and Maynard (2000) find that the hegemony of Western feminism means that the range of women's issues (e.g., work) tends to be narrowly and parochially conceived, especially in the use of concepts that are not easily translated into English (or Spanish in this case). The authors argue that non-Western concepts must be moved from margin to center stage. This is relevant to my discussion of work and *ayuda*, and the Zapotec basis of these concepts, even in Spanish-speaking communities.

The valley Zapotec word for work, *zèèi'ny* (Munro and Lopez 1999), refers specifically to cash labor, with fixed hours and a *patrón* or boss (de la Cruz, see note 16). Work, then, is labor remunerated in cash. There is considerable overlap in the concepts of work and ayuda, as well as the concept of *hogar*.

I have not (re)discovered the *hilo negro* (roughly, the wheel), but rather confirmed the concerns of many in the literature: women's work (paid and unpaid) is undervalued and undercounted. The important conclusion I draw from these data is that women's work, or *ayuda*, or whatever you want to call it, is vital in the sustenance of households in the central valley of Oaxaca, accounting for almost half of the total household food budget. Elsewhere I have analyzed migration and remittance patterns (Rees et al. 1991; Gijón et al. 2000; Rees 2000b) and concluded that 26 percent of migrants send no remittances. Those who do, don't send much (an average of $p846/month, or $US100, the median is $p500/month or $US59), but this amount makes an important contribution to household maintenance. Higher remittances are related significantly only to consumer goods (such as televisions), indicating that migrant remittances are mainly consumed (not invested) (Rees 2000b). Women's work is necessary for household survival and may also make (male) migration possible, even though women do not appear to work more if there are more migrants, or less if there is more remittance money coming in. I conclude that women's work makes household survival possible, and has been doing so for quite a while, regardless of male migration patterns.

Elson (1992, 41) argues that migration is a male strategy and although it reduces household expenses (male consumption), it also usually reduces resources even more. The recent increase in the number of female migrants to the United States (Rees and Coronel 2000) may indicate that this is no longer the case. In this sample, migration is not solely a male strategy; in spite of low remittances, the number of migrants is positively related to consumer goods. Not all Mexican migrants cut themselves off from their families, not all operate solely as "free agents" or individuals, but remain tied to their households and communities of origin.

SOCIAL REPRODUCTION

This is all related to community and social reproduction. Social reproduction includes not only the biological replacement of the social group, but the production of sufficient goods for the subsistence and biological reproduction of the group, as well as the social and ideological relations that make it up (Bourdieu 1990/1972, 59). In a social formation with simple reproduction (biological reproduction of the group, and production of sufficient goods for subsistence and biological reproduction and the reproduction of the social and ideological relations) (Bourdieu 1990/1972, 59), there may be contradictory interests. In the case of the pig (refer to table 4.3), the male and female head of household may have conflicting interests; migrants may have different interests from workers at home. The household cannot be treated as a homogeneous unit (Mackintosh 1977).

This perspective on women helps us critique accounts of household labor, and takes unpaid, invisible, devalued labor into account, requiring a new look at household reproductive and productive labor. Not taking women's labor into account misses an important part of household activity. In addition, taking language use into account adds cultural and linguistic concepts to our perspective, resulting in the conclusion that Western, often male, categories cannot be used to freely translate concepts from other languages. Not only do we undercount unpaid labor (male and female) but we also have inadequate categories to talk about it.

I have described the historical and current remunerated activities of women heads of household (*jefas*) in the central valleys of Oaxaca; commercial activity has increased, while many other activities have basically stayed the

same. The data show that women supply over a third of household maintenance. This analysis leads me to conclude that our definitions of work, help,
and household labor are not adequate to describe women's contribution to
household maintenance.

Overall, women provide their households with food, tortillas, and other ba-
sics. Men's income is for construction, cash crops, utilities, ritual (such as
quinceaños, a girl's fifteenth birthday/coming-out party), illness, and other "ex-
tras." Men can migrate because they know their wives have their own income and
their children won't go hungry. Women produce (cash income or agricultural
products) in order to reproduce (including the biological reproduction of the
unit, but also the culture, language, all things symbolized by ritual, community,
and land tenure). They reproduce, and in so doing, produce and export labor.

NOTES

Thanks to Laurel Smith, University of Kentucky, for insightful comments on an
earlier draft of this chapter. Colleagues at the 2001 annual meetings of the Society of
Economic Anthropology (Milwaukee, Wisconsin, April 27–28, 2001), where an
earlier version of this chapter was presented, made substantial useful comments.

1. National Science Foundation #9729824, Women and Migration in the Central
Valley of Oaxaca, Mexico. Analysis was carried out at the Centro de Investigaciones y
Estudios Superiores en Antropología Social-Istmo, Oaxaca, Mexico, with the support
of the Fulbright Foundation.

2. One of the limitations of these data is that they do *not* include all female workers
in the household, just the self- and household-designated head.

3. Martha Rees, Dolores Coronel Ortiz (IIS-UNAM), and Isabel Pérez Vargas
(Chapingo, Georgia State University), with help from Danyael Miller, Shaunda
Blackwell, and Michelle Patterson (supported by an NSF REU grant) designed the
instruments and carried out the survey research. Limitations to the study include the
fact that only municipal head towns were selected. We could suppose that smaller,
nonhead towns might have different characteristics.

4. Rees, Coronel, and Pérez carried out the ethnographic surveys with help from
Vishwanie Persaud, Kelly Taylor, Iyonka Strawn, and Shawn McClain. Data were
analyzed with the help of Kelly Taylor and Currey Hitchens, with the support of an
NSF REU grant and Agnes Scott College.

5. Elsewhere (Rees 2000a), I conclude that language is not a sufficient indicator of ethnicity, since "traditional," "indigenous" behavior—*guelaguetza* (roughly, reciprocity, see below), *tequio* (labor tax), and *cargo* (civil or religious post) do not sort out by language use.

6. There are other female workers than just the *jefa*, and their remunerated labor may reflect generational and educational changes.

7. Discrepancies in interviewers and coders was a problem; probably all women would have included *hogar* in their list of activities if we had elicited it.

8. Names have been changed to protect informants' identities.

9. I've successfully used this technique of estimating household income by eliciting household expenditures elsewhere (Rees 2001). Expenditures may not equal income, but they surely come close in most households, including my own.

10. I use median instead of mean to compensate for skewed data.

11. Because there are fewer work histories that begin before 1950, I limit this analysis to the period 1950–1998.

12. It isn't clear what the definition of development being used is.

13. Not to be confused with the twentieth-century folklore dance show, Oaxaca's largest tourist attraction, wherein urban dancers depict "traditional" dances of the different regions of Oaxaca.

14. Peasants are small agriculturalists who mainly produce with (unpaid) household labor for their own consumption (Wolf 1966).

15. Barabas (1986) has a similar analysis for the Chatino of Oaxaca.

16. Special thanks to linguist María Teresa Pardo, CIESAS-Istmo, for her interpretation and help with the concepts discussed here, especially *ayuda* and *yela*. Victor de la Cruz, CIESAS-Istmo, gave me the definitive interpretations of *ayuda*, *yela*, work, and other concepts.

REFERENCES

Afshar, Haleh, and Mary Maynard. 2000. "Gender and Ethnicity at the Millennium: From Margin to Centre. Introduction." In *Ethnic and Racial Studies* (special issue) 23(5):805–19.

Barabas, Alicia M.1986. "Organización económica de los chatinos de Oaxaca." *Mexico Indígena* 11:16–22.

Beals, Ralph. 1975. *The Peasant Marketing System of Oaxaca, México.* Berkeley: University of California Press.

Benería, Lourdes. 2000. "The Enduring Debate over Unpaid Labour." *International Labour Review* 138(3):287–309.

Berik, Günseli, and Cihan Bilginsoy. 2000. "Type of Work Matters: Women's Labor Force Participation and the Child Sex Ratio in Turkey." *World Development* 28(5):861–78.

Bonfil Batalla, Guillermo. 1989. *México profundo: Una civilización negada.* Mexico: Grijalbo. (In English, University of Texas Press).

Bourdieu, Pierre. 1990/1972. *Outline of a Theory of Practice.* Cambridge: Cambridge University Press.

Cerrutti, Marcela. 2000. "Economic Reform, Structural Adjustment and Female Labor Force Participation in Buenos Aires, Argentina." *World Development* 28(5):879–91.

Cook, Scott. 1968. "The Obsolete Anti-Market Mentality: A Critique of the Substantive Approach to Economic Anthropology." *American Anthropologist* 68(2):323–45.

Cook, Scott, and Leigh Binford. 1990. *Obliging Need: Rural Petty Industry in Mexican Capitalism.* Austin: University of Texas Press.

Cook, Scott, and Martin Diskin, eds. 1976. *Markets in Oaxaca.* Austin: University of Texas Press.

Coyle, Saowalee, and Julia Kwong. 2000. "Women's Work and Social Reproduction in Thailand." *Journal of Contemporary Asia* 30(4):492–506.

de Avila B., Alejandro. 1992. "La diversidad biológica de Oaxaca: Un seguro de vida para un estado temporalmente pobre." *Oaxaca, Población y Futuro* (Revista del Consejo Estatal de Población) 9:14–17.

DeWalt, Billie R., Martha W. Rees, and Arthur D. Murphy. 1994. *The End of Agrarian Reform in Mexico: Past Lessons, Future Prospects.* San Diego: Ejido Reform Research Project. Center for U.S.-Mexican Studies, University of California, San Diego.

Diskin, Martin. 1979. "The Peasant Family Archive: Sources for an Ethnohistory of the Present." *Ethnohistory* 26(3):209–29.

Diskin, Martin, and Scott Cook. 1975. *Mercados de Oaxaca.* Colección Secretaría de Educación Pública-Instituto Nacional Indigenista, 40. Mexico City: Instituto Nacional Indigenista y Secretaría de Educación Pública.

Donahoe, Debra Anne. 2000. "Measuring Women's Work in Developing Countries." *Population and Development Review* 25(3):543–76.

Dutta, Mousumee. 2000. "Women's Employment and Its Effects on Bengali Households of Shillong, India." *Journal of Comparative Family Studies* 31(2):217–29.

Economist, The. 2001. "Africa's Women Go to Work. Small Sums Help Poor Africans Set Up Small Businesses." *Economist* (January 12): 43–44.

Elson, Diane. 1992. "From Survival Strategies to Transformation Strategies: Women's Needs and Structural Adjustment." In *Unequal Burden,* ed. Lourdes Benería and Shelley Feldman, 26–49. Boulder, CO: Westview Press.

England, Paula, Joan A. Hermsen, and David A. Cotter. 2000. "The Devaluation of Women's Work: A Comment on Tam." *American Journal of Sociology* 105(6):1741–51.

Gijón-Cruz, Alicia Sylvia, Martha W. Rees, and Rafael G. Reyes Morales. 2000. "Impacto de las remesas internacionales en el ingreso y calidad de vida de las familias de los emigrantes en el valle de Tlacolula, Oaxaca." *Ciudades* 47:34–42.

INEGI (Instituto Nacional de Estadística Geografía e Informática). 1990. *Resultados Preliminares. XI Censo General de Población y Vivienda, 1990.* Mexico: INEGI.

———. 1995. *Oaxaca por Distrito. Resultados Definitivos. Tabulados Básicos.* Mexico: INEGI.

Kramer, Karen L., and Garnett P. McMillan. 1999. "Women's Labor, Fertility, and the Introduction of Modern Technology in a Rural Maya Village." *Journal of Anthropological Research* 55(4): 499–520.

Krasny, Michael. 2000. "Thinking with Her Hands." *Whole Earth* (Winter): 72–76.

Lin, Maya. 2000. *Boundaries.* New York: Simon and Schuster.

Mackintosh, Maureen. 1977. "Reproduction and Patriarchy: A Critique of Claude Meillassoux, Femmes, Greniers et Capitaux." *Capital and Class* (2):119–27.

MacNabb, Valerie A., and Martha W. Rees. 1993. "Liberation or Theology? Ecclesial Base Communities in Oaxaca, Mexico." *Journal of Church and State* 34:723–49.

Mammen, Kristin, and Christina Paxson. 2000. "Women's Work and Economic Development." *Journal of Economic Perspectives* 14(4):141–64.

Margulis, Mario. 1979. *Contradicciones en la estructura agraria y transferencias de valor.* Mexico City: Colegio de México.

Meillassoux, Claude. 1981. *Maidens, Meal and Money.* Cambridge: Cambridge University Press.

Munro, Pamela, and Felipe H. Lopez. 1999. Di'csyonaary X:tée'n Díi'zh Sah Sann Lu'uc. San Lucas Quiaviní Zapotec Dictionary. Vols. 1, 2. Los Angeles: UCLA Chicano Studies Research Center Publications.

Murphy, Arthur D., Martha W. Rees, Karen French, Earl W. Morris, and Mary Winter. 1990. "Informal Sector and the Crisis in Oaxaca, Mexico: A Comparison of Households 1977–1987." In *Perspectives on the Informal Economy,* ed. M. Estellie Smith, 147–59. Lanham, MD: University Press of America/Society for Economic Anthropology.

Murphy, Arthur D., and Alex Stepick. 1991. *Social Inequality in Oaxaca: A History of Resistance and Change.* Philadelphia, PA: Temple University Press.

Nahmad, Salomón, Alvaro González, and Martha W. Rees. 1988. *Tecnología indígena y medio ambiente.* Mexico City: Centro de Ecodesarrollo.

Pepin-Lehalleur, Marielle, and Teresa Rendón. 1983. "Las unidades domésticas campesinas y sus estrategias de reproducción." In *El campesinado en México: Dos perspectivas de análisis,* ed. K. Appendini. Mexico City: Colegio de México.

Rees, Martha W. 1993. Household Dynamics in Crisis: Women's Work, Migration and Craft Strategies in the Central Valleys of Oaxaca, 1960–1990. Paper presented at the annual meeting of the Society for Economic Anthropology, April.

———. 1996. "Ethnicity and Community in Oaxaca: Nursery, Hospital, and Retirement Home." *Reviews in Anthropology* 25:107–23.

———. 1999. Grassroots Development? Migration in the Central Valley of Oaxaca, Mexico. Paper presented at the annual meeting of the American Anthropological Association, Chicago, November.

———. 2000a. Etnicidad regional: Migración y trabajo en las comunidades indígenas de los valles centrales de Oaxaca. Paper presented at the Primer Congreso

Internacional: Desafíos del Desarrollo Regional—Hacia el Tercer Milenio. Instituto Tecnológico de Oaxaca. November.

————. 2000b. Migración y la comunidad: Efectos locales de la migración en los valles centrales de Oaxaca. Paper presented in the IV Simposio Bienal de Estudios Oaxaqueños, Centro Cultural Santo Domingo, Oaxaca, Oaxaca, July 6.

————. 2001. "How Many Are There? Ethnographic Estimates of Mexican Women in Atlanta, Georgia. Latino Workers in the Contemporary South. Proceedings of the Southern Anthropological Society," ed. Arthur D. Murphy, Colleen Blanchard and Jennifer A. Hill, 36–43. Athens: University of Georgia Press.

Rees, Martha W., and Dolores Coronel. 2000. Tapachula, Oaxaca, San Quintín and LA: Historical Trends in National and International Migration from Oaxaca. Paper presented at the annual meeting of the Society for Applied Anthropology, Merida, Yucatán, March 27.

Rees, Martha W., and Josephine Smart. 2001. "Introductory Thoughts." In *Plural Globalities in Multiple Localities: New World Borders*, ed. Martha Rees and Josephine Smart. Society for Economic Anthropology Monograph Series, vol. 17. Lanham, MD: University Press of America.

Rees, Martha W., Arthur Murphy, Earl Morris, and Mary Winter. 1991. "Migrants to and in Oaxaca City." *Urban Anthropology* 20(2):15–30.

Rothstein, Frances Abrahamer. 2000. "Declining Odds: Kinship, Women's Employment, and Political Economy in Rural Mexico." *American Anthropologist* 101 (3):579–93.

Seguino, Stephanie. 2000. "Gender Inequality and Economic Growth: A Cross-Country Analysis." *World Development* 2(7):1211–30.

Stephen, Lynn. 1991. *Zapotec Women*. Austin: University of Texas Press.

Williams, Aubrey W., ed. 1979. *Social, Political, and Economic Life in Contemporary Oaxaca*. Nashville, TN: Vanderbilt Publications in Anthropology.

Wolf, Eric. 1966. *Peasants*. Englewood Cliffs, NJ: Prentice-Hall.

Zanhe Xbab, SA. 1995. *Diccionario. Reglas para el entendimiento de las variantes dialectales de la Sierra*. Oaxaca: Zanhe Xbab SA.

II

FIRMS AND CORPORATE ENTITIES

The researchers in this section weave the threads introduced by authors of household labor—control of labor, risk, social networks, migration, gender, and identity—to which are added new themes of resistance and union organizing. Like all the authors in the book, these scholars question existing theory and contribute alternative and more powerful explanations for an economic anthropology of labor.

Ortiz refines transaction cost theory, to which she adds the important factors of agency and structure, making this theory even more powerful as an explanatory tool. Ortiz shows how seasonal migrant labor brings flexibility, but also hidden transaction costs for citrus and coffee growers, including the risk factor of limited information on unfamiliar laborers. She builds on Scott's theory of resistance on the part of migrant workers, introducing a concept that runs through Reichart, Marshall, and Pulskamp. Another thread that links these chapters is the organization of labor, and labor resistance, through unions. Ortiz shows the economic benefit of social relations between coffee planter and workers, and the importance of communication between worker and employer, in setting conditions of work and political factors involved in labor, for which the union is not especially effective. This contrasts with research by Pulskamp, Reichart, and Zlolniski on unions as tools of labor resistance. How wages are set, and the larger issue of how labor organization has been transformed, also ties in elsewhere.

Reichart, like Rees, challenges the theory that views women's work as devalued and invisible. According to Rees, the Zapotec concept of reciprocal labor views women's labor as substantial, while the misinterpretation of women's labor as unimportant stems from a linguistic misapplication by Western academics. Reichart argues that women play a critical role in the organization of labor in West Virginia mines, even as they are rendered invisible twice—by industrial capitalism and by historians. Nonacquiescing behavior in the private domain, she argues, has often been interpreted as passivity. On the contrary, women's strategies of resistance during union strikes were extremely effective. These strategies, which have gone unrecorded, include "poundings" based on reciprocity under conditions of risk and uncertainty. "Poundings" were organized through networks and distributed through the informal economy.

All the authors in this section look at resistance in one form or another. Marshall, like Rees and Reichart, considers the links between resistance and gender ideology. Marshall shows that networks of women's cooperatives form as resistance to waged labor employment and the control of labor. But, he argues, while women's work can be interpreted as resistance to the control of women's labor and a challenge to the power structure (by changing the marketplace, the context in which goods are produced and distributed), it cannot be interpreted as challenging gender ideology. Women have not organized to control their work schedules as a challenge to their traditional roles as caretakers. Rather, women control their work schedules in order to continue to meet these standards of care for their families, standards they hold as sacred. In a different time and place, Bowie will show the failure of resistance to the control of labor.

Pulskamp brings the discussion of control of labor, identity, and resistance to bear on the transformation of the workplace. With the transfer of power to the employer comes the proletarianization of the professional worker. Proletarianization of professionals—management breaks down professional jobs and coordinates them so professionals become workers selling labor rather than skills—is a step on the way to becoming abstracted labor, like general laborers who just sell labor or workers in the temporary labor market. The result is a loss of status and blurring of identity. Resistance comes in the formation of organization/union, but it faces a major obstacle—the inability to relinquish identity as a professional and take on the mantle of a worker.

5

Bargaining Wages and Controlling Performance: Harvest Labor in Coffee and Citrus

Sutti Ortiz

Scholars have argued that as agriculture has become modernized and more closely integrated into capitalist economies, farmers cease to retain permanent laborers and hire them only when needed (Bardhan 1980, 1984). Capitalist farmers prefer contracts-at-will (i.e., contracts that allow partners to terminate the relations for whatever reason or no reason at all) because they regard them as lowering the total wage bill and enhancing managerial flexibility. These contracts allow farmers to shift from one laborer to another depending on the talents of each, and facilitate the prompt firing of unsuitable workers (Epstein 1985). Not surprisingly, neoliberal economists recommend legislation that allows contracts-at-will. Citrus and coffee producers are now relying on seasonal laborers for the harvest. Both favor piece-rate contracts.

However, these contracts have hidden transaction costs. The term "transaction cost" refers to the opportunity costs that buyers have to assume to gain information about the laborer's ability, reliability, and attitude, and to ensure that the transaction is completed satisfactorily. Farmers, who have limited information about the ability and commitment of unfamiliar laborers, must repeatedly screen prospective laborers to ensure quality performance and their timely availability (Bardhan 1984; Eswaran and Kotwal 1985; Binswanger and Rosenzweig 1984; Platteau and Nugent 1992; Stanley 1996; Collins and Krippner 1999).

The contract of choice is not necessarily a one-sided solution. As the transaction cost argument suggests, the farmer makes an initial bid that is countered either openly or indirectly by the laborer. In other words, the contract is bargained until a compromise is reached between the farmer (principal) and the laborer (agent). This seems to be the case for citrus workers in Belize (Kroshus 1992). Williamson (1986) assumes that the initial bidding only serves to set the contracting process in motion. As new transaction costs become apparent, the contracts are renegotiated. By assuming that the contract is bargained (Bush and Horstmann 1999), transaction cost theories acknowledge the role of all actors. What we need to add to the model is the impact of cultural and class perspectives on actors' evaluations of transaction costs, their ability to bargain, and the rules they have to abide by when bargaining. In other words, we have to integrate structure and agency considerations (Long 1977, 1992).

Contracts, however, are not always openly bargained. In some cases, farmers do not allow counterbidding and may even fail to disclose the terms of the contract (Breman 1985; Jarvis, Monitor, and Hidalgo 1993; Barger and Reza 1994; Sosnick 1978; Ortiz 1999). The coffee harvesters in the first case study, at least, had the market power to force farmers to increase the piece-rate offered. In Argentina, the situation is more complex. A politically powerful labor movement has forced citrus growers to negotiate an industry-wide collective agreement. The agreement, however, sets general rules and does not empower the laborers of a firm to negotiate necessary adjustments. The laborers are also hampered by the use of labor contractors and a weak market power. The result is that the piece-rate adjustment does not fully reflect farm conditions and laborers seem powerless to force farmers to comply. Differential rates paid to lemon harvesters, thus, cannot reflect the laborers' ranking of preferences—as was the case in the two coffee farms—but a unilateral accommodation by the farmer. As we shall see, it is a costly accommodation.

James Scott has argued that workers who have few options and limited means to fundamentally change their situation resort to everyday forms of resistance to express their protest (1985, 247, 290). He cites, as examples, absenteeism excused as illness and improper threshing to leave more rice to glean (256). These acts are essentially similar to coffee and citrus harvesters' failure to follow harvesting rules and citrus harvesters' high rate of absenteeism. They have an element of instrumentality as well as protest (Pelzer White 1986; Russell 1994). Disregard of work rules allows coffee and citrus harvesters to increase the volume of berries and fruit and compensate for income below what they consider a "fair wage," but it brings berries and fruit of lower quality. Inconsistent attendance represents a stronger expression of disappointment over work-site conditions; it also makes the management of the harvest more costly. Shirking and poorer work performance choices should then be treated as transaction costs associated with specific hiring procedures and not simply as the cost of monitoring work performance related to specific work formats (Ortiz 1999; Thompson 1983; Toth 1993; Turton 1986). If these costs are included in our analysis, we then have to question the contractual strategy of one of the lemon agro-industries. The transaction cost paradigm does not help us to explain this behavior.

An informed transaction cost analysis must then consider how the existing governance rules protect each of the bargaining parties. Since the ability to bargain also hinges on political and economic power, we cannot ignore how differential access to factors of production, to coercive forces, or to political privilege constrains an agent's modes of bargaining (Bates 1994; Russell 1987; Ortiz 1992). Bilateral and economic power also affects the cost of gathering information and controlling performance (Leathers 1999). The two case studies illustrate both the potential and the limitations of the transaction cost paradigm.

THE FIRST CASE STUDY: MODERNIZATION OF COFFEE PRODUCTION IN COLOMBIA

During the decade of 1970, coffee production in Colombia intensified in response to market incentives and subsidies to encourage farmers to replant orchards with a new variety of trees.[1] Between 1955 and 1976 the area planted in coffee was not only renovated but also increased by 26 percent. The impact of these developments on labor markets was significant: It consolidated localized labor markets and altered the mix of labor contract and management practices (Ortiz 1999; Urrea 1976; Errazuriz 1989; Junguito and Pizano 1991).

The first contracts to be eliminated during the expansion and boom years were share and labor service contracts. The demise of share contracts was not surprising since they had never been very popular. Labor service contracts were more commonly used by farmers to attract a readily available core of workers. In exchange for a commitment to work as wage laborers when needed, laborers were offered a house and some land where they could plant food crops for consumption and sale. They also received wages for work performed, though probably at lower than market rate. As the price of coffee increased so did the value of coffee-producing land and the cost of labor service contracts. Furthermore, permanent laborers, under the new legislation, had many more fringe benefits. Farmers were obliged to pay family subsidies if the laborer's income was below a certain figure. They also had to cover some medical costs and a dismissal indemnity. Some of the costs of these fringe benefits were also shared by the laborers. Nevertheless, the burden of the dismissal costs amounted to 26.4 percent of the wage, according to the 1968 Ministry of Labor annual report. A dismissed permanent laborer was entitled to forty-five days' pay for every year that he worked for an employer. As is the case in Argentina, permanent laborers are also paid a Christmas bonus that amounts to a month's pay. Farmers, consequently, evicted many of these laborers, retaining only some under different contractual terms: free housing without access to land for their own crops, for example.

Optimistic about profit, farmers did not think of altering the management of the harvest. They continued to pay harvesters on a piece-rate basis and to attract the mounting number of laborers required by responding to their wage increase demands. They opposed the use of labor contractors. They argued that they would incur higher costs because of the price of the contractor's service and inadequate supervision. They feared higher damage to trees and poorer quality coffee beans.

Piece-Rate Harvest Contracts in Coffee Agriculture

Coffee farmers and laborers value piece-rate contracts for several reasons. Laborers feel rewarded for their effort; it also allows them to enhance their income with family helpers and feel free to shift employment if take-home pay is below what they expect. Farmers believe that piece-rate encourages productivity, since laborers are paid only for what they do. It also allows them to hire all local laborers without having to assume the cost of inexperience (Brown and Phillips 1986). However, piece-rate contracts encourage opportunistic behavior. Harvesters, aiming to increase their earnings, are likely to transgress two main rules: to pick only ripe berries and not damage trees. To control opportunistic behavior, farmers must supervise them carefully. Coffee farmers use permanent wage laborers as crew supervisors, hoping that these privileged workers are willing to confront harvesters. Contrary to what many writers have assumed, attachment to a farm does not ensure the loyalty and commitment of permanent laborers. At the time of my field research, farmers could use two different strategies to foster trust and loyalty. They could be very transparent about mutual contractual obligations, adding that they would comply with the labor legislation (including compensation for dismissal). Alternatively, the farmer could foster dependence and some loyalty through patronage (Platteau 1995). Both strategies entailed costs. Hence, a significant saving could be attained if the proportion of harvester per supervisor could be increased.

Shortly before the harvest, the farmer or his supervisors began the search for workers. With the help of their attached laborers, they contacted their regular workers, encouraging them to bring others. They would then wait for harvesters to drop by; sometimes farmers would go to the town square to look for others. Whether the farmer encountered the laborers singly or in groups, each worker would be hired as an individual. All of them would be informed of the piece-rate and work rules. This hiring policy was time-consuming, but it disallowed group leaders and reduced the chance of organized protest (Wells 1996, 166). One important characteristic of the harvest labor market in coffee agriculture was the openness of bargaining and the transparency of the offers made to the laborers. This mode of hiring laborers changed drastically after the harvest.

Once the offer was made, farmers expected to hear acceptance or rejection of the offer; they were not put off by negative comments. They did not entertain individual counteroffers, but they responded to mounting comments and rejections by increasing the rate paid per kilogram of harvested berries. At the start of the harvest, farmers offered the same rate that prevailed at the end of the last harvest. They increased it progressively if they had trouble recruiting enough laborers. They also kept an eye on rates paid by farmers with coffee groves similar to their own.

Farmers preferred laborers who resided locally. They regarded outsiders as untrustworthy and careless. Migrant laborers also had to be housed and fed. Fights were constant in the large dormitories that house single men. Thus, large groups of migrants could be costly and problematic. The laborers, particularly the migrants, tried to avoid the very large farms, though it was not always possible. When asked, they responded that they preferred a good quality grove and not too large a farm. Local laborers were equally mindful of the distance they had to travel. Although laborers and farmers accepted offers or hired harvesters without asking too many questions, they promptly corrected disappointing experiences. Laborers failed to show up the second day of work if the take-home pay was too low. Farmers fired laborers on the spot if caught damaging trees or consistently bringing too many leaves or green berries. High rates of absenteeism sent powerful messages to farmers. Not surprisingly, harvest take-home pay was high, higher than wages paid in construction and other agricultural industries in Colombia (Errazuriz 1989, 1993; Ortiz 1999).

Earning Differentials and the Laborers' Preferences

Given the competitive nature of the harvest market, the urgency of organizing a reliable crew, and the market power of laborers, one would expect little difference in earnings across local farms. When differences existed, they were expected to reflect the agent's preferences. Earnings in two of the large farms in the area of the study illustrate the weight of preferences and the openness of the bargaining process in the coffee market during the 1985–1986 harvest.

The two farms were equally productive. They were well run and both had good reputations among local laborers. They were not close to each other. The question is not why laborers chose one over the other, but why one farm had to offer a higher piece-rate and spend more on supervision—one supervisor per twenty-five laborers instead of forty-four laborers. In other words, why did one farm have to incur a higher transaction cost in order to attract enough harvesters?

The only significant differences between the two farms were their size and location. Farm A was somewhat smaller and located at a higher altitude than Farm B. In Farm A, the harvest was more prolonged as the berries ripened more slowly. The manager was able to hire a smaller crew of mostly local harvesters and retain them for a longer period than the manager of Farm B. About 25 percent of all occasional laborers were able to work in this farm most of the year (see figure 5.1). The manager of Farm B had to attract a larger number of harvesters and a higher proportion of migrants. He could retain less than 10 percent of the occasional laborers that he needed at the peak of the harvest (see figure 5.2).

Table 5.1.   Harvesters' Earnings in Two Large Coffee Farms
(Earnings Are Expressed in Colombian Pesos)

	Farm A	Farm B
Average seasonal piece-rate	$9.12	$10.81 (16% more)
Kg. berries per day per worker	78 kg	73 kg (6% less)
Weekly cost per laborer	$5,815	$6,258 (7% more)
No. laborers per supervisor	44 laborers	25 laborers
Percentage migrants	24%	38%

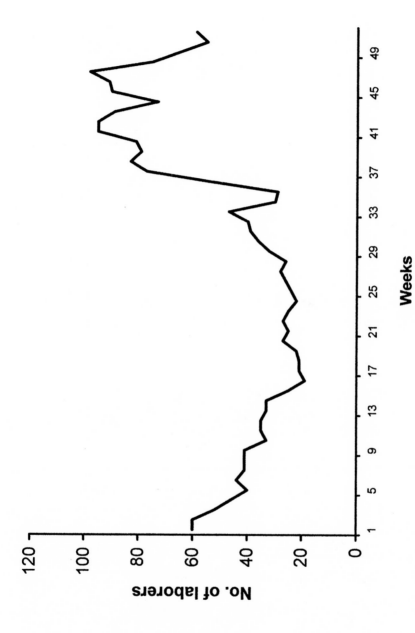

FIGURE 5.1
Number of Occasional Laborers per Week in Farm A (March 1985 to March 1986)

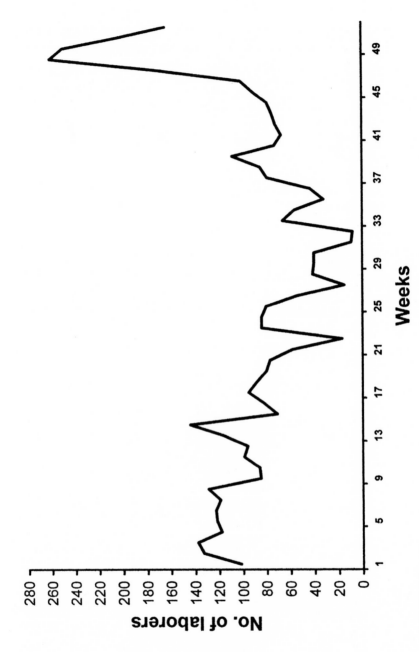

FIGURE 5.2
Number of Occasional Laborers per Week in Farm B (January 1985 to December 1985)

At the beginning of the season, the manager of Farm B offered $9 (all amounts are in Colombian pesos) per kg of berries. However, he had to increase it several times and, by the end of the season, he had to pay $11 per kg of berries. The seasonal average was $10.81, despite the fact that they hired a large number of women harvesters. Farm A, instead, initially offered $8 per kg and $10 at the end of the season; the seasonal average was $9.12. Both farms managed to retain their laborers and avoid confrontations. Records of Farm A show very low absenteeism, despite the lower rate. It was not possible to compare the quality of the work in each farm, but I assume that there was no significant difference. In both cases, the harvesters' daily take-home pay was above the legal minimum wage of $452 and the average preharvest wage of $460. However, in Farm A, 22 percent of the harvesters received a take-home pay that did not match the highest preharvest wage paid in the region, while in Farm B only 2 percent of them did so. Furthermore, in Farm A only 13 percent of the laborers managed to earn what was considered to be a "fair harvest wage" ($1,000) in 1986, while 77 percent of the harvesters did so in Farm B.

The contrast in incomes raises three related questions:

1. Why did one farm raise the piece-rate a number of times throughout the season while the other one did not?
2. Why more laborers tolerated lower incomes in one farm than in the other?
3. Why laborers in Farm A were not able or willing to force the farmer to increase the piece-rate?

The answers to these questions fit the predictions based on a transaction cost paradigm. Farm A could satisfy the laborers' preference of steadier employment during most of the year. As figures 1 and 2 indicate, Farm A can retain a higher proportion of laborers throughout the year by switching them from harvesting to maintenance tasks. The owner also gave small lots of land for house building to encourage laborers to settle near the farm. Most of the core crew resided in the settlement that emerged. The owner of Farm B used the same strategies but he had to cope with greater fluctuations in labor demand and the need for many more harvesters. He had to attract a higher proportion of migrants who were not interested in more permanent employment.

The predictions of the transaction cost paradigm are confirmed but only because a number of bargaining conditions prevail:

1. The laborers are hired by the agent who is responsible for paying them and is free to set the rate he will pay.
2. The laborers have clear preferences that are relatively easy to rank. They are also verbal about their preferences. Higher income is one of their preferences.
3. The market is competitive.
4. The urgency of the harvest and the limited number of locally available workers give harvesters considerable bargaining power. They are quite aware of it. As they explained to me, "The harvest is when we rule." Bargaining conditions are very different during the slack period.

THE SECOND CASE STUDY: LEMON PRODUCTION IN TUCUMÁN, ARGENTINA

Spanish and Italian migrants planted citrus trees when they settled in Tucumán around 1870.[2] But it was not until 1960 that lemons attracted the attention of local investors. In response to incentives offered to revitalize the provincial economy, farmers and industrialists built better packing establishments and lemon processing factories. Lemons and lemon products became exportable commodities. The first shipment of fresh lemons reached Europe in 1971. The success of these ventures led to an astronomical growth in area planted in lemons; it has grown almost fourfold since 1969 (Batista and Naterras Rivas 1998). In the year 2000, Argentina became the number one world producer of lemons and began exporting not only to Europe and Asia but also to the United States. As with coffee in Colombia, the expansion of the lemon orchards resulted in a higher labor demand. These producers, however, did not have to struggle to attract them. Regional unemployment was 14 percent during 2000, and many of the farms are located near the larger urban centers.

There are four other significant differences between these two case studies. In the first place, the growth of the lemon industry was accompanied by a concentration of land in the hands of four very large, vertically integrated enterprises that control the export and industrial market (Batista and Naterras Rivas 1998; Aparicio and Benencia 1999). These enterprises process not only the fruit they produce but also fruit grown by medium and small producers.

They handle 63 percent of the fruit exported and they process 87 percent of the fruit that is industrialized (Asociación Tucumana de Cítrus 2000, 23). To ensure quality and to control the flow of fruit to their packing premises, these enterprises purchase 90 percent of the fruit on the tree. In other words, these four enterprises assume responsibility for the harvest of a large quantity of fruit in farms spread over a wide area. Although these enterprises have considerable economic power and can influence provincial policies, they cannot expect support for repressive forms of labor control.

The second significant difference between coffee and lemons is the perishability of the commodity. The quality of lemons destined for the factory is not too problematic. But lemons that are to be packed for export must show no blemishes. They cannot be handled while moist with rain or dew, particularly early in the season. The fruit bruise easily if held too tightly or bumped against each other. The lemon should not be pulled from the branch but carefully cut with special scissors, leaving a short stem and avoiding piercing the skin. Consumers are also fickle and each market demands a different size and type of fruit. To some extent, the fruit can be selected when packed but, early in the season, the harvester is also asked to select the fruit by size. Only orchards with factory-quality fruit can be harvested by hand at a fast pace. In most other cases, the fruit sent to the factory has been harvested for export but is discarded by the packers. Careful performance is thus very important to most producers. Nevertheless, farmers and enterprise managers prefer piece-rate contracts. They try, instead, to control carelessness through supervision and sanctions. Coffee producers do not face such stringent quality requirements and thus avoid very high supervision costs.

The third important contrast is the protection and benefits that Argentine harvesters are entitled to receive (Aparicio et al. 1987; Alfaro 1999, 2000; Formento and Francia 1997). Harvest laborers must be hired as seasonal laborers and recalled in subsequent years. They must be registered in the official payroll that is submitted to the office of the provincial department of labor. They are granted health coverage and family subsidies and are entitled to retirement benefits. The cost of these benefits is covered by contributions from employers (25 percent of wages) and a 17 percent deduction from the laborers' take-home pay. Seasonal workers also have a right to Christmas bonus (paid in two installments) and sick and vacation pay. If they work on Sundays and holidays, they have a right to double pay. Most employers avoided complying with the law. They had no trouble attracting laborers, since most young unmarried men prefer to avoid heavy deduction from their pay, even at the expense of qualifying for social services and retirement benefits. In the past two years, however, government surveillance has made it more difficult to avoid compliance. Large enterprises now register most or all of their laborers. In Colombia, seasonal workers received no benefits and very little protection.

The fourth difference is that in Argentina, labor unions are important actors in the rural setting. Since the 1970s, UATRE (Unión Argentina de Trabajadores Rurales y Estibadores, or Union of Argentine Rural Laborers and Stevedores) has represented the citrus laborers of Tucumán. In recent years, representatives of this union meet every three years with citrus growers to negotiate the terms of the labor contract. UATRE is a national organization that, since 1990, also administers the health clinics that serve their members. All laborers registered in the labor office are automatically enrolled in the union; the membership fee is deducted from their paychecks (2 percent of their pay and another 1.5 percent for burial insurance). The collective agreement is rather brief. It lists the fringe benefits and responsibilities that employers must assume. It also sets the base wage that each category of worker must receive and defines the minimum weight of fruit that he must harvest to attain it. By custom, the piece-rate is adjusted twice a year to reflect early harvest and high harvest changes in the productivity of labor. Since it varies with the condition of the orchard and harvesting equipment used, the piece-rate differs from employer to employer. UATRE is not a combative organization and has not pushed to increase wages. The last strike they supported was in 1994 when some small wage gains were achieved. Laborers from one of the large enterprises walked out of the orchards during the harvest of the year 2000, but the union did not support them and asked them to return to their jobs. Harvesters are very critical of the union and have no contact with their leaders. Very few of the crews have union representatives. Nevertheless, UATRE has a considerable political presence.

From Permanent to Occasional Contracts

As orchards expanded and farms specialized in a single crop, the number of seasonal laborers required was increased. It became very costly to handle most of the farmwork with a contingent of permanent laborers. Farmers also became convinced that permanent laborers had become less productive. I have not been able to evaluate the veracity of the first assumption, but it is still keenly felt by small farmers and managers of very big enterprises. Slowly, the large enterprises began to mechanize maintenance tasks and to negotiate the dismissal of their permanent laborers, a costly procedure that has to be carried out a step at a time. Most large enterprises retain some permanent workers, some of whom become supervisors. Piece-rate contracts became the contract of choice when harvesters have to be hired. Because they had enjoyed decades of secure employment and protection, citrus workers do not prefer these contracts. Their loss of institutional protection was also coupled to a loss of market power.

Labor Contractors

Lemon producers have decided to subcontract the harvest. Threats of industrial action, unionization, and large fringe benefits are all associated with the use of labor contractors (Vandeman, Sadoulet, and Janvry 1991; Polopolus and Emerson 1991). The first labor contractors appeared in the citrus industry of Tucumán during the late 1980s, as the large enterprises emerged. By 1992, most of the currently active large harvest service firms were in operation. These firms have offices, computers, some permanent administrative and supervisory personnel, small trucks, and some equipment. Each of them recruits from 1,000 to 2,000 harvesters and crew leaders each season. Their task is to transport the laborers to the farms, supervise the crews, pay them, and handle all relevant payroll responsibilities. They are not represented, however, during the negotiation of the collective agreement. These large service firms harvest most of the fruit purchased by the vertically integrated enterprises, as well as the fruit produced by other large farmers. Smaller firms handle mostly the harvest of medium producers and packers, though occasionally they serve large clients. Labor contractors who only have a truck and minimal harvesting equipment serve only the small growers who sell their fruit to the factories or in the regional fresh fruit market. There are an unknown number of these contractors, none of whom complies with any labor regulations. They handle at most 10–13 percent of the industrialized fruit. In this account, I limit my discussion of contractors to the large service firms that serve two of the four enterprises. One of these enterprises handled 33 percent of all of the fruit exported in 2000; the other firm handled only 11 percent. The factory of the first firm processed 38 percent of the industrialized fruit and the other firm processed 11 percent during the same period.

The use of labor contractors, however, is problematic and costly. Labor contractors are also paid by volume of fruit harvested, a method that encourages opportunistic behavior on their part. Thus, the enterprises that hire them do not entirely entrust them with the supervision of the harvesting crews. They send their own set of supervisors who monitor quality and the volume that must be harvested on a particular day. The service firms' supervisors also monitor quality but are more responsible for discipline in the workplace and the coordination of activities. Also present is a representative of the producer, who checks that trees are not damaged and that fruit is not left on the tree. It is a very expensive form of controlling opportunistic behavior. In effect, these enterprises delegate only a few responsibilities. They not only continue to supervise but they also program the harvest, and set the method of harvesting the fruit and the piece-rate that harvesters should be paid. The large enterprises also contribute some of the equipment used to move the fruit. Consequently, a service firm with more than one client might have to pay different rates and use more than one harvesting system.

Although the service firms officially hire the harvesters, the person who searches for the harvester and communicates with him is the foreman. Before the harvest starts, the service firms contact their regular foremen and ask them to organize crews with a given number of harvesters. These foremen, in turn, call on their habitual laborers and let it be known that they might need others. During these encounters the foreman is asked for whom he is working this year and when they are going to start. Two other frequent questions are whether workers will be paid weekly or fortnightly and whether the firm will offer advances. Some may ask if they are expected to bring their own cutting instruments. Heads of households with young children are likely to convey that they would like to be registered in the formal payroll so that they are entitled to benefits. Laborers have to wait, usually until the first day of harvest, to hear from the firm's supervisor what the piece-rate will be. When the crew first arrives at the farm, the foreman gathers them and informs them what harvesting system they will use and what work rules they must follow. Returning laborers who were once registered in the payroll (they are labeled as permanent but discontinuous) find it difficult and time-consuming to reregister under a new employer. They risk a long delay in receiving fringe benefits if they change employment or risk not receiving fringe benefits at all. However, if the day wage is very disappointing, the harvester might still be tempted to miss a few days at a time and work as well for an employer who hires him clandestinely. A harvester with children, for example, can commit himself to work for a contractor that offers social security benefits and compensate for low pay and high payroll deductions by occasionally joining a crew that offers higher take-home pay. This option becomes more costly if the contractor pays them the 8 percent bonus to which workers are entitled for not missing more than a day of work each fortnight. However, few of them seem to comply. Thus, legal hiring practices and the attendance bonus limit the room that laborers have to express their protest and to adjust their income, but it does not entirely curtail it.

Day Wage Differential

Although enterprises have to comply with the base pay and number of bags required to earn the base pay, each one has to adjust the piece-rate to reflect farm conditions and harvesting method used. The largest and most innovative of all the enterprises (no. 1, table 5.2) asked the service firms they hired to pay laborers the rate set in the collective agreement. As indicated in table 5.2, the set rate allowed laborers to earn at least the daily wage of $12 as specified in the collective agreement. Enterprise no. 12, instead, set the piece-rate much higher. Yet many harvesters earned less than what the agreement specifies and a smaller proportion earned above it. Table 5.2 documents the earnings of laborers in five different crews, hired by the same service firm but harvesting in the two enterprises mentioned.

Table 5.2. Harvesters' Earning and Absenteeism in Two Enterprises Harvest of Year 2000

	Average Daily Earning in Dollars % of Laborers in Each Income Category (1)					% Laborer Absent (2)	Average Bags per Harvester (3)
Enterprise	<12	12–14	15–19	20–24	>24		
1	5	17	30	35	13	12	57
1	—	22	61	16	1	18	43
12	—	49	43	8	—	15	30
12	14	38	33	13	2	47	30
12	31	57	12	—	—	32	25

1. Enterprise 1 paid $0.393 per 20-kilogram bag and Enterprise 12 paid $0.50.
2. Only more than two days' absences per week are considered. Laborers may be absent on Mondays and Saturday to drink rather than to protest or to work elsewhere.
3. The average is estimated for the whole crew. Piece-rate is measured in terms of 20-kilogram bags harvested.

The earning differential is due in large part to the harvesting method chosen by each enterprise. Enterprise no. 1 had invested in equipment that facilitated the task of the laborers and protected the fruit from damage. Bins for depositing the fruit are placed very near the tree where the harvester works. Once filled, they are transported to the loading area with new equipment used to reduce bruising of fruit. This enterprise has also invested in expensive monitoring costs. They label the bins, which allows supervisors to trace the laborers responsible for the fruit in it. At the end of the day, the bins are sampled for quality and the information is given to the service firm and the foreman of the crew. The responsible laborers are sanctioned if the discard is higher than 15 percent and warned if it approaches that figure. Enterprise no. 12 uses an older and more inefficient harvesting system. Laborers have to carry their loaded bags to where a truck with bins is parked. They often have to stand in line to wait for the fruit to be quickly scanned for quality. If acceptable, they are given a chip, which is used later to confirm the amount each laborer has harvested. It is a system that does not enhance the productivity of laborers, but it is much cheaper.

Enterprise no. 12 does not offer any other benefits that could offset the lower pay the laborers receive. The laborers tolerate it for the following reasons:

- They are not given the opportunity to negotiate the rate with the agent who sets it. They negotiate, instead, with the service firm, which does not have the power to set contractual terms.
- When hired, they are not informed for what client their crew will work.
- Their opportunity wage is very low; because of high unemployment, they have few employment alternatives.

Although laborers do not quit and seldom strike, they respond with absenteeism, as the table indicates. They might also respond with more careless handling of the fruit, but I was not able to measure it because the enterprises used totally different methods of monitoring quality. Absenteeism does not serve to successfully pressure the enterprise to increase the piece-rate. The managers of enterprises deny the link between earnings and absenteeism. They ascribe it to ineffectual disciplining of the service firm's supervisor or the lack of work ethics of the laborer. Enterprise managers have become too removed from the problems associated with recruitment to pay attention to the message of irregular attendance—yet absenteeism can be costly since it affects the daily volume of fruit that arrives for packing. I have not yet been able to determine how problematic it might be for each one of the enterprises mentioned here.

CONCLUSION

The transactions cost paradigm serves to adequately explain income differences between two large coffee producers. Laborers in one of the farms benefited from trading-off lower wages for secure income. The farmer profited not only from a lower wage bill but also from the commitment of his workers, which allowed him to cut costs of supervision. The other farm needed to attract a higher proportion of migrants, who could be retained only with high short-term returns. The higher cost represented a trade-off for a timely harvest and high-quality dry beans.

Income differences in citrus production cannot be explained as bargained solutions of principal and agent's preferences. No other benefit countervailed the lower income of laborers in Enterprise no. 12. Furthermore, the laborers in both enterprises were not able to bargain effectively, either directly or indirectly. Income differences, instead, were an unintended consequence of contrasting investment policies. One enterprise favored a cheaper harvesting system with probably higher fruit discard. The other enterprise wanted to invest in higher productivity and fruit quality.

One may still argue that the transaction cost paradigm helps to explain the unilateral decision about the mix of labor process strategies. For example, that the higher transaction cost related to volume fluctuation and perhaps of fruit discard of Enterprise no. 12 was balanced by the lower investment cost required.[3] Such arguments, however, assume that the managers who set the rate are mindful of the message sent by the laborers. It does not seem to be the case. The information on absenteeism was not available to the harvest manager of the enterprise; I had to obtain it from the service firm. Only Enterprise no. 1 kept detailed records about quality of fruit brought by each crew. The weakness of the laborers' bargaining position and use of service firms interfered with the enterprise's ability to gather information about shirking factors. The explanatory power of transaction cost arguments rests on the assumption that agents are able to bargain and effectively communicate their opposition to offers. That was the case for coffee but not for lemons.

Protective labor legislation and union representation, ironically, did not effectively improve the well-being of citrus harvesters. Their income, by local standards, is considered a hunger wage. The bureaucracy of fringe benefits and subcontracting has also hindered the ability of individual laborers to protest in an effective and timely fashion. It is hard for them to redress situational disadvantages. Coffee laborers, by contrast, earned enough to save money for the lean months that awaited them. They were also in a better position to force farmers to increase the piece-rate since they benefited from a market advantage. Coffee growers, paradoxically, refused to bring cheaper laborers. This allowed laborers to bargain.

In all cases producers attempted to reduce the opportunism that flaws piece-rate contracts. The two coffee farmers mentioned balanced supervision with incentive: higher wage or longer employment. It is very likely that this dual strategy served to reduce the transaction cost of piece-rate contracts, but this is very difficult to prove. No incentives are offered to laborers in the citrus enterprises cited. Their strategy is to develop a "fair" and effective system to monitor and sanction the performance of laborers and evaluate the service of the labor contractor. A group of smaller farmers, however, is experimenting with a system of bonus payment for high-quality harvested fruit. These two divergent citrus strategies (sanctions versus bonuses) rest on different ideological premises: the viability of trust and the perceived "obligation and responsibility" of laborers (Ortiz and Aparicio forthcoming).

The more stringent quality control methods used by citrus growers obviously relate to the perishability of the fruit. In both cases, damage to the tree will affect future yields. Both coffee and lemons have to be harvested selectively, but only the latter have to be handled with care after it is cut from the tree. Citrus harvesters, in the large enterprises, are also more likely to be tempted by speed than are coffee harvesters. Their income is lower and they are no longer allowed family helpers. In Colombia, the less-adept coffee harvesters could bring young daughters or a wife to help with the task. Frustration about their inability to earn enough harvesting lemons or choose a work site discourages commitment to the stipulated work ethics. I have already mentioned absenteeism as a means of redressing pay shortcomings. Another is to disregard fruit-handling rules and cover up the evidence. In the larger of the two enterprises mentioned, 10.31 percent of the fruit was either badly cut or incorrectly selected; another 4.75 percent was bruised by the time it was placed in the bin. By the time it reaches the packinghouse, new bruises or unnoticed blemishes will appear; a very large proportion of the fruit has to be sent to the factory. Improper harvesting has been described as forms of protest. Coffee and citrus producers, however, interpret this behavior as reflections of poor work ethics and try to correct it with sanctions and, recently, by refusing to rehire those who use it or firing them after a number of warnings.

NOTES

1. The data here presented are based on a field study of coffee agriculture in two municipalities of Risaralda and one in Cundinamarca. It was funded by the National Science Foundation (BNS 8570614).

2. Susana Aparicio, University of Buenos Aires, has been researching the transformation of the citrus industry. Her help and advice were invaluable. I first went to Tucumán in 1999 and then again in 2000, to look at labor contracting in sugar cane and compare it with contracting in the citrus industry. The collapse of the sugar industry and rapid mechanization of the harvest convinced me to concentrate on the labor process of citrus producers. I returned to the field in October 2001 to reinterview labor contractors, enterprise managers, and interview farmers, crew leaders, and laborers. My field research has been supported by the Wenner Gren Foundation (Gr 6546).

3. However, since all enterprises pay the same rate to service firms, they are unlikely to factor in labor costs when making decisions about harvesting systems. Labor costs were the same for both enterprises since they paid the same rate per weight of fruit to the service firm. The latter compensated for losses related to lower productivity by reducing supervision, which contributed to poor work performance.

REFERENCES

Alfaro, María Inés. 1997. Notas en torno a las luchas de los trabajadores rurales en la Argentina. Paper presented to the Conference on Rural Employment and Flexible Policies, National University of Buenos Aires, December.

———. 1998. Los asalariados rurales en un mercado de trabajo moderno: Posibilidades para la construcción de la protesta social. Unpublished manuscript.

———. 1999. "Los espacios para la negociación laboral en la citricultura Tucumana: Actores y estrategias." *Revista Estudios del Trabajo* 18 (segundo semestre), ASET.

———. 2000. Marco regulatorio de la contratación y organización sindical en el mercado de trabajo citrícola en Tucumán. Informe (Unpublished manuscript).

Aparicio, Susana, and Roberto Benencia. 1999. "Empleo rural en la Argentina: viejos y nuevos actores sociales en el mercado de trabajo." In *Empleo rural en tiempos de flexibilidad*, ed. Susana Aparicio and Roberto Benencia, 29–82. Buenos Aires: La Colmena.

Aparicio, Susana, Mónica Catania, María Iturregui, and Marte Palomares. 1987. "La legislación del trabajo agrario: análisis y propuestas." Series: *Aproximaciones*. Buenos Aires: CEPA.

Asociación Tucumana de Citrus. 2000. *Noticiero*, 23. Tucumán, Argentina.

Bardhan, Pranab K. 1980. "Interlocking Factor Markets and Agrarian Development: A Review of Issues." *Oxford Economic Papers* 32:82–98.

———. 1984. *Land, Labour and Rural Poverty: Essays in Development Economics*. New York: Columbia University Press.

Barger, W. K., and Ernesto M. Reza. 1994. *The Farm Labor Movement in the Midwest: Social Change and Adaptation among Migrant Farmworkers*. Austin: University of Texas Press.

Bates, Robert H. 1994. "Social Dilemmas and Rational Individuals: An Essay in New Institutionalism." In *Anthropology and Institutional Economics*, ed. James Acheson, 43–66. Monographs in Economic Anthropology, 12. Lanham, MD: University Press of America/Society for Economic Anthropology.

Batista, Ana Ester, and Juan José Nateras Rivas. 1998. Expansión de la actividad limonera y repercusiones sobre los pequeños productores en la Provincia de Tucumán. *Baetica* 20:7–20.

Binswanger, Hans P., and M. Rosenzweig, eds. 1984. *Contractual Arrangements, Employment and Wages in Rural Labor Markets in Asia*. New Haven, CT: Yale University Press.

Breman, Ian. 1985. *Of Peasants, Migrants and Paupers*. Oxford: Clarendon Press.

Brown, Martin, and Peter Phillips. 1986. "The Decline of the Piece-Rate System in California Canning: Technological Innovation, Labor Management, and Union Pressure, 1890–1947." *Business History Review* 60:565–601.

Bush, Lutz-Alexander, and Ignatius J. Horstmann. 1999. "Endogenous Incomplete Contracts: A Bargaining Approach." *Canadian Journal of Economics* 32:957–75.

Collins, Jane, and Greta R. Krippner. 1999. "Permanent Labor Contracts in Agriculture: Flexibility and Subordination in a New Export Crop." *Comparative Studies in Society and History* 41:510–34.

Epstein, Richard A. 1985. "Agency Costs, Employment Contracts and Labor Unions." In *Principals and Agents: The Structure of Business*, ed. John W. Pratt and Richard J. Zeckhauser, 127–48. Boston, MA: Harvard Business School Press.

Errazuriz, María. 1989. *Mercado de trabajo y empleo en la caficultura*. Bogotá, Colombia: Fedesarrollo.

———. 1993. "El empleo y los salarios durante la crisis: que muestran la evidencia empírica?" In *Economía cafetera: Crisis y perspectivas*, 159–88. Bogotá, Colombia: Centro Editorial Javeriano.

Eswaran, M., and A. Kotwal. 1985. "A Theory of Contractual Structure in Agriculture." *American Economic Review* 75:352–67.

Formento, S., and A. Francia. 1997. Flexibilidad laboral y modalidades contractuales en el sector agropecuario: una perspectiva legal. Paper presented at the International Conference on Rural Employment, University of Buenos Aires.

Jarvis, Lovell S., Cecilia Monitor, and Mauricio Hidalgo. 1993. "El empresario fruticultor: fortalezas y debilidades de un sector heterogeneo." *CIEPLAN* (Corporacion de Investigaciones Economicas para Latinoamerica) *Notas Técnicas, 154.* Santiago, Chile: CIEPLAN.

Junguito, Roberto, and Diego Pizano. 1991. *Producción de café en Colombia*. Bogotá, Colombia: Fondo Cultural Cafetero, Fedesarrollo.

Kroshus, Medina Laurie. 1992. Power and Development: The Political-Economy of Identity in Belize. PhD diss., Department of Anthropology, University of California, Los Angeles.

Leathers, Howard D. 1999. "What Is Farming? Information, Contracts and the Organization of Agricultural Production: Discussion." *American Journal of Agricultural Economics* 81:621–23.

Long, Norman. 1977. *An Introduction to the Sociology of Rural Development*. London: Tavistock.

———. 1992. "From Paradigm Lost to Paradigm Regained? The Case of an Actor-Oriented Sociology of Development." In *Battlefields of Knowledge: The Interlocking of Theory and Practice in Social Research and Development*, ed. Norman Long and Ann Long, 16–46. London: Routledge.

Ortiz, Sutti. 1992. "Market, Power and Culture as Agencies in the Transformation of Labor Contracts in Coffee Agriculture." In *Understanding Economic Process*, ed. Sutti Ortiz and Susan Lees, 43–60. Monographs in Economic Anthropology, 10. Lanham, MD: University Press of America/Society for Economic Anthropology.

————. 1999. *Harvesting Coffee, Bargaining Wages: Rural Labor Markets in Colombia.* Ann Arbor: University of Michigan Press.

Ortiz, Sutti, and Susana Aparicio. Forthcoming. "Management Response to the Demands of Global Fresh Fruit Markets: Rewarding Harvesters with Financial Incentives." *Journal of Development Studies.*

Pelzer White, Christine. 1986. "Everyday Resistance, Socialist Revolution and Rural Development: The Vietnamese Case." In *Everyday Forms of Peasant Resistance in South-East Asia,* eds. James Scott and Benedict J. Tria Kerkvliet, 49–63. London: Frank Cass.

Platteau, Jean Phillipe. 1995. "A Framework for the Analysis of Evolving Patron-Client Ties in Agrarian Economies." *World Development* 23:767–86.

Platteau, Jean Phillipe, and J. Nugent. 1992. "Share Contracts and Their Rationale: Lessons from Marine Fishing." *Journal of Development Studies* 28:386–422.

Polopolus, Leo C., and Robert D. Emerson. 1991. "Entrepreneurship, Sanctions and Labor Contracting." *Southern Journal of Agricultural Economics* 23:57–68.

Russell, Susan. 1987. "Middleman and Moneylending: Relations of Exchange in a Highland Phillippine Economy." *Journal of Anthropological Research* 43:139–61.

————. 1994. "Institutionalizing Opportunism: Cheating on Baby Purse Seiners in Batangas Bay, Philippines." In *Anthropology and Institutional Economics,* ed. James Acheson, 87–107. Monographs in Economic Anthropology, 12. Lanham, MD: University Press of America/Society for Economic Anthropology.

Scott, James. 1985. *Weapons of the Weak: Everyday Forms of Peasant Resistance.* New Haven, CT: Yale University Press.

Sosnick, Stephen H. 1978. *Hired Hands: Seasonal Farm Workers in the United States.* Santa Barbara, CA: McNally and Loftin West.

Stanley, Denise L. 1996. Labor Market Outcomes in a Natural Resource Boom: The Case of Mariculture Exports in Honduras. PhD diss., Department of Anthropology, University of Wisconsin, Madison.

Thompson, Paul. 1983. *The Nature of Work: An Introduction to Debates on the Labour Process.* London: Macmillan Press.

Toth, James. 1993. "Manufacturing Consent and Resistance in Peripheral Production: The Labor Process among Egyptian Migrant Workers and Egyptian National Development." *Dialectical Anthropology* 18:291–335.

Turton, Andrew. 1986. "Patrolling the Middle-Ground: Methodological Perspectives on 'Everyday Peasant Resistance.'" In *Everyday Forms of Peasant Resistance in South-East Asia*, ed. James Scott and Benedict J. Tria Kerkvliet. London: Frank Cass.

Urrea, Fernando. 1976. *Mercado de trabajo y migraciones en la explotación cafetera.* SENALDE, Migraciones Laborales, 9. Bogotá, Colombia: Ministerio de Trabajo y Seguridad Social

Vandeman, Ann, Elizabeth Sadoulet, and Alain de Janvry. 1991. "Labor Contracting and the Theory of Contract Choice in California Agriculture." *American Journal of Agricultural Economics* 67:681–92.

Wells, Miriam J. 1996. *Strawberry Fields: Politics, Class, and Work in California Agriculture.* Ithaca, NY: Cornell University Press.

Williamson, Oliver E. 1986. "The Economic of Governance: Framework and Implications." In *Economics as a Process: Essays in the New Institutional Economics*, ed. Richard N. Langlois. Cambridge: Cambridge University Press.

6

We're to Stand Side by Side: Household Production and Women's Work in Rural Mining Communities

Karaleah S. Reichart

Much research attention in anthropology and the social sciences has been directed to understanding the complex distinctions between "domestic" labor—such as household production, mother-child relationships, and "female" work—and labor in the "public" sphere, including participation in government, wage occupations, and the "male" realm. Feminist scholars have explored the strategies used cross-culturally by women to negotiate the demands made on their labor and economic resources by families, and specifically their husbands. The ongoing process of economic and social change allows for the elucidation of multiple connections between micro-level processes and structures at the regional and national levels, effectively linking the household and the family to the wider set of political economic processes in which they are embedded. By analyzing social formations historically, we can see relationships among women in conjunction with the rise of global industrial capitalism.

One of the primary means of investigating these interconnections is by turning our attention to the rural economy as a focal point of social change with the transformation from subsistence agriculture to industrial capitalism. Under conditions of relatively equal gender status, the spheres of domestic and public labor are not sharply delineated. As demonstrated by Sanday (1974), however, the stratification of power according to gender increases significantly when the relative economic contribution of men is either much more or much less than resource inputs received from women's economic activities.

Many Marxist analyses are centered upon the reliance on women's domestic or household labor for the reproduction of the labor force under capitalist systems of production. It stands to reason that if the division of wage labor in the workplace is strictly based on gender, then necessary work conducted within the household is implicitly linked to the opportunities for women's entrance into the wage-labor market. As a result, the conflation of culturally accepted gender roles and household organization serve to restrict women's participation in the formal economy. This observation of women's participation in the formal economy, however, is only as relevant as the historical context in which it is made, and is dependent on the recognition of a variety of political economic circumstances that serve to shape these outcomes. It remains to demonstrate how productive relations specifically interact with social norms of household organization and gender roles.

Political economic approaches to the gendered division of labor have been criticized as functionalist, based on their emphasis on the sexual and household relations of production as determined by the capitalist division of labor. Indeed, it has been argued that while capitalism has transformed the processes of production and reproduction, these transformations have been equally affected by existing forms of gender and social relations (Bozzoli 1983), and that the attribution of all social change to the rise of industrial capitalism is fundamentally incorrect. I demonstrate in my research, however, that in consideration of historical contingency and the context of social change, in many cases capitalist stakeholders *are* the primary agents of social change, and use their power to order not only the relations of production but the social and gender relations of a community as well. The focus of my research rests at the heart of the multifaceted history of capitalist production, rural development, and the gendered division of labor in single-industry communities in the central Appalachian coal-mining region of the United States.

THE GENDERED ECONOMICS OF COAL PRODUCTION
The development of the coal mining industry in Appalachia has been identified with widespread labor strife, including armed violence and the proliferation of company-union animosity among single-industry communities across the state. Beginning with the movement to organize coal miners in the early 1900s and continuing with today's issues of mountaintop removal and environmental awareness, women's roles in community labor disputes have changed consider-

ably. Although coal companies did not directly employ women, I discuss how women's roles as community stakeholders shaped household economic dynamics and destabilized gender categories during strikes.

The gendered division of labor, as it is socially constructed and promoted by the production systems of extractive industries, has been the focus of much research during the twentieth century in the United States. The Appalachian coal industry provides yet another elegant example of the colonial model of resource distribution as applied to the contemporary United States. Between 1890 and 1920, the population of the southern coalfields increased fivefold, two-thirds of which included recent European immigrants who were lured to America by overseas advertisements and promises of great riches from the mining of "black gold" (Corbin 1981, xiv). To house this fresh population influx, companies engineered and constructed "coal camps" complete with company-owned churches, stores, dentists, doctors, cinemas, and police forces. In addition, companies routinely exchanged a miner's labor for scrip, company-specific cash that could only be redeemed for goods at the company store. During these early days of industrialized coal production, more miners of West Virginia lived in company towns than those in any other state.

To maintain control of these communities and avert the constant threat of the labor organization and unionization among the miners, companies across southern West Virginia utilized complex systems of surveillance to monitor the activities of miners and their families. Through a combination of superstition, rural geography, and the historic fraternal structure of local branches of the United Mine Workers of America, women were systematically prevented from entering the mining wage-labor force during the early twentieth century. Until the late 1970s, women were routinely forbidden from entering large underground mining operations, although in small family-owned operations women had been mining coal since the early nineteenth century. The relative isolation of these coal communities also limited the opportunities for women to bring alternative sources of wages into the household. Undoubtedly, if a miner's wife did happen to find work outside of the camp, her cash wages would be exchanged at the company store for a much higher rate, which also discouraged the acquisition of standard U.S. dollars.

Companies enjoyed no strategic advantage by encouraging women to seek employment outside of the coal camp. Rather, by decreasing a miner's dependence on wages from his wife, the company was encouraging a miner's dependence on the company and hence ensuring the smooth operation of the mine. The strict division of women and men into separate spheres of labor and community interaction was a strategy in which women were relegated to the private sphere. At the same time, however, women were highly visible components of the community and were observed meticulously through random house inspections of company-owned houses, often leading to what would be considered by today's standards unbearable amounts of housework and domestic labor. The fact of being constantly seen, and of always being able to be seen by company management, maintained discipline in the company town and thwarted many early activist efforts among women in these communities.

The United Mine Workers of America, however, did successfully organize the southern coalfields, and the ensuing labor conflicts split communities into union miners and "scabs," or replacement workers. During these violent conflicts and strikes, women assumed a variety of roles in the community, including participation in political activism, civil disobedience, and armed resistance against company police. Without this public yet informal support from women, the strike efforts of union miners would have certainly collapsed under the considerable structural power wielded by paternalistic company management. Indeed, it is important to understand how women were involved in shaping the local political economy in southern West Virginia.

The relationships witnessed in Appalachia between the capitalism of extractive industry and strict gender roles exhibit an inherent contradiction: company operators and miners have competing interests in women's labor. While women produce and reproduce the informal means of existence, including food and clothing, they are also engaging in social reproductive activities to maintain the coal community. During periods of relative labor-management peace, or when unionization activities were successfully suppressed by company surveillance, women engaged in household activities and the daily maintenance of the home, including cleaning, raising children, and preparing meals. These domestic-sphere activities were directly in support of the functioning of the coal town economy, as the mining labor force was being successfully reproduced from day to day and one generation to the next. When strikes and labor disputes arose, however, women's labor immediately served a very different purpose. Women in coal communities under siege by labor conflict were no longer directing their efforts to the reproduction of the labor force; rather, many women chose to prolong the strike by participating in nonviolent resistance and political action, thus allowing the dispute to continue until the most favorable labor-management contract settlement was reached.

Because of the very specific economic strains that strikes imposed on the maintenance of the family and household, the goals and interests among women during these conflicts were not always in support of the goals of the miners' union, or their husbands. This separation of objectives often resulted in active participation in labor-industrial disputes on behalf of women in support of their own interests, which contributed to the destabilization of the strict public-private dichotomy and precipitated culture change and the reformation of gender roles. In fact, women's narratives that I obtained throughout the course of this research reflect a complex process of decision making that facilitated changes in gender roles during strikes that often divided women in the community. In this context, a woman's withdrawal from participation in a particular strike event did not imply that she was acquiescing to the public dynamics of power surrounding the labor-industrial dispute. Rather than ceasing to be an agent of social change by removing herself from a public conflict, in some cases a woman in southern West Virginia was actually promoting her own interests and goals. By not agreeing to pool scarce resources during conflicts, such as miners' strikes that were not popular among women in the community, women prevented miners from promoting their own interests and effectively ended such disputes by shifting the balance of power back into the hands of the coal operators.

The gendered division of labor was expressed as an integral part of daily work life in coal communities across southern West Virginia during the first half of the twentieth century. Thus, the gendered Victorian stereotypes of labor divisions emerged in the material reality of coal towns in southern West Virginia and continued into the second half of the twentieth century. Women were effectively relegated to the "domestic" sphere, fulfilling the responsibilities of maintaining the household and child-rearing duties (under the direct supervision of coal operators), while their husbands and fathers mined coal for scrip wages. Companies implemented these divisions to reinforce the political-economic conditions in which they were constructed and utilized.

To overlook the gendered household labor in coal communities as "private," however, is to misunderstand the role of women's work within the context of the political-economic dynamics of the coal industry. The portrayal of women as losers or victims within the paternalistic machinery of the coal industry would imply that they were passive participants in the system, essentially reinforcing the various ideologies of control promoted by the coal producers. Given that the coal town system was so precise and obvious in its gendered division of labor, it stands to reason that women would evolve strategies to adjust to and resist this level of surveillance and control. In fact, my research examines the early historic shifts in visibility of women's labor and demonstrates that women played an important role in shaping work structures and gender roles in their communities by actively participating in arguably the most divisive form of "public" conflict in their culture—labor-industry disputes. Although the rigid coal company towns of the past no longer exist, women continue to initiate and participate in a variety of activities during coal town labor conflicts; including political activism, community organizing, civil disobedience, media campaigning, and picketing.

This chapter briefly evaluates historical data pertaining to the early development of the coal industry, approximately 1880–1920. Based on four years of ethnographic and historical fieldwork in the coalfields, I elucidate some of the complex relationships between wage labor and household labor in coal camps, and how these practices are complicated by women's involvement in community labor-industrial disputes. I address three central issues pertaining to household production and conflict in coal towns: (1) how women negotiated the precise and obvious gendered division of labor imposed during the transition from subsistence agriculture to industrial capitalism; (2) what strategies evolved to shape household work structures and gender roles to accommodate women's interests following large-scale industrialization; and (3) how these complex relationships between household and wage labor are complicated by the expression of women's interests as stakeholders during industrial disputes.

COLONIZATION AND POWER

Following much heated debate on the floor of Congress, the American Civil War eventually led to the secession of West Virginia from the state of Virginia, and the establishment of its own statehood on June 20, 1863. Antebellum West Virginia had experienced rapid population growth and cultural changes that accompanied the institutionalization and proliferation of the coal industry in the southern and north-central parts of the state. After company towns were built to house the new influx of miners and their families, services monitored and owned by coal interests often included churches, company stores, dentists and doctors, entertainment and movie theaters, and company-hired police forces.

The rise of this monopolistic system of absentee ownership within the coal industry led many scholars to view the central Appalachian coal mining region as a sort of colony, by which a hegemony of power among industrial economic interests was exercised over indigenous rural mountain populations (Gaventa 1980). The initial stages of colonization included the seizure of land and mineral rights, which created an unprecedented economic boom in the mountainous region. The benefits of this economic development, however, were not passed on to the laboring class. Rather, these rapid social changes created economic inequalities and monopoly power, the residuals of which still haunt the region today. The solidification of the political-economic apparatus of power was wrought by the election of state government officials who were affiliated with the interests of coal. Essentially, industrialization in the central Appalachian region brought the establishment of an ideology that would ensure the reduction of participation in government by the non-elite mining class.

According to Justin Collins, a local company superintendent, coal operators must "never lose sight of the fact that the sole purpose of the organization is to make money for their stockholders, and matters of conduct . . . that tend to produce a contradictory result should be promptly squelched with a heavy hand" (letter from Justin Collins to Jarius Collins, 1896). Most coal companies adopted the widespread and controversial practice of remuneration through scrip. Buying goods outside of the company town was severely discouraged, not only by social pressure but also by restrictive monetary exchange policies. If company clerks agreed to exchange scrip for U.S. dollars, this exchange was routinely conducted at a rate that allowed for gross profit to the company.

The social institutions of the company town were owned and operated by company management, which paid for the land, building construction costs, and salaries of the employees. Independent Protestant, Catholic, and Baptist churches were replaced with company-sponsored clergy, all operating within the confines of the company town. For example, an announcement by the West Virginia Coal Operator's Association stated, "The coal companies are intensely interested in their communities and give every instance of developing the spiritual nature of their employees and their families. It is a good business proposition for any coal company to take an interest in and assist in the building up of religious and community activities" (West Virginia Coal Operators Association 1925).

Another "good business proposition" that was frequently employed by coal operators to manage social activities in the company town was the community school system. In an attempt to attract competent teachers, coal companies constructed rent-free "teacherages" that included bedroom suites, kitchen-dinette furniture, and living-room furniture. The coal companies, which blamed miners for mining accidents, believed that by educating the workforce, accidents would decrease and coal production would increase (Reynolds and Reynolds 1912). Companies often used the public schools to make early and aggressive attempts at "Americanizing" the illiterate black and immigrant workforce, while simultaneously indoctrinating European children with various "American" antiunion sentiments.

Some coal companies even went so far as to create separate schools for the coal miners to instruct them on how to read, write, and speak English in an attempt to increase productivity in the mines. Coal companies argued that by educating the workforce, they would also become "educated" about the evils of unionization. In a U.S. Senate Committee investigation, one coal operator stated, "We have, on the average, a more illiterate class of people working in the mines than almost any other occupation. This is taken advantage of by a great many people; in other words, this ignorance is taken advantage of by the disturber of the peace, the UMWA organizer" (Senate Committee on Education and Labor 1922, 1658–59). Paradoxically, the only true vehicle for community and social interaction and expression that was not overtly sanctioned and monitored by company management emerged with the proliferation of labor organizations throughout southern West Virginia.

Many coal miners and their families reported the ubiquitous practice of keeping their rented company houses dirt free. The need for this level of cleanliness was twofold: the companies required that their houses be kept immaculate under pressure of eviction; and the conditions were so unsanitary in the camps that good housekeeping was required to minimize the occurrence of disease. This work was further complicated by the fact that most company towns had no electricity or running water—women in these communities were forced to carry water, sometimes several miles, from the local creeks and streams to perform necessary cleaning duties.

World War I had a major impact on the miners of southern West Virginia, as did the mass labor uprisings of 1919, which were undoubtedly attempts to preserve the powerful political position of labor that was achieved during the war. Samuel Gompers, the leader of the American Federation of Labor, supported many of these struggles, saying that World War I "demonstrated to me that the pacifism in which I believed and which I faithfully advocated was a vain hope. I realized that the struggle in defense of right and freedom must ever be maintained at all hazards" (Gompers 1925, 524). The struggle to unionize southern West Virginia often resulted in brutal battles between coal miners and company-hired police forces. The United Mine Workers of America had tried for twenty years to fully unionize southern West Virginia, and eventually expressed its frustration by writing in the *United Mine Workers Journal* and *National Labor Tribune*, "we have often wondered what kind of animals they have digging coal in West Virginia and have never been able to successfully solve the problem. Their ignorance must be more than dense, their prejudice more bitter and their blindness more intense than that of any other body of miners we have ever heard tell of" (United Mine Workers of America 1899).

Between 1912 and 1922, this region experienced some of the most dramatic and violent events in the American labor movement. According to labor historian David Corbin,

> These episodes included the bloody and protracted Paint Creek-Cabin Creek strike of 1912–13 that saw a labor-management dispute turn into civil war; a shoot-out in the streets between the citizens of Matewan and the representatives of law and order in the coal fields that cost the lives of eleven men; a ninety-mile armed march of 20,000 coal miners bent on the overthrow of two county governments; and the formation of a dual union in opposition to the United Mine Workers of America. (1981, xiii)

As a result of these events, over five hundred coal miners were indicted for insurrection and treason. There were four declarations of martial law.

The Paint Creek-Cabin Creek strike was one of the first major battles of the mine wars in southern West Virginia. Coal camps lined both valleys, but union tent-colonies that housed displaced miners and their families who were evicted by management during the strike replaced these "model" communities. Families lived in alarming conditions, with mud floors, sodden blankets, and outdoor cooking stoves. Multiple diseases flourished in the cramped conditions, including smallpox, diphtheria, and measles (Williams 1984, 131). The importation of strikebreakers and heavily armed mine guards to protect them from the armed miners and their families contributed to the violence and prolonged the labor dispute.

During these early strikes that sparked in response to the colonial political-economic structure that was being established and reinforced by large coal companies in Appalachia, many reports of violence and resistance were documented by the United Mine Workers of America, the lawyers for the coal industry, and independent journalists. None of these reports, however, addressed the critical role of women in the early power dynamics of the region. To glean information about women's relative positions of power during these formative years of the American labor movement, I conducted multiple life-history interviews with women in Logan County, West Virginia, between 1997 and 2000. I also reviewed archived documents and transcripts of oral histories at the Center for the Study of Ethnicity and Gender in Appalachia (CSEGA) at Marshall University in Huntington, West Virginia. I then consolidated historical and archival documents from research centers like CSEGA, with ethnographic data I obtained from field research, to form a comprehensive understanding of norms of household production and the gendered division of labor in coal communities.

Division of Labor

During the transition from rural agricultural production to industrial capitalism and the accompanying proliferation of coal company domination in the area, women of southern West Virginia faced a variety of challenges to negotiate the imposed gendered division of labor in coal towns. For example, the following interview excerpt reflects the views of one of my informants as she recalled her experience of living in a company-owned house:

> We had to live around the coal fields 'cause that was all my father knew, that was his way to make a living. But [my mother] lived, they lived, in like a company-owned house, and the thing that was bad was they would send the inspectors around, and they would check to make sure that your house was clean, your children had to be clean, you had to tell them what you served your children. That's why to this day I despise oats.... That was the best thing that you could get to feed the kid then, they said, was "Mother's Quick-Cooking Oats."... They had inspections like, oh, every two or three months. Mother became such a fanatic about the house that she would scrub and clean and cook and carry on. We weren't allowed to play outside the yard because we might get our shoes dirty, and they might come and inspect the house. (Interview with author, July 10, 1997)

While women and men experienced many of the same social problems in company towns, women were also faced with what today would be considered unbearable amounts of housework and physical and psychological stress. Women were responsible for keeping their houses clean, which was a daunting task given the high levels of coal dust and black grime that accumulated on the company houses from the mining processes. Two women describe their experiences with the imposed levels of cleanliness in company towns in the following interview excerpts:

> My mother worked, from the minute her feet hit the floor, she was scrubbing on the house, scrubbing on the kids, wash by hand, carry water from the pump that was down in the street, no water in the house, no toilet, outside johnny, and coal. We had a little coal stove, and she burned coal to cook with . . . she wouldn't even let us get dirt on our shoes. She was afraid if we played outside, that that would be the day the coal company would inspect. And so, we had to stay on the porch, or, we just couldn't get dirty. We couldn't be like other children. And that really was no life for a child. (Interview with author, July 31, 1997)

> Livin' in a coal camp, I guess you're just inclined to keep your house clean. I mean, I always did. It was always two or three of us that worked together, even, and helped each other when we had our babies and all. I always had two or three really good women close to me, and I'd help them. We always kept our house clean. We'd mop and wax every weekend, cleaned windows every two weeks and all that, and curtains. I don't know why we did that. (Interview with author, August 8, 1998)

On average, women in coal camps devoted several days of every week solely to washing clothes without the convenience of running water (Women's Bureau 1925, 54–56). One of my informants remembered that her mother "had everything to do. It's mind-boggling how much you had to do. At least a man knew what he had to do. He had to get up, go to work, put in his shift. He came home, took his bath, and then he could work in the garden . . . but she had to do everything—cooking, sewing, and two little kids, I don't see how she coped" (Interview with author, July 31, 1997).

Women in coal communities often relied upon informal economic networks to share the burden of household labor and the constant surveillance of the coal company officers. The informal economy in West Virginia is defined here as encompassing a series of economic activities that require little start-up capital and fall outside the realm of wage labor. Many cross-cultural studies of the informal economy exemplify how women engage in petty commodity production to meet basic household needs in the absence of capital resources (for examples, see Arizpe 1977; Mintz 1971; Mueller 1977). The process of using the informal economy for protection, however, resembles the grassroots networks discussed in studies of the "irregular economy" in the urban context (Ferman and Ferman 1973).

During labor disputes, coal companies customarily prohibited union miners and their families from purchasing foodstuffs and necessary household supplies at the company store. To compensate, women organized what were called "poundings," during which women would obtain large baskets and move from house to house in a coal camp, collecting money, food, and clothing throughout an entire day. They would then take the full baskets and redistribute the collected goods to families that most needed the resources. In this way, women were able to negotiate the surveillance tactics and mobilize support against the pressures exerted by coal companies during strikes, as recounted by a coal town resident:

> I don't know why it was called a pounding, but it was called a pounding. You would go to church, because that's where you would find out about it, and everybody would know, well so-and-so is having a hard time. And they did it in a way as to not embarrass the family. It was done through the church; it wasn't done by one particular person. And the women, everybody would get together and they'd organize and they'd get a big old laundry basket and go from house to house and collect whatever. If it was money, or food, or if it was clothing, they'd do it all day long. They would just go from place to place until they would have anywhere from five to ten baskets that they thought would help this family. And they would take it to the family's home, and like I say it was done in such a way as to not make the people feel bad, because it was from the church, it was from your neighbor, it was from people who cared about you and your family. They wanted to see to it that you had what it took to see that you were okay. (Interview with author, June 30, 1997)

Reciprocity was an implicit characteristic of these community mobilization efforts. If one woman donated resources during a given pounding event, she knew that she might very easily be the recipient of other goods during the next pounding. Because of the economic uncertainty created by strikes and the unionization effort, resources were readily volunteered. In addition to goods provided for survival, members of the community also engaged in counter-surveillance, a variety of "community watch" to protect union miners and their families, as described in the following excerpt:

We had to stay safe, because back then, they'd just come in on you and whip you good. We had the Ku Klux Klan that would do that. You know how they used to go in on people. They would target the whites, they didn't pick. They would, if they thought somebody was in the wrong or trying to cause trouble, they saw trouble coming. . . . They'd set them in order. And they'd bring in the switch, and lay it in your doorway. You'd better not look up and see that, you know what that represents. . . . They'd get that out of you, they expected you to walk the line, as they say. Because a company, you know, they work undercover. (Interview with author, July 14, 1997)

Women who organized and distributed resources and protective services in the informal economy were deliberately bypassing the officially recognized political-economic activities of the coal company. Hence, they were actively engaged in resisting company power and the omnipresent devices of social control expressed by coal company interests, particularly during conflicts between the United Mine Workers and company management. This informal production, however, was not only a means of resistance and adaptation to inhospitable economic conditions during strikes. Because of the gendered division of labor that was codified and reinforced by coal producers, women were not typically engaged in wage-labor production during labor conflicts or during periods of relative peace in the coalfields; rather, their participation in gardening and petty commodity production (and the subsequent informal redistribution of these resources) was practiced continuously during the era of coal company towns. The informal infrastructure that was initially created as an adaptation to company control persisted during strikes, and evolved into a major structuring force in culture change in these communities.

STRATEGIES OF STAKEHOLDER INVOLVEMENT

By breaching the public/private boundary established by coal companies, women were actively shaping their experiences in rural mining communities. The occurrence of labor disputes emerged as a nexus of social change, in which women could promote their own interests during labor negotiations. Participation and involvement among women included nonviolent civil disobedience, political action, and violent engagement with company police. Nonviolent actions among women in industrial conflict situations included walking the picket lines with striking miners, holding "poundings" to gather resources for neighboring families, and disrupting the day-to-day operations of company business by blockading coal trucks.

While nonviolent involvement in conflicts was perhaps the most common form of dispute interaction among women in coal communities, modes of violent participation have sometimes either been overlooked entirely by historians, or attributed to the limited extension of the "private" sphere into the "public" sphere during times of community crisis. Many women, for example, viewed replacement workers as "thieves" of their husband's income during periods of conflict, and they witnessed firsthand how their families suffered as a result. Interviews suggest that strong family socialization against crossing picket lines was utilized as a mechanism to deter strikebreaking and increase community solidarity. One woman explained that "you had to be careful what you said because you didn't dare work. You couldn't cross the picket line. To this day, if someone in a union is picketing a store, I won't go in. I will not cross a picket line. Because, that was one thing, if you did, you could just end up with no head. I mean, they [union members] did not fool around" (Interview with author, July 15, 1998).

In the early twentieth century, women engaged in armed resistance against company management, and particularly against scabs. In one account of the armored "Bull Moose Special," a coal train that routinely passed by union camps and opened fire, Maud Estep witnessed the death of her husband by company gunfire and organized the people around her. She took her husband's gun and shot at the armed guards on the train. Later, several women gathered together and damaged the train tracks to prevent the Bull Moose Special from returning (Senate Committee on Education and Labor 1913). Industrial violence often took emotional, political, and economic tolls on women in coal communities. Wives of known union agitators were sometimes threatened by company guards in an attempt to intimidate others and suppress union efforts in the community. Women, like Maud Estep, sometimes lost their husbands during violent altercations, and thus also lost their primary means of support. During strikes, men were not risking their lives in the mines, but in gun battles and situations of intense conflict.

Women were generally not employed as miners until the 1970s. While some women chose to participate in physically nonviolent or violent situations of industrial conflict, others chose to engage in broader political action, which is exemplified by the proliferation of women's political organizations and activist groups in the region. The participation of women in these groups extends women's roles to the public sphere, forging a link between the "public" and the "private" that is even more dynamic during community labor disputes.

All of these forms of conflict participation implied the direct involvement of women as stakeholders. When conflicts were stagnant and strikes were initiated, women aided miners by obtaining alternative forms of income and providing food and supplies to striking men. When the conflict escalated, women often turned from nonviolent to violent participation, engaging in the historical armed conflict of the mine wars and tactics of scab intimidation.

SUMMARY AND IMPLICATIONS

From ethnographic interviews and historic documents, it is clear that the coal industry of the early twentieth century established a series of gender norms that supported and reinforced the complex relationships of industrial production and labor reproduction in these communities. Women's active participation in labor disputes, however, serves to challenge these established roles. While gender norms changed over the twentieth century, so too did the fabric of social life in these coal communities. As a result, labor disputes served as the nexus of community transformation and the emergence of new political-economic relationships of gender in southern West Virginia.

As these new interactions developed, relationships of power and status were shifted to reflect these changes in the relations of production. Coal companies began losing influence over their workforce at the macro-level following the decline in demand for coal after World War II. At the community level, women were gaining influence by expressing their interests as public participants and stakeholders in labor disputes. The dichotomy of gender norms established to organize the labor force in southern West Virginia became less relevant as women's actions extended into the public sphere and were recognized as a major group of stakeholders in these communities.

In conclusion, my research extends beyond conventional Marxist analyses of labor and industrial relations and issues of capitalist development to evaluate complex longitudinal relationships among community, power, women and political economy. The integration of historical documentation with the rich descriptions of social phenomena gleaned from life-history interviews contributes to the development of empirically based modern understandings of employment relations as they pertain to gendered interactions at the nexus of work and community.

NOTES

The author acknowledges financial support for field research from the Dispute Resolution Research Center at Northwestern University and from the Wenner-Gren Foundation for Anthropological Research (Grant #6486).

REFERENCES

Arizpe, Lourdes. 1977. "Women and the Informal Labor Sector: The Case of Mexico City." In *Women and National Development: The Complexities of Change*, ed. Wellesley Editorial Committee, 25–37. Chicago: University of Chicago Press.

Bozzoli, Belinda. 1983. "Marxism, Feminism and South African Studies." *Journal of Southern African Studies* 9(2):139–71.

Collins, Justin. 1896. Papers. Morgantown, WV: West Virginia University Library, Manuscript Collection.

Corbin, David Alan. 1981. *Life, Work and Rebellion in the Coal Fields: The Southern West Virginia Miners, 1880–1922*. Urbana: University of Illinois Press.

Ferman, Patricia R., and Louis A. Ferman. 1973. "The Structural Underpinning of the Irregular Economy." *Poverty and Human Resources Abstracts* 8:3–17.

Gaventa, John. 1980. *Power and Powerlessness: Quiescence and Rebellion in an Appalachian Valley*. Urbana: University of Illinois Press.

Gompers, Samuel. 1925. *Seventy Years of Life and Labour: An Autobiography*. Vol. 2. New York: E. P. Dutton.

Mintz, Sidney. 1971. "Men, Women and Trade." *Comparative Studies in Society and History* 13:247–69.

Mueller, Martha. 1977. "Women and Men, Power and Powerlessness in Losotho." In *Women and National Development: The Complexities of Change*, ed. Wellesley Editorial Committee, 154–66. Chicago: University of Chicago Press.

Reynolds, Sam, and W. H. Reynolds. 1912. "Human Element in Coal Element." *Coal Age* 1 (May 11): 1021.

Sanday, Peggy. 1974. "Female Status in the Public Domain." In *Woman, Culture and Society*, ed. M. Z. Rosaldo and L. Lamphere, 189–206. Stanford, CA: Stanford University Press.

Senate Committee on Education and Labor. 1913. *Conditions in the Paint Creek District, West Virginia.* 63rd Congress, First Session, vol. 1. Washington, DC: Government Printing Office.

———. 1922. *West Virginia Coal Fields: Hearings to Investigate the Recent Acts of Violence.* 67th Congress, First Session, vol. 2. Washington, DC: Government Printing Office.

United Mine Workers of America. 1899. *National Labor Tribune* (April 13): 1.

West Virginia Coal Operators Association. 1925. "Religious Work in Coal Towns." *West Virginia Review* (August 1).

Williams, John Alexander. 1984. *West Virginia: A History.* New York: W. W. Norton.

Women's Bureau. 1925. "Home Environment and Employment Opportunities of Women in Coal-Mine Families." *Women's Bureau Bulletin,* no. 45:54–56. Washington, DC: Department of Labor.

7

The Emergence of Worker Cooperatives in Japan among Middle-Aged, Middle-Class Housewives in the Late Twentieth Century

Robert C. Marshall

Cooperatives emerge where markets fail: middle-aged, middle-class house-wives are the last abundant labor source not yet fully integrated into Japan's market economy. Government policies designed to bolster a "breadwinner plus housewife" family system reinforce the particular ways Japan's labor market fails women. Worker cooperatives offer an opportunity for housewives in Japan's new middle class to work part time and, by controlling the conditions of their own labor, manage their time and energy in ways that still let them meet their own exacting standards of care for their families. Over the past fifteen years an emerging movement dedicated to organizing worker coopera-tives has attracted increasing numbers of women in the Tokyo-Yokohama region. As many as 12,000 women now work at women's worker cooperatives (WWCs) (Watanabe n.d.; Iwami 2000, 234–58).

In December 1982, a handful of women in Kanagawa Prefecture started Ninjin, Japan's first WWC (Sato 1988, 393). "Ninjin" means "carrot" in Japa-nese; the business began as the workforce for a consumer cooperative's produce distribution center. But these women write the name of their business using duplicate characters with the meaning "person" or "people." In colloquial American English, Ninjin should be taken as "The People People," just how these women think of themselves. Extending Ninjin's breakthrough, women opened another fifteen WWCs over the next two years. The decade following Ninjin's founding saw 7,000 women start over 250 WWCs (Kanagawa Worker

Collective League 1994, 1). The authoritative roster compiled by Workers' Collective Network Japan, the official organ of the WWC movement, lists 463 WWCs in business in February 2000 (Iwami 2000, 234–58). They call their cooperatives *wākāzu korekuteibu,* the Romanization of the Japanese transcription of the phrase "workers' collective," adopted from usage current in the 1970s on the West Coast of North America.

The women owning, running, and working in these WWCs are overwhelmingly middle-aged and middle-class. Over 80 percent are between forty and sixty years old, more than half in their forties (Sumitani 2000, 35; Kutsuzawa 1998, 82). Their household incomes, rates of homeownership, and educational accomplishments are well above national averages (Kutsuzawa 1998, 82–84). WWCs' many different business activities arise from the knowledge, skills, interests, and values members developed as well-educated wives and mothers, and in consumer cooperatives. A partial list of business activities spun off from Ninjin alone includes recycling shop, cooking class, lunch restaurant, home-care service, day care, culture class (*karuchā kyōshitsu*), marriage counseling, handmade goods, ice cream making, soap making, welfare cooperative, bread bakery, display group, translating, printing, editing, international exchanges, video production, consumer cooperative office work, delivery service, "and so on" (Utsuki 1993, 8). WWCs practice principles of workplace democracy, ownership equality, and social responsibility.

Its critics assert that the WWC alternative to the economic status quo can only continue as long as these women remain dependent on their husbands' substantial incomes. A 1999 survey of 221 members of WWCs found more than two-thirds with spouse's annual income above $50,000; more than one-fifth were above $100,000; 15 percent did not answer the question (Sumitani 2000, 37). In 1995 more than two-thirds of WWC members reported annual household incomes above $80,000 (Kutsuzawa 1998, 82). The average income for working households in 1999 was $68,490 (Japanese Government 2001). In Sumitani's (2000, 37) judgment, "The common perception is that the women in worker cooperatives do not work from economic necessity, and these figures bear out that view substantially." The movement's critics frame a paradox from which we can appropriately launch analysis: why do these women so eagerly bite the hand that feeds them so well? (Kutsuzawa 1998, 88–89; Iwao 1993, 266–70).

A first approximation to an answer is not difficult to come by: the appeal and success of worker cooperatives for these women spring from the combination of three particular conditions in their lives. First, the frequency by age curve of the labor market for women has two modes, and is commonly described as "M-shaped": women in the new middle class typically work full time for several years after graduation, "retire" to bear and raise a small number of children, and then reenter the market for part-time labor in different, usually much less attractive, occupations some years later.

Second, Japan's income tax law hits a household's "secondary income" astonishingly hard above a quite low maximum in the middle-income brackets, a phenomenon infamous as the "Million Yen Wall": "A wife who earns in excess of 1.03 million yen loses her dependent status and has to pay her own social security taxes and health insurance" (Mason and Ogawa 1998, 15). Here, ¥1 million yen arbitrarily though not unrealistically equals US$10,000 (Horioka 1998, 3). Effectively, the first $10,000 a dependent wife earns is tax exempt; the next $7,000 to $10,000 will all go to taxes of one kind or another. At the low hourly wages typical of jobs available to them, middle-aged women must expect to work twenty to twenty-five hours per week to earn $10,000. Vanishingly few jobs paying more than $20,000 are available to the women who start WWCs. In the deeply sarcastic words of Komori Chie (1993, 32), director of the Labor Project for the Kanagawa Women's Conference, in her keynote address to WWC activists at a conference celebrating the tenth anniversary of the founding of Ninjin, "If you don't make over a million yen, and are a wife who diligently raises her children to become superior company warriors, waits up for the return home of her husband and fixes him a delicious meal [laughter], your husband's taxes will be reduced." The Equal Employment Opportunity Law (1985) and the Young Childcare Leave Law (1992) are of a piece with tax law, designed to prop up a family structure in which economically dependent wives devote much of their time to the care of their rarely divorced husbands, fewer than two children, and the world's longest lived parents-in-law.

Third, almost all members of WWCs have long belonged to the Seikatsu Club Consumer Cooperative (SCCC), internationally extolled for its motto "Stop Shopping," its social activism, and its distinctive structure of networked small groups. SCCC intentionally incubated the first several WWCs as part of its overall aim to create alternatives in Japanese society.

Taken together, these three circumstances mark out a category of Japanese women predisposed toward cooperation and prepared to experiment with cooperation in its less familiar forms. Looking for appealing work once again, these

women can create, with family savings they themselves manage, work opportunities where they control their own labor and schedules, as they are accustomed
to do as housewives, consumer cooperative members, and even cooperative and
social activists. Conservatively, hundreds of thousands of Japanese women might
see themselves in this specific description. According to a 1987 survey by the
Kanagawa Prefecture Consumer Cooperative League, slightly less than half of
member housewives were employed, half of those remaining without work
wanted it, and half of those wanting work wanted it at their consumer cooperative (Iwami 2000, 54). In 1999, over 20 million members owned more than 650
consumer cooperatives in Japan (Co-op Japan 2001). From the late 1960s to the
early 1990s, the singular SCCC itself grew to over a quarter of a million members, 95 percent of whom are women (SCCC 1993, 2). The resources these novice
entrepreneurs bring to their businesses, coupled with the advantages to them of
working cooperatively (Marshall 1995), have allowed them to succeed and their
movement to grow steadily from the mid-1980s through the present during successive phases of intense speculation, collapse and recession, and continuing
stagnation and turmoil in Japan's market economy.

     A second approximation toward an answer that comprehends this move-
ment must take into account the binds or contradictions as well as the opportunities working cooperatively in this context presents to these women.
The prominent theme of the desirability of women's "independence" and
"self-reliance" (*jichi, jiritsu*) echoes throughout the movement (Kutsuzawa
1998, 74; Utsuki 1993, 12), and from which point of view the Million Yen Wall
and other forms of discrimination are strongly decried. The independence
most women working in WWCs want, however, is from waged employment
and the constraints of current tax law, not from their families or communities. Independence from families or communities has not been a reason
Japanese women mention for taking employment (Roberts 1994, 70). So while
many women want to work more hours in their WWCs than they do, many
other women resist pressure within their WWC to work more hours by letting
the Million Yen Wall deflect coworkers' unspoken accusations of selfishness.
The sharp limit on their work hours, whether they want to work only part
time or not, lets these women better fulfill their obligations to family and
community, obligations SCCC philosophy prominently embraces as the
essence of personal life, the best of a way of life that is being destroyed by the
commodification of the skills and relationships needed for daily living (Utsuki

1993, 8; Tsuchiyama 1986, 44). Rather than themselves work more, many women would prefer men to work less, and in different ways (Iwao 1993, 208–12; Kawamoto 1993, 30; Lam 1993, 220).

WWC members' motives, ambitions, and convictions are more complex, more diverse, more imaginative than their critics or supporters give them credit for, and the movement continues to grow steadily because it offers multiple, flexible, interesting, ambiguous, and income-earning opportunities to middle-aged, middle-class women. Characterizations of revolution, reaction, reform, or mere adaptation all fail to comprehend adequately this complex movement's creation of appealing alternatives to the economic status quo. Later in this chapter, I explore and elaborate on this general pattern with participant observation data from my 1994 fieldwork at the WWC lunch-catering restaurant Shun, from Kutsuzawa's (1998) 1995 ethnography of a similar site, and from a variety of survey and interview data produced within and around the WWC movement itself. Sections examining the labor market for women in Japan and government policies affecting women's waged work and status as dependents follow a look at how women work at Shun and the relation of the WWC movement to the SCCC.

WORKING AT A WOMEN'S WORKER COOPERATIVE

Fourteen housewives, forty to sixty-two years old, own and operate the lunch-catering restaurant (*shidashi-bentoya*) Shun ("In Season"). All members of SCCC, these women replied independently to a notice in the SCCC newsletter that Seikatsu Club Saitama wanted to start a WWC lunch restaurant in its soon-to-be-built prefectural headquarters building. To get Shun off the ground, each woman bought one ¥100,000 share. In its fourth year when I went to work there, Shun was already finding its space cramped, but they remain in business at this same address to the present moment.

Shun serves a lunch that any of its members would make for a friend visiting her home, and their friends do often drop by Shun to lunch and chat. Shun's meals are all handmade home cooking, from wholesome Seikatsu Club ingredients. They serve a different lunch every day. Each member cooks everything in Shun's repertoire of some 100 main dishes and as many side dishes. No one's appearance suggests she is not at home, cooking in her own kitchen. Shun explicitly decided not to wear uniforms (*oshikise*), so common in Japanese businesses of all kinds. They favor slacks, even jeans, and blouses, even sweatshirts, and big colorful aprons with big pockets. They told me their first year was hard because no one would be frank. Since then it's been busy but fun. After only one month in business, one of the original members quit—the work was just too hard. Her investment was returned to her whole. No one has quit since and three additional members have joined.

The space and equipment were designed and installed by the Saitama SCCC to be a WWC lunch restaurant from the start. A half-wall and divided curtain (*noren*) split the space into a kitchen in back and a lunch counter and tables out front, an area they call "omise," their "shop." On a typical day six women make 125 lunches, 30 of which they serve out front and the rest they deliver to five or six customers. A slow day might reach only half that number of lunches. On a busy day as many as ten members cook 200 or more lunches in the overcrowded kitchen. Orders from a PTA meeting or a local consumer cooperative conference generate even occasional 300-lunch days. Shun's members work long days, from 8:30 a.m. to 7:00 p.m. or later, but everywhere in Japan "part time" means long days and often hours even as long as those of "regular" employees (Kondo 1990, 289–90; Hendry 1993, 236).

Mornings start slowly, sometimes with a cup of tea and a bun on slower days while a few late customers phone in small orders, hoping to be squeezed in. The bulk of orders are placed days in advance or left standing by their best customers, particularly SCCC and Saitama Consumer Cooperative members and employees, and Saitama Prefectural Government office workers. The pace speeds up gradually, timed to get the deliveries all out the door in a burst, hot, and into the waiting delivery cars at 11:30 a.m. Shun then serves lunch out front to walk-in customers until 1:00 or so, as long as the food holds out. The cooks eat their own cooking for lunch from 1:00 to 2:00, that day's meal when any remains. Today's cooks plan tomorrow's menu while eating lunch and just after. They wash the pots, pans, and then the dirty lunch boxes from 2:00 until done, often 5:00 or later, and then get started cooking tomorrow's meal until 7:00.

Rarely does anyone work two full days in a row, though a late afternoon followed by a whole day is common enough. Between the fourth of January and the thirtieth of March, the period of my stint, chance composed the same crew, seven workers, only twice, February 7 and February 14. For a small worker cooperative of part-time workers to succeed for ten years, it cannot depend overmuch on any one or two members. Shun even had three members get training as bookkeepers. In general, no member works more days than she wants to work and several not nearly as many. Shun did a great deal of hour-juggling to avoid anyone hitting the Million Yen Wall as the end of the fiscal year approached.

One Saturday morning each month they clean their restaurant from top to bottom and then talk over their business for two to three hours after lunch. An annually elected director chairs these meetings, but has no unique authority otherwise. At Shun, emphatically no one is in charge. While they had once talked about putting one person in charge of each day's work on a rotating basis, the sort of system Kutsuzawa (1998, 118) documents for the WWC lunch restaurant Sō, the desire for maximally flexible scheduling ultimately came to determine their practice.

The current happy state of their business does not represent the pinnacle of success to all of these women. In separate conversations four members told me of their hopes to open restaurants, bakeries, or cooking schools of their own. Several of the fourteen members would like Shun to grow and diversify. To this end Shun bid on and won the catering for the Saitama Teachers Union's 400-guest party thrown to celebrate the opening of the union's new office building. The days before the party were hectic with preparation. Shun closed on the date of the event itself. On the night before the party, four members slept upstairs in the tatami room of the SCCC office building that houses their kitchen. Two members did not work on the party, one ill with flu and another keeping previous arrangements made for a ski vacation with her family.

WWCs AND SCCC

A little more than a third of WWCs are in the food industry (Sumitani 2000, 38), not surprising in a movement started by a consumer food cooperative. Unlike other consumer cooperatives, however, SCCC continues to develop ever-greater member activism on several fronts rather than turn the cooperative into a chain of stores. In the words of Yokota Katsumi, one of the founders of Seikatsu Club Kanagawa, "It is not our ultimate purpose in life, as individuals, to buy safe reliable consumer goods at reasonable prices" (Yokota 1991, 11).

Two hundred Tokyo housewives started SCCC in 1965 to buy whole milk, rather than the reconstituted milk alone available in industry channels. Early in its history SCCC developed the three fundamental and interrelated practices that continue to distinguish this organization as a consumer cooperative: small group ordering and distribution (*han seido*) by cooperative procurement (*kyōdō kōnyū*) directly from the producer (*sanchoku*). Together, these three systems take the place of stores and shopping. But they also require carefully coordinated activity among members, especially at the level of the small group, the *han*, whose eight to fifteen members stay in frequent contact. Seikatsu Club activism extends outward from *han* solidarity.

The organization's history shows annual increases in membership and increasing activism by members over a spreading range of activities. Members founded Ninjin in 1982, and elected SCCC's first ten women representatives to municipal assemblies in 1983. Membership in the consumer cooperative underpins the rest of SCCC member activism.

The mid-1980s saw the percentage of full-time housewives drop below half for the first time (Ueno 1987, S80). As part-time employment began to rise even among SCCC members, many SCCC members also began to experience schedule conflicts between their part-time jobs and their *han* activities (Sato 1995). The depot emerged from SCCC's efforts both to accommodate employed members and to provide an alternative form of work for unemployed members (Kutsuzawa 1998, 73). Ninjin started at "Depot," the Kanagawa distribution center. Introduced in 1981, the depot system solved two problems for SCCC at a single stroke: busy members could have their orders prepared for pick-up separate from the rest of their *han*, and members who wanted to make money through SCCC could join a co-op and work at their depot—at first, office work and member order handling (Utsuki 1993, 6).

This plan dovetailed closely with SCCC's other activities in politics and environmentalism designed to reach out to a wider population. The SCCC's so-called soap movement illustrates their creation of imaginative alternatives that reach out to recruit through networked activism. Following their initial success organizing a consumer cooperative, activists within SCCC began a petition drive to have synthetic detergents banned in 1977. In Japan wash water is not treated but discharged directly into the "gray water" stream. Synthetic detergents are a major and serious pollutant throughout Japan's waterways, and also a source of allergic reactions among infants from laundered diapers (Utsuki 1993, 6). Housewives are linked to a second substantial source of water pollution when they rinse used cooking oil down the kitchen sink into the "gray water" system where it too enters, remains in, and kills rivers, streams, and wetlands.

The genius of the SCCC "soap movement" was to create networks among SCCC members for the collection and manufacture of soap from used cooking oil. Individual housewives collect and turn in their used cooking oil, and use the easily biodegradable soap made from it in place of synthetic detergents in their homes; movement activists collect used oil and make soap in public places, and educate and recruit around these environmental problems; and WWCs make soap from the used oil on a larger scale and distribute it through the SCCC. Other worker cooperatives in Japan design and manufacture appropriate-scale soap-making machines; a washing machine designed to be especially effective using this soap rather than synthetic detergent is on the horizon (Marshall 1997). SCCC activists made the Kanagawa Prefectural legislature's failure to act on their petition into the springboard from which to launch SCCC member candidates. Over 100 SCCC members had been elected to local and regional assemblies by 1995 (see Iwao 1993, 242–64). SCCC members have used their organization to create an expanding array of social, political, and above all alternative economic opportunities, first for consumption and more recently for production.

WOMEN AT WORK IN JAPAN

Many women want work connected to their consumer cooperatives because employment opportunities for women returning to the labor market are unattractive. Ueno (1987, S80) stresses the fact that "part-time work was an invention of employers rather than the result of women's demand to work," arising from a constant labor shortage in Japanese industry into the 1970s and again in the 1980s. By the late 1970s, high rates of economic growth had given way to an economy characterized by the oxymoronic "stagflation." Middle-class, middle-aged women began to take employment to provide households with supplementary incomes, money that would be spent predominantly on their children's education and on housing. This desire to be better mothers brought many more women into the growing market for part-time labor in the "bubble" economy of the late 1980s.

Since the early 1970s, an increasing fraction of women has continued to enter a market for part-time labor that presents them no unambiguously attractive opportunities. Numerical views and interpretations of many aspects of women's labor in Japan are widely available in English (Japanese Government 2001; Ogasawara 1998; Sugimoto 1997; Roberts 1994, 1996; Iwao 1993; Ōmori 1993; Chambers 1989). By 1991 women made up more than 40 percent of the total paid workforce, and by 1991 more than 50 percent of women between the ages of fifteen and sixty-five engaged in waged labor. Virtually all women in Japan marry, and by 1983 the ever-increasing fraction of married women working at waged labor crossed the one-half mark for the first time. By 1991 this number had reached almost 60 percent. Single women now make up only about one-third of the female labor force.

Unlike men, "a large number of women leave the labor market after marriage and childbirth" (Ogasawara 1998, 18). While over 75 percent of Japanese women in their early twenties are now employed for wages, this fraction drops to about one-half for women in their early thirties. When women complete the reproductive and child-rearing phases of their lives, many reenter the labor force: about 70 percent of women in their late forties are now working for wages outside the home. However, "regular full-time jobs are not usually available for women over thirty years of age" (Ōmori 1993, 97). Lebra (1993, 371) records from survey data that only 16 percent of women favored a continuous work career, and that over 50 percent preferred that their second-stage work be part-time.

Only negligible numbers of women work in upper-management career tracks in companies with more than 100 employees even today (Ogasawara 1998, 19–20), fifteen years after the passage of Japan's Equal Employment Opportunity Law (Creighton 1996; Lam 1993). However, the "trough of the M" hits its low point at about 50 percent of thirty-year-olds; variation in age of marriage and first birth notwithstanding, a significant fraction of women, about 20 percent of their cohort a decade ago (Ueno 1987, S80), does actually remain employed from school door to final retirement with extremely little time off (Roberts 1996, 241). With regard to the kinds of opportunities for waged work available to SCCC members who start or join WWCs, it is notable that the low point in the middle of the M does only fall to 50 percent. The number of women employed by the smallest firms rises steeply with age (Roberts 1994, 27): the majority of employed women move from the largest firms in the first peak of the M to the smallest firms in the second peak of the M, where pay, working conditions, and job security are all worse.

Lo (1990) captures this important index of class difference as the distinction between "office ladies and factory women." The women factory workers whose work lives Roberts (1994) documents make up a "regular" permanent, not a part-time temporary, female blue-collar workforce who return in the long second stage of their work careers to factory jobs much like those they left briefly for childbirth, but often to smaller factories and at lower pay. "Office ladies," the young women employed before marriage at the largest firms in wholesale and retail, and finance, insurance, and real estate especially (Ōmori 1993, 81), are "not only offered inducements [to retire upon marriage], but sometimes actively discouraged from continuing work" (Ogasawara 1998, 64). Once they leave, "office ladies" are replaced by younger women, rarely returning to their old firms or to their old work, and never to both.

In the popular imagination "office ladies" retire to marry, raise children, and care for their white-collared husbands, becoming *sengyō shufu*, "professional housewives" (Lo 1990, 9). The notion that a housewife might be "professional" did not arise until the early 1970s when the term emerged to contrast with the category *kengyō shufu*, a woman with part-time employment in addition to her undiminished and unshared activities as housewife (Ueno 1987, S80; Long 1996, 159). The emergence and transformation of the professional housewife of the new middle class is well documented (Vogel 1978; Imamura 1987, 1996; Ueno 1987; Hendry 1993; Iwao 1993). The WWC movement began to grow just as Ueno (1987, S80) was observing that "the middle-class ideal, however, is rapidly becoming inaccessible." In this ideal the mistress of the house does not work for a wage, but nurtures her husband, their children, and his parents.

When we ask what a professional housewife actually does, and what forces shape her decisions, however, answers become more complicated. The house-wifely ideal took on its current shape for Japanese women over a century ago as the Meiji-era modernizers melded dependence and nurturing in the phrase *ryōsai kenbo*, "good wife, wise mother" (Long 1996; Hendry 1993). Women may acquire a great deal of knowledge and autonomy in order to nurture well, but these acquisitions do not lead to independence. Self-reliance does not lead to self-sufficiency. Women remain extremely vulnerable to accusations of self-ishness. What women do must still be justified by how it benefits those who depend on them and upon whom they also depend, if for different things.

Hendry (1993) and Iwao (1993) discuss the role and activities of professional housewives who incidentally also happen to be SCCC members. The increasing professionalization of household management seen in the search for higher quality and lower prices moves housewives toward consumer cooperatives (Hendry 1993, 227), but the housewife's role does not carry expectations of vol-unteerism and community service (Imamura 1987, 124–29). While housewives' efforts to perform their tasks more effectively have led many out of and well beyond their homes, few women have abandoned, or even disparaged, the housewifely role itself as their fundamental identity. SCCC activist candidates for public office draw support by running as "ordinary housewives" (*futsū no shufu*). They present themselves to voters as "proxies" (*dairinin*) for their support networks, rather than use the conventional term "representative" (*daihyō*), in order to distinguish themselves from professional office seekers. "As long as it remains relatively difficult for middle-aged women to find work that accommodates the demands of family and home, political involvement . . . may offer an appealing alternative" to employment (Iwao 1993, 258). And as long as public policy remains focused on inducing married women's dependence on their husbands' incomes to keep them available as unpaid caregivers for family members, activist housewives will continue to focus on the necessity of changing public policy through political action.

WOMEN'S WORK AND PUBLIC POLICY

Under some circumstances, areas of incompatibility between dependence and caregiving become conspicuous, but public ideology and government policy insist that these components are indissolubly fused. To the extent caregiving requires autonomy and independent judgment, and yet remains a "totalizing experience" (Long 1996, 166) requiring devotion parallel to men at work, women's experiences lead them to clash with public policy and the dominant ideology. Yet women's practices may also produce, even among allies, radically different interpretations of those practices, which can in turn become a source of conflict over the direction and form women's political pressure on policy ought to take.

Policy now assumes that women must be induced to remain economic dependents. Both SCCC philosophy and government policy join in resisting, although for different reasons, the further commodification of caregiving (especially for the increasing numbers of elderly), while they come to opposing conclusions on keeping middle-aged women dependent on their husbands' incomes. At present two separate bodies of law, equal employment opportunity law (EEOL) and tax law, create effects of dependency of wives on their husbands' incomes. The WWC movement concentrates its attention more intensely on tax law iniquity, but I will discuss the effects of EEOL first.

Japan's 1985 Equal Employment Opportunity Law is generally understood as a weak step taken to placate critics of continuing discrimination in employment against women, and as such is fundamentally criticized for its lack of teeth (Creighton 1996, 196): "The EEO Law does not have enough power to prevent employers' sex-based personnel policies" (Lam 1993, 219). Such discrimination continues even in major department stores, easily the employer most responsive to women's circumstances. While department stores employ many women because women are better able than men to sell to women customers, "the interests of the predominantly female employees run counter to the interests of a largely male management" (Creighton 1996, 193).

EEOL continues to be interpreted in ways that maintain prohibited harmful practices based on the distinction between male and female employees. Companies are not required to treat all female and male employees equally, only those employees in the same track. There are two tracks, permanent and not permanent, in the world of pink-collar work; women returning to work after childrearing are hired as nonpermanent employees. They remain at a wage disadvantage because "the Japanese seniority-based permanent employment system grants higher pay rates for consecutive years of employment with the same company" (Creighton 1996, 195). While women in their teens and twenties earn about 80 percent of what men of the same age earn, women in their forties and fifties earn only about half what men of that age earn (Oshima 1998, 200).

The Young Childcare Leave Law, which went into effect in 1992, explicitly states that both parents must be allowed to take extended leave after the birth of a child. Few men, however, even in companies with progressive policies that expressly allow such leave independent of the law, take childcare leave. In 1999, 97.6 percent of Young Childcare Leave takers were women (Rōdōshō 2000). "Thus, even the passage of a childcare leave law that includes fathers does not indicate that gender role distinctions have vanished or that men and women will easily take advantage of their newly defined legal rights" (Creighton 1996, 200). Child care remains an exclusively female activity in Japan, an activity of each child's own mother.

The great majority of Japanese women "are not prepared to accept the type of 'equal opportunities' offered by their employers," which are exactly those offered to men, requiring long hours, an uninterrupted career, a willingness to accept distant assignments, and "that the occupational sphere remains aloof from the domestic sphere" (Lam 1993, 220). Few women choose to live merely diminished versions of men's lives, unable to marry and mother, and pursue a professional career simultaneously. Among the women in managerial positions Creighton randomly met and interviewed for her study of department stores, not one had ever been married (1996, 211).

The WWC movement focuses more political effort on the dependent status of women because tax law affects women in WWCs so much more directly, both immediately and after final retirement. Professor Kuba Yoshiko used her keynote address at the May 1993 symposium sponsored by the National League of Women Tax Accountants, "Thinking about the Million Yen Wall and Part-time Employment," to review the many ways the formula "Female equals Dependent" does not square with reality (Kawamoto 1993, 30). Ninjin board member Kawamoto Reiko then walked WWC activists through Kuba's material in her tax workshop "Tax and Women Supporting the Twenty-first Century" at the conference celebrating Ninjin's tenth anniversary. The following two paragraphs adumbrate the content of these presentations.

The worker cooperative is not a legally recognized form of enterprise in Japan, but those who work in them have their earnings from them taxed as wage income. What remains after the ¥680,000 waged-income deduction is taken out is subject to taxation. From total income there is also a ¥350,000 basic deduction, so the income tax on income up to ¥1,030,000 is zero. Tax must be paid on anything above ¥1,030,000. When the husband is the primary income earner in the family, if the net income of the wife is less than ¥350,000 and the taxable income of the main income earner is less than ¥1,030,000, a "spousal exemption" of the ¥310,000 resident tax (jūminzei) can be taken. Beyond this, the "spousal special exemption" is available if the husband's total income is below ¥1,030,000 and the wife's income is within ¥1,350,000. In such cases the maximum tax from the wife's income is ¥350,000 and the resident tax is exempted. The amount of the exemption changes in proportion to the wife's income, and by combining "spousal deduction" and "spousal special deduction," a tax schedule is developed in decrements of ¥50,000 from ¥750,000 to zero yen. The household income, or at least the total net income of the husband and wife when the income of the wife surpasses ¥1,030,000 if they must pay both income and resident taxes, increases as the wife's income increases.

If the wife works and exceeds this framework of tax (and social security for covered dependents), there occurs an "income reversal phenomenon" (Kawamoto 1993, 28), a decrease in after-tax income. If the wife earns more than ¥1,030,000, or in some rare cases ¥1,300,000, the couple will lose exemptions of up to ¥680,000 depending on how much more she earns, in addition to having to pay social security and health insurance premiums for both husband and wife. In brief and in general, only the first $10,000 (or in extremely rare cases, $13,000) married women make can be tax exempt, and the next $6,500 to $9,500 they earn all go to taxes in one form or another. If a married women earns $10,000 a year working about twenty to thirty hours per week, it cannot be worth her while to work even much more except at much higher wages, and there are no jobs with such high pay available for middle-aged women returning to the labor market. Because most women's families will lose her dependent's deduction of $6,500 as soon as she earns more than $10,000, it is a dead loss for her to earn between $10,000 and $16,500. Because of this, the phrase "Million Yen Wall" was born.

A questionnaire answered by forty-four of sixty-six participants circulated after Kawamoto's tax workshop. Only one of the forty-four respondents was single. Thirty-one of the forty-four wanted to work more hours than they did, but did not work more because of the Million Yen Wall. Thirty-four of forty-four said they would participate politically to topple the Million Yen Wall, and thirty-four also made less than ¥1,300,000 (with five above ¥1,300,000 and five giving no answer).

Among comments gathered from participants after Kawamoto's tax workshop was the following: "As long as we let our work be guided by the Million Yen Wall, we are participating in a secret plan (*hisaku*) which worker cooperatives' operations too keep on maintaining. We aim at jobs (*shigoto*) and independence (*jiritsu*), but these things are not possible, I realized once again" (Kawamoto 1993, 31). Another participant's comment focused the cause of her irritation somewhat nearer at hand: "Although I am now thinking about joining social security, I feel acutely the lack of consciousness among members of WWCs, and irritation at their lack of support for people aiming at independence and crossing the Million Yen Wall" (Kawamoto 1993, 31). Yet the reason surveyed WWC members overwhelmingly gave for working at all is to create *ikigai*, "a purpose in life," followed by "help out with the family budget" and "revive my experience." *Keizaiteki jiritsu*, "economic independence," finished out of the money, ahead of only "make better use of my leisure time" (Sumitani 2000, 54). At this point, that some WWC members do not support economic independence for other WWC members through their co-ops must surprise no one, but certainly few WWC members can care to have such different desires aired openly in their own WWC. Where then might the WWC movement bring its deepest solidarity to bear most effectively?

POLICY IMPLICATIONS AND CONCLUSION

WWCs are much more likely to have success with another legislative priority, a national worker cooperative law. Many WWC members already link this goal directly to their tax complaints as well. Forty percent of WWC members Sumitani surveyed think that tax, insurance, and social security problems are rooted in the government's failure to recognize the particular characteristics of worker cooperatives and provide in law for their differences from regular businesses (Sumitani 2000, 65). These same WWC members also think for this reason enactment of a worker cooperative law should be the movement's highest priority for activism. In this goal, they have allies among other businesses in Japan's wider worker cooperative movement (Marshall 1994) as well as among politicians, bureaucrats, newspaper editorial boards, activists, and academics.

Even after a national Worker Cooperative Law is passed, however, and the pending issues of social security premium payments, insurance eligibility, business tax liability, and dividend distribution are resolved in a rational way for those who work in Japan's worker cooperatives, for the women who work in WWCs and see themselves as part of a growing movement for social alternatives, the status of women as dependents will not have changed and will not become more likely to change. It may be even less likely to change. Many women will continue to prefer to work part-time in order to be better caregivers and better human beings, rather than "shopping robots" or "worker bees."

How much part-time work will be worth their while will remain a problem for many of these women. While over 70 percent of WWC members are dissatisfied with their earnings, WWC members overwhelmingly believe themselves better off than if they had to accept conventional part-time employment, entirely because they are able to control their own work (Kutsuzawa 1998, 86). Both despite and because of the Million Yen Wall, the WWC movement will remain an attractive possibility to the large number of middle-class women looking for ways to create a life worth living once their children are well along in school, a life that does not lapse into the short-term, part-time employment of so many middle-aged women, does not emulate the life-long full-time employment of their husbands, and that does not even evolve into full-time work in a women's workers cooperative.

NOTES

Research for this article was conducted in Japan during the summer of 1991 and the twelve months from September 1993 to September 1994. This research was supported by grants from the Social Science Research Council, the U.S. Department of Education Fulbright-Hays Faculty Research Abroad Program, and Western Washington University Bureau for Faculty Research. I thank particularly Tomizawa Kenji for his generous hospitality during my 1993–1994 residence as visiting research professor at Hitotsubashi University Institute of Economic Research while he was director of that entirely estimable institute, and Tsukamoto Ichiro, who guided me to and around the already large and still rapidly growing Japanese language literature on Japan's worker cooperatives. The staff and members of the Japan Institute of Cooperative Research (JICR) as well extended to me every consideration and several opportunities to present my ideas for criticism and comment while I developed them. Their collective remarks were always helpful. Current JICR director Sakabayashi Tetsuo provided extensive comment on an earlier version of this chapter. Ninjin member and former Kanagawa Prefectural Assembly member Watanabe Mitsuo and her anonymous tax accountant have vetted my numbers and done their best to keep them accurate. Remaining inaccuracies are my own responsibility. Tom Roehl, Kathy Saunders, and Betsy Pernotto all helped me separate what was from what wasn't important in earlier drafts. Translations from Japanese language materials are my own.

REFERENCES

Chambers, Norma J. 1989. *Industrial Relations in Japan: The Peripheral Work Force.* London: Routledge.

Co-op Japan. 2001. Co-op Japan Homepage. At www.co-op.or.jp (accessed January 4, 2001).

Creighton, Millie R. 1996. "Marriage, Motherhood and Career Management in a Japanese 'Counter Culture.'" In *Re-imaging Japanese Women,* ed. Anne E. Imamura, 192–220. Berkeley: University of California Press.

Hendry, Joy. 1993. "The Role of the Professional Housewife." In *Japanese Women Working,* ed. Janet Hunter, 224–41. London: Routledge.

Horioka, Charles Yuji. 1998. "Do the Japanese Live Better Than Americans?" In *Japan: Why It Works, Why It Doesn't,* eds. James Mak, Shyam Sunder, Shigeyuki Abe, and Kazuhiro Igawa, 3–10. Honolulu: University of Hawaii Press.

Imamura, Anne. 1987. *Urban Japanese Housewives at Home and in the Community.* Honolulu: University of Hawaii Press.

————, ed. 1996. *Re-imaging Japanese Women*. Berkeley: University of California Press.

Iwao Sumiko. 1993. *Japanese Women*. Boston, MA: Harvard University Press

Iwami Takashi, ed. 1986. Nihon no Wākāzu Korekuteibu (*Japan's Workers Collectives*). Tokyo: Gakuyō Shobo.

————. 2000. Shigoto to shokuba wo kyōdō de tsukurō: Wākāzu kōpu to shinia kōpu (*Let's Create Work and Workplaces with Cooperation: Workers Co-ops and Seniors Co-ops*). Tokyo: Shakai Hyoronsha.

Japanese Government. 2001. Statistics Bureau Homepage. At www.stat.go.jp/english/156b.htm (accessed January 4, 2001).

Kanagawa Worker Collective League, ed. 1994. Shinpan hatarakizukuri, machizukuri gaidobukku (*A Guide to Creating Jobs and Building Cities, new edition*). Yokohama: Kanagawa Worker Collective League.

Kawamoto Reiko. 1993. "Jiritsushita hatarakikata wo mezasu" ("Aiming at an Independent Way of Working"). In *Wākāzu Korekuteibu Zenkoku Kaigi Kirokushu* (Workers Collective National Assembly Collected Records), ed. Wākāzu Korekuteibu Zenkoku Kaigi Jikkō Iinkai (Workers Collective National Assembly Executive Committee), 28–31. Tokyo: Wākāzu Korekuteibu Zenkoku Kaigi Jikkō Iinkai.

Komori Chie. 1993. "Hanashi" ("Remarks"). In *Wākāzu Korekuteibu Zenkoku Kaigi Kirokushu*, (Workers Collective National Assembly Collected Records), ed. Wākāzu Korekuteibu Zenkoku Kaigi Jikkō Iinkai (Workers Collective National Assembly Executive Committee), 32. Tokyo: Wākāzu Korekuteibu Zenkoku Kaigi Jikkō Iinkai (Workers Collective National Assembly Executive Committee).

Kondo, Dorinne K. 1990. *Crafting Selves*. Chicago: University of Chicago Press.

Kutsuzawa Kiyomi. 1998. Gender, Work and the Politics of Identity: Work Collectives and Social Activism among Middle-Class Housewives in Contemporary Japan. PhD diss., Department of Anthropology, University of Connecticut.

Lam, Alice. 1993. "Equal Employment Opportunities for Japanese Women: Changing Company Practice." In *Japanese Women Working*, ed. Janet Hunter, 197–223. London: Routledge.

Lebra, Takie. 1993. "Gender and Culture in the Japanese Political Economy: Self-Portrayals of Prominent Businesswomen." In *Cultural and Social Dynamics*. Vol. 3 of *The Political Economy of Japan*, ed. Shumpei Kumon and Henry Rosovsky, 364–422. Stanford, CA: Stanford University Press.

Lo, Jeannie. 1990. *Office Ladies, Factory Women*. London: M. E. Sharpe.

Long, Susan O. 1996. "Nurturing and Femininity: The Ideal of Caregiving in Postwar Japan." In *Re-imaging Japanese Women*, ed. Anne E. Imamura, 156–76. Berkeley: University of California Press.

Marshall, Robert C. 1994. "Working in a Seikatsu Collective and Other Japanese Worker Co-ops." *Grassroots Economic Organizing Newsletter* 13:6–7.

———. 1995. The Culture of Cooperation in Three Tokyo Worker Co-operatives. Paper presented at the annual meeting of the American Anthropological Association.

———. 1997. Social and Political Networks, and Economic Support among Tokyo's Worker Cooperatives. Paper presented at the annual meeting of the American Anthropological Association.

Mason, Andrew, and Naohiro Ogawa. 1998. "Why Avoid the Altar?" In *Japan: Why It Works, Why It Doesn't*, ed. James Mak, Shyam Sunder, Shigeyuki Abe and Kazuhiro Igawa, 11–20. Honolulu: University of Hawaii Press.

Ogasawara Yuko. 1998. *Office Ladies and Salaried Men: Power, Gender and Work in Japanese Companies*. Berkeley: University of California Press.

Ōmori Maki. 1993. "Gender and the Labor Market." *Journal of Japanese Studies* 19(1):79–102.

Oshima, Harry. 1998. "Is Japan an Egalitarian Society?" In *Japan: Why It Works, Why It Doesn't*, ed. James Mak, Shyam Sunder, Shigeyuki Abe, and Kazuhiro Igawa, 195–204. Honolulu: University of Hawaii Press.

Roberts, Glenda. 1994. *Staying on the Line: Blue-Collar Women in Contemporary Japan*. Honolulu: University of Hawaii Press.

———. 1996. "Careers and Commitment: Azumi's Blue-Collar Women." In *Re-imaging Japanese Women*, ed. Anne E. Imamura, 221–43. Berkeley: University of California Press.

Rōdōshō. 2000. Josei Koyō Kanri Kihon Chōsa (*Women's Employment Management Basic Survey*). Tokyo: Rōdōshō Joseiyaku (Labor Ministry, Women's Bureau), Government of Japan.

Sato Yoshiyuki, ed. 1988. Joseitachi no seikatsu nettowāku: Seikatsu kurabu ni tsudou hitobito (*Women's Networks: The People Who Come Together at Seikatsu Club Consumer Cooperative*). Tokyo: Bunshindo.

————. 1995. Joseitachi no seikatsu-sha undō: Seikatsu kurabu wo sasaeru hitobito (*Women's Grassroots Activism and Seikatsu Club Consumer Cooperative Members*). Tokyo: Marujyū.

Seikatsu Club Consumer's Co-operative. 1993. *Facts and Figures*. Tokyo: Seikatsu Club Consumer's Co-operative Union.

Sugimoto Yoshio. 1997. *An Introduction to Japanese Society*. Cambridge: Cambridge University Press.

Sumitani Zemi. 2000. Wākāzu korekuteibu de hataraku josei no rōdō seikatsukan (Survey of Work and Lifestyle of Women Working in Women's Worker Cooperatives). Unpublished manuscript. Tokyo: Ōtsuma Women's College, Department of Social Communications.

Tsuchiyama Yuji. 1986. Risaikuru wo tōshita nettowākuzukuri ("Building Networks through Recycling"). In Nihon no Wākāzu Korekuteibu (*Japan's Workers Collectives*), ed. Takashi Iwami, 43–46. Tokyo: Gakuyō Shobo.

Ueno Chizuko. 1987. "The Position of Japanese Women Reconsidered." *Current Anthropology* (supplement) 28(4):S75–S84.

Utsuki Tomoko. 1993. Kichō hōkoku ("Keynote Report"). In *Wākāzu Korekuteibu Zenkoku Kaigi Kirokushu* (Workers Collective National Assembly Collected Records), ed. Wākāzu Korekuteibu Zenkoku Kaigi Jikkō Iinkai (Workers Collective National Assembly Executive Committee), 5–16. Tokyo: Wākāzu Korekuteibu Zenkoku Kaigi Jikkō Iinkai (Workers Collective National Assembly Executive Committee).

Vogel, Suzanne H. 1978. "Professional Housewife: The Career of Urban Middle-Class Japanese Women." *Japan Interpreter* 12:16–43.

Watanabe, Mitsuo. N.d. Personal Communication.

Yokota Katsumi. 1991. *I among Others: An Introspective Look at the Theory and Practice of the Seikatsu Club Movement*, ed. Iwanami Takashi. Yokohama: Seikatsu Club Seikyō Kanagawa.

8

Proletarianization of Professional Work and Changed Workplace Relationships

John R. Pulskamp

In this chapter I discuss the proletarianization of professional work, drawing attention to the struggle for power in the worker/employer relationship. This struggle, as seen here, is not limited to the loss of power by the professional workers and the resulting accrual of power by employers. It includes strategies and tactics employed by the workers to maintain and regain control of power in the changed environment exemplified by efforts on the part of professionals to organize into labor unions, and employers' responses to such maneuvers.

To clarify the distinctions intended here between professional and proletarian work, and to put forward an intended meaning of "proletarian" as used here, I point to the following contrasts as examples. Whereas one engaged in professional work expects a high degree of autonomy on the job regarding levels of productivity, sequence of tasks, techniques and tools to be used, and so forth, proletarian work is typified by high degrees of oversight, supervision, and direct control by the employer. A code of ethics for a profession is developed and enforced by the profession itself; deviations from ethical work conduct on the part of those engaged in proletarian work are addressed by the employer. Professionals are perceived, or at least self-perceived, to hold their service to the community to be of greater significance than their own remuneration; the proletarian worker is understood to be driven more directly, or even solely, by the needs to establish security and generate income for one's self.

The status and identifying characteristics of professional workers have changed dramatically during the past century. In the past those fields of work considered to be professional were limited to a very few. Traditionally, characteristics of professions have been their association with predominantly intellectual activity requiring a lengthy period of specialized training and education, the commitment to service above personal gain on the part of the practitioner of such work, and the broad range of autonomy and personal responsibility retained by the practitioner. Of particular importance in worker/employer relationships is the range of worker autonomy. "The professions have claimed autonomy as the key to the integrity of professional practice and work. Implicit in this claim is the argument that the professional must be granted special rights and working conditions not accorded other workers, namely, the relative or absolute freedom from external authority and the privilege of peer or self-supervision" (Derber 1982, 13).

Today, in addition to the traditional professions, there are many new professions: engineering, social work, teaching, computer programming, and so on. These are considered professions, yet the set of characteristics associated with professions has been altered, partly as a result of the influx of the new professions into the fold. The inclusion has tended to blur the distinctions between professions and other categories of work. Even more important, the set of defining characteristics has been deconstructed so that particular characteristics may be excluded while others are retained, thus further changing the meaning of the word "professional." The blurring of professional distinction along with the elimination or diminishing of autonomy has resulted in the "proletarianization" of professional categories of work. That is, the reduced autonomy associated with professional work has rendered it increasingly similar to other kinds of work. Management presents this change—maintenance of individual responsibility but with diminished autonomy—as inevitable and necessary (Bottery 1998, 163).

This proletarianization of these types of work has had the effect of transferring power from the professional worker to the employer. This shift in power has in turn changed the ways in which such workers can attempt to exercise some control over the worker/employer relationship. Today the relationship of both the new and the traditional professions to the economic system is that of the working class. These professionals typically have little work-related autonomy, and have little to do with the means of production other than the sale of their labor (Braverman 1974, 403).

CLASSIC DESCRIPTIONS OF A PROFESSION

It has been opined that currently there would be a lack of agreement in any attempt among a group of scholars, or a group of workers themselves, to identify a list of occupations to be considered as "professions." Correspondingly, it is likely that there would also be a lack of agreement, with any degree of precision, on the meanings of the words themselves (Blankenship 1977, 2; Pavalko 1988, 17; Rabban 1989, 1835). Regardless of this, many scholars do have some level of agreement on the classic meaning of "profession" or "professional." In this sense, categories of work that were typically considered to be professional fields were those such as the clergy, physicians, attorneys, university professors, and so forth.

Effectively, the meanings of the words "professional" and "profession" have been undergoing a change, as have the professions themselves (Oppenheimer 1975, 34). Changes in technology and ways of organizing work have in turn promoted other changes, such as the professionalization of new, and in some cases preexisting but heretofore nonprofessional, categories of work. Additionally, because of the enhanced status inferred by the use of the words, there has been increasingly frequent application of "professional" and "profession" to workers and types of work not entitled to these descriptors within the classic use of the words. This lack of precision and the fluid nature of the meanings of these words further blur the boundaries between professions and other classes of work.

There is general agreement among scholars regarding some of the identifying traits of professions in the classic sense. The sets of parameters defining professions are arbitrary constructs employed by authors discussing the issue, but workers themselves have much more flexible and varied definitions of "professional," and do not necessarily subscribe to the same rigid sets of required characteristics to identify a professional. Some who have written on the subject (e.g., Hoffman 1976, 1) list as few as three attributes to identify a profession. Others propose a more extensive list of as many as eight or more identifying characteristics (Lieberman 1956, 1–6). These sets of criteria are in agreement, at least implicitly, in several major areas of concern. Professional autonomy is a principal element. The long period of specialized training provides the prospective professional with the distinct set of skills and esoteric knowledge that can then be utilized for some service to society. It has been the possession of these specialized skills and knowledge that has justified professionals to employ high levels of autonomy over their work (Rothstein 1973, 159; Stinnett 1968, 276–77). The conscientious self-policing of a profession based on its code of ethics helped to legitimize its right to a level of autonomy not associated with nonprofessional categories of work. Autonomy is an essential component of a profession. Like any other worker, the professional sells his or her labor, but unlike other workers, in the traditional sense, autonomy is not relinquished (Haber 1991, 360).

These sets of identifying attributes describe a classic understanding of the parameters of a profession, but do not present criteria necessarily used by workers when introspectively determining whether or not they themselves are professionals. Workers apply a wide range of definitions to the word "professional." Although Hoffman, Lieberman, and others present us with workable sets of criteria for arbitrarily determining if a given person is a professional, it is an external imposition of a definition. It is not how workers or managers and supervisors of the workers make the determination.

WORKERS' UNDERSTANDINGS OF "PROFESSIONAL"
To provide insight into attitudes of workers in regard to the question of professionalism, and to highlight the ambiguity of the meaning of the word even among professional workers themselves, three workers will be introduced to discuss their concepts of "professional."[1] The three of them worked at a large municipal utility company in Southern California. The first of these workers is a senior computer operator who believes that membership and participation in his labor union plays a role in his sense of professionalism. He had had no previous experiences or involvement in labor organizations prior to coming to the company, and initially joined the union only because the cost of the agency fee was virtually the same as that of union dues, and he felt he might as well belong. Later he assumed a minor elected office in his union. Having accepted this position, he took the responsibility seriously and eventually ran for and was elected to another more responsible position where he participated on various negotiating committees.

He considers himself a professional, as do the other two individuals discussed here. To some degree he ties his professionalism to his involvement and responsibilities with the union. He says "Being a member of the union—being an active member of the union—I have to consider what people are looking at when they see me. And I think I have been very good at projecting myself as a professional, because people come to me and they ask me, 'What's going on with the union?'" He believes that his participation in the union has raised his level of professionalism. His understanding of a relationship between professionalism and unionism is not unlike an attitude occurring among some groups such as schoolteachers (Cole 1969, 8; McDonnell and Pascal 1988, vi). A union's demands and accomplishments can increase the level of professionalism on the job, and even be a "major source of their professional identity" (Bascia 1994, 7). The Los Angeles Public Library Guild has also postulated that union involvement can enhance professionalism (Guyton 1975, 85).

Although when asked about his professionalism, he credited his union involvement with being at least a partial source of his professional status, his discussion also divulged an understanding of a relationship between education and professional status. This understanding is in accordance with the classic descriptions of "professional."

Another worker, a systems analyst at the time of the interview who has since retired, also considers himself a professional, but with a slightly different meaning than expressed by the senior computer operator. None of the positions he has held required a college degree at the times of his appointments. However, he now holds a degree in information systems and one in computer science. He earned his degrees while working and feels that his academic efforts have helped him attain status as a professional.

The union that represents these workers is the recognized bargaining agent for several different bargaining units, including the administrative and professional units. As a systems analyst, this worker believes that his civil service class, which is currently in the administrative unit, should be in the professional unit. This desire to be in the professional rather than the administrative unit is of interest because for at least the previous two decades there had been no differences in wage and benefit increases between the two bargaining units. During an interview he stated, "The people in that class [civil service classification] are professionals. The majority, you might say, 85 percent of them are degreed. . . . I think of myself as being a professional." Like the case with the senior computer operator, this systems analyst recognizes the importance of education for one to be considered "professional" but again, as with the other worker, he ties his description or definition of the word to another characteristic. He describes a professional (in speaking of an electronic data processing development effort) as "the person that has had the experience, has had the education, and the blend—in putting it all together." He puts a high value on the experiential knowledge, an important facet of a professional's qualifications (Haug 1973, 203).

The third worker is an electrical engineer. He began his career with the company as an electrical engineering assistant immediately after graduating from college with a bachelor of science degree in electrical engineering. He had worked on a series of important design and construction projects during his career, including substations, switching stations, and receiving stations. He played a significant role in the design and construction of a major hydroelectric power plant, both in town during the design phase and then as field engineer in charge of electrical engineering on site with the responsibility to oversee the work of all the electrical inspectors and electrical testers during construction. He also worked on the design and construction of a high-tech center for the control of electric energy distribution and transmission for the city, and later in addition to this strictly engineering work, he also developed a scheduling and cost control system that had been intended for adoption by the company for all engineering projects.

He holds a master's degree in electrical engineering, is a registered professional engineer in California, and a member of several professional societies. He was quick to draw attention to his status as a registered professional engineer and his membership in the various professional societies as definite indications of his professional status. Of the three workers discussed here, he is the only one who started his employment already holding a college degree. As part of his formal training, he had been taught to regard engineering as a true profession even before joining the workforce. This is somewhat characteristic of engineers (Raelin 1986, 95). Although like the workers previously discussed he placed importance on education as a factor in identifying one as a professional, the difference is that for the other two, education was secondary to some other factor. For the senior computer operator, union involvement has been a major factor in establishing and developing his sense of professionalism. For the systems analyst, it has been the ability to do high-quality work, or professional work. By virtue of the type of work with which he had been involved, the electrical engineer is also the one who had been able to exercise the most autonomy. Because of the nature of his work, his formal education in actual preparation for his chosen field of work, and his membership in various professional societies, his case is the one most nearly meeting the classic description of professional.

BECOMING PROLETARIAN—LOSING AUTONOMY

Usually, the conversion from autonomous professional to proletarian worker happens incrementally and is not likely to startle or even attract the attention of the workers involved. Trying to observe the change is something akin to watching a baby grow or a flower bloom. The change is not noticeable without the use of time-lapse photography or isolated observations interspersed with relatively long periods of absence. Growing numbers of professional workers today, like any other workers, are employed by bureaucratic companies or agencies with multiple levels of supervision and management above them exercising various but undeniable degrees of control over them (Abrahamson 1967, 7; Meiksins 1982, 122). The bureaucratization of a field of work diminishes its level of professionalism (Macdonald 1995, 61), and each level of management has a propensity to constantly attempt to monopolize power. This is accomplished by the introduction of sets of standards and procedures, operating rules, and policies (Derber 1982, 17). The imposition of these rules makes conspicuous management's power and is a primary means of asserting authority over professionals (Benveniste 1987, 20). The relationship between the meaning of "profession" and the change of the characteristics of professional work is cyclic, each feeding the other. That is, as increasing varieties of work not previously considered professional in the classic sense are identified as professional, the meaning of the word "profession" changes to encompass the added categories of work. The converse is also true. As the meaning of the word changes, additional types of work can be accumulated under the title.

The ambiguity of definition of a professional is manipulated and compounded by managerial strategies to the detriment of the professional workers and the general benefit of management, creating a situation where professional workers are expected to provide their services on a professional level and with a professional sense of duty and responsibility, but without the benefits, rights, and privileges traditionally afforded the professional.

Managers, logically enough, have therefore changed the definition of professional, which, for them, has all the advantages of the old guild organization and none of its disadvantages. Professionalism for programmers as it has emerged in management literature means the establishment of universal job descriptions and standards, formulated, of course, by managers; common training programs; and perhaps a common certification process similar to that found among traditional engineering employees. On the other hand, the managers' image of professionalism does *not* [emphasis in original] include certification by an authority controlled by the programmers' peers; it does not include, certainly, licensing, nor does it foresee under any circumstances making independent entrepreneurs out of software workers. Management's vision, in other words, is of a profession without professionals. Such a "profession" would allow managers to work both sides of the street. Job "performance standards" would be established—presumably at high "professional" levels—but the standards would be set by managers. In short, the managers' notion of professional programmers is one which gives them, and not the programmer, the power to define what programming is. (Kraft 1977, 95)

Unlike most of the professions, the occupation of computer programmer is new and has evolved and changed quickly enough for one generation of programmers to have seen and noticed the change. The changes that have taken place during the past four decades in the field of computer programming at the utility company discussed here provide an example of change occurring rapidly enough that one generation of workers could experience the entire metamorphosis. Braverman (1974, 329) has also noted this rapid change in the field of data processing.

In 1963, the company had just acquired its first computers used for business applications. At that time scientific or engineering applications were developed for use on analog computers because of the limited capacity of the digital computers to handle the large numbers in those types of applications. This was a time when slide rules were still the badge of an engineer, and only a few years removed from a period when accounting clerks wore green visors and made journal entries by hand. Scores of clerks still spent their working hours punching in their calculations on full-keyboard adding machines and cumbersome old comptometers. The fields of programming for scientific and engineering applications, and programming for business applications at this company were in their infancy and developed within somewhat parallel but separate spheres of influence. I will discuss programming for business applications. This included things such as payroll, timekeeping, billing, inventory, purchasing, accounts receivable, and accounts payable systems (Braverman 1974, 329).

For quite a number of years preceding the acquisition of computers, much of the business data processing at the company had been somewhat automated. Source documents such as time cards, meter read sheets, and so forth would be put into batches and sent off to the "key-punch girls"[2] (some of whom had been on the job for over twenty years) where the handwritten data would be read and punched into paper cards variously known as Hollerith cards,[3] IBM cards, or simply tab cards or punched cards. The tab cards would then be sent to the tabulating section where tabulating equipment operators would hand wire circuit boards to control the electronic accounting machines (E.A.M. equipment) through which the tab cards would be fed to produce various accounting reports.

The workers responsible for operating the E.A.M. equipment needed to understand the logic required to produce the various reports from the punched cards in order to wire the circuit boards controlling the machines. The wiring of these circuit boards might be thought of as "proto-programming." In this company, it was from the ranks of these workers that most of the earliest programmers came. Most of the original programs written for the company's new computers were produced by some of the more senior supervisors in the tabulating section. They had the understanding and knowledge required, and by virtue of their supervisory positions had enough flexibility in their duties to spend some time learning how to program the new machines. It is also likely that they were instructed by management to do so. Soon, others from the tabulating section began learning to program and began producing small programs that would enable some of their work to be done faster on the new computers than on the E.A.M. equipment, but these efforts were not their assigned tasks and constituted only a minimal contribution. It was done during slack time or during nonwork hours.

By the mid-1960s, civil service classifications had been established specifically for programmers and the company had begun to hire and train people whose primary duties would be programming computers. They were sent to classes given by IBM and other private computer companies. Although their abilities lacked the sophistication of today's programmers, by the late 1960s, as these workers developed skills and experience, they quickly became very highly valued within the company and very marketable outside the company. Their ability to perform apparent feats of wizardry with the computers, the fact that others around them including their managers could not do what they could do, and their high marketability outside the company put them in position as elites within the division's workforce (Braverman 1974, 329). Because they were virtually the only ones who knew how to do the required work, they were often able to do it with minimal managerial control. Sometimes managers would insist on specific approaches to the work, but often would simply assign a project to a group consisting of several programmers and supervisors, and let them determine how the work was to be approached, segmented, and designed, what programming language was to be used, and the sequence in which it was to be done.

During this period the individual programmer controlled all aspects of the work. A programming task would be assigned with the general requirements indicated, the programmer would perform the analysis to identify the particular detailed requirements; design the logic; code, test, and debug the program; develop documentation for its use; put it into production; and then support and modify it as needed. This was done with a sense of dedication and professional satisfaction not unlike that of some New York firefighters who in their work were able to "oversee the 'whole product,' probably one of the more satisfying, least common attributes of work in industrialized society" (Kaprow 1991, 98). They exercised a high level of autonomy.

This changed over time. Programmer autonomy has been reduced. Programmers working for this company still enjoy relatively more autonomy than many other workers. Though more restricted, autonomy has not been eliminated. This is the case for other professions as well (Moore 1970, 195). Programmers continue to take breaks when they want to and skip breaks if they feel that is needed to complete a critical task, and to a large degree they plan their own work for the day and work at their own pace. Other things have changed. Increasingly, standards have been established, and as Kraft (1977, 95) has noted, these standards have been imposed by management. They have not been developed by programmers. Work has been broken down into smaller components, and some of it turned over to nonprogrammers to do. Bureaucratization has increased.

As an example, in the past there were management-imposed guidelines regarding program documentation, but it was primarily up to the programmer how and whether to do it. A program could be developed and put into production before or after the documentation was completed. The programmer could control the timing and coordinate synchronized implementation of a series of programs into production. Often this could be done on rather short notice to accommodate a particular need. With more management-imposed standards and procedures, and the segmentation of the work, the programmer has lost much of the control over the process. Documentation technicians now review documentation produced by programmers not only to see that it meets the standards, but often edit what programmers have written, sometimes insisting that the programmer change wording that may have had a specific meaning because of the particular wording used. If the documentation technician refuses to sign off on the documentation, data control clerks, who also now have veto power over the programmers' desire to install a program and are the parties who actually submit the computer task causing a program to be installed, will not permit the program to be put into production. If the programmer had been attempting to install several programs that worked together and were required to be installed at the same time or in a particular sequence, but one was held up by documentation technicians or data control clerks, the result could be corrupted data or bad and/or inaccurate reports. Yet it is the programmer who carries the principal responsibility for resolving the problem. The programmer has lost autonomy and control over the process, but continues to have a "professional" responsibility to resolve resulting problems.

The power of the professional to control work and work decisions is diminished by the segmentation of work into smaller identifiable tasks to be parceled out to others. This parceling out of related tasks creates a class of de-skilled workers who are able to perform their specialized tasks well, but are typically unable to perform work required for an entire process. This is an approach management has taken in many industries (Kaprow 1991, 97). Redefinitions of work and even the titles of the workers themselves facilitate this process. The result is lost autonomy, but often continued responsibility for the professional. The work is broken down into units along an industrial model where each task is simple for one worker to master, but no one worker is to be able to learn and control a whole process. Management is attempting to increase the productivity of professional workers by assuming a position of authority over them and using an industrial model as a template for organizing professionals' work, regarding it as an invisible assembly line (Stamp 1995, 6–15).

PROFESSIONAL WORKER RESISTANCE AND INFLUENCE

Today, the typical work relationship is not a professional/client relationship, but rather an employee/employer relationship. Forces acting to diminish the

professional workers' autonomy and control over their work have not been ig-
nored by professionals, but their sense of ethics—including stated and sub-
conscious dedication to service—may inhibit them from taking actions or
pursuing resolutions to perceived wrongs in the same manner as other workers. A form of resistance taken by many professionals is to coalesce into an organization and use the weight and leverage of the organization to influence
management in an attempt to establish, reestablish, or maintain some level of
professional autonomy in the workplace. Professionals often do not agree on
the appropriate nature of such organizations. Should it be strictly a scholarly
association that espouses no particular viewpoint on workplace issues faced
by the members, or perhaps a slightly more militant association that addresses
issues directly with the employer, or could it even appropriately be a labor
union with bargaining power (Hoffman 1976, 4)? The traditional professional
associations operated with an assumption that they and the employer shared
a common interest and responsibility to produce high-quality service (Kleingartner 1967, 105). The association did not see itself as oppositional to management. Traditionally, professional associations or societies, rather than labor
unions, have been the choice of professional workers, but with the changing
status of professionals labor unions become increasingly attractive (Derber
1982, 28; Oppenheimer 1975, 34).

On occasion, professional workers have formed unions or elected to be represented by an existing union. Other times professional associations have begun to behave like unions, and even evolved into unions. However, unionism
has often been perceived to be unprofessional. The workers discussed earlier
were represented by a union that had begun as a professional association and
evolved into a union.

In 1994, their union published a commemorative brochure in celebration
of its centennial.[4] It included a condensed history of the union written by a
publicist who had been hired to produce the booklet. The following description of the union's history borrows from that article, especially in regard to
events and conditions from 1894 through the 1950s.

The organization had originated in 1894 as a professional association. It
encouraged high levels of professionalism among its members, disseminated
information regarding changing technology, and helped provide advice regarding employment opportunities and professional improvement. At that
time, it was very definitely not a union but exclusively a professional associa-

tion. It did not provide labor relations assistance to its members and certainly would not have considered job actions. The attitude of the typical worker was that professionals did not need representation when confronting management. As professionals they were above that!

These attitudes began to change during the 1940s and 1950s. Association members noticed the progress being made by blue-collar union workers. While the professionals had their status, the craft workers were making progress in the areas of wages and working conditions. "Perhaps the decisive factor galvanizing these 'formerly aloof' public employees into action was the fact that less educated and less skilled working people were leaping ahead of them both in pay and fringe benefits" (see endnote 4). It was during this period that a practice of "collective begging" began. This involved lobbying, presenting logical arguments at public meetings of various governing bodies, and mobilizing the membership to exert political pressure to advance their cause.

The association began to behave like a union although at that time it was not yet a recognized bargaining agent. In the mid-1950s the association conducted a two-hour work stoppage, and in the mid-1960s officially supported a successful candidate for mayor because of his pro-worker orientation. So, without legal recognition, and certainly without a legal right to strike, the association began to effectively manipulate the political system. With the passage of a city ordinance in 1971 permitting unions to be recognized bargaining agents for city workers, the association found itself in an increasingly difficult position in attempting to protect its relationship with its members. This was a result of unions' interests in representing the bargaining units encompassing the association's members. During that time several unions, some of which had been maneuvering to gain the support of workers who had traditionally been affiliated with the association, went on strike against the utility company. The association participated in the strike, not only to press management but also to maintain connections with its members. Shortly thereafter, elections were conducted and the association was chosen to represent the professional workers. At this point there was no question as to the organization's status as a union in spite of the fact that its membership continued to refer to it as an association. In 1993, the union was embroiled in another strike against the utility company. The workers there had been working without a contract for more than a year. The city had originally offered a 0 percent wage increase and some reductions in benefits. Eventually, a 9 percent wage package over four years was agreed upon.

Even at the time of the walk-out in the mid-1950s, though, the organization was not a union and generally saw itself as a professional association. In
years since, it has moved into full unionhood by engaging in all activities normally associated with unions. Although the vestiges of the professional association attitudes continue, the willingness to take job actions has probably
impelled growing numbers of members in the organization to see themselves
as a union. However, as recently as a few years ago, members of the union's
board of governors generally avoided use of the term "union" when referring
to the organization in deference to the word "association." During one board
meeting the word "union" had been used in reference to the organization. One
board member became quite indignant, scolding the offender and stating,
"We are an association, not a union. If [the organization] is a union, I will re-
sign from the board!" (personal observation). Since the most recent strike, it
has become virtually unheard of for anyone to suggest that the organization is
an association and not a union. Today, it is routinely referred to by its members, officers, staff, and management as "the union."

This question of union versus professional association is not unique to the
group of workers presented here, although it may be more prevalent with engi-
neering-oriented workers than with some others. According to Hoffman (1976,
i), "In nursing, teaching and college teaching the associations are using collective bargaining as a method, while eschewing 'unionism' as an organizational label. In science and engineering, however, associations are not engaged in
collective bargaining, and there still appears to be opposition not only to unionism as an organization, but also to collective bargaining as a method." From its
inception in 1915 until 1972, the American Association of University Professors
(AAUP) rejected the ideas of strikes and collective bargaining, and when the
AAUP did adopt the practice of collective bargaining it resulted in considerable
internal strife and an initial loss in membership (Hoffman 1976, 54).

Not only management but also the professional workers themselves sometimes stifle their own movements toward the unionization of professional
work. It is understandable that professionals may be reluctant to appear too
different from their managers. Many professionals aspire to become part of
management, and often managers are selected from the ranks of the professionals. Although many professionals are unionized, many continue to consider it to be unprofessional. In subtle ways management reminds professionals
of their status with the implication that they should behave differently than

other workers. Sometimes, in not so subtle ways, management has tried to actually prevent professionals from organizing by claiming that professionals are exempt under the National Labor Relations Act. The National Labor Relations Board, though, has carefully differentiated between professionals, and supervisors and managers who are exempt (Rabban 1989, 1778–1805).

CONCLUSIONS

A professional today is not what one was in the past. The number of various kinds of callings considered to be professions has increased tremendously due to changes in technology, new fields of work, and inclusion of preexisting types of work now deemed as professional when they had not been so in the past. Under the classic meaning, the term "profession" could be applied only to a small number of occupations usually limited to the clergy, physicians, attorneys, university professors, and perhaps a few others. The meaning of the word itself has changed.

> In the past, being a professional was ennobling. It presumed a calling—a vocation—and a dedication to service. A physician (one who healed) served the needs of a patient (one who suffered). A professor (one who professed) served the needs of a student (one who studied). Today we question whether concepts such as "student" and "teacher" are appropriate in the postmodern age. Do we have students, or are they customers, clients, stakeholders, constituents, or (indeed) products? Do faculty members profess, or do they manage, coordinate, or facilitate learning? While we engage in arcane debates about words, my local branch of a discount clothing chain no longer refers to salespeople as clerks, but as "educators" (because "an educated consumer is our best customer"). So in our brave new world, professors are coordinators, while clothing clerks are educators. (Birnbaum 2000, 225–26).

With the changing meaning of the terms come changing conditions. Through imposition of rules, standards, and policies not developed within the professions, management has dismissed and limited autonomy, which had been the hallmark of professionals. Management has also segmented what had been professional work and distributed various components of once unitary tasks to other workers, putting control of a process in the hands of management through their authority over workers, rather than in the hands of professionals. With lost or diminished autonomy, professionals have become little different from other workers in their relationship with employers. This change, in turn, has been reflected in the way professionals have been willing to attempt to maintain some autonomy in the workplace. With increasing frequency they have joined or formed labor unions. To many professionals, especially those coming out of programs of formal education that had prepared them to think of themselves as professionals in terms of the classic descriptions, joining or forming labor unions was initially distasteful. It appeared "unprofessional."

Today's professional working for a bureaucratized company or public agency, though paid higher wages perhaps, is not very different from any other wage earner within the economic system. One worker, from a family of professionals in the classic sense (his father had been trained in law at the university in Vienna and his brothers were both physicians), put it this way: "These people don't recognize the fact that whether they are laying bricks or taking people's temperature, or taking a history, a medical history—they're working in a large organization as a relatively small cog."

NOTES

1. Remarks about, and the quotations of, particular workers are based on interviews taken during research done during 1995–1998 and in 2001 with workers from a municipally owned utility company in Southern California. If not indicated otherwise, other specific examples of worker behavior and attitudes presented here are based on personal observations occurring during that research and/or my thirty-five years working for the same agency as the workers referenced in the interviews. Those thirty-five years were spent in the field of data processing, or information technology, a field of work that could be considered one of the "new" professions.

2. Most of the workers who operated the E.A.M. equipment at the time were males with the exception of a number of women who had probably been hired during the male worker shortage of World War II. Braverman (1974, 329) suggests that because the keypunch process utilized a keyboard it had been "immediately recognized as a job for 'girls.'"

3. Named after Herman Hollerith who, in 1888, invented a system of codes based on holes punched in thirteen rows across eighty columns of a paper card. Each of the eighty columns could contain hole combinations to represent one numeral, alphabetic character, or special character (Maynard 1981, 88).

4. Neither the union, nor the title of its 1994 commemorative booklet, is named here because at the time of the interviews it was agreed with the informants that they and their union would remain anonymous.

REFERENCES

Abrahamson, Mark. 1967. *The Professional in the Organization.* Chicago: Rand McNally.

Bascia, Nina. 1994. *Unions in Teachers' Professional Lives: Social, Intellectual, and Practical Concerns.* New York: Teachers College Press.

Benveniste, Guy. 1987. *Professionalizing the Organization: Reducing Bureaucracy to Enhance Effectiveness.* San Francisco: Jossey-Bass

Birnbaum, Robert. 2000. *Management Fads in Higher Education: Where They Come From, What They Do, Why They Fail.* San Francisco: Jossey-Bass.

Blankenship, Ralph L. 1977. "Professions, Colleagues and Organizations." In *Colleagues in Organization: The Social Construction of Professional Work,* ed. Ralph L. Blankenship, 1–50. New York: John Wiley and Sons.

Bottery, Mike. 1998. *Professionals and Policy: Management Strategy in a Competitive World.* London: Cassell.

Braverman, Harry. 1974. *Labor and Monopoly Capital: The Degradation of Work in the Twentieth Century.* New York: Monthly Review Press.

Cole, Stephen. 1969. *The Unionization of Teachers: A Case Study of the UFT.* New York: Praeger.

Derber, Charles. 1982. *Professionals as Workers: Mental Labor in Advanced Capitalism.* Boston: G. K. Hall.

Guyton, Theodore Lewis. 1975. *Unionization: The Viewpoint of Librarians.* Chicago: American Library Association.

Haber, Samuel. 1991. *The Quest for Authority and Honor in the American Professions, 1750–1900.* Chicago: University of Chicago Press.

Haug, Marie R. 1973. "Deprofessionalization: An Alternative Hypothesis for the Future." In *Professionalization and Social Change,* ed. Paul Halmos, 195–211. Staffordshire, UK: University of Keele.

Hoffman, Eileen B. 1976. *Unionization of Professional Societies.* New York: Conference Board.

Kaprow, Miriam Lee. 1991. "Magical Work: Firefighters in New York." *Human Organization* 50(1):97–103.

Kleingartner, Archie. 1967. *Professionalism and Salaried Worker Organization.* Madison: Industrial Relations Research Institute, University of Wisconsin.

Kraft, Phillip. 1977. *Programmers and Managers: The Routinization of Computer Programming in the United States.* New York: Springer-Verlag.

Lieberman, Myron. 1956. *Education a Profession.* Englewood Cliffs, NJ: Prentice-Hall.

Maynard, Jeff. 1981. *Dictionary of Data Processing.* 2nd ed. London: Butterworths.

Macdonald, Keith M. 1995. *The Sociology of the Professions.* London: Sage.

McDonnell, Loraine M., and Anthony Pascal. 1988. *Teacher Unions and Educational Reform.* Santa Monica, CA: RAND.

Meiksins, Peter F. 1982. "Science in the Labor Process: Engineers as Workers." In *Professionals as Workers: Mental Labor in Advanced Capitalism,* ed. Charles Derber, 121–40. Boston: G. K. Hall.

Moore, Wilbert E. 1970. *The Professions: Roles and Rules.* New York: Russell Sage Foundation.

Oppenheimer, Martin. 1975. "The Unionization of the Professional." *Social Policy* (January/February): 34–40.

Pavalko, Ronald M. 1988. *Sociology of Occupations and Professions.* 2nd ed. Itasca, IL: F. E. Peacock.

Rabban, David M. 1989. "Distinguishing Excluded Managers from Covered Professionals under the NLRA." *Columbia Law Review* 89(8):1775–1860.

Raelin, Joseph A. 1986. *The Clash of Cultures: Managers and Professionals.* Boston: Harvard Business School Press.

Rothstein, William G. 1973. "Professionalization and Employer Demands: The Cases of Homeopathy and Psychoanalysis in the United States." In *Professionalization and Social Change,* ed. Paul Halmos, 159–78. Staffordshire, UK: University of Keele.

Stamp, Daniel. 1995. *The Invisible Assembly Line: Boosting White-Collar Productivity in the New Economy.* New York: American Management Association.

Stinnett, T. M. 1968. *Professional Problems of Teachers.* 3rd ed. New York: Macmillan.

STATES: PREMODERN
TO TRANSNATIONAL

As with previous chapters, the authors in this section bring into question economic theory and neoclassical economics. They all address the reorganization of, and control over, labor, the links between social networks and transnational migration. Flexibility, recruitment of labor, risk, resistance, and unions are continuing themes that tie these studies to the previous chapters.

Kowalewski and colleagues look at the relationship between control of labor and urban transformation. In a challenge to current archaeological theory, they argue that military violence, not technological change, was a factor in the reorientation of labor and urban transformation, and that it was intensive community-level collective labor that built the fortified, terraced hilltowns, not a hierarchical and centralized control of labor. These self-ruling hilltop communities may also have supplied seasonal migrant labor for the valley floor towns. Seasonal migration figures in Ortiz's research on contemporary Latin American, which here reaches back into the archaeological past.

Steinberg, like Kowalewski, regards control of labor as an explanation for political and economic change. Steinberg documents the settlement of Viking Age Icelandic migration to avoid living under a state controlled by Harald Finehair, and the subsequent rapid colonization of a chiefdom-level society. Like others in this volume, Steinberg challenges economic theory: In Viking Age Iceland, a political economy was based on scarce, but highly productive, labor, not land as claimed by neoclassical economics. Steinberg argues that the first settlers of settlement and commonwealth Iceland chose not to own more productive land, but rather land that required the least labor. Secondary settlers would have a greater need of labor to make their less productive land yield adequate crops, and were thus dependent upon these first settlers who held control over labor. For several hundred years, Icelandic chiefly social organization was able to maintain its power by its differential control over labor.

Bowie addresses the intersection of two ongoing themes, resistance and control of labor, but with a different outcome. While Marshall, Pulskamp, and Reichart document effective strategies of resistance, Bowie explains how resistance can be thwarted. Lack of peasant resistance and revolt in northern Thailand are explained by strategies of labor control. Fragmentation of labor strengthens political and economic power as it weakens peasantry. Migration played a role in the studies by Ortiz, Koenig, Rees, and Kowalewski et al. Bowie shows how migration can be a tool of exploitation. She argues that migration that results from village tensions between ethnic groups is one aspect of the strategy of fragmentation used by those in power to weaken the peasantry.

The ongoing themes of migration, control of labor, resistance, networks, and unions, as well as challenges to neoclassical economic theory, coalesce in Zlolniski's study of the Silicon Valley. With globalization and the new economy, there is an increase in subcontracting that utilizes flexible, unskilled, and semiskilled immigrant labor and taps into their social networks for labor recruitment and control. These same networks are used by union organizers in mobilizing collective labor resistance. Paid workers draw on unpaid, invisible household labor, as entire families perform one janitorial job. The skilled professional workers in Pulskamp's study, and the unskilled and semiskilled workers in Zlolniski's chapter (and Reichart's West Virginia miners), have much in common—for all collective labor is organized into unions for resistance. Like others in this book, Zlolniski challenges economic theory. It is with the household as a social unit, not with the individual as claimed by neoclassical economics, that allocation of labor takes place.

Wilson documents how laborer and employer alike utilize worker networks. Here we see the relationship between capitalization, transnational migration, and networks. What migrants have in common is not atomization relative to capital but networks, which can function both negatively and positively. Zlolniski shows how subcontractors tap into the social networks of immigrant workers for labor recruitment and control, while union organizers use these same networks to mobilize collective labor resistance. Wilson shows how widely dispersed networks facilitate transnational migration for both the laborer and employer. For both laborer and employer, networks allow for greater access to information and thus diminish risk.

Dilly brings a new dimension to the discussion of social networks and labor mobilization in this volume—volunteerism. Volunteer labor is characterized by the informal economy, reciprocity, and social networks. Dilly argues that the cultural value of volunteer labor production is the reproduction of a viable rural culture in a deteriorating economic environment. Although all chapters document economic responses to changing economic environments, here labor is used to ratify withdrawal from the global market and reinforces the sociability of rural community. This approach challenges neoclassic theory (demand for public goods and maximization of personal benefits), as well as the sociological approach that looks at volunteer labor as social networks organized for social good.

9

Hilltowns and Valley Fields: Great Transformations, Labor, and Long-Term History in Ancient Oaxaca

Stephen A. Kowalewski, Gary M. Feinman, Linda M. Nicholas, and Verenice Y. Heredia

The great transformations in history involve at their heart profound changes in the way people work. New dispositions of labor, in turn, require fundamental alterations in many other aspects of culture. The Industrial Revolution was one such totalizing, great transformation. A great transformation in a preindustrial context took place in Oaxaca, Mexico. It began about 500 B.C. and its consequences were still reverberating eight hundred years later. This chapter examines to what extent labor was transformed during this epoch of change in Oaxaca. This was not a case of major change being due to technological innovations allowing greater energy capture and central appropriation of new means of production. Here, there were no new technologies. Military violence played a key role, and new community formations were built on principles more corporate or collective than centralizing or apical.

The first section describes the archaeological data on which the chapter is based. Unusually large-scale surface surveys and broad excavations at specific sites provide a suitably complicated context. The next section outlines the great urban transformation in Oaxaca, emphasizing how totalizing it was. With the large-scale surveys, we now know that the process of transformation worked out differently in the different regions of central Oaxaca. The Valley of Oaxaca underwent a period of demographic and hierarchical growth, while the Mixteca Alta suddenly became a militarized landscape of defensible hilltowns. Agricultural work had to adjust, everywhere, and especially in the Mixteca Alta where people now lived on high knobs at considerable distance from their former fields.

Oaxacan hilltowns were dense, fortified settlements and community-scale architectural creations. Whole mountaintops were sculpted. Excavations at El Palmillo, in the Valley of Oaxaca, show how walls and residential terraces must have been planned and constructed as suprahousehold efforts. Using insights from the El Palmillo excavations, we make some broad estimates of the labor that must have gone into terrace and civic-ceremonial construction at hilltowns in the Mixteca Alta. As in other recent studies in which archaeologists have estimated the amount of labor in construction, our results do not indicate astounding toil over many years, but they are revealing of the organization and direction of social labor.

We draw on full-coverage archaeological surface surveys from the Valley of Oaxaca (Kowalewski et al. 1989), its southern peripheral Ejutla Valley (Feinman and Nicholas 1990), its southwestern peripheral Sola de Vega Valley (Balkansky 1997), its mountainous western periphery (Finsten 1996), the Cuicatlán Cañada to the north, which apparently was conquered by the Valley of Oaxaca (Spencer and Redmond 1997), and our recent surveys of the central Mixteca Alta (Balkansky et al. 2000). We also draw on surveys of the Nochixtlán and Yucuita regions of the Mixteca Alta by Spores (1972) and Plunket (1983), and the Guirún eastern periphery of the Valley of Oaxaca (Feinman and Nicholas 1996, 1999). These surveys found, mapped, and dated virtually all the visible settlements in a part of the world where most archaeological sites have left substantial remains on the surface. The total area covered in this contiguous block is about 7,000 km², large enough to be genuinely multiregional in its cultural evolution.

Residential terraces had been excavated prior to Feinman and Nicholas's work at El Palmillo, especially at Monte Albán, ancient capital of the Valley of Oaxaca (Kuttruff and Autry 1978; Winter 1974), and Finsten (1995) has done intensive mapping and surface collecting at groups of interconnected residential terraces at Jalieza in the Valley of Oaxaca. Feinman and Nicholas have intensively mapped several hilltowns in eastern Tlacolula and are in the third year of excavations at El Palmillo, described below (Feinman and Nicholas 2001). For more detail on the great transformation in Oaxaca, see the works by Marcus and Flannery (1996) and Blanton, Feinman, Kowalewski, and Nicholas (1999). Spores (1969) and Kirkby (1972) have described agricultural terracing in the Mixteca Alta.

Abrams (1994) has produced some of the most detailed estimates of the various labor costs in construction for the Classic-period Maya city of Copán. Chaco Canyon archaeologists (e.g., Wills 2000; Windes and McKenna 2001) have used labor cost estimates for great houses and great kivas as evidence for suprahousehold organization. Particularly relevant is the study by Hard, Zapata, Moses, and Roney (1999) on the labor time in residential terrace construction in Chihuahua, which they estimated by making an experimental terrace. Robles García's (1994) ethnoarchaeological study documents details of stone quarrying near Mitla, Oaxaca.

THE URBAN TRANSFORMATION IN OAXACA

Oaxaca was at the center of pre-Hispanic Mesoamerica. It is mostly mountainous. Central Oaxaca, the focus of this chapter (figure 9.1), consists of several upland drainage basins, with valleys as low as 600 meters above sea level (asl), the Cuicatlán Cañada, to the more typical 1,600 meters (the Valley of Oaxaca) or 2,000 meters (valleys in the Mixteca Alta). Mountain ranges separating the valleys rise as high as 3,200 meters. Permanent habitation has mainly been confined to below 2,500 meters. Climates are warm to hot, semiarid, with dry winters. Higher elevations, as in much of the Mixteca Alta, receive the most rain, although frost can limit the growing season and orographic effects create drier locales. The Cañada is hot and dry, but it has good irrigation resources in its valley bottom. The Valley of Oaxaca and its peripheral valleys have some irrigation resources but quite a lot of the land must depend on spotty rainfall for agriculture.

Oaxaca was home to a long-standing, plant-food-collecting and hunting adaptation, out of which developed the indigenous Mesoamerican diet based on domesticated and collected plants and small amounts of meat. The transition to settled farming villages took place by at least 1500 B.C. The typical Early Formative pattern in central Oaxaca was for a valley pocket to have a cluster of settlements, with small hamlets gravitating around a larger town (we refer to this as a "head town/satellite hamlet" settlement pattern). Higher and more rugged areas had little or no permanent habitation (see the column sections prior to 500 B.C. in figure 9.2). Each settlement cluster may have had up to two thousand people. Houses were of wattle and daub. Public architecture in head towns (such as San José Mogote in the Valley of Oaxaca) and some smaller villages suggests a two- or three-tiered civic-ceremonial hierarchy above the level of the basal hamlet. There was regular exchange of locally available and exotic items within and between the settlement clusters in central Oaxaca. There is

FIGURE 9.1

little evidence of mobilization or division of labor beyond that found in many chiefdoms. The Mixteca Alta clusters were demographically on a par with those in the Valley of Oaxaca.

The urban transformation has its first manifestation in the Valley of Oaxaca about 500 B.C. Outside of Oaxaca, other regions in Mesoamerica seem to have undergone major reorganizations about this time. In the Valley of Oaxaca the process began with the founding of a new capital, Monte Albán, on a previously uninhabited mountaintop. Monte Albán grew quickly to a population of some 5,000 people, which created new demands for provisioning. Production for tribute and exchange affected household formation, activities, and time budgets. Individual household storage began to decline, presumably in

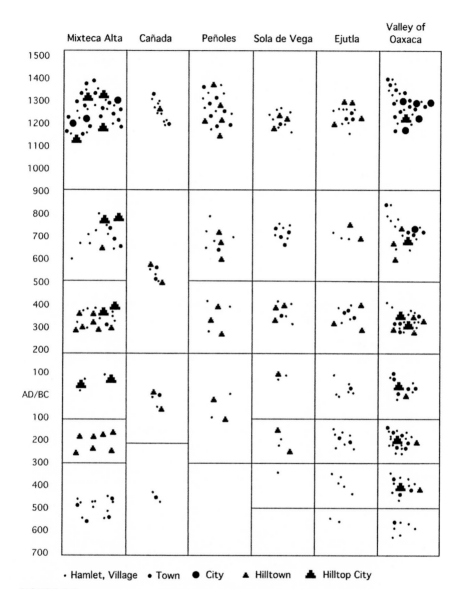

| | Mixteca Alta | Cañada | Peñoles | Sola de Vega | Ejutla | Valley of Oaxaca |

· Hamlet, Village · Town ● City ▲ Hilltown 🔺 Hilltop City

FIGURE 9.2
Settlement pattern histories in several regions in Oaxaca, showing how the urban transformation played out somewhat differently.

favor of daily market procurement; cooking habits changed (more tortillas); wattle and daub gave way to masonry as the preferred house construction style; the family tomb replaced less elaborate pit burials; and a transformed ideology strong on fertility symbolism was evident in rituals at every level from the capital to the individual household. Within four centuries of the founding of Monte Albán, the Valley of Oaxaca had 50,000 inhabitants, 17,000 of whom lived in the urban center. The civic-ceremonial hierarchy grew from two or three levels before Monte Albán to at least five levels by 100 B.C.—the most outstanding episode of political growth ever in Oaxaca. State-sponsored violence was displayed in sculptures on Monte Albán's main plaza. Although most people and most settlements were around the valley floor, the earliest terraced hilltowns apparently date to a century or two after 500 B.C. By about 100 B.C., Monte Albán itself was fortified.

The valley's immediate peripheries were only lightly occupied (Sola de Vega and Ejutla) or not inhabited at all (perhaps Peñoles) as late as 300 B.C. The fertile Cuicatlán Cañada continued the "head town/satellite hamlet" pattern as late as 200 B.C. Our current knowledge of the Mixteca Alta would suggest a similar pattern, with some growth continuing until 300 B.C.

Either in response to external threats or internal consolidation, depending on the interpretation followed (Blanton et al. [1999] or Marcus and Flannery [1996]), Monte Albán's founding mobilized households in novel ways, and this in turn kicked off a cascade of consequences affecting every aspect of culture in the Valley of Oaxaca. The Mixteca Alta and the Cañada were part of the process, but they were to reorganize in different ways.

By 300 or 200 B.C., every region in central Oaxaca underwent major settlement change, the farther from the Valley of Oaxaca, the more profound. Ejutla had fairly strong rural growth in the two centuries after 300 B.C., but no hilltowns were built. Sola de Vega saw the construction of fortified hilltowns for the first time. The mountainous Peñoles region was occupied by small hamlets, at least some fortified, after 300 B.C.

In the Cuicatlán Cañada, village burning and abandonment, violent death, a trophy skull rack, new fortified hilltowns, and a sculpture on the main plaza at Monte Albán showing it as a war trophy all point to conquest and subjugation by the Valley of Oaxaca state. This occurred by 200 B.C.

The transformation in the parts of the Mixteca Alta was different still, and no less dramatic. As depicted in figure 9.2, before 300 B.C. everyone lived in open-ground dispersed settlements in the head town and satellite hamlet pattern; after 300 B.C. virtually everyone lived in newly constructed fortified hilltowns, especially west of the Nochixtlán Valley. This was a militarized landscape. Hilltowns were situated several hundred meters in elevation above valley floors. In the Nochixtlán and Coixtlahuaca Valleys of the eastern Mixteca Alta, urban centers on hilltops included Monte Negro, Yucuita, and Coixtlahuaca. Pre-Hispanic agricultural terrace systems (*lama-bordo*) are associated with many of these hilltowns and urban centers. *Lama-bordos* are strings of cross-drainage check dams that catch soil and water flowing from eroding side slopes. *Lama-bordo* fields require fairly intensive maintenance but their agricultural productivity is outstanding. It is likely that *lama-bordo* systems grew as a consequence of slope disturbance in and near hilltowns and that they were maintained as a high-yield alternative to valley-floor fields for milpa, cactus, fruit trees, and other crops.

Between 100 B.C. and A.D. 200, all regions of central Oaxaca underwent, to a greater or lesser degree, a similar process of settlement nucleation, consolidation into somewhat fewer but larger towns, and abandonment of some settlements and locales. It may also have been a time of some demographic slowdown after the growth of the previous period. Nowhere was this more dramatic than in the Mixteca Alta, where the shakeout among hilltowns produced wholesale abandonment of some areas and consolidation into larger, fortified urban agglomerations in just a few places. Some of the earlier urban experiments, like Monte Negro, failed, but the surviving urban agglomerations (Huamelulpan and Yucuita) were in size the peers of Monte Albán.

To put this urban transformation into better perspective, we carry the story forward for another three centuries into the Early Classic period (A.D. 200–500). This was a time of population growth and settlement expansion in all parts of central Oaxaca. Areas that had been abandoned between 100 B.C. and A.D. 200 were now recolonized. Central Oaxaca had quite a few cities and towns in the range of 5,000–15,000 inhabitants, and there were many more smaller towns and villages. Regional systems were not dominated by very large primate centers; instead, each region, and the whole area under consideration here, was composed of networks of neighboring cities and towns. Hilltowns were part of the mix in these regional systems. Their size, amount of civic-ceremonial architecture, military importance, and amount of craft specialization varied considerably with the role or place they had in regional systems.

In sum, the urban transformation in central Oaxaca involved all its constituent regions. It began about 500 B.C. when Monte Albán was founded, probably in response to political events both local and external. This triggered a chain of unforeseeable events, including transformation of daily life and hierarchical growth in the Valley of Oaxaca, and everywhere, but especially in the Mixteca Alta, an increase in military concerns. An initial period of growth was followed by a period of abandonment and competitive consolidation, and then by the Early Classic, another major expansion in landscapes of cities and towns that were urbanized in every respect. The division of labor took on all the characteristics of preindustrial urbanism. During the urban transformation, labor became mobilized in entirely new ways. Labor was uprooted, untied from place, but incompletely, in some regions more than others, and as we shall see, the process of uprooting and mobilizing may also have created new, collective institutions by which workers could organize themselves into communities that were relatively self-ruling.

The history of urbanism in central Oaxaca has a lot of hilltowns in its genealogy. In the next section we focus on hilltowns as objects of work and reflections of the changing ways in which labor was organized.

HILLTOWNS

Hilltop sites with residential terraces have a 2,000-year history in Oaxaca. Monte Albán was the earliest and most famous hilltop terraced site, but there are hundreds of others. They share three common features that make them very distinct from other settlements: location on mountaintops high above valley floors and away from traditional farmland and water resources, densely packed houses on multiple artificial terraces, and defensive properties provided by the same terrace retaining walls. Hilltop terraced sites can be quite different from one another in size, form of the terraces, proportion of civic-ceremonial architecture, degree of military function, craft specialization, permanence of occupation, and so forth.

Here we describe the hilltowns that played a role in the urban transformation, 500 B.C. to A.D. 500. Many hilltop terraced sites have been severely eroded, plowed, or obscured by later occupation, so our interpretations must be drawn from a smaller selection of better preserved sites.

The earlier (Ramos, Monte Albán Late I–II, 300 B.C.–A.D. 200) hilltop terraced sites (apart from Monte Albán) tend to have the form of a doughnut ring-ing a round or oval knob (figure 9.3). The terrace retaining walls are massive rock walls (revetments) arranged in multiple concentric rings broken in only a few places by ramps from one level to the next. In cross-section, the sites would look like a multitiered wedding cake (rather like the glyphs of the conquered places on Mound J at Monte Albán (Caso 1947). The walls average two to three meters in height. The terraces themselves are long and narrow (averaging more than thirty meters long by five to seven meters wide). Houses were built on the back, uphill side of the terrace, and it is not uncommon at all to find multiple houses sharing a single terrace and retaining wall. The top of the hill was leveled to form one or a small number of flat areas. These may be plazas, but none have been excavated so we do not know if these flat areas instead may have supported domestic or public structures. Typically, these sites have one or more small mounds, which were the basal platforms for civic-ceremonial architecture. The total civic-ceremonial area of possible plazas and mounds was relatively small. We interpret these early sites as hilltowns, that is, full-function communities whose populations live entirely within the defensive walls.

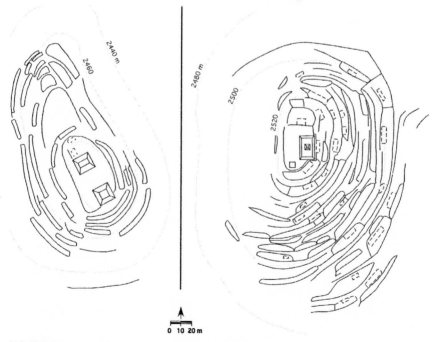

0   10   20 m

FIGURE 9.3
Two examples of fortified hilltowns: SAL-16 (left) and SJG-11 (right).

By the Early Classic period, there was more differentiation and variation in hilltop terraced sites. Some continued the older hilltown form. In other cases the strongly concentric form was lost, and the terraces and retaining walls were much shorter. Ridgelines and side slopes might be almost continuously covered by cascading strings of small residential terraces. At some sites the mean terrace area is under 100 m², that is, the entire house and house lot took up less than 1,100 square feet. These were single-household domestic units. Some hilltop terraced sites grew to city scale, some were more specialized military garrisons, some had considerable craft specialization and others little, and some were prominent places in the civic-ceremonial hierarchy while others of similar size had only low-level civic-ceremonial functions. We suspect that labor-rich but resource-poor hilltowns may have supplied workers for land-rich but underpopulated valley-floor estates. In other words, as urban central place hierarchies differentiated, horizontally and vertically, so too did hilltop terraced sites assume different roles and configurations.

El Palmillo

El Palmillo is a mountaintop site in the eastern Valley of Oaxaca. It has over 1,400 terraces packed into less than one square kilometer, and at its maximum between A.D. 250–750 it had a population of at least 5,000 people.

Excavations totaling 500m² have been carried out on four adjacent terraces. Terrace building at El Palmillo was a monumental undertaking. Terraces were made by building a massive rock wall (revetment) and filling in behind it with sediment. On the lower slopes of the site, the two-meter-high retaining walls are long and arranged in concentric rings or steps. From below, the whole hill slope must have appeared sculpted, and the closely packed houses and their roofs, plus the terrace retaining walls, would have presented a totally integrated look. El Palmillo and other hilltop terraced sites were not only defensive works, they were community-scale architectural statements.

The excavated houses consisted of long, rectangular structures, flanked by adjoining units, opening onto a central patio. These were well-made, stone masonry and lime plaster constructions. There were also several other one-room structures. As the surface surveys observed at many sites, these excavations show the house situated at the back of the terrace, with a narrow "walkway" or cleared area of one- to two-meter width in front, along the retaining wall. So much of the terrace area was built on and paved that there would have been room for only a few ornamental plants—milpa would have been out of the question. Both the terraces and the structures were renovated several times, and these modifications, plus repetitive use of burial areas, demonstrate considerable continuity in the use of domestic space.

The long, common retaining walls of the concentric terrace rings, the arrangement of gates and roads through these walls, and the overall coordination required for building densely packed fill platforms and rock walls must have required suprahousehold organization of work. House building probably required a few skills not universally shared, but the labor for house building need not have been coordinated beyond the domestic unit.

El Palmillo is in one of the drier, rockier parts of the Valley of Oaxaca. The excavations found quite a bit of evidence for specialized craft activities in the domestic units. Today the site is profusely covered with economically useful plants: agave, yucca, *cazahuate, tunillo,* amole, nopal, *copal,* and others. These plants are much less frequent on the neighboring hills, which were never occupied, so it seems likely that they are the descendants of colonies maintained by the ancient town's inhabitants. The excavations have found ovens for roasting maguey hearts, similar to the ovens in use today in nearby Santiago Matatlán's mescal industry. Scrapers, bone battens, perforators, awls, and spindle whorls attest to textile production. Local chert was worked, and there is a notable amount of deer bone. Although sufficient controlled surface collections and excavations have not yet been carried out in the Mixteca Alta hilltowns, it is our impression from their surface artifacts that specialized craft activities were not as intense as at some of the Valley of Oaxaca hilltop terraced sites like El Palmillo and Jalieza. The intense craft activity seen at some Classic-period hilltop sites in the Valley of Oaxaca does not seem to have been a feature of the early hilltowns in the Mixteca Alta.

Labor Estimates

How much work did it take to make one of the early hilltowns? Is there anything about the labor involved that would speak to community or task organization? We draw on a recent study of a terraced site in Chihuahua, in which Hard and colleagues (1999) built a replica terrace and recorded the labor time. In their work, site clearing and layout took less than two hours, less than 3 percent of the total time. Most of the work involved moving stone and earth for the retaining berm and the terrace fill. This and other studies suggest that a person can dig and move a cubic meter of sediment in about two hours. To estimate the volume of materials moved, Hard et al. used the civil engineering technique of calculating an average cross-sectional area for the terrace, and multiplying by the terrace length to obtain the volume of fill.

Terrace fill volumes vary with the geometry of the cut and fill operation. The most economical way to make a terrace is to cut half the desired terrace width into the back side of the slope and move that fill to the front, behind a retaining wall. Pure fill or pure cut operations, in which the entire terrace width is built out or cut into the slope, have a much greater cross section and retaining wall height. The El Palmillo excavations demonstrate that there was little cutting into the slope, and our observations of retaining wall heights suggest that the Oaxaca terraces were much closer to pure fill operations rather than cut-and-fill, or what we called the "dog-scratch" method. In our calculations of terrace volumes, we therefore assume the larger cross sections.

The other crucial variable in terrace construction is slope, because terrace width and retaining wall height vary with slope angle. We computed average slope for the terraced portions of the hilltops in our study sample, and used this angle to calculate expected retaining wall heights for terraces of given widths. We checked the cases where we had measured retaining wall heights against the formula expectations, and verified that on average the formula was a good proxy. We could therefore use our field measurements of terrace width, length, and slope angle to estimate broadly the amount of fill per terrace, and from this, the amount of labor time involved in terrace making.

Moving dirt represents the largest portion of labor time in terrace construction, but there are other steps in the making of a hilltown that we do not control, for example, removing trees. People quarried stone on site, but we don't know how much. Other studies suggest a person would need 2.5 days to quarry a cubic meter of stone from bedrock. In most cases, quarried stone probably represented a small fraction of the materials in the initial construction of hilltowns. We are also not counting labor in houses or public buildings beyond the making of the basal platforms. According to Abrams's figures (1994, 64), building the basic house in the Copán area would have required on average about 80 six-hour person-days.

Table 9.1 summarizes labor time estimates for all the construction we mapped at seven hilltop terraced sites in the Mixteca Alta. We selected these sites because they were well-enough preserved so that most of their terraces

Table 9.1. Construction Estimates for Selected Mixteca Alta Hilltowns

Site	Period	% Slope	No. of Terraces	Mean Terr. Length (m)	Mean Terr. Width (m)	Est. Wall Ht. (m)	Tot. Terr. Person/ Days	Mean Terr. Person/ Days	No. Civ.- Cer. Strs. & Plazas	Civ.- Cer. Person/ Days	Civ.- Cer. Days/ Terr. Days	Residential Population	Tot. Days for ½ Resid. Pop.
SJG-11	Ramos	36	55	37	7	2	7464	136	10	473	0.06	450	35
SJA-10	Ramos	40	20	29	8	3	2556	128	4	389	0.15	250	24
SMP-13	Ramos	34	14	23	6	2	840	60	2	46	0.05	600	3
SAL-16	R,LF	40	30	47	5	2	3802	127	4	2347	0.62	250	49
SVN-10	LF,R	43	72	55	9	4	52952	735	3	663	0.01	900	119
SVN-13	Las Flores	22	52	32	6	1	3733	72	7	345	0.09	3500	2
YPD-1	Las Flores	33	21	31	5	2	1096	52	12	6068	5.54	400	36

could be mapped, and because we could be confident that their construction dated to one or two phases. Some of the variation in these sample sites is probably due to the difference between the early hilltowns and the later, Classic-era sites that tend to vary in function according to their place in more complex regional systems. All of these sites are on high, fairly steep knobs and ridgelines. The number of terraces varies from fourteen to seventy-two but at two sites (SMP-13 and SVN-13) we could not map all the terraces that once existed. Terraces tend to be long, a few as long as 150 meters, but the site averages range from twenty-nine to fifty-five meters in length, and thus the average terrace was probably a multihousehold unit. Mean terrace widths range from five to nine meters. Mean retaining wall heights (estimated and measured) are usually two meters or more. The retaining walls are stone and earth, piled nearly vertical in some cases. Each is a formidable obstacle, and in most of these sites the terraces are arranged in concentric rings so ascending the hill means negotiating at least four or five walls, which is easiest done using the ancient ramps and stairs between terrace levels.

The total amount of labor on the residential terraces—that is, the time it took to move the estimated wall and fill volume—is expressed as the number of six-hour person-days. Most of the sites in this sample could have been built at a cost of 1,000–7,000 person-days, but one site, SVN-10, may have required over 50,000 person-days because of its steep slope and the fact that people chose to construct some very wide terraces. With the exception of SVN-10, the average amount of labor per terrace ranges between 50 and 140 person-days. (Hard et al.'s experimental terrace of 17 x 8 meters on a more gentle slope with a retaining wall one meter high took ten person-days to make.) The larger terraces at Valley of Oaxaca and Mixteca Alta sites would have required more labor than a single household could afford in a year without sacrificing other necessary activities.

To construct the largest of the four terraces excavated at El Palmillo would have required sixty person-days. Many of the El Palmillo terraces are quite small; the average for the four excavated terraces is about thirty-six person-days. The 1,453 terraces at El Palmillo (not all built at once) represent 52,000 person-days. We are not accounting for quarrying, obtaining and moving fill over distances, building the houses (with foundations of large stones, and plaster floors), and the various remodelings.

The volume of material moved for the mounds and plazas at the focal point of the hilltown was, in most cases, much less than that moved to make the residential terraces. In the Mixteca Alta sample (table 9.1), at five sites, including all the earliest ones, the public architecture labor cost was only 1 to 15 percent of the residential terrace labor. One site, SAL-16, which may be a little later in time, has two large plazas, so its public architecture labor cost was somewhat larger. YPD-1 is a totally different hilltop terraced site, an Early Classic civic-ceremonial center with public buildings six times as costly as the few surrounding residential terraces.

With the population estimates in table 9.1 we can address one final, simple question. These estimates are for the total population of the site, including terraced and nonterraced areas, if any, and are based on five to ten people per house where house counts could be made, or ranges of people per hectare under varying house-density conditions. The question is simply, "How long would it take a community to build its terraced hilltown, including the public and residential areas?" With all the above assumption in place, assuming half the population works on the project, and initially counting only the earth-moving, the answer is, one dry season, that is, the time between harvest in the fall and planting in June. Four of the seven sites could have been constructed in twenty-four to forty-nine days. If we add another 10 percent for quarrying, eighty person-days to build each house, and several hundred days for some good public buildings, the whole project is feasible within a single dry season.

CONCLUSIONS

From these very approximate labor cost estimates and the varying form of hill-towns and other hilltop terraced sites, we draw the following six conclusions that bear on the transformation of society in Oaxaca from 500 B.C. to A.D. 500.

1. Building hilltop terrace sites required suprahousehold, probably community-level, coordination, and work gangs instead of individuals or families working independently. Many residential terraces were multihousehold units. Many terraces had long, common retaining walls and must have been built as single units. The concentric rings of long terraces, with ramps, gates, and roads, found at many early hilltowns and into the Classic period, as at El Palmillo, required broad planning as well as collective effort. Such large-scale efforts required coordination in conception, layout, procurement of fill, and interrelationships of so many deep-fill platforms adjacent to or on top of one another. Some areas of later hilltop terraced sites have whole slopes given over to

strings of small terraces, and these may be "subdivisions" expanded with household-scale labor.

2. Early hilltowns, especially in the Mixteca Alta where so many are known and preserved, had organization more communal than hierarchical. The reasons for concluding that these towns and villages were more communal than apical or hierarchical are (1) the focal, public architecture took up a very small proportion of the total amount of labor expended on early hilltown construction, and (2) so far, no portable artifact or architectural patterns strongly distinguish potential elite and commoner residential areas; that is, the early hilltowns may be relatively homogeneous socially. (This requires more intensive surface collecting and excavation, but even with the current data, the early hilltowns look much more homogeneous than some of the later ones in which artifactual and architectural indicators are fairly apparent.) Perhaps aspects of these community institutions continued on in Classic times, for there are many hilltop terraced sites from the Classic and Epiclassic periods that had collective construction and relatively little public architecture.

3. The early hilltowns could have been (and in our opinion were) constructed quickly. Our labor calculations show that the members of a community could have constructed a hilltown, including all the terraces, walls, houses, and public facilities, in a single dry season, between harvest and planting. We think that something like that happened in the Mixteca Alta around 300 B.C., when almost all open settlements were abandoned and local populations consolidated in densely packed, fortified residential sites on hilltops. LeBlanc (1999, 64–66, 220) points out that certain Southwestern pueblo construction styles lend themselves to defense, and fast construction using work gangs.

4. On the basis of their communal rather than hierarchical organization, the consolidation due to military pressure, the collective labor efforts, and the relatively flat and undifferentiated array of central places across the Mixteca Alta just after 300 B.C., we can entertain Korotayev's (1995) idea of "mountain democracies" as a model for community organization in parts of central Oaxaca affected by but not incorporated into the urbanizing hierarchies of core states. Korotayev observes that mountain societies at the peripheries of the great Eurasian civilizations centralize less rapidly, but have a "higher level of community autonomy (and often . . . correspondingly higher levels of complexity in the communal structures themselves)"

(1995, 62). Internally these communities may develop "democratic" as opposed to oligarchic government, as in the polis of the Greek world, especially in the mountains and around the periphery of the Classical world. Such communities are often parts of loose confederacies.

5. After a rough time of competition, abandonment, and consolidation, first in the core states and by the Early Classic period everywhere in central Oaxaca, population and settlement expanded again under a regime of urban hierarchical differentiation. As part of that growth, many new (and old) hilltop terrace sites were occupied, but with varying mixes of military, craft specialty, civic-ceremonial, and labor functions. We hypothesize that communal institutions developed earlier may have lived on in the internal organization of hilltop towns of the Classic period. Conceivably, self-governing communal organization was another product of the great urban transformation. We hypothesize that internally self-ruling hilltop towns may have supplied labor for wealthy valley-floor towns or estates. This may have entailed seasonal or longer-duration migration across the region (Mixtec migration, famous in our time, has a prehistory), and if we are approximately correct, it would have meant a movement of individuals back and forth between self-ruling commune at home and subordination to apical authority at work.

6. The urban transformation in Oaxaca involved at its core profound changes in the way people worked. In the Valley of Oaxaca, for example, specialized production for tribute and market exchange meant intensified agriculture, sometimes with canal irrigation. Households responded to new scheduling demands by altering food procurement, storage, and preparation. More effort and costlier materials went into house construction. At every level from the household to the capital of the state there is evidence for ideological and ritual innovation symbolically expressing (or perhaps resisting) the new order. In the Mixteca Alta, the abandonment of lower-elevation settlements and the establishment of hilltowns led to agricultural intensification in the form of *lama-bordo* terrace systems near the new towns.

Reorientation of labor contributed significantly to the total urban transformation, through demographic increase, settlement pattern and community form, the labor process, organization of work, social relations of production, household time scheduling, and associated ritual and iconography. In short, people had to work more intensively and in many cases, more collectively, and in turn the reorientation of labor had profound consequences on many other aspects of culture.

REFERENCES

Abrams, Elliot M. 1994. *How the Maya Built Their World: Energetics and Ancient Architecture.* Austin: University of Texas Press.

Balkansky, Andrew K. 1997. Archaeological Settlement Patterns of the Sola Valley, Oaxaca, Mexico. PhD diss., Department of Anthropology, University of Wisconsin.

Balkansky, Andrew K., Stephen A. Kowalewski, Verónica Pérez Rodríguez, Thomas J. Pluckhahn, Charlotte A. Smith, Laura R. Stiver, Dimitri Beliaev, John F. Chamblee, Verenice Y. Heredia, and Roberto Santos Pérez. 2000. "Archaeological Survey in the Mixteca Alta of Oaxaca, Mexico." *Journal of Field Archaeology* 27(4):365–90.

Blanton, Richard E., Gary M. Feinman, Stephen A. Kowalewski, and Linda Nicholas. 1999. *Ancient Oaxaca: The Monte Albán State.* Cambridge: Cambridge University Press.

Caso, Alfonso. 1947. "Calendario y Escritura de las Antiguas Culturas de Monte Albán." In *Obras Completas de Miguel Othón de Mendizábal,* vol. 1, 113–44. Mexico City: Talleres Gráficos de la Nación.

Feinman, Gary M., and Linda M. Nicholas. 1990. "At the Margins of the Monte Alban State: Settlement Patterns in the Ejutla Valley, Oaxaca, Mexico." *Latin American Antiquity* 1(3):216–46.

———. 1996. "Defining the Eastern Limits of the Monte Albán State: Systematic Settlement Pattern Survey in the Guirún Area." *Mexicon* 18:91–97.

———. 1999. "Reflections of Regional Survey: Perspectives from the Guirún Area, Oaxaca, Mexico." In *Settlement Pattern Studies in the Americas: Fifty Years since Virú,* ed. Brian R. Billman and Gary M. Feinman, 172–90. Washington, DC: Smithsonian Institution Press.

———. 2001. "Excavations at El Palmillo: A Hilltop Terrace Site in Oaxaca, Mexico." *In the Field* 72(2):2–5.

Finsten, Laura. 1995. *Jalieza, Oaxaca: Activity Specialization at a Hilltop Center.* Vanderbilt University Publications in Anthropology, 48. Nashville, TN: Vanderbilt University Press.

———. 1996. "Periphery and Frontier in Southern Mexico: The Mixtec Sierra in Highland Oaxaca." In *Precolumbian World Systems,* ed. Peter N. Peregrine and

Gary M. Feinman, 77–96. Monographs in World Archaeology, 26. Madison, WI: Prehistory Press.

Hard, Robert J., José A. Zapata, Bruce K. Moses, and John R. Roney. 1999. "Terrace Construction in Northern Chihuahua, Mexico: 1150 B.C. and Modern Experiments." *Journal of Field Archaeology* 26(2):129–46.

Kirkby, Michael J. 1972. *The Physical Environment of the Nochixtlán Valley, Oaxaca.* Vanderbilt University Publications in Anthropology, 2. Nashville, TN: Vanderbilt University Press.

Korotayev, Andrey V. 1995. "Mountains and Democracy: An Introduction." In *Alternative Pathways to Early State,* ed. Nikolay N. Kradin and Valeri A. Lynsha, 60–74. Vladivostok: Institute of History, Archaeology, and Ethnology, Russian Academy of Sciences Far Eastern Division, and DalŌnauka.

Kowalewski, Stephen A., Gary M. Feinman, Laura Finsten, Richard E. Blanton, and Linda M. Nicholas. 1989. *Monte Albán's Hinterland, Part II: Prehispanic Settlement Patterns in Tlacolula, Etla, and Ocotlán, the Valley of Oaxaca, Mexico,* 2 vols. Memoirs, 23. Ann Arbor: Museum of Anthropology, University of Michigan.

Kuttruff, Carl, and William O. Autry Jr. 1978. "Test Excavations at Terrace 1227." In *Monte Albán: Settlement Patterns at the Ancient Zapotec Capital,* ed. Richard E. Blanton, 403–15. New York: Academic Press.

LeBlanc, Steven A. 1999. *Prehistoric Warfare in the American Southwest.* Salt Lake City: University of Utah Press.

Marcus, Joyce, and Kent V. Flannery. 1996. *Zapotec Civilization: How Urban Society Evolved in Mexico's Oaxaca Valley.* London: Thames and Hudson.

Plunket, Patricia S. 1983. An Intensive Survey in the Yucuita Sector of the Nochixtlán Valley, Oaxaca, Mexico. PhD diss., Department of Anthropology, Tulane University.

Robles García, Nelly M. 1994. *Las Canteras de Mitla, Oaxaca: Tecnología para la Arquitectura Monumental.* Vanderbilt University Publications in Anthropology, 47. Nashville, TN: Vanderbilt University Press.

Spencer, Charles S., and Elsa M. Redmond. 1997. *Archaeology of the Cañada de Cuicatlán, Oaxaca.* Anthropological Papers, 80. New York: American Museum of Natural History.

Spores, Ronald. 1969. "Settlement, Farming Technology, and Environment in the Nochixtlán Valley." *Science* 166:557–69.

————. 1972. *An Archaeological Settlement Survey of the Nochixtlán Valley, Oaxaca.* Vanderbilt University Publications in Anthropology, 1. Nashville, TN: Vanderbilt University Press.

Wills, W. H. 2000. "Political Leadership and the Construction of Chacoan Great Houses, A.D. 1020–1140." In *Alternative Leadership Strategies in the Prehispanic Southwest,* ed. Barbara J. Mills, 19–44. Tucson: University of Arizona Press.

Windes, Thomas C., and Peter J. McKenna. 2001. "Going against the Grain: Wood Production in Chacoan Society." *American Antiquity* 66(1):119–40.

Winter, Marcus C. 1974. "Residential Patterns at Monte Albán, Oaxaca." *Science* 186:981–87.

10

A Political Economy from Increasing Marginal Returns to Labor: An Example from Viking Age Iceland

John M. Steinberg

In this chapter, I argue that inequality in Viking Age Iceland can be best understood as a result of control over labor in an environment of increasing marginal returns. Viking Age Iceland was created by a rapid colonization of a chiefdom-level society in an uninhabited land. In Viking Age Iceland, labor was the key resource that needed to be controlled for an elite class to exist. A political economy based on scarce but highly productive labor can create stable societies that seem to defy classical and neoclassical economic doctrines and have some unusual features that can be attributed to specific institutions of property that develop in such an environment.

DIMINISHING RETURNS

The law of diminishing marginal returns states that when other factors are constant, the output from extra units of any factor of production will eventually fall. David Ricardo (1817) imagined that an empty environment with land resources of variable quality would be settled in a predictable manner and that the settlement would produce a socially differentiated society. He thought that the best or most productive resources or land would be claimed first—land that new settlers later claimed would be inferior, or as he called it, marginal. He imagined that the same amount of labor would be required to produce anything on any land, regardless of the land's quality, but that the same labor on the best land would produce more, a quantity he called rent, which would be unequally distributed, just as the best land was unequally distributed. The unequal distribution of rent (or land) made the people who owned the best land—probably inheriting it from their ancestors—richer than those on inferior lands, creating social inequality. Like Thomas Malthus (1985/1789), Ricardo imagined that as population expanded, not only would some have more than others but that eventually some would be forced to use land that was barely productive enough to support them. Since Ricardo held that this marginally productive land constituted the majority of the land and, like Malthus, supposed that people inherently multiplied, he thought that eventually most people would be living at the edge of subsistence.

Because the best land is taken first, and because it is inherently more productive than secondary or marginal land, the rent that the best land generates goes straight into the pockets of the owners. Ricardo proposed the fundamental relationship between labor and property in the creation of social differentiation: better land made labor more efficient and created social stratification. The theories now used to understand the development of social inequality as evidenced in the archaeological record usually identify the important but scarce resources with diminishing marginal returns that incipient elites are able to control (e.g., Hayden 1995; Sahlins and Service 1960) and on the whole, it is land (Finley 1973).

Ricardo's scenario is tenable in an environment in which property rights are enforced, a scenario characteristic of a state society. Morton Fried (1967), putting Ricardo's ideas into an evolutionary framework, realized that unequal distributions of property rights—an organization he called stratified—without state enforcement was inherently unstable because of the problem of defending property rights. Fried argued that stratified societies must create institutions of state enforcement to protect claims to differential access to resources. Without such institutions, society would collapse because vital rights of the elite could not be defended.

Another reason archaeological theory has unquestionably adopted diminishing marginal returns as a base of prehistoric economics is that primary civilizations seem to develop in environments where good land is becoming scarcer. Scarce resources, particularly land, provide opportunities for both managerial and predatory elite (see contributions to Earle 1991; Ehrenreich, Crumley, and Levy 1995; Hunt and Gilman 1998; McIntosh 1999; Price and Feinman 1995; Renfrew and Shennan 1982; Winterhalder and Smith 1981). A predatory elite can prosper when land is scarce and labor abundant (i.e., where there is population pressure), because returns to labor for the majority of the population move to a level close to subsistence; and the majority is easily exploited by a property-owing elite class (Engels 1986/1884). The spread of complex societies need not be based on the same economic foundations as their origins. According to Ricardo and most of classical and neoclassical economics, the existence of abundant productive land should be a temporary situation. Abundant land can be created by a variety of events beyond discovery or population reduction, such as technological or environmental change. General trends in the evolution of human societies associate newly abundant land with a reduction in social complexity (Johnson and Earle 2001). On the other hand, expansion of complex societies into areas of uninhabited or underutilized land should be a common event in the archaeological record and an economics of scarce labor and abundant land may well help us understand complex societies in these unusual environments.

INCREASING RETURNS

Ricardo held that as new resources were opened up, the most productive would be captured first. Simply being first, regardless of which land is chosen, is important and is a central idea in economic theories of path dependence and other founder effects (Arthur 1989, 1990; Goodstein 1995; Mueller 1997; Pierson 2000). That is, once an economic organization is in place and standards are established, it becomes difficult to change the system, even though the change would increase productivity in the long run. Ricardo's emphasis was not on being first, but on claiming the best land. He has been criticized for his emphasis on the scarcity of land, especially since he witnessed much of the New World being opened up (Galbraith 1998; Pollard 1995, 1997).

Few economists have dared to propose an alternative simplification of the relationship of land and labor for fear of ending up in the dustbin of the history of economic thought. One of those who did propose such a theory was Henry C. Carey (1848) who took great notice of how America was being settled. In most situations, he observed increasing, not decreasing, marginal returns to land. That is, land that could be put into production quickly and with minimal labor investment was settled first. Marginal land was that which required substantial labor to put into production, but once in production was, in the long run, quite possibly more productive than land claimed first. This scenario is almost the opposite of a Boserupian sequence that outlines the events close to carrying capacity (Boserup 1965; see also Hunt 2000; Lee 1986; Wood 1998).

If increasing marginal returns to land and labor is a better description of colonizations, especially those observed in the archaeological record, then we must adjust our economic assumptions accordingly (Winfrey and Darity 1997). The concept of increasing marginal returns is different from economies of scale, but it has the same outcome—greater returns to additional inputs, or even to a single input. Increasing marginal returns assumes fundamental resource abundance—a world usually inhabited only by Robinson Crusoe in economic textbooks (e.g., Samuelson and Nordhaus 1992). Crusoe must decide which activities warrant his labor because that is what is scarce, not his resources.

The basic difference between diminishing and increasing marginal returns is to be found in assumptions about the relative amount of labor necessary to put land into production. Under the scenario of diminishing marginal returns, Ricardo assumes that the same amount of labor could be applied to both the best land and to marginal land and that both would produce something. Carey supposes that some land would not produce anything until a substantial amount of labor had been input. He argues that the land that would ultimately yield the most would need substantial labor input before it would produce anything. For example, before farming could take place, trees would have to be cut down, swamps drained, and fields flattened. The start-up costs for agriculture would be substantial. In many cases, the greater the start-up costs, the more productive the land would be in the long run. For example, the more dense the tree growth, the more productive the land, once the trees were cut. From this point of view, his general rule of increasing marginal returns makes some sense. Under specific conditions, the more labor needed to put land into production, the more productive that land would be. That is, the more labor input, the greater the long-run productivity or, as he called it, increasing marginal returns.

Carey was a protectionist, an abolitionist, and early founder of the Republican Party. At the same time, Marx praised him as the "only original economist among the North Americans" (Marx 1993). These seemingly inconsistent characterizations are the outcome of his theory of increasing marginal returns and high start-up costs that essentially inverted Ricardo's ideas (Conkin 1980;

Dawson 2000; Marx 1967/1867, 706). He felt that fledgling industry had to be protected, not only for its own sake but also to keep workers' salaries high. Therefore, for Carey, the interests of workers and capitalists were not necessarily at odds, in contrast to the ideas of Malthus and Ricardo. That is, the inherent differences in the quality of land did not produce social stratification, control over labor did.

Carey worried that in situations of increasing marginal returns, profit was not only to be made by owing good land and using it efficiently but also by reducing the cost of labor to an absolute minimum. That is, an economic system characterized by increasing marginal returns could degenerate into a relatively short-term economic program in which the reduction of labor costs was paramount in order to make a profit. The extreme form of the reduction of labor costs is slavery—the un-economic control over labor. For Carey, classes were not an inherent part of complex society with a healthy division of labor but the misguided result of apparent free trade. He believed that the forceful control over labor was really responsible for social stratification. He argued that protectionism was necessary to end slavery.

Following on the heels of Carey, Herman Nieboer (1900) proposed an understanding of the conditions under which slavery could exist that was systemized by Evsey Domar (1970). In the strong version, they propose that free land, free peasants, and nonworking landowners cannot exist simultaneously. If good land is abundant, then a nonworking landowner elite can only exist if there is a state organization in place to keep peasants unfree. Therefore, slavery and slave societies are most common in conditions of state expansion into land-abundant environments—the classic examples being the southern United States and the Roman Empire (see contributions to Engerman, Drescher, and Paquette 2001). In land-abundant environments, social stratification is a result of the control over labor, with slavery being an extreme form.

Both Carey and Ricardo see production at the margins as a key factor in understanding the overall political economy. Marginal productivity is the link between economic activity and social stratification. Both models of marginal production employ the concept of margin to the fullest, seeing it as both the addition of extra labor and the addition of extra land to increase production. From there, the two models diverge. Ricardo sees the combination of marginal land and marginal labor as fundamentally less productive but with similar setup costs. That is, extra people and extra land are and will be inherently poor, making social classes inevitable. Carey sees the combination of marginal land and labor as greatly productive but with almost prohibitively high setup costs. That is, extra land and extra people could be greatly productive, if not for the inability to take advantage of it. In Carey's optimistic view, as opposed to Marx' gloomy Ricardian view, workers and capitalists made a natural match, since industrial wages would be inherently high.

IMPLICATIONS OF INCREASING MARGINAL RETURNS

There are some very good reasons for exploring the implications of increasing marginal returns to labor because it seems to be an excellent description of broad economic activities (David and Wright 1997; Romer 1996). Human economic history, since the beginning of the Neolithic, has been characterized by increasing returns to labor because of advances in technology and organization. While it is true that at a given technology and organization, diminishing returns are inevitable, Adam Smith's (1976/1776) fundamental idea was that the division of labor essentially creates increasing marginal returns. Classical and neoclassical economics have always been torn between the gloomy predictions based on the fundamental scarcity of land (diminishing marginal returns) and the optimistic predictions for the unlimited possibilities of manufacturing (increasing marginal returns) due to better technology and better labor organization (Buchanan and Yoon 1999; Foley 2000).

Archaeologists usually understand labor—like land—under conditions of diminishing marginal returns (e.g., Arnold 1993; Bogucki 1993; Friedman and Rowlands 1977; Milisauskas 1977, 1978; Stone, Netting, and Stone 1990; Webster 1990). Flannery (1972) and others have recognized that the goal of elites is to get more people to work harder, but this is usually attributed to the power of ritual and ideology (DeMarrais, Castillo, and Earle 1996; Mann 1986), in keeping with classical economic paradigms.

Another key reason that Ricardo's model holds broad appeal to prehistorians is that it inherently explains social stratification as a result of the substantial advantages of being first. The best strategy, according to Carey, would be to move into an environment where substantial labor had already been input, and then to take advantage of the substantial increases in productivity. While Carey's optimism is commendable (Marx [1993] called it naïve), it is unlikely that people who owned improved resources would share them voluntarily.

Carey imagined that within sight of highly productive land, early colonizers would be barely eking out a living on inferior land because they did not have access to the labor necessary to put that good land into production. Carey assumed that the first land settled would be rather unproductive at any level of labor input. While low productivity is critical for Ricardo's model, there is nothing in Carey's model that requires it. All that is necessary for Carey's model to be consistent is that land first claimed be subject to lower increasing marginal returns and that it would reach the point of diminishing marginal returns sooner than land claimed later. If land that is claimed first were quite productive at low labor inputs—but rather unproductive at high inputs—there would be tremendous advantages to claiming land first.

This small twist—land chosen first is productive at low labor inputs, but land still available, while unproductive at low labor inputs, is much more productive when production is intensified—makes the Careyan model much more applicable to archaeological societies. According to this alternate formation of Carey's model, the first settlers into a landscape would take land that was quite productive at low labor inputs, most likely under extensive exploitation strategies. Later settlers would take land that would need higher labor input and actual investment into the land and environment. In the long run, this investment into the land would produce much greater returns to additional labor than the first land settled. The conditions under which this augmented Careyan model can take place are relatively specific. First and most obvious, productive resources would have to be highly variable. The most productive resources would only be available with substantial initial investment. Second, technology and labor organization would have to play a critical role in subsistence in a nonmobile adaptation. Third, there would have to be a technological or organizational change where previously underutilized resources became central to the economic system.

There are three consequences of this model for the development of social stratification. First, secondary settlers would be in dire need of labor and other resources that the earlier settlers might possibly possess. The loan of resources from earlier settlers to secondary settlers would create a debt that later settlers would have to repay. Second, because of the increased investment of the secondary settlers into the landscape, the secondary settlers would be locked into the land and the high returns it produced. Any time there are advantages to being first, especially combined with mechanisms for lock-in (Gilman 1991) and the creation of debt (Parker-Peterson 1982), the refusal costs can easily become greater than the compliance costs, and complex societies can develop (Haas 1982). In the scenario described above, this can happen even in the presence of abundant land (Hayden 2000; Junker 1999) because later settlers would be both in debt to and easily exploitable by earlier settlers. Finally, property rights could be stable, from the beginning, even without state institutions to enforce them (Hirshleifer 1995). There is incentive to respect property rights simply because land that, in the long run, might be better is still unclaimed. Although the unclaimed land may require more labor to put into production, the effort might be about the same as that required to take an existing claim.

Following this logic, the social differentiation in land-abundant situations would be different from the situations close to carrying capacity. There is much description of the difficulty encountered by initial colonizers dependent on intensive technology (Andrews 1934; Ellickson 1993; Scott 1977) as they pave the way for later colonizers. However, the level of exploitation is limited because land is not a scarce resource that can be controlled. This might lead to a situation where the elite who arrive early compete with each other, each wooing later entrants to be part of their entourages. In this situation, stratified groups would not be land based, but settler based. The overall effect is that elites might start out the sequence as functional, increasing the overall production of the society, and become parasitic as the lock-in became more effective. This means that complex societies based on scarce labor should have two very distinct phases: a rush phase, where there is a race to claim resources first (Anderson and Hill 1990; Haddock 1986; Lueck 1995; Schiff 1995), and a developed phase, where the increasing returns to labor are exploited.

ICELAND DURING THE VIKING AGE

Iceland was settled as part of a population expansion that was apparently driven by political and economic desires, rather than any necessity brought about by population pressure. Once in Iceland, the chiefdoms established by the immigrants were not territorially defined. Furthermore, the location that the earliest and most powerful original settlers chose does not seem to be associated with long-term success. These observations are all consistent with a chiefdom where social stratification is achieved by differential control over labor.

Both the nature and causes of Scandinavian expansion has been a topic of substantial debate (e.g., Barrett et al. 2000; Griffith 1995; Haywood 1995; Ólafsson 2000; Sawyer 1971). Although large areas of Northern Europe were at one time or another under Viking control, Iceland and the Faeroe islands were the only permanent and successful extensions of the Viking world. In other areas, settlements either died out or were assimilated into local cultures. While the long-term success of Viking expansion was limited, they were relatively successful during the power vacuum of early medieval Europe (Roesdahl 1998).

The western Viking expansion, which started about A.D. 793, covered various parts of France and England as well as Iceland and Greenland. Prior to the Viking expansion, the Scandinavian states themselves started to develop. Denmark, with its relatively homogeneous and rich soils, was the first to consolidate in about 750. Much of the impetus for state formation was a Danish fear of Frankish expansionism (Griffith 1995). Almost 150 years later, state formation in Norway was complete, as Harald Finehair, during a lull in Danish influence, began to control the sea passage between the coastal islands and the Norwegian mainland. In the sagas, Icelanders attribute their immigration to their wish to avoid living under a state controlled by Harald Finehair (Durrenberger 1992). Almost three hundred years later, Sweden, the most environmentally variable, with small patches of good agricultural land and large tracts of sparsely populated forest, began to consolidate. Finally, one hundred years later, in 1264, pastoral Iceland was incorporated into the Norwegian state.

Slavery played an important role in the economic development of all four states. Not only were slave raiding and slave trading important but slaves themselves (thralls) also seem to have been an important part of Viking Age farm productivity (Karras 1988). The voluntary abandonment of slavery (and its usual replacement with serfdom) is generally associated with an increasing abundance of labor and a relative scarcity of land (Bloch 1975). Scandinavia only partially follows this pattern and the same forces that produced states over 515 years of consolidation do not seem to correlate with the 175 years over which slavery was abandoned (table 10.1). In fact, slavery ends first in Iceland (before state formation) and last in Sweden (well after state forma-

Table 10.1. Dates of State Formation and Manumission in Scandinavia

Country	State Formation (A.D.)	End of Slavery (A.D.)
Denmark	750	1250
Norway	890	1200
Sweden	1172	1325
Iceland	1265	1150

tion), indicating that the processes involving population densities that produce states are very different from those of manumission.

Iceland was settled as part of the westward Viking expansion, mostly from Norway. This island society produced a remarkable literature that relates not only Icelandic events and myths but also much of Viking Age history (e.g., Sturluson 1964). Some of the stories are actually histories, written down immediately after the events (e.g., McGrew 1970; McGrew and Thomas 1974), while the more famous family sagas (e.g., Smiley and Kellogg 2000) and the laws (Dennis, Foote, and Perkins 1980) were written down several hundred years after the supposed events. The documents (Pálsson and Edwards 1972) and the archaeology (Vésteinsson 2000) concur in showing that Iceland was settled starting about A.D. 874. By the end of the *landnám* (land-taking or settlement period, A.D. 930), Iceland is said to have been fully claimed and its population numbered between 40,000 and 100,000 (Sveinbjarnardóttir 1992, 16). The rush phase of settlement lasted just over fifty years but most of the habitable areas were occupied within a few years (Vésteinsson 1998, 2000).

During the following Commonwealth (A.D. 930–1264), the island was divided into quarters and each quarter had about nine chieftains, for a total of thirty-six. This developed phase lasted over three hundred years. After A.D. 1180, individuals having more than one chiefdomship, as well as extraordinarily wealthy farmers, became more common. In the early thirteenth century, most of the Icelandic chieftaincies fell into the hands of just seven families. By mid-thirteenth century, these families were engaged in a bloody struggle for power. In 1264 the last claimant to chiefly title killed his only remaining rival and became a subordinate to the king of Norway.

In Viking Age Iceland, the household was the basic unit of production (Smith 1995). In some areas of Iceland, before 1300, grain was grown but sheep and cattle were the main source of subsistence and wealth (Amorosi et al. 1997; McGovern et al. 1988; McGovern 1990). One of the lures of expansion into the islands of the North Atlantic was the extensive grazing land. Nonetheless, collecting enough fodder to bring livestock though the winter would have been a major labor bottleneck (Durrenberger 1990). Winter fodder was predominantly grass cut with iron scythes. Increasing grass yield with manure or flooding, along with properly scheduled labor, would be critical for intensifying farm production. In particular, access to labor during the harvest would have been essential to increase herd size and thereby to generate wealth.

Archaeologically, a household is a farmstead, and in medieval Iceland, it usually consists of one large central building and several smaller outbuildings spread out over a hectare or so of infield used to grow grass fodder (Eggertsson 1992; Friðriksson 1973). The pastoral economy that required winter fodder prescribed a dispersed settlement pattern (Gibson 1988). During the Commonwealth, large long-halls, housing between twenty and ninety people (Wallace 1990), punctuated the landscape (Vésteinsson 1998). As Iceland was being incorporated into the Norwegian state, architecturally related central-passage manor houses began to develop (Sigurðardóttir 1998). While the timing of the appearance of smaller farms is unclear (Sveinbjarnardóttir 1992), it appears that the overall settlement pattern was in flux during the Commonwealth.

The Commonwealth chieftaincies are essentially Germanic chieftains (Engels 1986/1884; Gilman 1995; Tacitus 1999). The Icelandic chiefdoms were neither circumscribed by landmarks nor delineated by specific houses, farms, or fields. Chieftaincies were heritable and alienable property that were assigned to a given quarter, not to a particular region. Within a quarter, chieftains had to vie with each other for entourages of followers by giving gifts and feasts as well as support in disputes. Conversely, farmers had to pledge allegiance to a chieftain from within their quarter, although the farmers could switch their allegiance yearly. The location of a farm did not dictate the patron to whom a farmer would give allegiance.

The lack of territoriality means that elite finance did not come from owning the land, the most common source of chiefly wealth (Earle 1997). Durrenberger (1998) argued that chiefs gained followings and thus power by enforcing property rights of other settlers while Gelsinger (1981) emphasized control over foreign trade as a source of chiefly finance. These and other proposed sources of chiefly wealth revolve around control over labor: armed labor to resolve disputes and to enforce property rights, and productive labor to generate wool for export.

Petty chiefs emigrating from Norway did, in fact, claim proportionally larger areas than did other settlers. However, these early large land claims do not seem to be directly connected to the long-term locations of chiefly activity. The *Landnámabók*, written in the early twelfth century, describes the land claims of approximately 450 individuals and their retinues who settled Iceland between A.D. 874 and 930 (Pálsson and Edwards 1972). The first settlers apparently removed large tracks of coastal scrub birch to grow grass for animals

(Buckland et al. 1990; Hallsdóttir 1987). The trees may have been used for fodder as well or possibly for fuel for iron production (Friðriksson 1973). In Skagafjörður, a fertile northern fjord valley where my research takes place, the *Landnámabók* outlines thirty-one original land claims. The description specifically designates three of the settlers as leading men from Norway and that their status carried over to Iceland where they were chieftains. In general, these three chieftains took larger areas than other recorded claimants (table 10.2) and have spaced themselves so as to be as far apart as possible (figure 10.1). The *Landnámabók* also mentions that the west side of the valley was settled before the east side of the valley. The slopes on the west side are more gradual and there are a number of north-running tributaries, as opposed to the steeper east side where the tributaries primarily run westward. On the whole, land claims on the west side are also larger than those in other parts—except for the lower-productivity uplands in the south of the valley, which are the largest.

Although the chieftains did take large land claims, their size is either much smaller than would be expected in a hierarchical society or, from another perspective, the size of nonchiefly land claims are greater than expected. Figure 10.2 is a Lorenz curve of the distribution of the size of land claims as a percentage of the claimants. The shaded areas measure the relative inequality. In this depiction, the largest 10 percent of claims (which do not include any chiefs) control about 24 percent of the land, the top 25 percent (which does include the chieftains) control almost 50 percent of the land. Conversely, the bottom 50 percent of the land claims control 27 percent of the land. These proportions are only slightly skewed and are indicative of an evenly distributed land area.

Table 10.2. Original Claim Size by Location and Status as Described in *Landnámabók* (Pálsson and Edwards 1972).

Area	Claims	Mean Size (Sq Km)
By Region		
Coast	11	1.0
West	6	1.2
East	5	0.7
Side Valleys	5	0.5
Upland	4	2.1
By Status		
Common	28	1.0
Chiefly	3	1.8
All	31	1.6

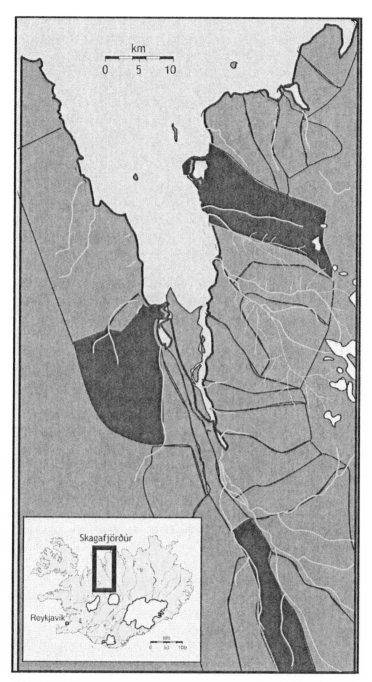

FIGURE 10.1

Skagafjörður with original land claims described in *Landnámabók* outlined in black (Pálsson and Edwards 1972). Shaded claims indicated chiefly ownership. Not all land claims in Skagafjörður (Table 10.2) are shown on this map.

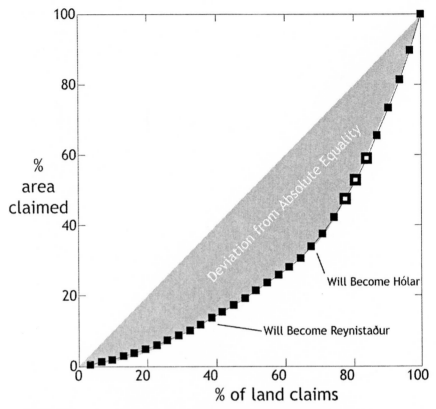

FIGURE 10.2
Inequality of the area of original land claims described in *Landnámabók* (Pálsson and Edwards 1972). The three chiefly land claims have white box centers.

By 1300, inequality of land control in Skagafjörður has become much greater. There are over four hundred farms in the region, and by 1400, the bishopric at Hólar controls about one hundred of them. Hólar is most powerful in 1550 when it controls over three hundred farms. Census data is most complete from 1710 when Hólar controls 180 farms. At that time, 34 farms (7 percent) control 300 other farms (63 percent). Of the 35 farms that own more than one other farm, the top two—Hólar and Reynistaður—control 213 farms (45 percent). A comparison of the inequality of the top thirty-four farms (figure 10.3) puts the relative equality of the settlement (figure 10.2) into perspective. The hierarchy, described in the documents at the beginning of the Commonwealth, does not seem to be related to differential control over

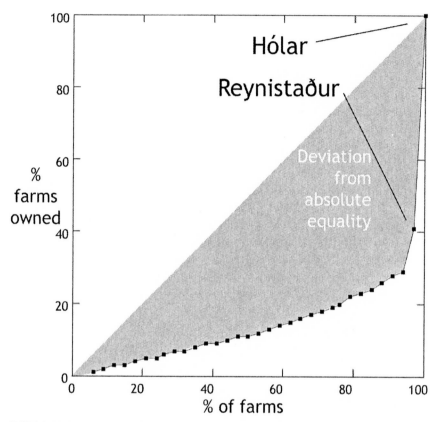

FIGURE 10.3
Inequality of the ownership of farms in 1714 based on the Jardabók (Magnússon and Vídalín 1927).

land. After 1300, when the state-level medieval manorial system had super-seded the chiefdom organization, inequality of land control is apparent.

The locations of chiefly settlements in Skagafjörður were not the same as in the later medieval manorial centers. There does not seem to be a strong rela-tionship between claiming large areas and chiefly power. Furthermore, neither Reynistaður nor Hólar is located on an original chiefly settlement. On the east side, the area that would become the bishopric at Hólar was first claimed by Kolbein, who then gave that valley to Hjalti, whose descendants then gave part of their claim for the bishopric. Hólar, one of the most powerful farms in Ice-land, would have been one of the last areas in Skagafjörður to be occupied. It would seem that any advantages to being first to claim land, or any advantages of ownership of slightly larger settlements do not translate into long-run power.[1]

Orri Vésteinsson (1998) has proposed a comparable model for the settlement of Iceland. After a very short period of trial and error, the first settlers chose wetland areas and those early settlements eventually formed into large estates. Slightly later settlers established smaller farms in between those estates. A second phase of settlement that lasted into the second millennium saw the land of lesser quality divided into small units and occupied by final immigrants and later generations of Icelanders. In this model, the best land is both easy to put into production and highly productive under more intensive agricultural regimes. Furthermore, these productive locations chosen by the first settlers are also ideally situated to take advantage of nonagricultural resources (e.g., upland pasture, fish, building material, bird eggs). While the model emphasizes the role of labor (by calling attention to early sites with multiple contemporary houses), it places a primacy on the ownership of good land in the creation of social stratification. Similar to the augmented Careyan model presented above, Vésteinsson's model suggests that substantial inequality between households should appear very early in the settlement sequence. The difference is that the Careyan model predicts a reorganization of the political economy, while Vésteinsson's model underscores the continuity of social differentiation. Both of these models are in contrast to the more common interpretation, hinted at in the sagas, of equal and independent farms dotted throughout the landscape during the whole of the Commonwealth period (e.g., Byock 2001).

To sum up, I argue that the social structure of Settlement and Commonwealth Iceland seems to be best explained by a Careyan sequence in which land that requires the least labor to be put into production is chosen first. The advantages to being first are not a result of owning more productive land but rather in controlling labor. Secondary settlers, in greater need of labor and resources to put their land into production, would have been dependent on early settlers and chieftains for labor. Once settled, these settlers would have been locked into their improved farms, making them easy prey for an exploitative elite. In the long run, the secondary settlers would have chosen more productive land. The medieval manorial state organization that arose several hundred years after the colonization was based on control over land (Júlíusson 1995) and, therefore, it is understandable that there should be little relationship between the medieval manorial organization and the chiefly

Commonwealth. For a few hundred years it would appear that differential control over labor maintained the Icelandic chiefly social organization.

CONCLUSION

Viking Age Iceland may not be unusual. For some years, Peter Bogucki (1988, 1993) has been working on a similar argument for north-central Europe. He argues that labor is the limiting factor of Neolithic production. More recently, he has augmented this position with an application of complex adaptive systems based on increasing returns to the spread of agriculture (2000). He outlines a theory in which Neolithic agriculture expanded rapidly across north-central Europe because increased knowledge of the environment and how to make it productive would have substantially reduced start-up costs (cf. Romer 1986). Bogucki argues that this knowledge explains the rapid and homogeneous settlement across the European plain. Household interdependence, he elegantly argues, produces the social differentiation of the north-central European Neolithic. The argument made here for Iceland is similar, relying on increased returns to explain a punctuated settlement.

I differ from Bogucki in arguing for substantial and even ever-increasing start-up costs—not for reduced start-up costs—as the cause of social stratification. Under specific conditions in which the most productive resources would only be available with substantial initial investment, there would be advantages to being first to claim the most productive land that required the least labor. Later entrants would face ever-greater start-up costs, and once invested, would be both in debt to earlier settlers and locked in to their now-productive resources, making them easy targets for exploitation.

A Careyan model is, oddly enough, much more in keeping with ideas of agency (e.g., Blanton et al. 1996; Johnson 1989) than is a Ricardian model. Following Ricardo, agency is usually concerned with controlling surplus labor (e.g., Saitta 1994) and its application to scarce resources, rather than with choices under conditions where labor is critically scarce. According to Ricardo, people on marginal land are marginal themselves and they follow the lead of those on the best land. This means that social stratification is as fixed as the variation in the land. Conversely, in the augmented Careyan model, secondary entrants control very productive resources. The result is a dynamic political economy where social change could be an inherent part of increasing marginal returns.

The augmented Careyan model presented above and applied to Viking Age Iceland is as simplistic as Ricardo's model (Pollard 1997). The correct application of either model depends on a whole series of factors, including the type of production, its start-up costs, the population densities, carrying capacity, and the rate of technological change. The type of returns to labor is an empirical question and it may well be that the type of marginal returns (increasing or decreasing) are very different foundations for alternate pathways to complex societies.

NOTES

1. Recent excavations by Fornleifastofnun Íslands at Aðalstræti in downtown Reykjavík suggest that the very first Icelander did choose the land that would become the center of the Icelandic capital. Despite its historic beginnings and present importance, Reykjavík was not an important place in the Middle Ages or early modern times.

REFERENCES

Aley, James. 1996. "The Theory That Made Microsoft (The Theory of 'Increasing Returns')." *Fortune* 1338:65–68.

Amorosi, Thomas, Paul C. Buckland, Andrew J. Dugmore, Jón Haukur Ingimundarson, and Thomas H. McGovern. 1997. "Raiding the Landscape: Human Impact in the Scandinavian North Atlantic." *Human Ecology* 25:491–518.

Anderson, Terry L., and Peter J. Hill. 1990. "The Race for Property Rights." *Journal of Law & Economics* 33:177–97.

Andrews, Charles McLean. 1934. *The Colonial Period of American History.* New Haven, CT: Yale University Press.

Arnold, Jeanne E. 1993. "Labor and the Rise of Complex Hunter-Gatherers." *Journal of Anthropological Archaeology* 12:75–119.

Arthur, W. Brian. 1989. "Competing Technologies, Increasing Returns and Lock-In by Historical Events." *Economic Journal* 99(394):116–31.

———. 1990. "Positive Feedback in the Economy." *Scientific American* 262(2):92–99.

Barrett, James H., Roelf P. Beukens, Ian A. Simpson, Patrick Ashmore, Sandra Poaps, and Jacqui Huntley. 2000. "What Was the Viking Age and When Did It Happen? A View from Orkney." *Norwegian Archaeological Review* 33:1–39.

Blanton, Richard E., Gary M. Feinman, Stephen A. Kowalewski, and Peter N. Peregrine. 1996. "Agency, Ideology, and Power in Archaeological Theory: A Dual-Processual Theory for the Evolution of Mesoamerican Civilization." *Current Anthropology* 37:1–14.

Bloch, Marc, ed. 1975. *Slavery and Serfdom in the Middle Ages: Selected Essays by Marc Bloch*, trans. by William R. Beer. Center for Medieval and Renaissance Studies, 8. Berkeley: University of California Press.

Bogucki, Peter. 1988. *Forest Farmers and Stockherders: Early Agriculture and its Consequences in North-Central Europe*. Cambridge: Cambridge University Press.

———. 1993. "Animal Traction and Household Economies in Neolithic Europe." *Antiquity* 67:492–503.

———. 2000. "How Agriculture Came to North Central Europe." In *Europe's First Farmers*, ed. T. Douglas Price, 197–218. Cambridge: Cambridge University Press.

Boserup, Ester. 1965. *The Conditions of Agricultural Growth*. Chicago: Aldine.

Buchanan, James, and Yong Yoon. 1999. "Generalized Increasing Returns, Euler's Theorem, and Competitive Equilibrium." *History of Political Economy* 31:511–23.

Buckland, Paul C., Andrew J. Dugmore, D. W. Perry, D. Savory, and Guðrún Sveinbjarnardóttir. 1990. "Holt in Eyjafjallasveit, Iceland: A Paleoecological Study of the Impact of Landnám." *Acta Archaeologica* 61:252–71.

Byock, Jesse L. 2001. *Viking Age Iceland*. London: Penguin Books.

Carey, Henry Charles. 1848. *The Past, the Present, and the Future*. Philadelphia: Carey & Hart.

Cipolla, Carlo M. 1994. *Before the Industrial Revolution: European Society and Economy, 1000–1700*. 3rd ed. New York: W. W. Norton.

Conkin, Paul. 1980. *Prophets of Prosperity: America's First Political Economists*. Bloomington: Indiana University Press.

Cowgill, George L. 1975. "On the Causes and Consequences of Ancient and Modern Population Changes." *American Anthropologist* 77:505–25.

Coy, Peter. 2002. "Commentary: Deregulation: Innovation vs. Stability." *Business Week* 128:56–58.

David, Paul A., and Gavin Wright. 1997. "Increasing Returns and the Genesis of American Resource Abundance." *Industrial and Corporate Change* 6:203–45.

Dawson, Andrew. 2000. "Reassessing Henry Carey (1793–1879): The Problems of Writing Political Economy in Nineteenth-Century America." *Journal of American Studies* 34:465–85.

DeMarrais, Elizabeth, Luis Jaime Castillo, and Timothy K. Earle. 1996. "Ideology, Materialization and Power Strategies." *Current Anthropology* 37:15–32.

Dennis, Andrew, Peter Foote, and Richard Perkins. 1980. *Laws of Early Iceland: Grágás, the Codex Regius of Grágás, with Material from Other Manuscripts.* University of Manitoba Icelandic Studies, 3. Winnipeg: University of Manitoba Press.

Domar, Evsey. 1970. "The Causes of Slavery or Serfdom: A Hypothesis." *Journal of Economic History* 30:18–32.

Duby, Georges. 1974. *The Early Growth of the European Economy: Warriors and Peasants from the Seventh to the Twelfth Century.* Ithaca, NY: Cornell University Press.

Durrenberger, E. Paul. 1990. "Production in Medieval Iceland." *Acta Archaeologica* 61:14–21.

———. 1992. *The Dynamics of Medieval Iceland.* Iowa City: University of Iowa Press.

———. 1998. "Property, State, and Self-Destruction in Medieval Iceland." In *Property in Economic Context,* ed. Robert C. Hunt and Antonio Gilman, 171–86. Monographs in Economic Anthropology, 14. Lanham, MD: University Press of America.

Earle, Timothy K., ed. 1991. *Chiefdoms: Power, Economy and Ideology.* Cambridge: Cambridge University Press.

Earle, Timothy K. 1997. *How Chiefs Come to Power: The Political Economy in Prehistory.* Stanford, CA: Stanford University Press

Eggertsson, Thráinn. 1990. *Economic Behavior and Institutions.* Cambridge: Cambridge University Press.

———. 1992. "Analyzing Institutional Successes and Failures: A Millennium of Common Mountain Pastures in Iceland." *International Review of Law and Economics* 12:423–37.

———. 1998. "Sources of Risk, Institutions for Survival and a Game against Nature in Premodern Iceland." *Explorations in Economic History* 35:1–30.

Ehrenreich, Robert, Carole L. Crumley, and Janet E. Levy, eds. 1995. *Heterarchy and the Analysis of Complex Societies.* Archaeological Papers of the American Anthropological Association, 6. Washington D.C.: American Anthropological Association.

Ellickson, Robert C. 1993. "Property in Land." *Yale Law Journal* 102:1315–1400.

Engels, Frederick. 1986/1884. *The Origins of the Family, Private Property and the State.* New York: Penguin Books.

Engerman, Stanley L., Seymour Drescher, and Robert L. Paquette, eds. 2001. *Slavery.* Oxford: Oxford University Press.

Finley, I. Moses. 1973. *The Ancient Economy.* New York: Penguin Books.

Fitzhugh, William W. 2000. "Puffins, Ringed Pins, and Runestones: The Viking Passage to America." In *Vikings: The North Atlantic Saga,* ed. William W. Fitzhugh and Elisabeth I. Ward, 11–25. Washington, DC: Smithsonian Institution Press.

Flannery, Kent V. 1972. "The Cultural Evolution of Civilizations." *Annual Review of Ecology and Systematics* 3:399–426.

Foley, Duncan K. 2000. "Stabilization of Human Population through Economic Increasing Returns." *Economic Letters* 86:309–17.

Friðriksson, Sturla. 1973. *Líf og land, um visfræði Íslands.* Reykjavík: Varði.

Fried, Morton H. 1967. *The Evolution of Political Society.* New York: Random House.

Friedman, Jonathan, and Michael J. Rowlands. 1977. "Notes towards an Epigenetic Model of Evolution of 'Civilization.'" In *The Evolution of Social Systems,* ed. Jonathan Friedman and Michael J. Rowlands, 201–76. London: Duckworth.

Galbraith, John Kenneth. 1998. *The Affluent Society.* New York: Houghton Mifflin.

Geertz, Clifford. 1963. *Agricultural Involution.* Berkeley: University of California Press.

Gelsinger, Bruce E. 1981. *Icelandic Enterprise: Commerce and Economy in the Middle Ages.* Columbia: University of South Carolina Press.

Gibson, D. Blair. 1988. "Agro-Pastoralism and Regional Social Organisation in Early Ireland." In *Tribe and Polity in Late Prehistoric Europe,* ed. D. Blair Gibson and Michael N. Geselowitz, 41–68. London: Plenum Press.

Gilman, Antonio. 1981. "The Development of Social Stratification in Bronze Age Europe." *Current Anthropology* 22:1–23.

———. 1991. "Trajectories towards Social Complexity in the Later Prehistory of the Mediterranean." In *Chiefdoms: Power, Economy and Ideology,* ed. Timothy Earle, 146–68. Cambridge: Cambridge University Press.

———. 1995. "Prehistoric European Chiefdoms: Rethinking 'Germanic' Societies." In *Foundations of Social Inequality*, ed. T. Douglas Price and Gary M. Feinman, 235–51. New York: Plenum Press.

Goodstein, Eban. 1995. "The Economic Roots of Environmental Decline: Property Rights or Path Dependence?" *Journal of Economic Issues* 29:1029–44.

Griffith, Paddy. 1995. *The Viking Art of War*. London: Greenhill Books.

Haas, Jonathan. 1982. *The Evolution of the Prehistoric State*. New York: Columbia University Press.

Haddock, David D. 1986. "First Possession versus Optimal Timing: Limiting the Dissipation of Economic Value." *Washington University Law Quarterly* 64:775–92.

Hallsdóttir, Margret. 1987. *Pollen Analytical Studies of Human Influence on Vegetation in Relation to the Landnám Tephra Layer in Southwest Iceland*. Vol. 18 of *Lundqua Thesis*. Lund: Lund University, Department of Quaternary Geology.

Hastrup, Kirsten. 1985. *Culture and History in Medieval Iceland: An Anthropological Analysis of Structure and Change*. Oxford: Clarendon Press.

Hayden, Brian. 1995. "Pathways to Power: Principles for Creating Socioeconomic Inequalities." In *Foundations of Social Inequality*, ed. T. Douglas Price and Gary M. Feinman, 15–86. New York: Plenum Press.

———. 2000. "On Territoriality and Sedentism." *Current Anthropology* 41:109–12.

Haywood, John. 1995. *The Penguin Historical Atlas of the Vikings*. London: Penguin Books.

Hedeager, Lotte. 1992. *Iron-Age Societies: From Tribe to State in Northern Europe, 500 B.C. to A.D. 700*. Oxford: Blackwell.

Hirshleifer, Jack. 1995. "Anarchy and Its Breakdown." *Journal of Political Economy* 103:26–52.

Hunt, Robert C. 2000. "Labor Productivity and Agricultural Development: Boserup Revisited." *Human Ecology* 28:251–77.

Hunt, Robert C., and Antonio Gilman, eds. 1998. *Property in Economic Context*. Monographs in Economic Anthropology, 14. Lanham, MD: University Press of America.

Johnson, Allen, and Timothy K. Earle. 2001. *The Evolution of Human Societies*. Stanford, CA: Stanford University Press.

Johnson, Matthew H. 1989. "Conceptions of Agency in Archaeological Interpretation." *Journal of Anthropological Archaeology* 8:189–211.

Junker, Laura Lee. 1999. *Raiding, Trading, and Feasting: The Political Economy of Philippine Chiefdoms.* Honolulu: University of Hawai'i Press.

Júlíusson, Árni Daníel. 1995. Bónder i pestens tid: Landbrug, godsdrift og social konflikt in Senmiddelaldernes Icelandske Bondesamfund. PhD diss., Department of History, University of Copenhagen.

Karras, Ruth Mazo. 1988. *Slavery and Society in Medieval Scandinavia.* Yale Historical Publications, 135. New Haven, CT: Yale University Press.

Lee, Ronald. 1986. "Malthus and Boserup: A Dynamic Synthesis." In *The State of Population Theory: Forward from Malthus,* ed. David Coleman and Roger S. Schofield, 96–103. Oxford: Basil Blackwell.

Lindkvist, Thomas. 1996. "The Origins of a State Society in Medieval Sweden." In *Rome and the North,* ed. Alvar Ellegård and Gunilla Åkerström-Hougen, 62–97. Studies in Mediterranean Archaeology and Literature, 135. Jonsered: Åström.

Lueck, Dean. 1995. "The Rule of First Possession and the Design of the Law." *Journal of Law & Economics* 38:436.

Magnússon, Arni, and Páll Vídalín. 1927. *Jardabók.* Copenhagen: Hid Islenska Frædafélag í Kaupmannahöfn.

Malthus, Thomas. 1985/1789. *An Essay on the Principle of Population, as It Affects the Future Improvement of Society.* New York: Penguin Books.

Mann, Michael. 1986. *The Sources of Social Power.* Cambridge: Cambridge University Press.

Marx, Karl. 1967/1867. *The Process of Capitalist Production.* Vol. 1 of *Capital: A Critique of Political Economy.* New York: International Publishers.

———. 1993/1857–1858. *Grundrisse: Foundations of the Critique of Political Economy.* New York: Penguin Books.

McGovern, Thomas H. 1990. "The Archaeology of the Norse North Atlantic." *Annual Review of Anthropology* 19:331–51.

McGovern, Thomas H., Gerald F. Bigelow, Thomas Amorosi, and Daniel Russell. 1988. "Northern Islands, Human Error, and Environmental Degradation: a View of Social and Ecological Change in the Medieval North Atlantic." *Human Ecology* 16:225–70.

McGrew, Julia H. 1970. *Saga of Hvamm-Sturla and the Saga of the Icelanders.* Vol. 1 of *Sturlunga Saga.* Library of Scandinavian Literature, 9. New York: Twayne.

McGrew, Julia H., and R. George Thomas. 1974. *The Shorter Sagas of the Icelanders.* Vol. 2 of *Sturlunga Saga.* Library of Scandinavian Literature, 10. New York: Twayne.

McIntosh, Susan Keech, ed. 1999. *Beyond Chiefdoms: Pathways to Complexity in Africa.* New Directions in Archaeology. Cambridge: Cambridge University Press.

Milisauskas, Sarunas. 1977. "Adaptations of the Early Neolithic Farmers in Central Europe." In *For the Director: Research Essays in Honor of James B. Griffin,* ed. Charles E. Cleland, 295–316. Anthropological Papers, 61. Ann Arbor: University of Michigan Press.

———. 1978. *European Prehistory.* New York: Academic Press.

Miller, William I. 1990. *Bloodtaking and Peacemaking.* Chicago: University of Chicago Press.

Mueller, Dennis C. 1997. "First Mover Advantages and Path Dependence." *International Journal of Industrial Organization* 15:827–42.

Nieboer, Herman J. 1900. *Slavery as an Industrial System: Ethnological Researches.* The Hague: Martinus Nijoff.

Ólafsson, Haraldur. 2000. "Sagas of Western Expansion." In *Vikings: The North Atlantic Saga,* ed. William W. Fitzhugh and Elisabeth I. Ward, 143–45. Washington, DC: Smithsonian Institution Press.

Pálsson, Hermann, and Paul Edwards. 1972. *The Book of Settlements: Landnámabók,* trans., with Introduction and Notes, Hermann Pálsson and Paul Edwards. Winnipeg: University of Manitoba.

Panter-Brick, Catherine, Robert H. Layton, and Peter Rowley-Conwy, eds. 2001. *Hunter-Gatherers: An Interdisciplinary Perspective.* Biosocial Society Symposium Series. Cambridge: Cambridge University Press.

Parker-Peterson, Mike. 1982. "Mortuary Practices, Society and Ideology: An Ethnoarchaeological Study." In *Symbolic and Structural Archaeology,* ed. Ian Hodder, 99–113. Cambridge: Cambridge University Press.

Pierson, Paul. 2000. "Increasing Returns, Path Dependence, and the Study of Politics." *American Political Science Review* 94:251–69.

Pollard, Sidney. 1995. "Marginal Areas: Do They Have a Common History?" In *Towards an International Economic and Social History*, ed. Bouda Etemad, Jean Batou, and David Thomas, 121–36. Genève: Editions Passé Présent.

———. 1997. *Marginal Europe: The Contribution of Marginal Lands since the Middle Ages*. Oxford: Clarendon Press.

Price, T. Douglas, and Gary M. Feinman, eds. 1995. *Foundations of Social Inequality*. New York: Plenum Press.

Randsborg, Klavs. 1980. *The Viking Age in Denmark: The Formation of a State*. London: Duckworth.

Renfrew, Colin, and Stephen J. Shennan, eds. 1982. *Ranking, Resource and Exchange: Aspects of the Archaeology of Early European Society*. Cambridge: Cambridge University Press.

Ricardo, David. 1817. *Principles of Political Economy and Taxation*. London: Chiswick Press.

Roesdahl, Else. 1998. *The Vikings*, trans. Susan M. Margeson and Kirsten Williams. London: Penguin Books.

Romer, Paul M. 1986. "Increasing Returns and Long-Run Growth." *Journal of Political Economy* 94:1002–37.

———. 1996. "Why, Indeed in America? Theory, History and the Origins of Modern Economic Growth." *American Economic Review* 86:202–6.

Sahlins, Marshall D. 1972. *Stone Age Economics*. Chicago: Aldine.

Sahlins, Marshall D., and Elman R. Service, eds. 1960. *Evolution and Culture*. Ann Arbor: University of Michigan Press.

Saitta, Dean J. 1994. "Agency, Class and Archaeological Interpretation." *Journal of Anthropological Archaeology* 13:201–27.

Samuelson, Paul, and William Nordhaus. 1992. *Economics*. 14th ed. New York: McGraw-Hill.

Sawyer, Peter H. 1971. *The Age of the Vikings*. London: Edward Arnold.

Schiff, Maurice. 1995. "Uncertain Property Rights and the Coase Theorem." *Rationality and Society* 7:321–27.

Scott, William B. 1977. *In Pursuit of Happiness: American Conceptions of Property from the Seventeenth to the Twentieth Century.* Bloomington: Indiana University Press.

Sigurðardóttir, Sigríður. 1998. *Þróun torfbæja trfhleðsla.* Varmahlíð: Byggðasafn Skagfirðinga.

Sigurðsson, Jón Viðar. 1999. *Chieftains and Power in the Icelandic Commonwealth.* Odense: Odense University Press.

Smiley, Jane, and Robert Kellogg, eds. 2000. *The Sagas of Icelanders: A Selection.* New York: Viking.

Smith, Adam. 1976/1776. *An Inquiry into the Nature and Causes of the Wealth of Nations.* Chicago: University of Chicago Press.

Smith, Kevin P. 1995. "Landnám: The Settlement of Iceland in Archaeological and Historical Perspective." *World Archaeology* 26:319–47.

Stone, Glenn Davis, Robert McC. Netting, and M. Priscilla Stone. 1990. "Seasonality, Labor Scheduling, and Agricultural Intensification in the Nigerian Savanna." *American Anthropologist* 92:1–27.

Sturluson, Snorri. 1964. *Heimskringla: History of the Kings of Norway,* trans. Lee M. Hollander. Austin: University of Texas Press.

Sveinbjarnardóttir, Guðrún. 1992. *Farm Abandonment in Medieval and Post-Medieval Iceland: An Interdisciplinary Study.* Oxbow Monograph, 17. Oxford: Oxbow Books.

Tacitus, Cornelius. 1999. *Germania,* ed. James Rives. Clarendon Ancient History Series. Oxford: Clarendon Press.

Turgot, Anne-Robert-Jacques. 1973/1766. *Turgot on Progress, Sociology and Economics: A Philosophical Review of the Successive Advances of the Human Mind, on Universal History [and] Reflections on the Formation and the Distribution of Wealth,* trans. Ronald L. Meek. Cambridge: Cambridge University Press.

Vésteinsson, Orri. 1998. "Patterns of Settlement in Iceland: A Study in Prehistory." *Saga-Book* 25:1–29.

———. 2000. "The Archaeology of Landám: Early Settlement in Iceland." In *Vikings: The North Atlantic Saga,* ed. William W. Fitzhugh and Elisabeth I. Ward, 64–174. Washington, DC: Smithsonian Institution Press.

Wallace, Brigitta Linderoth. 1990. "L'anse aux Meadows: Gateway to Vinland." *Acta Archaeologica* 61:166–97.

Webster, Gary S. 1990. "Labor Control and Emergent Stratification in Prehistoric Europe." *Current Anthropology* 31:337–66.

Winfrey, William, and William Darity. 1997. "Increasing Returns and Intensification: A Reprise on Ester Boserup's Model of Agricultural Growth." *Metroeconomica* 48:60–80.

Winterhalder, Bruce, and Carol Goland. 1997. "Evolutionary Ecology Perspective on Diet Choice, Risk, and Plant Domestication." In *People, Plants, and Landscapes: Studies in Paleoethnobotany,* ed. Kristen J. Gremillion, 123–60. Tuscaloosa: University of Alabama Press.

Winterhalder, Bruce, and Eric Alden Smith, ed. 1981. *Hunter-Gatherer Foraging Strategies.* Chicago: University of Chicago Press.

Wood, James W. 1998. "A Theory of Preindustrial Population Dynamics." *Current Anthropology* 39:99–136.

Þórarinsson, Þórarinn. 1974. "Þjóðin lifði en skógurinn dó" *[The Nation lived but the forest died].* Ársrit Skógræktargélags Íslands (1974): 16–29.

11

Of Corvée and Slavery: Historical Intricacies of the Division of Labor and State Power in Northern Thailand

Katherine A. Bowie

Conceptual models of peasant-court relations can be categorized into three ideal types: (1) an independent peasantry with minimal links to the court; (2) a contented peasantry with significant positive links to the court; and (3) an oppressed peasantry with significant negative links to the court. Scholars of the Thai kingdoms of mainland Southeast Asia have most frequently characterized peasant-court relations as benign theater-states or exemplars of an Asiatic mode of production. Thus, drawing upon Clifford Geertz's notion of a "theater-state," Stanley J. Tambiah argues that the Thai kingdoms were "galactic polities" held together "not so much by the real exercise of power and control as by devices and mechanisms of a ritual kind" (1976, 125).[1] Tambiah, while noting that the court extracted corvée (unpaid labor) and tribute from the subordinate peasantries, viewed the peasantry as economically self-sufficient and independent of the court. He argues that the "rice-growing, land-based sector of the economy could . . . not put directly in the hands of the center large economic resources that it could disburse and manipulate and thereby control the recipients" (1976, 129).

Scholars such as Chatthip Nartsupha and Suthy Prasartset (1978) have glossed traditional Thai kingdoms as being characteristic of an "Asiatic mode of production." Although this phrase has been defined variously,[2] the Thai application refers to self-sufficient peasantry sending a nominal tribute of luxury goods to the court. In this view, the court has little effect on village daily life. As in the galactic polity model, the peasantry is seen as primarily independent of the court.

In this chapter, I explore the role of labor in the constitution of the political economy of the Lanna kingdoms of northern Thailand during the mid to late nineteenth century. I argue that understanding the Lanna court's control of labor, while far from benign, reveals both the underpinnings of the political and economic strength of the Lanna court and the political and economic weakness of the Lanna peasantry. I first explore how control over labor provided the Lannathai state with significant and varied economic resources. The Lanna court extracted economic wealth from the peasantry both by direct access to labor through slavery and corvée, and indirect access through tribute and taxation. Taking various peasant revolts as illustrations, I then consider how this system of labor control, while contributing to the strength of the state, weakened the peasantry. Thus, understanding the Lanna system of labor control explains both the overall lack of major peasant uprisings and the structure of those that did occur.

My analysis is based upon both archival sources and oral histories gathered from some 550 villagers, most over age eighty, living in some 400 villages throughout Chiang Mai Valley. The Lanna kingdom of Chiang Mai was centered in the Chiang Mai Valley; the city of Chiang Mai has long been Thailand's second-largest urban center.[3] Until its incorporation into the modern nation-state of Thailand, this kingdom was independent, albeit with tributary relations with the central Thai court. The society was divided into three main social statuses: aristocrats, free persons (sometimes translated as "serfs"), and slaves. The kingdom was administered by five ruling lords (*chaw khan haa baj*). Village headmen were responsible for administering affairs in their respective villages. Headmen in turn came under subdistrict leaders (*khwaen* or *kamnan*), the highest ranking of whom bore the title of *phrayar* and reported to the ruling lords.

Located in a fertile rice-growing valley surrounded by mountain forests, the Chiang Mai kingdom was the largest and most important of the Lannathai polities. David Edwardes, a British official who traveled to Chiang Mai in 1875, gives the following description of its size:

> It extends northwards from the borders of Raheng for a distance of nearly 200 miles, and its main breadth cannot be much less than 100 miles.
>
> The greater part of the population, which probably numbers about 300,000 people, is to be found on the banks of the river leading to Bangkok, and in the numerous villages and hamlets which stand in the extensive plain on which the

town of Chiengmai [Chiang Mai] is built, and which, in some directions from Chiengmai, is nearly two days journey in extent. (Edwardes in Nartsupha and Prasartset 1978, 175–76)

LABOR CONTROL AND THE STRENGTH OF THE STATE

The Lanna court extracted economically significant resources from villagers who were integrated into the overall productive system of the kingdom in different and varied manners. The court had direct access to labor through slavery. In addition, the court gained access to the labor of its "free" peasantry (*phrai*) directly through corvée and indirectly through the extraction of goods offered as payment of tribute or taxes. In this section, I describe the court's intricately differentiated control of peasant labor.

Direct Control of Labor through Slavery

Although many scholars have assumed that debt slavery was the dominant form of slavery in Southeast Asia, I have argued that northern Thai sources suggest that a clear majority of slaves were war captives (Bowie 1996).[4] Dr. Richardson, in his diary of his journeys to Chiang Mai in the 1830s, noted that three-quarters of the kingdom's population were war captives (Richardson 1829–1836, 143). General McLeod wrote of his trip to Chiang Mai in 1837 that war captives "comprise more than two-thirds of the population of the country" (Hallett 1890, 202). The American missionary John Freeman estimated that about half of the populations of the adjacent kingdom of Lamphun were descendants of war captives (1910, 100). Data gathered from oral histories supports the presence of numerous war captives (Bowie 1988, 1996). Thus, there is a remarkable consensus amongst several independent nineteenth-century observers that the combined total of war captives together with other kinds of slaves must have comprised more than half of the population.[5]

The ruling lords of the northern kingdoms owned the vast majority of slaves. As Freeman succinctly writes, "The 'chow,' or native princes, are the principal slave-holders" (1910, 101). Other nineteenth-century observers provide supporting evidence. A. H. Hildebrand (1875) writes that the second chief had some 600 slaves living under his roof and another 600 or so slaves living elsewhere, thus owning a combined total of some 1,200 slaves. Archibald Colquhoun provides the most detailed breakdown, showing the Chiang Mai aristocracy owned thousands of slaves. He records that the first lord (Chaw Luang) had 1,500 slaves, the second lord had 1,000 slaves, the third lord had 800 slaves, and other lesser lords had 70–100 each. The ranking rural elite (*phrayars*) also had slaves, averaging fifteen to twenty each (Colquhoun 1885, 257). Slavery was an important source of royal labor, some slaves contributing to the everyday maintenance of the court and others contributing to the court's financial revenue.

Agricultural lands were owned by both lords and villagers. Royally owned lands were worked by a combination of corvée labor, serf-tenants, and slaves. Contrary to the prevailing view that "it was not in the Thai tradition to farm a lot of land and to use slave labor in farming" (Wedel 1982, 126), slave labor was heavily used in agricultural production. Of informants living in thirty-three villages that had royal lands worked by tenants, about half (sixteen) also recalled that such tenants were slaves (Bowie 1988, 255). Rice and other agricultural crops were important, not only to meet the subsistence needs of the court, but also as items of trade (Bowie 1988).

Slave labor was also important in the production of textiles and a range of other crafts. Weaving was a skill that crossed the social spectrum from poor to rich, from peasants to lords. Although ordinary clothing was woven from cotton, prestige textiles were made of silk. Both slaves and women in the court appear to have been most likely to weave silk goods. As Richardson writes as early as 1830, "The daughters and slaves of men of rank are employed in weaving and in embroydering" (1829–1836, 37). Carl Bock provides one eyewitness account of the wife of the second lord (Chaw Uparat) of Chiang Mai who "lived in a large, roomy, teak-built house, and was always busy making silken garments, while one of her slaves worked at the loom spinning silk thread" (1986/1884, 322). Edwardes (1875) records that the ruling lords had 300 slaves engaged in weaving alone.[6]

In addition to meeting internal court demands, silk was woven for export and likely served as an important source of revenue. Indications of a possible trade orientation can be gleaned from a variety of sources. The British official Hildebrand (1875) notes, "There is a good deal of trade capable of being done also in silk garments and silk fancy work, at which the slaves and others are great adepts." He writes that one of the chief sources of income for the ruling lord of Chiang Mai was "the sale of wearing apparel, etc., made by his several hundred slaves" (1875, 16). Elsewhere, Hildebrand comments that freeholders were corvéed to perform various tasks for the lord, with "slaves being employed on some more profitable occupation."[7] Lt. Younghusband introduces the interesting issue of gender exploitation with regard to profits from silk weaving when he writes in 1888, "A ready made wife can be bought for Rs. 50. This is an excellent investment, for his wife, if properly managed, will repay her husband double that amount in a year by the work of her hands. Indeed, the Lord Chief Justice's head concubine, an old lady, can in five days weave a silk lungi valued locally at Rs. 18" (1888, 58).

In addition to weaving, slaves also provided the court with a variety of other artisanal skills. The Chiang Mai kingdom was famous for its gold and silver work. As Freeman writes, "Repousse work in silver and gold is done with much skill in all Laos [Lanna] cities" (1910, 62). The American missionary Hugh Taylor notes that the neighboring king of Lampang "kept some of his slaves, each dry season, washing out gold" (1888–1930, 166–67). The manufacture of lacquerware was another important slave industry; Freeman describes its importance: "One of the most curious and important industries of the Laos is the manufacture of lacquerware. From Chieng Mai this ware is not only sent all over the Laos states, but to Bangkok as well. . . . The gum from which the lacquer is prepared is found in the Laos forests, and forms an important article of export" (1910, 62).

Other handicrafts of significance in which slave labor was utilized included woodworking and the production of silk umbrellas, of largely ceremonial significance and used primarily by royalty and monks (see Bowie 1988, 254).[8]

Elephants were another major source of royal income and military power in which slave labor played an important role. Edwardes records of his trip to Chiang Mai in 1879 that "there are many thousands of these animals in Chiangmai and numbers of these are daily to be seen. They are reared in Chiangmai and are also brought from the northeastern Laos States" (in Nartsupha and Prasartset 1978, 180–81). Holt Hallett notes that "elephants were very numerous in the country: there were fully 8000 in both Zimme [Chiang Mai] and Lakon [Lampang], even more in Nan, and about half that number in Peh [Phrae]" (1890, 104).

Archival and oral histories suggest that elephants were virtually entirely owned by lords. The *Mengraisat* declared ownership of elephants to be a royal monopoly (Aroonrat 1976). As late as the nineteenth century, the northern Thai lords reserved "to themselves the sole right to hunt the elephant and rhinoceros" (Bock 1986/1884, 269; Freeman 1910, 76, 85). Colquhoun gives some idea of the relative scale of ownership among the elite: "In the Siamese-Shan states, the chiefs, besides slaves and serfs are possessed of numerous elephants. The tsobua, at the time of our visit, owned over a hundred and fifty; the kyou-koopone, or sister-in-law of the tsobua, one hundred and thirty-five; the chao hona, a hundred; and every chao, from five to twenty" (1885, 256; for more details, see Bowie 2000).

Elephants served a variety of purposes. In times of war, elephants "were trained to tear down obstacles and, above all, to kill" (Edwardes 1875, 99). In addition, elephants "were used as a means of transport by the Siamese and Burmese armies in great numbers" (Colquhoun 1885, 96). In peacetime, elephants were symbolically grandiose, politically intimidating, and economically important. Elephants played important roles in transporting people and goods. As William Dodd explains, "Owing to the state of the roads, through the jungle, over high mountain ranges, through almost impassable bogs and deep streams, the elephant was almost the only mode of travel for journeys of any distance" (1923, 253–54). As H. Warington Smyth writes, "For hauling teak, for collecting rattans, or jungle grass, for carrying tobacco, rice, or cotton, and for any journeying away from home, he is indispensable to his master" (1898, 108–9). Dragging logs to the riverbanks, elephants had a major role in the teak-logging industry. Elephants also were important in the development of new agricultural fields and irrigation canals to clear rocks and tree stumps.

Elephants were also bought and sold. According to the British trade report of 1858, no fewer that 1,060 elephants and 10,000 head of cattle were purchased from the Chiang Mai region alone (FO 69/30; Bowie 2000, 337). Edwardes mentions elephants in 1870 costing anywhere from 600–2,300 rupees (Nartsupha and Prasartset 1978, 180–81). Smyth suggests that a "really experienced teak-hauling elephants with good tusks may fetch Rs. 3,000" (1898, vol. 2, 107). Given wages at the time, an elephant cost the equivalent of about twenty years' wages for a hired agricultural laborer (Bowie 2000, 337). Thus, while the profits being made from the care and export of elephants accrued to the lords, slaves fed the elephants, kept watch over them, and served as their mahouts.

Direct Control of Corvée Labor

In addition to control over slave labor, the lords of Chiang Mai also had access to labor corvéed from "free" peasants. Although many of the royal land-holdings were worked by slaves, royal lands were also worked through corvéeing villagers. Villagers often described corvée as "working for nothing" (*ia hyy pyan bo daj*). One villager, after explaining his village's corvée duties, added, "There is no way that would be tolerated today. Whoever tried it would meet with a bullet." The element of coercion is revealed in various villagers' accounts:

> Villagers had to work one *rai* [*rai myang* or 0.1 acre] per person for them for nothing. And one had to do it properly. The lord's underlings would take a banana tree trunk and stick it upright in the field after it was plowed. If it fell over, that meant it was well plowed. Otherwise, one would have to keep on plowing it until the ground was soft.

The royal fields had to be planted first, before villagers could plant their own. The lord's servants would ride about on elephant to supervise villagers. If anyone wasn't working as supposed to, the servant would be sent on elephant back to summon the faulty party, who would be ridden on the elephant back to the lord, where he would then receive a whipping.

> Our grandparents were corvéed to work the royal fields. After everyone had threshed the rice, they burnt the rice stalks to make sure that if the lord or his underlings came around on inspection, they wouldn't find anything to get upset over. Otherwise if they came around and found rice still sticking to the stalks, they would say the rice hadn't been properly threshed. [For more details, see Bowie 1988, 278.]

Royal lands were worked both by tenant or slave labor, and by corvée labor. With tenant labor, the owner only receives a portion of the total crop; with corvée labor the lord could receive the full portion. The organization of royal agricultural corvée varied. In some areas, villagers were responsible for providing labor for the various phases of the agricultural cycle, from the planting, harvesting, threshing, and storing of the equivalent of approximately one *rai myang* of land.[9] In other areas, different villagers performed different phases of the agricultural cycle. Rather than participating in all phases of the planting and harvesting, in these areas certain villages were corvéed to plant; yet other villagers were corvéed to harvest. Villagers could be corvéed from great distances. As one informant recalled, "At harvest time, and whenever else we were wanted, we had to go to help. The lord's lands were not even close by. They would have to sleep overnight to reach lord's lands" (Bowie 1988, 258).

Corvéed agricultural labor contributed vast rice stockpiles to the royal granaries. As Richardson records in 1835, the royal harvest "from his rice grounds which are immediately in this neighborhood I am told amounts to 15 or 16,000 baskets" (1829–1836, 124–25). Corvéed village labor also played a role in the clearing and development of new royal landholdings (Bowie 1988; see also Cohen 1981; Anan 1984). Villagers were also corvéed to build irrigation dams, to clear new canals, and to repair existing irrigation networks, as well as the small earthen irrigation walls (*khannaa*) throughout the royal paddyfields.[10]

In addition to corvée on agricultural lands, corvée labor was also used in facilitating royal travel and transport. Forrest noted the royal use of corvée on a trip to Cambodia in 1857, a pattern that seems equally likely in northern Thailand and elsewhere. He writes, "The King and such of the nobles as are sufficiently powerful to undertake mercantile operations find it more to their advantage to use vehicles and beasts of burden, the corvée system placing those of the poorer classes at their disposal for a great part of the year" (FO 69/8). Sir Ernest Satow records the use of riverine corvée, complaining of the frequent delays caused by having to seek new river pilots:

> It is generally the *kamnan* or village mayor who performs the duty of pilotage, but sometimes his wife replaces him, which is not to be wondered at, for in this country, the women have quite as much intelligence, and more "go" than the opposite sex. But a mayor does not profess to be acquainted with any part of the river beyond the limits of his little district, and hence the frequent changes. Sometimes we found it difficult to get the mayor, for no payment is made for such services by Siamese Government officials. (Satow 1885–1886 [20/1], 25)

In northern Thailand, lords owned their own boats, often made by royal slaves, and had their own crews, also slaves. However, villagers were corvéed to help dredge the Ping River of its sandbars in order to facilitate the passage of royal boats. Villagers could also be corvéed to help portage goods or help passing the rapids. As one informant explained, "In villages nearest the rapids, everyone would be corvéed to go and help pull the boats past the rapids."

Villagers were corvéed to perform in a wide variety of other capacities, such as posting regular guard duty at the court, working as sawyers and carpenters building resthouses, and serving as bearers, messengers, and porters. Villagers who lived along routes between major towns seemed most liable to this last form of corvée.[11] When porters were needed, the local village headman was contacted to find the requisite number of men. A porter carried about twenty kilos. In some cases, porters were gone as long as a month or so. In other cases, the work of porting was done in stages, with different villagers corvéed for each stretch. Certain villages en route seem to have been designated as rest stops, charged with the obligation of providing food and shelter to the traveling porters.[12]

Indirect Labor Control through Tribute and Taxation

In addition to direct control over the subaltern population's labor through slavery and corvée, the Lanna state also gained access to the fruits of people's labor through tribute and taxation. Tribute is not easily differentiated from corvée since considerable labor was entailed in procuring many of the items of tribute. Betel, for example, was a fruit tree that needed to be planted and cared for. Once picked, the fruit was cut into small slices, strung and set out to dry. The cutting and drying of betel was very time-consuming. Coconut, sugar palm, and other such fruit trees involved less work, but were nonetheless cultivated trees. Similarly, chilies, sesame, and various vegetables were cultivated garden crops. Picking leaves for *miang* (fermented tea leaves) was arduous work; the fermentation process also involved specialized knowledge.[13] *Kapok* and cotton were only cultivated in certain areas; women were corvéed in big evening gatherings to pick out the seeds. Collecting forest products and hunting game also involved considerable time and specialized knowledge. To make saltpeter, villagers collected guano or bat-dung from caves; the guano was boiled down and the saltpeter crystallized out. To make lime for building, the limestone first had to be cut out from the mountain quarry. Kilns were made and wood to fire the kilns had to be collected in readiness. The lime was then broken into smaller rocks and loaded into the kilns, where it was baked for twenty-four hours. After firing, the lime was then pounded into a fine powder.[14] The labor involved in iron smelting and blacksmithing is intimated in Richardson's account of a village:[15]

> The village contains 60 or 80 houses, the inhabitants are all blacksmiths and are exempt from service or taxation on furnishing the Labong *Tsabwa* [ruling lord of Lampang] with elephant chains, spears, cooking pots and other iron ware during war and for military purposes. The iron is a red oxyd and is found in a hill about half day from this in NW direction—it is brought to the village on elephants. (1829–1836, 18)

Just as the division between corvée and tribute is vague, so is the division between tribute and tax. In one account, a nineteenth-century traveler suggests that the villagers paid a tax for the "privilege of working" the salt wells in Nan province (Anonymous 1895, 72). Yet this same traveler describes a similar arrangement at the salt beds at Muang La as tribute; he writes, "At that time, M. La had to send to Luang Prabang 300 lbs of salt as the annual tribute for the privilege of working the salt-beds" (Anonymous 1895, 122). In addition to salt, the ruling lords acquired additional rice and fish through exactions of tax/tribute. Some royal payments bordered on extortion. In one account, Richardson notes that Karen villagers were expected to pay a customary tax of cloth and beeswax; when the lord visited, they also "were obliged to furnish his party with rice and salt gratis" (1829–1836, 47; also 38). In another similar account, Richardson adds that the village headman "will not be set at liberty till all his demands on the village are satisfied" (1829–1836, 119–20).

Goods collected from villagers as tribute are remarkably similar to goods exported from Chiang Mai for sale on regional and international markets. The goods mentioned by villagers as items of tribute included forest products such as bamboo shoots, mushrooms, beeswax, honey, sticklac, kindling, firewood, orchids, and rattan; wild animals such as barking deer, wild boar, lizard, turtles, and various insects; fish; animal skins including deerskins, buffalo, and oxen hides; domesticated animals such as chickens and ducks; a wide range of plants and cultivated vegetables such as chilies, sesame, squash, cucumbers, eggplant, soybeans, and the like; betel nuts and serivine; *miang*, a variety of fruits such as coconuts, sugar palm, and jackfruit; cotton, kapok, and cloth; limestone and saltpeter. In addition to items useful for the maintenance of the court, virtually all were goods sold through local and regional market networks. Items such as sticklac, *miang*, cotton, chilies, betel, serivine, saltpeter,[16] and animal hides were particularly important items of export, responsible for significant royal revenue.

LABOR FRAGMENTATION: A WEAKENED PEASANTRY

Villagers produced a variety of goods and services that the court extracted through direct and indirect control of village labor. This intricate division of labor, although contributing to the political and economic strength of the Lanna state, undermined the political and economic position of the Lanna peasantry. In this section, I consider three avenues by which Lanna peasants were fragmented: economic specialization, social diversity, and internal village heterogeneity.

Geographical Diversity and Economic Specialization

The prevailing characterization of the traditional peasant economy as self-sufficient or subsistence oriented (see Bowie 1992 for a critique) minimizes the extent of poverty and class stratification in nineteenth-century Thailand. Inequality in landholdings was one of the primary factors contributing to poverty. Lords and members of the rural elite owned much of the best land. Consequently, the elite had large surpluses of rice while most ordinary villagers fell short (see Bowie 1988, 1998). Natural vicissitudes exaggerated this disparity, causing periodic famines. Describing a drought in 1892, Hugh Taylor, a missionary, records that villagers were begging for coconut husks to fill their stomachs. Taylor, who had organized some relief work, said, "We had to post a guard to keep the people from crowding in on us too hard . . . sifting the starving from the merely hungry" (1888–1930, 113). As Taylor continues:

> Yes, they were starving. More than three score starved to death in the next village down the river from us. . . . The Elders and Evangelists who were sent out to follow up those who had received help reported finding dead bodies in deserted houses. They set fire to the houses and cremated the bodies. They found village wells filled with starved bodies that the neighbors were too weak to bury. (1888–1930, 114)[17]

While famines of this severity were not the norm, evidence for the more general extent of agrarian poverty is provided by oral histories. In the course of my interviews, I routinely asked elderly villagers throughout the Chiang Mai valley if people in their villages fell short of rice in the past (generally defined as during their childhood or earlier), and if so, for how many months out of the year. Of a total of 273 villages, 97 percent of villages had at least some households who fell short of rice for at least two or three months each year. In nearly half (48.7 per cent) of the villages, the majority of households fell short of rice at least two or three months each year (Bowie 1988, 1998).

Villagers made ends meet by a range of activities, from collecting forest products and making a variety of handicrafts to hiring themselves out as wage laborers. In addition to agricultural labor, the main types of wage labor were as sawyers and porters. Far from being a "subsistence economy," villagers were integrated into a complex network of trade relations. Poverty and geographical diversity prompted exchange. Villagers living along rivers were able to catch fish; villagers living in the mountains had access to numerous forest products. Other villages were located near iron, salt, or gold deposits and specialized in mining. Tea leaves for *miang* were grown in certain mountain villages; betel trees were cultivated primarily in two districts near the Ping River, San Sai and Doi Saket.[18] Sugar cane was an upland crop; garden crops were most likely to be planted along the river banks where the plants could be most easily watered during the dry season. Villagers also specialized in the production of a variety of handicrafts such as blacksmithing, silversmithing, pottery making, roof making, rope making, mat weaving, bamboo weaving, paper making, making lacquerware, and cloth weaving (see Bowie [1992, 1993] for intervillage and interregional division of labor in textile production). Yet other villagers collected forest products. Villagers used boats, rafts, oxen, mules, and porters to distribute these goods.

That villages were heterogeneous and not homogeneous meant that they were less likely to undergo economic crises or political stresses simultaneously. An increased levy of tax or tribute on a certain village or certain item would not affect all villagers, but only specific ones. This heterogeneity made finding common ground for political protest more difficult.

Social and Ethnic Diversity

Given inequality in landholdings and pervasive rural poverty, it is not surprising that so many villagers had to borrow rice to see their households through to the next harvest. Although being a slave would not have been a desirable status in normal times, in times of famine and other hardships, slave status appears to have offered certain benefits. Sir John Bowring informs us that the slave master is under obligation to "furnish rice and salt fish, but not clothes" (1969/1857, 192). Hugh Taylor writes, in his account of the famine in Lampang, of his gratitude to one of his assistants who was a former trader and knew the people of the country; as they were distributing food to the starving, this assistant screened out slaves as "people who could otherwise get food" (1888–1930, 113). Indeed, this obligation of the master to his slaves suggests one way in which being a slave may have been better than being a freeholder— at least, during times of famine.

Thus, the rural population was divided, not only by economic specializations but also by differences in social status.[19] The status of slaves was ambiguous. Free villagers (*phrai*) had pity for those whose lot had deteriorated to the point of being slaves. Accounts remain of slaves whipped and treated mercilessly by their masters. One informant whose mother was a slave told how members of her family were sold separately, such that even the integrity of the family unit was destroyed. Free villagers avoided marriage with slaves, lest their offspring be classified as slaves, too. Nonetheless there were also a few slaves who acquired trusted positions with their masters, serving as overseers of their lands and other interests. If, during normal times, free villagers felt pity for poor slaves who were at the beck and call of their masters even more than free villagers, in times of hardship, the tides shifted. While free villagers were searching for a means of livelihood, slaves had a fundamental security, knowing that their masters would provide for them. Regardless of whether trusted or mistreated, slaves occupied a different economic and political position from free villagers.

Another social division separating villagers from each other and from the lords was ethnicity. These ethnic differences were a result of both forced and voluntary migrations. War captives were brought from as far away as Burma, China, and Laos. Although war captives were allowed to settle together in villages, efforts were made to separate villages from each other (see Richardson 1829–1836, 59). Thus, villagers captured from one region were relocated near villagers from a different area. In addition to forced relocations, new communities were also formed by peacetime migrations. Thus, northerners recognize a variety of "ethnic" subgroups such as Shan (Ngio), Mon, Khyyn, Lyy, Yong, Lawa, and Karen, in addition to various hill groups living in the mountains. Historical differences in geographical origin were reinforced by variations in linguistic accents and in such cultural practices as spirit beliefs and rituals. Even today, fights among village youths can be catalyzed by ethnic rivalries.

This ethnic diversity was likely an additional factor inhibiting the development of trust and cooperation across villages. Some indication of the possible role of ethnicity in dividing villagers is given in the Shan uprising of 1902. This revolt was largely caused by state policies that discriminated against the Shan (Taylor 1888–1930, 174; Bristowe 1976; Bunnag 1977; Ramsay 1979).[20] Missionary reports of 1901–1903 indicate the existence of a rice famine at this time, with very high prices and many villagers going hungry. Indeed, as one missionary (BOFM Briggs 271, 7) wrote, "The people had been sullen from some time for a multitude of reasons, but all circling round the Siamese as the cause of their troubles." The Shan uprising sent shockwaves throughout the north. However, these ethnic divisions hindered the ability of the Shan to form an alliance with other aggrieved villagers; their revolt failed.

Political Heterogeneity: Intravillage Stratification

Another factor affecting the ability of the peasantry to organize formal protests against government policy was the extent of socioeconomic divisions within village society. Village headmen occupied an ambiguous position. On the one hand, village headmen had close ties to the court. They coordinated royal demands for tribute and corvée; they oversaw local royal landholdings and irrigation systems. In recognition of their services, many were given royal titles (*phrayar* being the highest) and the regalia of rank. Headmen were generally the wealthiest men in their villages. They had the right to corvée labor for their own fields; hence they were able to maintain larger landholdings than ordinary villagers. These headmen were often intermarried with other members of the rural elite or with the court elite.

Although the rural elite identified with the court elite in many ways, they remained indigenous members of their communities. Thus, unlike societies in which the rural administrators are appointed and constantly rotate, Lanna headmen also shared certain interests in common with fellow villagers. Because of the strong local ties the Lannathai rural elite had with their home villages, any villager opposition to the court would have been difficult without the knowledge and involvement of the village heads. Indeed, the principal figures in those peasant revolts that occurred were often the *phrayars* and other village leaders.[21]

The *Phrayar* Phaab uprising in 1889 is illustrative. The state levied a new tax on betel nut. The American missionary Daniel McGilvary provides the following summary:

> A new tax, levied chiefly on areca [betel] trees, caused much exasperation throughout the country. As usual, the tax was farmed out to Chinese for collection. The local officers in various districts formed a coalition to resist to the uttermost the collection of the tax. Of course, this could not be allowed, since the collectors were the agents of the government.
>
> The resistance was centered chiefly in the districts to the eastward of the city, where *Praya* Pap [*Phrayar* Phaab], who had some reputation as a soldier, went so far as to gather a considerable force of the insurgents within a few miles of Chiengmai. A day even was set for their attack on the city. If they had made a dash then, they could easily have taken it, for the sympathy of the people was wholly with them, and the government was unprepared. (McGilvary 1912, 304–5)

Just why the attack never materialized has been given various explanations, ranging from interventions by monks to intervention by nature (a tremendous rainstorm). However, I believe that part of the explanation lies precisely in the fact that the uprising was centered in the region where betel nut cultivation was concentrated, namely areas of the San Sai-Doi Saket region east of Chiang Mai City. Thus, while solidarity with *Phrayar* Phaab and other betel producers was high in this region, the base of active support was restricted to this area. The rural elite had the most to lose with the imposition of this new tax since they had the largest betel nut orchards. Thus, rural revolts were most likely to occur when the grievances of the village elite coincided with their fellow villagers. However, these uprisings were likely to fail since ethnic and economic diversity contributed to the weakness of the Lanna peasantry.

CONCLUSION

In his last book, *Envisioning Power: Ideologies of Dominance and Crisis*, Eric Wolf writes, "The dominant mode of mobilizing social labor set the terms of structural power that allocated people to positions in society" (1999, 275). In this chapter, I have argued that understanding the system of control over labor provides insights into both the underpinnings of the strength of the Lanna court and weakness of the Lanna peasantry. The Lanna court extracted economic wealth from the peasantry by direct and indirect control over labor. The intricate division of labor provided the Lannathai state with significant economic resources, thus buttressing its political position. This same system of labor control, in its reliance on geographical and economic diversity, social and ethnic diversity, and intravillage stratification, weakened the Lannathai peasantry.

NOTES

1. Tambiah suggests the bonds between the peasantry were religio-cultural:

> This kind of galactic polity was integrated through collective cosmic rituals in which the king was the focal point and through the building of conspicuous public works whose utility lay at least partially in their being architectural embodiments of the collective aspirations and fantasies of heavenly grandeur. It was thus a theater-state providing the masses with an awe-inspiring vision of a cosmic manifestation on earth. (1976, 487).

2. See especially Anderson (1974, 462–549).

3. The Chiang Mai kingdom had close ties with other Lannathai kingdoms of Lamphun, Lampang, and Nan, and with satellite principalities of Fang, Phrae, Chiang Rai, and other smaller towns in the region of northern Thailand.

4. A similar argument can be made for central Thailand. See Bowie 1996.

5. Slaves were also acquired through kidnapping and sale. O'Riley writing in 1865 estimated "about 1,200 souls are annually captured" and sold to the Chiang Mai buyers (Mangrai 1965, 180–81; see also Richardson 1829–1836, 121).

6. The towns of San Khampaeng and Hot were centers for silk weaving. The tradition of silk weaving continues in San Khampaeng to the present day.

7. In the course of her oral histories, Patel met a trader who bought "valuable sarongs woven with gold and silver threads" from the lords of Lampang kingdom (1990, 125, 143).

8. The production of umbrellas was localized in the area of Bosang and continues today as a tourist attraction.

9. In practice, however, it does not seem that villagers actually marked out a *rai myang*, rather, on the designated day, the village headman would beat the temple gong to summon the villagers who then worked until the assigned job was done. With regard to plowing, one villager living adjacent to what had once been a huge royal landholdings said that members of his village were slaves and hence responsible for the plowing; other villagers from elsewhere were corvéed to plant and harvest.

10. Several of the northern Thai lords or the overseers of royal landholdings oversaw irrigation systems (see Bowie 1980 and Cohen 1981; see Pearson 1999 for historical overview).

11. Villagers who owned oxen would find themselves and their oxen conscripted to transport goods.

12. This practice of corvéeing villagers to serve as porters and laborers continued well into the twentieth century.

13. According to one informant, tribute amounted to one to two *pan kam* of *miang*. The average yield per producer was about ten *pan kam* (or one *myyn*), so that the tribute was about 10–20 percent of the yield (Bowie 1988, 243).

14. One informant recalled seeing mountains of limestone powder piled up underneath rain shelters built near the local headman's house. She recalled that each household had to give two to three *myyn* of limestone as tribute; the rest they sold (Bowie 1988, 243–44).

15. The Lawa village of Bo Luang.

16. Sticklac is the residue of an insect used to produce a red dye. The broad leaves of the serivine are chewed together with betel nut.

17. See also McGilvary 1912, 351. Satow recounts another drought in 1885, which also affected thousands of villagers (Satow 1885–1996, 30/33 [20/1], 200).

18. As one villager explained, "There were so many betel nut trees growing around here that dogs running around too fast would hit their heads on betel nut trees" (see Bowie 1988, 143).

19. Slaves appear to have been internally differentiated into two major categories, village slaves and household slaves (see Bowie 1996 for details).

20. According to J. S. Thomas, a missionary living in Phrae at the time of the uprising, the Shan list of grievances included:

1. The Siamese government refused them timber to build temples.
2. The Siamese refused to grant passports, and subjected the Shan to imprisonment for traveling without passports.
3. The taxes were exorbitant and increasing. For instance, no one could kill a pig or cattle without paying from one-sixth to one-fourth its value as a privilege tax.
4. It was becoming more and more impracticable for the Shan to procure homes and rice fields, or any property. (BOFM 271/93).

21. As far back as the days of the *Mengraisat*, the ancient Lanna legal code, village headmen were held accountable for the behavior of their villagers (Aroonrat 1976). During the turn of the twentieth century, villagers recounted a series of attacks on district offices, police stations, and distilleries. In cases where the government was able to apprehend rebel leadership, those who were imprisoned or executed were village leaders. The importance of village headmen in political organizing continues to the present. During the 1970s, the assassinated leaders of the Farmer's Federation of Thailand (FFT) were virtually all village headmen.

REFERENCES

Archival Sources
BOFM: Board of Foreign Missionaries. Presbyterian Church U.S. Siam Letters and Correspondence, 1840–1910. Microfilm. Philadelphia, Pennsylvania.

FO69: Foreign Office Series #69. Public Records Office, London, England.

Published Sources (Thai authors listed with first names first)
Anan Ganjanapan. 1984. The Partial Commercialization of Rice Production in Northern Thailand, 1900–1981. PhD diss., Department of Anthropology, Cornell University.

Anderson, Perry. 1974. *Passages from Antiquity to Feudalism.* London: New Left Books.

Anonymous. 1895. *An Englishman's Siamese Journals 1890–1893.* Bangkok: Siam Media International Books.

Aroonrat Wichienkhiew. 1976. Kaan wikhro sangkhom Chiang Mai samaj Ratanakosin ton ton tam ton chabap bajlaan naj phaak nya (An Analysis of Chiang Mai Society in the Ratanakosin Period based on Northern Thai Chronicles). Master's thesis, Chulalongkorn University, Bangkok, Thailand.

Bock, Carl. 1986/1884. *Temples and Elephants: Travels in Siam in 1881–1882.* Singapore: Oxford University Press.

Bowie, Katherine. 1980. In the Wake of the Lords: A Historical Perspective on the Role of Irrigation in the Political Economy of Northern Thailand. Master's thesis, Department of Anthropology, University of Chicago.

———. 1988. Peasant Perspectives on the Political Economy of the Northern Thai Kingdom of Chiang Mai in the Nineteenth Century: Implications for the Understanding of Peasant Political Expression. PhD diss., Department of Anthropology, University of Chicago.

———. 1992. "Unraveling the Myth of the Subsistence Economy: The Case of Textile Production in Nineteenth-Century Northern Thailand." *Journal of Asian Studies* 51(4): 797–823.

———. 1993. "Cloth and the Fabric of Northern Thai Society in the Nineteenth Century: From Peasants in Cotton to Lords in Silks." *American Ethnologist* 20(1):138–58.

———. 1996. "Slavery in Nineteenth-Century Northern Thailand: Archival Anecdotes and Village Voices." In *State Power and Culture in Thailand,* ed. Paul Durrenberger, 100–138. Southeast Asia Monograph Series, 44. New Haven, CT: Yale University Press.

———. 1998. "The Alchemy of Charity: Of Class and Buddhism in Northern Thailand." *American Anthropologist* 100(2):469–81.

———. 2000. "Ethnic Heterogeneity, Elephants and the State in the Nineteenth Century Lannathai Kingdoms of Northern Thailand." In *Civility and Savagery: The Differentiation of Peoples within the Tai-speaking Polities of Southeast Asia,* ed. Andrew Turton, 330–48. London: Curzon Press.

Bowring, John. 1969/1857. *The Kingdom and People of Siam*. Introduction by David Wyatt. 2 vols. Kuala Lumpur: Oxford University Press.

Bristowe, W. S. 1976. *Louis and the King of Siam*. London: Chatto and Windus.

Bunnag, Tej. 1977. *The Provincial Administration of Siam, 1892–1915*. Kuala Lumpur: Oxford University Press.

Chatthip Nartsupha and Suthy Prasartset. 1978. *The Political Economy of Siam, 1910–1932*. Bangkok: Social Science Association of Thailand.

Cohen, Paul T. 1981. The Politics of Economic Development in Northern Thailand, 1967–1978. PhD diss., London School of Economics and Political Science, University of London.

Colquhoun, Archibald Ross. 1885. *Amongst the Shans*. London: Field and Tuer.

Dodd, William Clifton. 1923. *The Tai Race: Elder Brother of the Chinese*. Cedar Rapids, IA: Torch Press.

Edwardes, D. J. 1875. *Journey to Chiang Mai*. MS, Foreign Office Series no. 69, vol. 62. Public Records Office, London, June 17.

Freeman, John H. 1910. *An Oriental Land of the Free*. Philadelphia: Westminster Press.

Geertz, Clifford. 1980. *Negara: The Theatre State in Nineteenth-Century Bali*. Princeton, NJ: Princeton University Press.

Hallett, Holt S. 1890. *A Thousand Miles on an Elephant in the Shan States*. Edinburgh: William Blackwood and Sons.

Hildebrand, A. H. 1875. *Report on Special Mission to Chiengmai*. MS, Foreign Office Series no. 69, vol. 65. Public Records Office, London, February 15.

Mangrai, Sao Saimong. 1965. *The Shan States and the British Annexation*. Southeast Asia Data Paper #57, Southeast Asia Series. Ithaca: Cornell University.

McGilvary, Daniel. 1912. *A Half Century among the Siamese and the Lao*. New York: Fleming H. Revel.

Patel, M. V. 1990. Silver Challenge Cups and a Bronze Frog Drum: Colonialism and the Development of Teak Capitalism in Northern Thailand. Master's thesis, Department of Anthropology, Macquarie University, Sydney, Australia.

Pearson, Ross. 1999. A Political Economy Analysis of the Impact of Agrarian Change and Urbanisation on Communal Irrigation Systems in the Chiang Mai Valley, Northern Thailand. PhD diss., Department of Anthropology, Macquarie University, Sydney, Australia.

Ramsay, James Ansil. 1979. "Modernization and Reactionary Rebellions in Northern Siam." *Journal of Asian Studies* 38(2):283–97.

Richardson, David. 1829–1836. *Journal of Dr. Richardson.* MS, Manuscript Division, British Museum, London.

Satow, Ernest. 1885–1886. *Journal of Sir Ernest Satow.* MS, Public Record Office Series no. PRO30/33 (21/1), Public Records Office, London, England.

Smyth, H. Warington. 1898. *Five Years in Siam: From 1891–1896.* London: John Murray, Albemarle Street.

Tambiah, Stanley J. 1976. *World Conqueror and World Renouncer: A Study of Buddhism and Polity in Thailand against a Historical Background.* Cambridge, MA: Cambridge University Press.

Taylor, Hugh. 1888–1930. *Autobiography of Hugh Taylor.* MS, Phayab College Library, Chiang Mai, Thailand.

Wedel, Yuangrat Pattanapongse. 1982. *Modern Thai Radical Thought: The Siamization of Marxism and Its Theoretical Problems.* Thai Khadi Research Institute Research Series, 4. Bangkok: Thammasat University.

Wolf, Eric. 1999. *Envisioning Power: Ideologies of Dominance and Crisis.* Berkeley: University of California Press.

Younghusband, G. J. 1888. *Eighteen Hundred Miles on a Burmese Tat.* London: W. H. Allen.

12

Immigrant Labor in the New U.S. Economy: Anthropological Notes

Christian Zlolniski

In the last chapter of *Europe and the People without History*, Eric Wolf (1982) writes about the "new laborers," the different types of working classes that emerged along with the transformation of the capitalist economy since the late nineteenth century. Among these groups are immigrant workers who deploy their labor in industrialized countries. The rise of an industrial pattern in the late twentieth century that combines high technology in some phases of production with labor-intensive manual production in others would have led to a rising demand for unskilled labor largely met by new working populations, especially immigrants (Wolf 1982). According to Wolf, the task of the social scientist is to examine the conditions for the emergence and the distinctive characteristics of each of these working class groups by taking a holistic approach that locates workers not only in relation to their experience in the workplace but also in relation to the economic, social, and political links they maintain with their communities of origin and the larger society as a whole (1982).

In this chapter, I want to contribute to this goal by examining the example of unskilled immigrant workers in today's U.S. economy. Rather than focusing on the structural forces that have led to the demand for low-skilled immigrant labor in the new economy, I focus on how anthropologists who rely on ethnographic research methods can contribute to the understanding of the ways in which this group organizes its economic livelihood in the spheres of production, consumption and distribution, and social reproduction. My argument is that economic anthropology has developed some theoretical concepts that can be fruitfully applied to understand low-skilled immigrants in today's U.S. capitalist economy—yet the usefulness of these concepts relies on avoiding a structural and mechanical perspective that permeates much of the contemporary literature on immigrant labor. Instead, we should treat workers as social actors in their own right in order to understand the dynamic interplay between structure and agency in their lives. Only by doing so will we be able to identify the opportunities and limitations that they encounter as a social group in the struggle to improve their working and living conditions in today's restructured capitalist economy, one of the principal goals of Wolf's approach to anthropology.

For this task, I focus on three concepts that have a long tradition in the field of economic anthropology: social networks, informal economy, and household economy. These help us to understand the form in which low-skilled immigrants are incorporated as laborers into the larger economy as well as the ways in which immigrants themselves organize for the production and reproduction of the goods and services that make their lives possible. The chapter is based on the ethnographic research I carried out among Mexican immigrants employed as low-wage laborers in the advanced economy of Northern California's Silicon Valley, one of the most celebrated examples of today's so-called postindustrial economy.

First, I provide a brief background of the growth of the high-tech economy and the rise of low-skilled Mexican immigrant labor in Silicon Valley. Then I address each of the three concepts mentioned above, discussing the various forms in which they reveal both the location of immigrants in the larger economic context and how immigrants as social actors organize their livelihood in their everyday lives. My aim is to stimulate the discussion about how to bring traditional concerns and concepts of economic anthropology to the arena of contemporary topics such as transnational immigrant workers in advanced industrialized economies.

THE CONTEXT: MEXICAN IMMIGRANT WORKERS IN SILICON VALLEY

The new U.S. "knowledge-based" postindustrial economy apparently has no need for low-skilled labor. According to the orthodox, neoclassical labor economics model, if unskilled workers still migrate to the United States, it is because high poverty and/or unemployment rates push them to look for better options beyond their own countries. Yet modern industrialized economies like that of the United States have less and less room for this kind of labor (e.g., Borjas 1994). At the same time, however, some of the most advanced technological regions in the United States attract a large contingent of low-skilled immigrant laborers, especially from Mexico and Central America. This is the case of the high-tech industrial complex in Silicon Valley in Northern California. Internationally known as the heart of the high-technology industry, up until the 1950s, Santa Clara Valley—the core of Silicon Valley—was an important agricultural and cannery center. The region started a rapid transformation when the microelectronics industry developed in the late 1950s for military purposes, experiencing an even faster growth with the development of the market for personal computers in the 1970s (Saxenian 1985). The success of the new industry fueled a period of intense economic and demographic growth in the region.[1] It also brought enormous wealth to the region, which soon became the epicenter of the new, postindustrial U.S. economy. As the high-tech industry evolved, Silicon Valley attracted a large number of skilled immigrants (from India, Taiwan, China, and other countries) who make up an important proportion of the scientists, engineers, programmers, and other highly educated workers who live in the region. But the development of the high-tech industry also attracted thousands of low-skilled immigrants to fill the manual and service jobs that were being created at a rapid pace. In the 1960s and 1970s, the robust growth of the electronics industry created a large number of unskilled, low-wage manufacturing assembly occupations that were mostly filled by women workers (Green 1983), including immigrants from Mexico, China, Vietnam, Korea, and the Philippines (Hossfeld 1988). Later, in the 1980s and 1990s, as the pace of manufacturing employment growth declined while employment in the service sector expanded, a new wave of immigrants, especially from Mexico, arrived in the region and became the bulk of the labor force employed in the low-wage segment of the service sector (Blakely and Sullivan 1989).[2]

Indeed, the high-tech industry in Silicon Valley was one of the earliest manufacturing sectors that went global when, in the early 1960s, semiconductor manufacturers began shifting their assembly operations to Asia (Alarcón 2000; Hossfeld 1988). A second stage in this decentralization process started in the 1980s when large corporations subcontracted several service and maintenance jobs to independent local firms. Unable to send these jobs abroad, subcontracting allowed these companies to reduce labor costs and reduce the number of in-house semi- and unskilled workers. Illustrative of this trend were building-cleaning jobs that went from in-house occupations for custodial employees to subcontracted jobs for recent immigrants employed by independent cleaning firms (Mines and Avina 1992). Mexicans, and to a lesser extent Central American workers, become the bulk of the workforce employed in this industry, contributing to the growth of unskilled labor migration to the region in the 1980s and 1990s.[3]

But how were these new laborers incorporated into the advanced, modern labor market economy of Silicon Valley? What does economic anthropology, whose theoretical tools are often developed from case studies in less industrialized economies, have to say about the modes in which contemporary immigrant workers are inserted into the larger economic context of complex industrialized societies? And how can such tools be used to illuminate the forms in which low-income immigrant workers organize their economic lives in the realms of production, consumption, and social reproduction traditionally studied by economic anthropologists?

SOCIAL NETWORKS AND THE ORGANIZATION OF PRODUCTION OF IMMIGRANT LABOR

The concept of social networks has an important tradition in the anthropology of complex societies. The concept stems from Barnes and Botts' studies on complex societies, which showed the important but often neglected role of personal interactions in social relations in industrialized societies dominated by market economies (Narotzky 1997). Networks are also a useful analytical instrument in economic anthropology for the study of the circulation of goods, services, and information in Western industrial societies, as well as for understanding how the information leading to the effective constitution of a labor market circulates (Narotzky 1997). In the field of immigration studies, the study of social networks is regarded as essential to explain both the development and consolidation of international labor migration, and the social ties that allow immigrant workers to find jobs, housing, and material and emotional support as they arrive to the new countries where they sell their labor (Massey et al. 1987).

In a context of today's restructured U.S. economy where labor subcontracting has replaced in-firm departments as a means for labor recruitment in many industries, the role of social networks is crucial to explain the process of labor recruitment and control (Narotzky 1997). This is clear in the Silicon Valley where most high-tech firms rely on independent contractors to have access to an abundant and flexible pool of immigrant labor for unskilled and semiskilled parts of the production process. A case in point is the building-cleaning industry in the region where independent contractors connected to immigrant workers by kinship, village, and social ties serve as brokers between large high-tech firms and undocumented immigrants employed as a cheap and flexible source for janitorial work. Social networks based on kinship, friendship, and *paisanaje* are the main mechanisms for labor recruitment and organization of immigrant workers in the building-cleaning industry in the region.

In the late 1980s, Sonix, one of the largest high-tech companies in Silicon Valley, replaced its former in-house custodial employees by subcontracted Mexican workers employed with a dozen small nonunion cleaning companies, some of which were formed by former custodial workers with social ties to the Mexican immigrant community. From the perspective of Sonix management, the advantages of using immigrant labor were not confined to economic factors alone (lower labor and operating costs) but also to the ability to implement a flexible organization of cleaning work in the workplace that critically depended on optimizing the social and cultural resources of immigrant workers' networks. Sonix management especially valued Mexican janitors' ability to send relatives or friends to substitute for them when they were sick or quit their jobs, the willingness to change their work routines, and the availability to work overtime with short notice. Rather than an obstacle to an efficient organization of the work process, Sonix managers saw Mexican workers' social and cultural traditions and values as valuable assets that, if wisely used, could help enhancing labor flexibility and productivity in the workplace. Summarizing the advantages of employing subcontracted Mexican workers, the head of Sonix maintenance division explained,

> We prefer working with small janitorial companies because they allow for more flexibility and better service, as for example when we request a non-scheduled service and have janitors respond promptly.... They are managed by their own boss who normally is on the site, which makes communication between us and these companies very easy, and which leads to a very good service. . . . [With these companies] we have instant service.

SOCIAL NETWORKS AND RESISTANCE

While the use of immigrants' networks as mechanisms for labor recruitment and control has been well documented (e.g., Durand 1998; Wells 1996), the way in which immigrants themselves use social networks to organize diverse forms of labor resistance has received comparatively little attention. The recruitment of immigrant workers through social networks in industries like building cleaning in Silicon Valley has also opened new possibilities for the organization of immigrants into labor unions as a form of resistance. The social organization and tactics of the Justice for Janitors campaign conducted by Service Employees International Union Local 1877 in Silicon Valley in the 1990s illustrate this point. Often coming from the same villages and regions in central and western Mexico, and related by kinship and friendship ties, immigrant janitors in the region built a web of social networks that facilitated the recruitment of members for the union's cause.

In 1992, after several years of working for a nonunion cleaning company subcontracted by Sonix, a group of Mexican janitors decided to contact Local 1877, the union that represents cleaning workers in the region, so that they could have some leverage in dealing with their employer. Shortly afterwards, about a dozen of these workers started to mobilize to gather the support of their peers. Being related by kinship and village-neighbor ties, these workers used the same network connections through which they obtained their jobs to build support for the union. The fact that many employees of this cleaning company were related by kinship and village ties facilitated this process and led to a rapid organization of workers, replacing traditional and more individualistic tactics of union recruitment. Likewise, the fact that many janitors often live in the same neighborhoods and/or extended households facilitated this recruitment process, despite the spatial isolation of janitors into numerous suburbs in Silicon Valley where more traditional tactics of union membership recruitment would have been difficult to implement (Fisk, Mitchell, and Erickson 2000).

Like employers of immigrant workers, the union also sought to mobilize workers' social ties to its advantage. For example, at a certain point into the campaign, Local 1877 decided to sponsor a soccer team formed by a group of janitors at Sonix who came from the same small rural village in the Mexican state of Michoacan and who were among the most vocal leaders of the union's cause. This team was officially registered in the region's soccer league under the name of this town, and its original founder and captain was one of the workers who first reached the union for its support. Once the union organizers realized that many of the workers they were trying to organize came from this and other neighboring villages, they decided to sponsor this soccer team as a form of cultivating the trust of other workers, which is a necessary ingredient for the success of this type of union campaign. In doing so, they were mobilizing the same social resources for janitors' union organization that employers and subcontractors had used in the past to recruit cleaning workers for Sonix.

Rather than a system of labor recruitment of the past doomed to disappear in the context of today's highly industrialized U.S. economy dominated by impersonal labor markets, the growth of labor subcontracting in regions like Silicon Valley demonstrates the centrality of social networks as informal mechanisms for both labor recruitment and collective forms of resistance. Indeed, as recent studies have shown, the unionization of thousands of immigrant workers in several industries in California in the recent past has been largely facilitated by the mobilization of the web of social connections upon which the labor forces in these industries is organized (Milkman 2000). Anthropologists with long experience in studying the economic and social value of networks in different economic and cultural contexts are best prepared to address the renovated role played by such networks in the labor market of the restructured capitalist economy in advanced industrialized countries.

THE INFORMAL ECONOMY AND IMMIGRANT LABOR

Closely related to the notion of social networks is the concept of informal economy that employs immigrant labor. The concept of the informal economy has been recognized as one of the most important contributions of anthropology to the study of the organization of the economy in state-level societies, particularly in industrialized societies and the urban sectors of developing countries (Halperin 1994). Brought to prominence by Keith Hart's work in Ghana (1973) to highlight the employment characteristics of workers who made a living outside the formal economic sector either as self-employed or casual workers, the informal economy concept soon gained currency beyond the realm of anthropology. In the 1980s, Marxist-oriented sociologists and social scientists borrowed the concept to explain the articulation of immigrant workers to the modern capitalist economy in advanced industrialized countries (Castells and Portes 1989; Sassen 1988). Saskia Sassen, for example, argued that

the de-skilling of the labor process along with the expansion of the service
economy and demand of personal services has led to a rapid growth of sweat-
shops, industrial homework, and different forms of labor subcontracting in industrialized countries that connect the most dynamic sectors of the economy
with large pools of unskilled immigrant workers in the informal sector (Sassen
and Smith 1992; Sassen 1988). In the hands of structuralist-oriented scholars,
however, the analysis of the informal economy has become rather static and
mechanical, losing the rich ethnographic baseline that, in the past, allowed anthropologists to discuss the logic that informal economic activities had for
workers themselves as economic actors.

Economic restructuring and the growth of labor subcontracting at the core
of the most advanced industrialized economies thus reveal the currency of the
informal economy concept well beyond the original context for which anthropologists first coined it. Here I want to highlight two particular aspects of the
informal economy in the Silicon Valley region where I conducted my ethnographic research. The first refers to the different forms in which labor subcontracting that operates on the basis of immigrants' kin and social networks
opens the door for a variety of informal labor arrangements. The building-
cleaning industry often uses unpaid family labor not included in the official
employment statistics. Because this industry largely relies on immigrants' networks as a system for labor recruitment, it facilitates the organization of the
work process around family and kin groups that often include the use of informal "family help" for jobs that otherwise would appear as within the confines of the formal economy.

A case in point is Building Service Systems, a large building-cleaning firm
with several contracts in this region. Among the numerous employees of this
firm are several members of Silvia's family. A fifty-five-year-old woman from
a small rural village in the state of Guanajuato, one of the Mexican regions
with long migratory tradition to the United States, Silvia lived in an extended
family household composed of two nuclear families formed by her oldest children, and her two unmarried children in their teens in a low-income urban
barrio in the Silicon Valley in San Jose. The principal, although not only,
source of income in this family were the wages that she and three other adult
members earned working as janitors for Building Service System. Silvia's family functioned as a single working crew in charge of cleaning several office
buildings in the nearby city of Fremont that have contracts with this company,

including a corporate law firm, a real estate company, a physician's office, an insurance company, and the headquarters of a California politician. In addition to these four family members formally employed as janitors by Building Service System, three other members would often work as "family help" in this crew. This often served to help Silvia, the oldest member of the crew, to complete her part of the job as well as to speed the whole cleaning process so that the strongest family members could take a second janitorial job in a different company. I found this type of family labor arrangements common among many Mexican immigrants employed as janitors in San Jose, as it served to optimize the use of family labor and the opportunities to generate an extra income. Employers benefit from using unpaid family labor, their clients enjoy access to a large and cheap supply of immigrant labor without the legal risks of directly employing undocumented and/or child labor, while immigrant workers' themselves use these informal arrangements to provide a supplemental income to the low wages they earn in low-skilled formal occupations.

THE INFORMAL ECONOMY AS ARENA OF RESISTANCE

Some Mexican immigrants use the informal economy as an employment alternative to labor exploitation in the formal sector by working as self-employed or casual employees. These Mexican workers value the flexibility, greater autonomy, and potential earnings offered by informal occupations as compared to employment in low-wage formal jobs. Arturo is a twenty-year-old Mexican immigrant from Puebla who migrated to San Jose in 1986 with his wife. He first worked as a janitor at $5 an hour in a formal cleaning company. After eight months, he decided to quit his job because he felt the work was hard, he resented his supervisor's treatment, and did not like to work in night shifts. His brother, who himself started working as a Popsicle vendor, convinced him to give it a try. In 1987 Arturo started working as a Popsicle street vendor for a local factory that used "self-employed" Mexican workers like him to sell its products. There is no formal agreement between the company and the vendors, nor do the latter pay any taxes on their profits, which they receive in cash. Most of the vendors are undocumented Mexican workers for whom this work represents their first job and an opportunity to enter the labor market. For others like Arturo, it constitutes an alternative and relatively stable source of employment. Arturo works normally from 11 A.M. to 7 P.M., selling Popsicles in some of the major Mexican urban enclaves in town. In

1992, he was earning \$30–\$40 a day, although his earnings were considerably higher in the summer season when he could make as much as \$80 a day. Despite the seasonal variations in his earnings, Arturo prefers this occupation to his former job as a janitor. He feels more independent and can determine his own schedule. He values not being under the direct control of a supervisor, and he makes about the same money as working in a regular unskilled job, while in the summer he earns considerably more. Like other immigrants who prefer to work in the informal sector rather than in minimum-wage jobs in the formal economy, he is willing to trade the risk of irregular earnings for the greater autonomy, work schedule flexibility, and independence from tight control management found in many occupations in the formal sector, especially among nonunion firms.

In most cases, however, working in the informal economy is a strategy to provide a supplement to family income generated in the formal economy rather than an alternative to work in the formal sector. In fact, the most common situation is that Mexican workers combine formal and informal occupations or move flexibly between formal and informal jobs. In the minds of many immigrant workers, unlike social scientists and policymakers, there is often little difference between the working conditions of low-paid formal and informal occupations, so they move between them in a rather dynamic manner depending on the specific circumstances and employment alternatives available at any given moment. In the context of advanced industrialized economies like Silicon Valley's, petty informal occupations are not marginal survival jobs created by unskilled immigrants who cannot find jobs in the formal sector. Rather, low wages and the harsh working conditions associated with unskilled formal occupations in which most immigrants are employed fuel the expansion of informal economic activities as either supplements or alternative sources of income for this segment of the working class.

THE HOUSEHOLD ECONOMY OF IMMIGRANT WORKERS

The household economy occupies a central place in the field of economic anthropology (Wilk 1989; Halperin 1994). For one thing, anthropologists have shown that it is one of the social institutions that most readily reflects and reacts to large-scale changes in the economy, often producing in turn important economic and demographic effects on a large scale. The household is also where people often mix and pool all kinds of income (Wilk 1989), and a good avenue to study issues of gender and generation conflict and inequality (Wolf 1992; Dwyer and Bruce 1988). In the anthropological literature on international migration, the household also represents a central unit of analysis (Kearney 1986), because it is this social institution—rather than the individual, as proposed by neoclassical economists—that is the principal arena where decisions regarding migration and the allocation of family labor take place.

The household economy also constitutes a heuristic tool to illuminate the forms in which low-income immigrant workers organize their economic lives in the realms of production and consumption. First, because of low wages and unstable employment, most Mexican workers live in different types of extended households, often in crowded conditions with several families sharing small apartments or single-family homes. These include extended family households composed of a simple nuclear family core and other kin, multiple family households containing two or more simple families, and nonfamilial family households comprising siblings and/or nonrelated roommates, frequently fellow villagers.[4] These households experience frequent changes in their composition and structure; what today is an extended family household, tomorrow may be a simple (nuclear) family household, and yet, in a few months, may become a multiple family household with the corresponding changes in internal budget arrangements. These transformations often respond to sudden and unexpected changes in the employment and economic fortunes of household, rather than changes in the life-cycle of the family. The household becomes a precise instrument to register the ups and downs of its members in the labor market. In fact, one of the most complicated tasks I encountered as an ethnographer in San Jose was to keep an accurate record of the numerous and rapid changes in the size and composition of the households of my informants.

As in the case of other working-poor groups studied by urban anthropologists, Mexican workers' households in Silicon Valley are also characterized by a great deal of income pooling and sharing. Housing (rent) and other basic living expenses such as food and utility bills are often shared by the members of these households, taking advantage of economies of scale—which explains their large size. Yet there is no single model of income pooling among Mexican immigrant families. In fact, rather than being the norm, the model of generalized reciprocity and income pooling represents just one of the numerous economic arrangements that can be found among Mexican immigrants' households. There are a large variety of budget arrangements, from open sharing and generalized reciprocity to minimum sharing and independent (nuclear family or single individual) budgets. As anthropologists have shown for other economic and cultural contexts (Wilk 1989), households that look similar in terms of size, money, and allocation of patterns (Roldan 1988) and structure may have rather different internal economic arrangements. Such arrangements are important because they are often associated with internal economic stratification among members of the same household along gender and immigration status lines. For example, undocumented immigrants, especially women, often occupy the most precarious and vulnerable economic position within extended households. Moreover, while in many households income pooling was the norm, in other cases pooling was used only to cover housing expenses, with members maintaining separate budgets for the rest of their needs, often with marked differences in their corresponding economic status and consumption levels.[5]

Informal economic activities centered on the household that rely on family labor are also critical to meet the consumption demands of low-income workers by producing supplemental income. These activities include the production and sale of homemade food items, child-care services, as well as selling a large variety of goods such as beauty products, household appliances, and candies. These activities are usually organized and coordinated by women, often working mothers, who combine them with child rearing and other household maintenance tasks. For example, several Mexican women I met in San Jose, in addition to their regular jobs, were providing child-care services at home to people who live outside the community, an activity that often involved the work of several family members, including their own children, so that they could go to work and attend to other household chores. In most cases, Mexican women use their kin and neighborhood social ties to recruit clients for their informal businesses. Thus, livelihood is deeply embedded in kinship and community, with kin and other social networks being mobilized as valuable resources for economic purposes to the extent that the distinction between social and economic relations within this immigrant community becomes rather blurred. Low-income immigrants cannot afford to maintain social relations for emotional and personal purposes alone while obtaining their livelihood from wage work in an independent economic sphere. Rather, in addition to wage work in the formal economy, they also have to use their kinship and social ties as economic resources to help them raise additional income in the informal sector.[6]

EXTENDED HOUSEHOLDS AS BASTIONS OF RESISTANCE

In the context of unstable and low-paid jobs that, by U.S. standards, are harsh (the case for most Mexican immigrants employed in San Jose), extended family households also serve as a refuge to those members who otherwise would have to endure such conditions. For example, it was not uncommon among the workers I met in my fieldwork to quit their jobs and look for better opportunities while relying on the help of kin members of their extended families. Thus, extended families with multiple wage earners often serve as bastions of resistance and refuge from a rather hostile environment. The degree, however, to which extended households serve as arenas of resistance with respect to the outside world depends on their internal economic arrangements: the more generalized reciprocity there is, the more often their members can use the household in this way. In those cases where there is little income sharing and strong internal household stratification, the situation can be the reverse: the most vulnerable members—usually working mothers— find in the external world (friendship ties, local government agencies, and nongovernment institutions) a relief from exploitative relationships within the household. It is thus essential to do a disaggregated analysis of immigrant laborers' households to move beyond the flat image of the general reciprocity, income-pooling model to a more nuanced portrait of the varied economic and social family arrangements by which these workers organize their daily livelihood in the context of modern urban economies like Silicon Valley.

CONCLUSION

Mexican and other Latino immigrants in regions like the Silicon Valley have become an important segment of a transformed urban working class in the restructured U.S. economy over the past two decades. The expansion of Mexican immigrant workers (many of them peasants from rural villages in central and western Mexico, others former rural-urban migrants with a proletarian background) in urban Silicon Valley, the heart of the new U.S. high-tech economy, seems to confirm Eric Wolf's idea that capitalism does not produce a single and uniform working class, but constantly recreates a variety of social classes of workers with different modes of insertion in the labor market (Wolf

1982; Palerm 2000). In this context, economic anthropologists are well suited to examine the varied ways in which different social groups organize their livelihoods and social reproduction. In doing so, we need to go beyond the wage nexus that links immigrants to their employers, often studied by neoclassical economists. Instead we have to take a broader holistic perspective that looks at the varied economic, social, cultural, and political resources and strategies used by immigrants to make a living in the local and transnational context in which their everyday lives take place. In doing so we can best understand both the range of options and the limits created by the larger economy and political context with respect to this particular group of workers as well as the active forms in which they respond to them.

In this chapter, I have argued that some concepts with an important tradition in the field of economic anthropology—social networks, informal economy, and household economy—can be fruitful to advance in this task. Together, these concepts help to illuminate the diverse forms in which immigrant workers go about the production and reproduction of the material goods and services that make their lives possible in a larger context in which their labor is inserted and where they are institutionally excluded by the state from social and economic benefits to which other social groups of the working class are entitled. First, networks based on kinship, friendship, and village ties often studied by anthropologists in other-than-Western market economies are crucial for understanding not only the recruitment and control of immigrant labor in important sectors of today's U.S. economy but also the social basis for the organization of resistance into labor unions where immigrant workers constitute the bulk of the membership. Likewise, the economic and social arrangements behind the expansion of the informal economy in places like Silicon Valley show the importance of going beyond impersonal, formal mechanisms for labor recruitment. Ethnographic case studies of the informal economy help us to understand how large companies in the formal economy are articulated with immigrant labor employed through subcontracting schemes, as well as the microtactics by which immigrants seek to resist labor exploitation in the formal economy and provide for their livelihoods. Finally, the household economy of Mexican workers reveals that it is a crucial institution for the organization of subsistence and social reproduction. Extended households are not the product of traditional social and cultural values immigrants bring with them, but the contemporary product of modern industrialized economies in which immigrants are inserted as a supply of cheap and flexible labor. At the same time, extended households follow the principles of generated and balanced reciprocity, and often serve as the bastions of resistance in the context of labor exploitation in the larger society.

If economic anthropology is to remain relevant in the study of today's global economy, it has to engage the fine-grained analysis of the diverse, heterogeneous effect of these global forces in particular localities affected by them, including transnational immigrant workers in advanced industrialized countries like the United States. We need, in short, to bring economic anthropology and its rich theoretical tradition back home to the study of contemporary immigrant workers embedded in global economic forces.

NOTES

1. High-tech employment alone accounted for 150,000 new jobs between 1975 and 1990 (Saxenian 1994). This explosive economic development was the major factor behind an equally impressive demographic growth: just between 1960 and 1980, the population of Santa Clara County almost doubled (from 658,700 to 1,265,200 people). And by the early 1990s, there were 1,497,577 people living in this former agricultural region (U.S. Department of Commerce 1991).

2. According to a study conducted by Blakely and Sullivan (1989), for example, by the mid-1980s Latinos, many of them Mexican immigrants, held almost 80 percent of the clerical and operating jobs in the low-wage service sector.

3. Between 1965 and 1990, for example, the demand for janitors in the Santa Clara Valley grew fivefold (Mines and Avina 1992).

4. The different subtypes found within each of these categories among Mexican immigrants in the United States have been explored in detail by Leo Chavez (1985, 1990, 1992).

5. For example, in one of the multiple family households I studied in San Jose composed of four nuclear families and a single mother living in a two-bedroom apartment, income pooling was used for covering only rent expenses, while all other expenses (food, phone bills, medical expenses, etc.) were independently handled by each of the different families in the household. Reflecting this situation was the presence of five refrigerators in the apartment, each belonging to one of the five social groups that made up this household.

6. For an analysis of the commodification of social relations among Central American immigrants in suburban New York, see Mahler (1995).

REFERENCES

Alarcón, Rafael. 2000. "Skilled Immigrants and Cerebreros: Foreign-Born Engineers and Scientists in the High-Technology Industry of Silicon Valley." In *Immigration Research for a New Century: Multidisciplinary Perspectives,* ed. Nancy Foner, Ruben Rumbaut, and Steven J. Gold, 301–21. New York: Russell Sage Foundation.

Blakely, Edward, and Susan Sullivan. 1989. The Latino Workforce in Santa Clara County: The Dilemmas of High Technology Change on a Minority Population. Study commissioned by the Latino Issues Forum of Santa Clara County, California.

Borjas, George J. 1994. "The Economics of Immigration." *Journal of Economic Literature* 32 (December): 1667–1717.

Castells, Manuel, and Alejandro Portes. 1989. "World Underneath: The Origins, Dynamics and Effects of the Informal Economy." In *The Informal Economy: Studies in Advanced and Less Developed Countries,* ed. Alejandro Portes, Manuel Castells, and Lauren A. Benton, 11–37. Baltimore, MD: Johns Hopkins University Press.

Chavez, Leo. 1985. "Households, Migration and Labor Market Participation: The Adaptation of Mexicans to Life in the United States." *Urban Anthropology* 14:4.

———. 1990. "Coresidence and Resistance: Strategies for Survival among Undocumented Mexicans and Central Americans in the United States." *Urban Anthropology* 19:31–61.

———. 1992. *Shadowed Lives: Undocumented Immigrants in American Society.* Fort Worth, TX: Harcourt Brace Jovanovich.

Durand, Jorge. 1998. *Política, Modelos y Patron Migratorio: El Trabajo y los Trabajadores Mexicanos en Estados Unidos. Cuadernos del Centro.* San Luis Potosí, México: El Colegio de San Luis.

Dwyer, Daisy, and Judith Bruce, eds. 1988. *A Home Divided: Women and Income in the Third World.* Stanford, CA: Stanford University Press.

Fisk, Catherine L., Daniel J. Mitchell, and Christopher L. Erickson, eds. 2000. "Union Representation of Immigrant Janitors in Southern California: Economic and Legal Challenges." In *Organizing Immigrants: The Challenge for Unions in Contemporary California,* ed. Ruth Milkman, 199–224. Ithaca, NY: Cornell University Press.

Green, Susan. 1983. "Silicon Valley's Women Workers: A Theoretical Analysis of Sex-Segregation in the Electronics Industry Labor." In *Women, Men, and the International Division of Labor,* ed. J. Nash and M. Fernández-Kelly, 273–331. Albany: State University of New York Press.

Halperin, Rhoda H. 1994. *Cultural Economies: Past and Present.* Austin: University of Texas Press.

Hart, Keith. 1973. "Informal Economic Opportunities and Urban Employment in Ghana." *Journal of Modern African Studies* 11(1): 61–89.

Hossfeld, Karen. 1988. Divisions of Labor, Divisions of Lives: Immigrant Women Workers in Silicon Valley. PhD diss., Department of Sociology, University of California, Santa Cruz.

Kearney, Michael. 1986. "From the Invisible Hand to Visible Feet: Anthropological Studies of Migration and Development." *Annual Review of Anthropology* 15:331–61.

Mahler, Sarah. 1995. *American Dreaming: Immigrant Life on the Margins.* Princeton, NJ: Princeton University Press.

Massey, Douglas, et al. 1987. *Return to Aztlan: The Social Process of International Migration from Western Mexico.* Berkeley: University of California Press.

Milkman, Ruth, ed. 2000. *Organizing Immigrants: The Challenge for Unions in Contemporary California.* Ithaca, NY: Cornell University Press.

Mines, Richard, and Jeffrey Avina. 1992. "Immigrants and Labor Standards: The Case of California Janitors." In *U.S.-Mexico Relations: Labor Market Interdependence,* ed. J. Bustamante, C. Reynolds, and R. Hinojosa-Ojeda, 429–48. Stanford, CA: Stanford University Press.

Narotzky, Susana. 1997. *New Directions in Economic Anthropology.* Chicago: Pluto Press.

Palerm, Juan Vicente. 2000. "Las Nuevas Comunidades Mexicanas en los Espacios Rurales de los Estados Unidos de América, a Propósito de una Reflexión del Quehacer Antropológico." In *La Diversidad Intelectual, Ángel Palerm in Memoriam,* ed. Virginia García Acosta, 63–112. México D.F., México: Ciesas.

Roldan, Martha. 1988. "Renegotiating the Marital Contract: Intrahousehold Patterns of Money Allocation and Women's Subordination Among Domestic Outworkers in Mexico City." In *A Home Divided: Women and Income in the Third World,* ed. Daisy Dwyer and Judith Bruce, 229–47. Stanford, CA: Stanford University Press.

Sassen, Saskia. 1988. *The Mobility of Labor and Capital: A Study in International Investment and Labor Flow.* Cambridge: Cambridge University Press.

Sassen, Saskia, and Robert C. Smith. 1992. "Post-Industrial Growth and Economic Reorganization: Their Impact on Immigration Employment." In *U.S.-Mexico Relations: Labor Market Interdependence,* ed. J. Bustamante, C. Reynolds, and R. Hinojosa-Ojeda, 372–93. Stanford, CA: Stanford University Press.

Saxenian, AnnaLee. 1985. "Silicon Valley and Route 128: Regional Prototypes or Historic Exceptions?" In *High Technology, Space, and Society*, ed. M. Castells, 81–105. Beverly Hills, CA: Sage.

———. 1994. *Regional Advantage: Culture and Competition in Silicon Valley and Route 128*. Cambridge, MA: Harvard University Press.

U.S. Department of Commerce, Economics and Statistics Administration, Bureau of the Census. 1991. *1990 Census of Population and Housing, Summary Population and Housing Characteristics, California*. Washington, DC: U.S. Government Printing Office, 1990 CPH-1-6.

Wells, Miriam J. 1996. *Strawberry Fields: Politics, Class, and Work in California Agriculture*. Ithaca, NY: Cornell University Press.

Wilk, Richard R. 1989. *The Household Economy: Reconsidering the Domestic Mode of Production*. Boulder, CO: Westview Press.

Wolf, Diane L. 1992. *Factory Daughters: Gender, Household Dynamics, and Rural Industrialization in Java*. Berkeley: University of California Press.

Wolf, Eric. 1982. *Europe and the People without History*. Berkeley: California University Press.

Crossing the Border from Jalisco, Mexico: Network-Mediated Entry into Micro-Labor Enclaves

Tamar Diana Wilson

A vast body of literature concerned with transnational wage-labor migration to the United States has shown that such migration tends to be network mediated: people go where they have kin or friends (Bach 1978; Boyd 1989; Durand and Massey 1992; DuToit 1975; MacDonald and MacDonald 1964; Massey 1987; Massey et al. 1987; Massey 1999; Massey and Espinosa 1997; Mines 1981; Wilson 1992, 1993, 1994, 1998a; Uzzell 1976; and others). As Massey et al. (1987, 153–62) have pointed out, over time migrants tend to form "daughter communities" in the United States; however, initial destinations that appear to be emergent daughter communities may cease to remain strong poles of attraction to future immigrants, while over time newer destinations may become incorporated into the "transnational migrant circuit" (Rouse 1989, 1991).

There is, nonetheless, an emerging dispute in the migration literature about the validity of using the descriptive term "migration networks." Goss and Lindquist (1995) propose that the concept of "migrant institutions" be substituted for "migration networks," arguing that the latter lack explanatory power because they are unable to explain how social networks become converted into migration networks. Defining institutions as "sets of rules and resources which govern the actions and interactions of agents who operate within them" (1995, 334), they suggest that "what has previously been identified as migrant networks be conceived as migrant institutions that articulate, in a nonfunctionalist way, the individual migrant and the global economy,

'stretching' social relations across time and space to bring together the potential migrant and the overseas employer" (1995, 335). The "social structure" of
immigration is often referred to when the "social relations" of immigration
would be a more valuable concept.

There are a number of conceptual problems involved in substituting "migrant institutions" for "migrant networks" or "migration networks" based on
social/kinship networks. First, it involves a reification of certain patently fluid
phenomena into an encapsulating structure that obfuscates the agency un-
derscored in the network concept. "Institution" implies a solidification that is
not found in the actual options of tapping network aid from various people
at various times in different geographical destinations. Second, and related to
the first point, "institution" implies a more static existence than is found in the
dynamism and elasticity of immigration networks. Over time networks expand to include new members; network members who begin their migratory
careers in one employment or in one locale may change jobs or move to other
places, widening the labor market options and geographical space through
which members may move with the expectation of obtaining aid from friends
or kin (DuToit 1975, 1990).

In this regard, migration networks constitute a form of "social capital" for
immigrants (Massey and Espinosa 1997; Massey et al. 1994, 1987; Gold 1994;
Portes 1995; Sassen 1995; Waldinger 1994, 1995; Wilson 1998a) enabling them
to find jobs while native-born workers may often remain unemployed. Census data and ethnographic research have shown that Latino immigrants, especially but not exclusively Mexican immigrants, are overwhelmingly
concentrated in the secondary sector or the restructured "subordinated primary sector" of the U.S. labor market, however (see Barrera 1979; Burawoy
1975; Chavez 1985; Chavez and Flores 1988; Gómez-Quiñones 1981; Hayes-
Bautista, Schink, and Chapa 1990; Jones 1995; Morawska 1990; Portes and
Bach 1985; Rodríguez 1987; Rouse 1991; Sassen and Smith 1992; Sassen-Koob
1981; Sassen 1985; Soja 1991; and others). Such menial jobs include farmwork, nonunionized or deunionized factory and restaurant work, and janitorial and other services. Latino immigrants are also overrepresented in the
informalized labor market, including jobs such as construction cleanup, clan-
destine garment manufacturing, and home-working, and in informal sector
activities such as street vending (Balmori 1983; Long 1987; Maram 1980;
Martí 1993; Portes 1983; Sassen 1990; and others). Commonly, initial work is

found through the same kin and friends who helped facilitate the move from origin to destination(s).

Social capital is seen as a property of networks. But does network-mediated migration into a particular job site or job type represent social capital for the employer, as Gold's article suggests, or for the worker? Or for both? The employer is ensured a workforce, the worker a job, however disagreeable the labor process involved and however inadequate the wages may be. The question becomes, with a "better," more expansive network, would access to more agreeable, better paying jobs be facilitated? Or do Mexican immigrants' networks always lead into the secondary sector of "dirty work?"

Functionalists tend to see positive effects for immigrants; structuralists have focused on the negative effects (Jones 1995). The effects of immigration are considered positive in that the primary goal of the wage-labor migrant (viz., finding employment) is secured. The effects are considered negative in that network recruitment may increase worker's vulnerability to exploitative employers. Whether hyperexploitability of workers need always result, given the multilocality of networks, will be broached in the concluding section.

Network-mediated recruitment of Mexican laborers has existed since Mexican immigrants, documented or undocumented, have been incorporated into the U.S. labor force. For example, since early in this century, Michigan sugar beet growers have depended on network recruitment by Mexican migrant workers to fulfill their farmworker quotas (Haney 1979). Stoddard (1976, 196) suggests that job placement of farmworkers through kin and friendship networks is one variable keeping the immigrant labor force docile; Mexican undocumented workers conform to exploitative labor requirements without protest or rebellion due to preexisting loyalties to relatives or friends—coworkers who recommended them for employment. It has also been suggested that networks facilitate the "super-exploitation" of members who feel obligated to superordinates who helped them through the maze of illegality involved in crossing the border and locating a job they hold only at risk (Heyman 1998).

This applies to immigrants, Latino or otherwise, who also locate jobs in urban centers through the aid of network members. Research on undocumented Central American and Mexican immigrants to Austin and San Antonio, Texas, revealed that new arrivals found work within days, due to network members' provision of information about available job openings (Browning and Rodríguez 1985, 286).

In tracing the jobs found by transnational immigrants from a village in Zacatecas, Mines (1981, 141–46) found that networks mediated entry into both
formal and informal sector jobs in rural and in urban areas in California.
Thus, in Santa Ana, the villagers worked in construction cleanup; in Los Angeles, in small dress shops in a subcontracting relationship with large manufacturers; in Watsonville, as strawberry sharecroppers; and in San Francisco,
in restaurant work. Entrepreneurs from this Mexican community have also set
up family factories in which cactus leaves are cut up and packaged; one, in Bell
Gardens, employed eighteen covillagers, paid on a piece-rate basis (Mines
1981, 146). Similarly, a community in the Los Altos region of Jalisco studied
by Cornelius (1991, 177) has emigrants working in Oregon orchards and
flower fields, in highway and bridge construction in Oklahoma City, in hotels
and restaurants in Palm Springs, and in services and light industry in the San
Francisco Bay area. As Massey and colleagues (1987) have documented, the
normative pattern is for a pioneering immigrant to find a job, perhaps rise in
rank from common laborer to foreman over the years, and begin to recruit
network members into job openings. Agricultural field foremen may even be
requested to form work groups as a condition of their being advanced to foreman status. Alternatively, once laborers from a certain source community are
hired, when there are job openings the employer often will ask them to recommend "friends" (which would include relatives).

In a study of immigrant workers in the New York City garment industry,
Waldinger (1985, 338) (a structuralist) found that network-mediated hiring
was functional for employers:

> To secure experienced sewing machine operators and skilled workers, employ-
> ers seek to mobilize the social networks among the workers already in their em-
> ploy. Network hiring serves two functions. It works as a predictive device in that
> employers use the attitudes and behavioral patterns of the existing workforce as
> a guide for screening potential recruits. It also acts as a mechanism of stabiliza-
> tion that implicates workers in the recruitment process, inducing them to screen
> out unqualified recruits and then exercise their own informal controls over be-
> havior in the workplace.

The value for employers of recruiting groups of undocumented immigrant
workers through networks has been elucidated by Rodríguez (1987, 21) in his
study of Central American immigrants in Houston:

An in-depth interview of a restaurant manager with experience in several restaurants in Houston revealed advantages that employers gain from employing a group of undocumented workers: an undocumented work group serves as recruiting means when additional workers are needed, as workers are anxious to find jobs for relatives, friends, or other household members; the social relations in the undocumented work group increase the efficiency of the labor process, as workers informally share tasks (this advantage increases with the homogeneity of the group, which reduces competition or conflict between workers); a work group with high national homogeneity performs the socialization of other workers.

Network-mediated migration into specific labor enclaves has also been found among other groups of undocumented workers such as Mayan Guatemalans in Houston (Hagan 1994) and Yucatecan Mayans in Dallas (Adler 2004); farmworkers from Mexico, Central America, Puerto Rico, and Haiti on the East and West Coasts of the United States (Griffin and Kissam 1995); and Brazilian immigrants to New York City (Margolis 1994). One fashionable Tex-Mex restaurant has employed as many as 200 Brazilians over the six-year period from 1985 to 1991 (Margolis 1994, 133). There is also network-mediated, word-of-mouth recruitment into call-cab driving, shoe shining, and construction work for men; into street vending, especially of books and foodstuffs for both men and women; and into the occupation of "go-go girl" in bars in New York, New Jersey, and on Long Island among Brazilian women. In Houston, more than 80 percent of Hagan's (1994) sample of Guatemalan Maya men worked for one retail supermarket chain; a pioneering immigrant who had found employment there had recruited them into jobs as maintenance and stockmen.[1]

Data I collected in a study of transnational wage-labor migration from a *rancho* (an unincorporated rural village) I call Los Arbores in Jalisco (Wilson 1992, 1993, 1994) show evidence of network-mediated migration into specific work sites and types of work, most belonging to the subordinated secondary labor market marked by seasonality, instability, and low wages.[2] Nonetheless, the multilocality of network members permitted immigrants to work in more than one geographical location and/or in more than one job, and over their migratory careers, many did. From a pool of sojourners working seasonally in agriculture, a few immigrants became "settlers," in that they remained for many years in Merced, California, where previously they had gone only seasonally to work in agriculture. Although the permanency through time of their status as Merced residents cannot be determined, 151 male heads of household interviewed in Los Arboles reported the following close relatives living in that town in 1989: four with sons, six with sisters, two with brothers. Most of those with close relatives in Merced have themselves worked in Merced. Of the thirty-six men who have worked in Merced three have sons there, five have sisters, and two have brothers living there. Other relatives resident in Merced in 1989, mentioned by both those who worked in Merced and those who didn't, include cousins, parent's siblings, parent's cousins, siblings' offspring, and wife's near and distant relatives.

The gradual rural to urban shift in destinations found by Massey and colleagues (1987) in their study of four communities in western Mexico and by Jones (1995) in his research on immigrants from Zacatecas and Coahuila is apparent as well among immigrants from Los Arboles. From a preponderance of agricultural fieldwork in various California, Arizona, and Texas towns during the Bracero Program period (1942–1965), immigrants after the 1970s tended to cluster in urban Los Angeles County or in Milwaukee.

For example, the first two men from Los Arboles who worked in Milwaukee were an *ejidatario*'s[3] son, whom I have called Juan Carlos, and his father's sister's son. They crossed together in 1973 with two friends from Los Arboles and an acquaintance from Guerrero. They first went to Chicago, Illinois, where Juan Carlos had first cousins and the man from Guerrero had close relatives, with whom they stayed. After several months in Chicago they moved on to Milwaukee, where siblings of Juan Carlos' Chicago-based cousins had relocated. Decades previously, in 1924, Juan Carlos' father had spent several months in Chicago, along with a brother; they worked in an electric light bulb and parts factory. Later, they moved on to Gary, Indiana, where they worked in a steel foundry. Notably, Juan Carlos' father and uncles were involved in armed conflict with the hired guns of local *hacendados* in the 1930s, which was marked by deaths on both sides. Although the *rancheros* reached their goal (viz., the establishment of the *ejido* portion of Los Arboles), killings in the Mexican countryside could, and still can, lead to cross-generational vendettas. One of Juan Carlos' father's brothers was killed during this conflict. Juan Carlos' uncles and aunts and their offspring moved permanently to Chicago shortly after this period of violence. Also pertinent is the fact that mother's and father's sisters would have little motivation to stay in Los Arboles, as only males were beneficiaries of the Agrarian Reform Law conferring *ejido* (individually tenured but unalienable) lands. If they married men from nearby *ranchos*, regional endogamy but *rancho* exogamy being common in the Los Arboles areas, their husbands would also have no claim on the lands being distributed from the hacienda on which Los Arboles had been located. Yet, as sisters of men who were involved in violence, their families would have been targets for revenge. From Chicago, parents' siblings' offspring probably moved on to Milwaukee to look for work, eventually becoming a bridgehead for cousins still resident in Los Arboles. Juan Carlos was one of these cousins. Two of Juan Carlos' brothers also came to work in Milwaukee, in the mid-1970s. Juan Carlos, on his four crossings to Milwaukee, and his two brothers, were accompanied, or joined in Milwaukee, by other relatives and friends from the *rancho*. Interestingly enough, Chicago never became a destination for male heads of household resident in Los Arboles. Only three have ever worked there, for several months, on their way to other destinations

Juan Carlos had previously crossed to work in the United States five times, three times under *bracero* contract to Arizona, California, and Texas in the 1950s, then in 1969 and 1971 to Los Angeles where he worked in a restaurant, without documents. After 1973, Juan Carlos continued to go to Milwaukee, working in a foundry in that city until the mid-1980s. He bought a house there in 1980 and his youngest daughter was born in Milwaukee. Due to mistreatment by an employer in California, in a temporary job there as a tractor driver, Juan Carlos decided not to return to the United States again. He sold his house in Milwaukee in 1985 and used the proceeds to buy a slaughterhouse in Guadalajara as well as land and cattle in Los Arboles. Five of his six sons and one of his three daughters continue living and working in Milwaukee, however. Given that land has become scarce in Los Arboles, it is quite possible that they will remain as permanent settlers within the United States. Juan Carlos' migratory career illustrates the multiplicity of geographical destinations and types of employment available to the potential migrant from a *rancho* with a multistranded migration network spread over various locations.

Concerning network-mediated migration into specific work sites or work types: Of the twenty-five men who have worked in Milwaukee, twenty-one (84 percent) worked in a foundry at some time while in that city and eighteen (72 percent) have worked only in foundries. All five men who had previously been employed as farmworkers in Merced, and who later crossed to Milwaukee, worked in foundries there.

Although network aid situated most Los Arboles men in foundries, members who found jobs elsewhere provided some other options. Migrants thus were enabled to leave one job for another, despite the fact that all of these jobs were in the secondary labor market. Clustering in certain types of jobs, and in specific work sites, did occur, however. Two of the total sample worked only in a tannery; one man began work in a foundry and later went to work in the tannery. One man moved from foundry work to employment in a chocolate factory in 1980. The wife of a man from Los Arboles had been working in this factory for two years previously and helped him get a job there. Two men worked exclusively in a repair shop, one as a solderer. One man was employed only in a restaurant.

All three of those who worked in tanneries found and held those jobs prior to 1975. No male heads of household interviewed on the *rancho* had crossed to Milwaukee prior to 1973, although Los Arboles–origin emigrants were present in Milwaukee by that time, suggesting a strong settlement process in that city in an earlier period. Of the total sample, 56 percent had gone to work in Milwaukee between 1973 and 1979 and 44 percent had gone to work there after 1980. Of the men who crossed for the first time to Milwaukee, or returned to that city after 1980, ten men (91 percent) had worked in a foundry at some point, and nine (82 percent) had worked exclusively in foundries.

The foundries were of diverse types: some alloying metals, some making car parts, some water pumps. Thus a particular type of foundry work was accessed, as well as specific work sites. Several of the men worked in more than one foundry. Friends and relatives advised newer immigrants of openings in the plants where they worked. In one case, a man whose parents had migrated into Los Arboles in the mid-1960s became a foreman in a water pump factory and successively placed five of his brothers there.

Notably, compared to the agricultural work force in Merced, the factory and foundry workforce in Milwaukee shows greater residential stability in their place of destination. As can be seen in figure 13.1, more people stayed greater lengths of time in Milwaukee on their first crossing to that city than those who went to Merced on their first crossing. Those who worked in Milwaukee stayed an average of twenty months, with the least time spent being four months, by someone who was deported, and the longest time, on first crossing, being forty-eight months (two cases).

On subsequent crossings, lengths of stay in Milwaukee were often greater: two men, for example, stayed five years on their second crossings. In Merced,

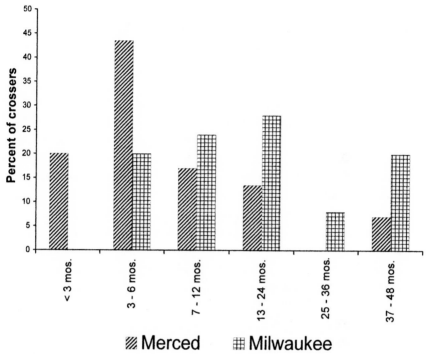

FIGURE 13.1
Immigrants' length of stay in Merced and Milwaukee

conversely, of the thirty men from whom information about their length of stay was obtained, the least time spent was one month (two cases), and the most time spent on any crossing was forty-eight months (one case). The average length of stay for men working in Merced, who continue to consider Los Arboles as their place of residence, was eleven months. Whereas only six men (20 percent) from among the Merced migrants stayed more than thirteen months, fourteen (56 percent) remained in Milwaukee for longer than thirteen months. Since agricultural work is seasonal, and obtaining full-time work means changing from one crop to another, certain crops being controlled by some companies and other crops by other companies, employment is less stable and subject to greater contingencies in Merced than it is in plants in Milwaukee, which accounts for the greater length of stay in the latter destination. Notably, the man who spent the longest time in Merced joined a brother's *compadre* who was a labor contractor.[4]

More Los Arboles male heads of household have relatives in Milwaukee than in Merced, as well, suggesting that local labor market conditions are a major factor in converting sojourners to settlers. Of the 151 male heads of household interviewed in Los Arboles, eight had brothers, three had sisters, and ten had both brothers and sisters residing in Milwaukee in 1989. Furthermore, fifteen had at least one son, one a daughter, and four both daughters and sons living in that city. For those who have worked in Milwaukee, the numbers are as follows: six have brothers, one a sister, five both brothers and sisters, and seven have sons living in Milwaukee. Besides these relatives, men who have worked in Milwaukee have reported joining mothers' and fathers' siblings and cousins, sisters' and brothers' sons, and wife's brothers, nephews, and cousins in that city. The availability of close relatives to join shows the greater network density in Milwaukee than in Merced (see figure 13.2). Thus, 36 percent of the male heads of household crossing to Milwaukee the first time joined close relatives (brothers) whereas only one person in the Merced sample (N = 36) joined a sibling.

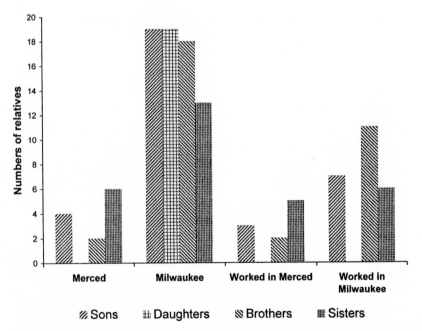

FIGURE 13.2
Density of networks in Merced and Milwaukee

Notably, of the five people crossing to Milwaukee prior to 1976, only one joined relatives (cousins); four joined friends. News of job opportunities in that city seem to have spread rapidly so that by 1976, all men going to Milwaukee had both distant *and* close relatives in that city. After 1976 only one man, who crossed with a number of friends and rented an apartment with them, did not join relatives at that destination. Thus Milwaukee's job opportunities acted as a magnet to pull in more network members from Los Arboles, as temporary, settled, or semisettled (long-term but eventually relocating) immigrants.

NEW AND FUTURE DESTINATIONS

Over time migration networks expand, often aided by the "strength of weak ties" (Granovetter 1973; Wilson 1998a), whereby acquaintances from other origins who congregate in the same places during their leisure time or work together (Massey et al. 1987) provide job information about locales and employment possibilities with which they are familiar. Once an immigrant from a specific source community accesses these locales and finds employment, they may become geographical nodal points for further network-mediated chain migration. Notably, new geographic locales accessed by male migrants may be mediated by female relatives, especially wife's relatives, when weak ties are converted to strong ties via marriage. Information about jobs in Massachusetts and Florida was obtained by Los Arboles immigrants through weak ties (i.e., through people not originally from the source community or region).[5] Nonetheless, over time, the placement in job sites in both states was facilitated by relatives among whom strong ties exist.

Migration of male household heads resident in Los Arboles to Florida and Massachusetts began in 1985. In 1985, the first male household head resident in Los Arboles crossed to Florida. There he joined two of his wife's brothers, whose origin was also Los Arboles, but who had been aided by their in-laws to find work there. These brothers-in-law helped him find work, first as a fieldhand, then in a plant nursery in Miami. He remained in Florida forty months. When he crossed the border again in 1988, now with amnesty, he returned to Miami to work in a nursery. A brother of his later joined him in Miami and was living there in 1989. In 1986 their father joined them in Miami and has worked in the plant nursery for several months each year since then.

Only two male household heads resident in Los Arboles in 1989 have worked in Massachusetts. Among five male household heads with relatives in Massachusetts, one had a sister, one a brother, one a brother and sister, one three of five sons, and one had one of five sons living in that state in 1989. The first man on record to work in Massachusetts was born in Los Arboles. While he was working in Milwaukee from 1986 to 1989, he and his wife went to visit his cousins in Westboro. There he worked in a pizza restaurant for two months before returning to his job in a foundry in Milwaukee.

The second man interviewed in Los Arboles who immigrated to work in Massachusetts was born on a nearby *rancho*. He married a woman from Los Arboles who has three brothers working in Westboro. He joined his wife's brothers there in 1988 and worked in a pizza restaurant. He plans to return to Massachusetts in the future: he feels one earns more money in Massachusetts than elsewhere in the United States. He crossed three times prior to going to Massachusetts, each time working in a restaurant, once each in Redondo Beach, Merced, and Lawndale, California. His wife's brothers are cousins of the man who left Milwaukee to work in Massachusetts. Thus, strong ties are pulling relatives into the same geographical location and into the same job type and even job site.

Notably, labor markets accessed have up to now been very limited in both Westboro, Massachusetts, where those interviewed all worked in pizza restaurants, and in Miami, Florida, where those interviewed worked in nurseries. If a wider selection of jobs can be tapped, both Miami and Westboro may attract more migrants from Los Arboles in the future, as friends and relatives have been or are now present in those cities, and may form new daughter communities.

DISCUSSION AND CONCLUSIONS

Networks facilitating migration may include members scattered in both the country of origin and of destination, and may even include members in two or more nations (Basch, Schiller, and Blanc 1994; Ho 1993; Uzzell 1976; Zabin and Hughes 1995). The establishment of friends or kin in one destination may lead to the expansion of the network to include destinations ever further afield. Rather than migrant "institutions," these must be seen as networks with a dynamic fueled by social relations and individual agency. In a study of Mixtec farmworkers from Oaxaca, Zabin and Hughes (1995) trace their early recruitment into farmwork in Sinaloa, Sonora, and Baja California to their expansion into California agricultural fields and Oregon berry picking. They argue (1995, 407) that Mixtec farmworkers employed in Baja California had greater access to information about work in the United States and more diverse networks to aid them in their transnational job search than did those Mixtecs who remained in Oaxaca. A number of men crossed with friends they had made while working in the Baja California fields. Thus, migration to one site may open up opportunities for migration to still other sites, as this chapter has tried to show in the case of transnational wage-labor immigrants from Los Arboles. Within the United States, transnational immigrants from Los Arboles who crossed to work in California agriculture were eventually given the option of working in Milwaukee foundries, Los Angeles restaurants, plant nurseries, factories, race tracks, Massachusetts pizza restaurants, or Florida plant nurseries, as their network members accessed new geographical locations. Rather than accepting a view of migrant institutions (suggesting solidification), circuit fluidity (Rouse 1989, 1991) and the dynamism of networks must take central place in the analysis of immigrant adaptations and options. Rather than the "social structures" of immigration, we must speak of the "social relations" of immigration.

The value of these expanding networks for immigrants is the greater freedom of choice provided in the job search; the value of migrant networks for the employers lies in their ability to recruit new workers, facilitate training of the workforce, and maintain loyalty (or "docility") of the workers due to the personal ties between them. Because many of the workers are undocumented, network recruitment into employment also leads to the vulnerability, and hence superexploitability, of even documented kin and friends.

In a study of farmworkers in the Southwestern U.S. lettuce industry, Thomas (1982, S95) found that harvest crews recruit and train new members: "Kinship often serves as an important avenue of entry into the crew. In addition, overlapping ties, such as distant family relations or common village origin in Mexico serve to bind the crew and to facilitate entry." Work crews tend to be composed of both documented and undocumented workers. Because of the presence of undocumented workers, Thomas (1982, S103) argues, the economic vulnerability of all crew members is increased: "When they are kin or friends of other crew members or when they are put into leading positions in the crew, the effect is the same: the fact of illegality becomes a lever with which the entire crew is moved into the direction of higher productivity."

Other evidence supports the contention that network recruitment can lead to greater exploitation of undocumented workers. Browning and Rodríguez (1985, 294) explain this dynamic as follows:

> When hired as individuals, *indocumentados* [undocumented immigrants] are a numerical minority in the firm and are individually incorporated into various work crews. Employers do not systematically make demands on them on the basis of their illegal status. When hired as members of a social group, *indocumentados* make up the majority of the work force, or at least their work crews are made up of *indocumentados*. Employers consider them as a distinct social group and often try to make extra demands on them because of such an identification.

As Browning and Rodríguez underscore (1985, 294), network-mediated entry into jobs leads to just such homogeneity.

Although working with kin and friends may make immigrants in a foreign country feel more comfortable, work-based networks can be used to institute divide-and-rule policies in multiethnic workplaces. Zavella (1987, 112), in her study of women cannery workers in the Santa Clara Valley of California, found that workplace networks not only created conflicts between various ethnic groups but between Mexicans and Chicanos as well (see also Browning and Rodríguez, 1985, 294). She notes (1987, 116): "Whether or not one ethnic group discriminated against another, women perceived ethnic discrimination. The fact that supervisors' work-based networks were of a different ethnic group from workers made the conflict over jobs and wages seem ethnically based, and in some cases it may have been."

In a similar fashion, network-mediated migration into job sites and job types can recreate divisions in the labor force (Bach 1986; Waldinger 1994, 1995). As Bach (1986, 148) describes this process,

> The secondary sector is characterized by antagonistic ethnic relations, in which the newcomers are segregated with members of their own group and native-born ethnic minorities. . . . Without access to alternative resources, these wageworkers must rely on networks within the community to locate jobs. Ethnically segregated job structures are reproduced through these organized social networks.

Thus network-mediated job procurement can lead to divisions both within the work site and within the labor markets accessed by immigrants.

Network-mediated entry into labor enclaves may thus be seen as having both immediate positive (as functionalists claim) and long-term negative effects (as structuralists argue) for undocumented (or documented) immigrant workers. Networks can unite people and form the basis for common efforts; but networks can also be played off against one another, leading to a minimization of consciousness of common interests among workers. Networks constitute "social capital," enabling their members to find jobs whereas other workers, including U.S.-born minorities, may not; on the other hand, they may merely channel network members into devalued jobs (Bach 1986; Coleman 1988; Massey and Espinosa 1997; Massey et al. 1987; Portes 1995; Sassen 1995; Waldinger 1994, 1995). Despite their negative potential, since network members may be scattered throughout a number of geographical locations (Cornelius, 1991, 1976; Massey et al. 1987; Wilson 1993, 1998a; see also Ho 1993; Uzzell 1976)—that is, since social networks are multilocal—if workers are highly dissatisfied with their jobs, they can join kin or friends in other occupations and/or locations. In other words, as shown by the work trajectories of wage-labor migrants from Los Arboles, network-mediated entry into the workplace also provides alternative employment possibilities. Nonetheless, these jobs usually remain within the secondary, "restructured subordinate primary" (Morales 1983), or informalized, labor markets and tend to involve a particular work site or work type.

Recent evidence suggests that social and kinship networks based in the place of origin, as well as social networks based on employment in previous job sites, can become the foundation for unionizing efforts (Milkman and Wong 2000; Zabin 2000). For example, the 1992 drywaller strike in Southern California rested on a bottom-up organizing of workers, which in turn depended partially on the network ties of men from a small village in Michoacán (Milkman and Wong 2000, 181).

According to Marxist class analysis, a "free" proletariat faces the capitalist class with nothing to offer but their labor power. From an atomized mass, organization will eventually develop, grounded in a common work experience, and the bourgeois order will be overthrown, the organized proletariat becoming the ruling class.

I would argue, based on the above evidence both from the literature and from the Los Arboles case studies, that the proletariat has never been atomized, nor are their commonalities based solely on their common situation of lack of access to the means of production. Rural to urban as well as transnational migration is marked by network mediation (Wilson 1998b); so is entry into specific work sites and into broad job categories or micro-labor enclaves. This chapter described the working of such networks in employment clustering as well as in employment opportunity expansion, using the case of transnational wage-labor migrants from a *rancho* in Jalisco to various cities and agricultural towns in the United States.

The problem for researchers is to determine whether, under what circumstances, and at what level of analysis, network recruitment has a restraining or a liberating potential; when, and under what conditions, networks are divisive and when they are enabling; and what type of economic resource they represent (i.e., do they only channel third world immigrants into low-wage, unstable employment, or are they useful in achieving social mobility?). The immigrant who finds jobs for friends and relatives in the same fields or factories may (or may not) foster employer's interests in order to maintain their own jobs and the social power they receive as brokers, reinforcing and recreating thereby the structures of exploitation. Nonetheless, networks develop and expand, and if the workers are dissatisfied with one job, in some cases they will be enabled to tap network aid to move to another perhaps less exploitative job, in a network-mediated trajectory, belying the randomness of atomization in the face of capitalist class relations.

NOTES

1. Many subsequently received amnesty under the 1986 Immigration Reform and Control Act.

2. Part of the Jalisco study was funded by a small grant from the Wenner-Gren Foundation for Anthropological Research, which enabled me to take two student interviewers from the Universidad Autónoma de Baja California, Mexicali, with me to the *rancho* for two months. My thanks go to Margarita Montijo Moreno and José Jesus Cano Paredes for having retrieved more than two-thirds of the preliminary interviews on which this study is based. I would also like to thank Robert Van Kemper for his encouragement of my work. The results of this study are based on interviews with 108 male heads of household present or intermittently present on the *rancho*. Seven other migration histories of men absent in the United States in the 1989 and 1990 periods were retrieved though interviews with their wives; these latter are omitted from this analysis.

3. Until recent changes in the Mexican Constitution instituted by President Salinas de Gortari, *ejidatarios* were beneficiaries of the 1917 Constitution's article 17, which distributed farmland to male heads of household. Such farmland, under earlier law, could not be sold, mortgaged, or rented, but could be passed on to offspring. If not worked for two years, it could be recovered, for redistribution, by the federal government. Constitutional changes proposed in 1992 and ratified in 1993 permit the sale, mortgaging, and rental of these lands, and preclude future distribution.

4. In 1979, he was hit by a car when he ran across the freeway near San Clemente to escape from the Border Patrol. Incapacitated by that accident for the rest of his life, he never returned to the United States again.

5. One man who worked in Florida in 1979 has no labor market network connections to those from Los Arboles who later worked in Florida, although he eventually had social ties with others from Los Arboles. He arrived in Los Arboles to reside in 1989. In 1979, leaving from a rancho in Zacatecas near the one where he was born, he went alone to Texas. There he made contact with a labor contractor who contracted him to work picking tomatoes, apples, cucumbers, and squash in Florida for six months.

REFERENCES

Adler, Rachel H. 2004. *Yucatecans in Dallas.* Boston: Pearson.

Bach, Robert L. 1978. "Mexican Migration and the American State." *International Migration Review* 12(4):536–58.

———. 1986. "Immigration: Issues of Ethnicity, Class, and Public Policy in the United States." *Annals of the American Academy of Political and Social Science* 485:139–52.

Balmori, Diana. 1983. *Hispanic Immigrants in the Construction Industry, New York City, 1960–1982.* Occasional Papers, 38. New York: Center for Latin American and Caribbean Studies, New York University.

Barrera, Mario. 1979. *Race and Class in the Southwest: A Theory of Racial Inequality.* South Bend, IN: University of Notre Dame Press.

Basch, Linda, Nina Glick Schiller, and Cristina Szanton Blanc. 1994. *Nations Unbound: Transnational Projects, Postcolonial Predicaments and Deterritorialized Nation States.* Basel, Switzerland: Gordon and Breach.

Boyd, Monica. 1989. "Family and Personal Networks in International Migration: Recent Developments and New Agendas." *International Migration Review* 23(3):638–70.

Browning, Harley L., and Néstor Rodríguez. 1985. "The Migration of Mexican *Indocumentados* as a Settlement Process: Implications for Work." In *Hispanics in the U.S. Economy*, ed. George J. Borjas and Marta Tienda, 277–97. New York: Academic Press.

Burawoy, Michael. 1975. "The Functions and Reproduction of Migrant Labor: Comparative Material from Southern Africa and the United States." *American Journal of Sociology* 81(5):1050–87.

Chavez, Leo R. 1985. "Households, Migration and Labor Market Participation: The Adaptation of Mexicans to Life in the United States." *Urban Anthropology* 14(4):301–46.

Chavez, Leo R., and Estevan T. Flores. 1988. "Undocumented Mexicans and Central Americans and the Immigration and Control Act of 1986: A Reflection Based on Empirical Data." In *Defense of the Alien*, ed. Lydio F. Tomasi, 131–56. Staten Island, NY: Center for Migration Studies.

Coleman, James. 1988. "Social Capital in the Creation of Human Capital." *American Journal of Sociology* 94 (Supplement): S95–120.

Cornelius, Wayne A. 1976. *Mexican Migration to the United States: The View from Rural Sending Communities.* Monograph Series in Migration and Development. Cambridge: Massachusetts Institute of Technology, Center for International Studies.

———. 1991. "Los Migrantes de la Crisis: The Changing Profile of Mexican Migration to the United States." In *Social Responses to Mexico's Economic Crisis of the 1980s*, ed. Mercedes González de la Rocha and Agustín Escobar Latapí, 155–94. La Jolla: University of California, San Diego, Center for U.S.-Mexican Studies.

Durand, Jorge, and Douglas S. Massey. 1992. "Mexican Migration to the United States: A Critical Review." *Latin American Research Review* 27(2):3–42.

DuToit, Brian M. 1975. "A Decision-Making Model for the Study of Migration." In *Migration and Modernization: Models and Adaptive Strategies*, ed. Brian M. DuToit and Helen Safa, 49–75. The Hague: Mouton.

———. 1990. "People on the Move: Rural-Urban Migration with Special Reference to the Third World: Theoretical and Empirical Perspectives." *Human Organization* 49:305–19.

Gold, Steven. 1994. "Patterns of Economic Cooperation among Israeli Immigrants in Los Angeles." *International Migration Review* 28(1):114–35.

Gomez-Quiñones, Juan. 1981. "Mexican Immigration to the United States and the Internationalization of Labor,1848–1980: An Overview." In *Mexican Immigrant Workers in the U.S., Los Angeles*, ed. Antonio Rios-Bustamante, 13–34. Los Angeles: Chicano Studies Research Center, University of California at Los Angeles.

Goss, Jon D., and Bruce Lindquist. 1995. "Conceptualizing International Labor Migration: A Structuration Perspective." *International Migration Review* 29(2):317–51.

Granovetter, Mark. 1973. "The Strength of Weak Ties." *American Journal of Sociology* 78:1360–88.

Griffin, David, and Ed Kissam. 1995. *Working Poor: Farmworkers in the United States*. Philadelphia, PA: Temple University Press.

Hagan, Jacquelíne María. 1994. *Deciding to Be Legal: A Maya Community in Houston*. Philadelphia, PA: Temple University Press.

Haney, Jane B. 1979. "Formal and Informal Labor Recruitment Mechanisms: States in Mexican Migration into Mid-Michigan Agriculture." In *Migration across Frontiers: Mexico and the United States*, ed. Fernando Camara and Robert Van Kemper, 191–99. Albany: State University of New York Press.

Hayes-Bautista, David E., Werner O. S. Schink, and Jorge Chapa. 1990. *The Burden of Support: Young Latinos in an Aging Society*. Stanford, CA: Stanford University Press.

Heyman, Josiah McC. 1998. "State Effects on Labor Exploitation: The INS and Undocumented Immigrants at the Mexico-U.S. Border." *Critique of Anthropology* 18(2):157–80.

Ho, Christine G. T. 1993. "The Internationalization of Kinship and the Feminization of Caribbean Migration: The Case of Afro-Trinidadian Immigrants in Los Angeles." *Human Organization* 52(1):32-40.

Jones, Richard C. 1982. "Channelization of Undocumented Mexican Migrants to the U.S." *Economic Geography* 58:156–76.

———. 1995. *Ambivalent Journey: U.S. Migration and Economic Mobility in North-Central Mexico*. Tucson: University of Arizona Press.

Keefe, Susan Emley. 1979. "Urbanization, Acculturation, and Extended Family Ties: Mexican Americans in Cities." *American Ethnologist* 6(2):349–65.

Long, Stuart. 1987. "Undocumented Immigrants in the Los Angeles Garment Industry: Displacement or Dual Labor Market?" *Journal of Borderlands Studies* 11(2):1–11.

MacDonald, John S., and Leatrice D. MacDonald. 1964. "Chain Migration, Ethnic Neighborhood Formation and Social Networks." *Milbank Memorial Fund Quarterly* 42(1):82–97.

Maram, Sheldon L. 1980. *Hispanic Workers in the Garment and Restaurant Industries in Los Angeles County*, with the assistance of Stuart Long and Dennis Berg. La Jolla: University of California, San Diego, Program in U.S.-Mexican Studies.

Margolis, Maxine L. 1994. *Little Brazil: An Ethnography of Brazilian Immigrants in New York City*. Princeton, NJ: Princeton University Press.

Martí, Judith. 1993. The Informal Sector and Municipal Government: Women Street Vendors in Nineteenth-Century Urban Mexico and Twentieth-Century Los Angeles. Paper presented at the annual meeting of the American Anthropological Association, Washington, DC, November 17–21.

Massey, Douglas S. 1987. "Understanding Mexican Migration to the United States." *American Journal of Sociology* 92(6):1372–1403.

———. 1999. "Why Does Migration Occur? A Theoretical Synthesis." In *The Handbook of International Migration: The American Experience*, ed. Charles Hirschman, Philip Kasinitz, and Josh DeWind, 34–52. New York: Russell Sage Foundation.

Massey, Douglas, Rafael Alarcón, Jorge Durand, and Humberto González. 1987. *Return to Aztlán: The Social Process of International Migration from Western Mexico*. Berkeley: University of California Press.

Massey, Douglas, S. Joaquin Arango, Hugo Graeme, Ali Kouaouci, Adela Pellegrino, and J. Edward Taylor. 1994. "An Evaluation of International Migration Theory: The North American Case." *Population and Development Review* 20(4): 699–751.

Massey, Douglas S., and Kristin E. Espinosa. 1997. "What's Driving Mexican-U.S. Migration? A Theoretical, Empirical, and Policy Analysis." *American Journal of Sociology* 102(4):939–99.

Milkman, Ruth, and Kent Wong. 2000. "Organizing the Wicked City: The 1992 Southern California Drywall Strike." In *Organizing Immigrants: The Challenge for Unions in Contemporary California*, ed. Ruth Milkman, 169–98. Ithaca, NY: Cornell University Press.

Mines, Richard. 1981. *Developing a Community Tradition of Migration: A Field Study in Rural Zacatecas, Mexico and California Settlement Areas.* La Jolla: University of California, San Diego, Center for U.S.-Mexico Studies.

Morales, Rebecca. 1983. "Transitional Labor: Undocumented Workers in the Los Angeles Automobile Industry." *International Migration Review* 17(4):570–96.

Morawska, Ewa. 1990. "The Sociology and Historiography of Immigration." In *Immigration Reconsidered: History, Sociology, and Politics,* ed. Virginia Yans-McLaughlin, 187–240. New York: Oxford University Press.

Portes, Alejandro. 1983. "The Informal Sector: Definition, Controversy, and Relation to National Development. Review." *Fernand Braudel Center for the Study of Economies, Historical Systems and Civilizations* 7(1):151–74.

———. 1995. "Economic Sociology and the Sociology of Immigration: A Conceptual Overview.'" In *The Economic Sociology of Immigration: Essays on Networks, Ethnicity, and Entrepreneurship,* ed. Alejandro Portes, 1–41. New York: Russell Sage Foundation.

Portes, Alejandro, and Robert L. Bach. 1985. *Latin Journey: Cuban and Mexican Immigrants in the United States.* Berkeley: University of California Press.

Rodríguez, Néstor P. 1987. "Undocumented Central Americans in Houston: Diverse Populations." *International Migration Review* 21(1):4–26.

Rouse, Roger. 1989. Mexican Migration to the United States: Family Relations in the Development of a Transnational Migrant Circuit. PhD diss., Stanford University.

———. 1991. "Mexican Migration and the Social Space of Postmodernism." *Diaspora* 1:8–23.

Sassen, Saskia. 1985. "Changing Composition and Labor Market Location of Hispanic Immigrants in New York City, 1960–1980." In *Hispanics in the U.S. Economy,* ed. George J. Borjas and Marta Tienda, 299–322. New York: Academic Press.

———. 1990. *The Mobility of Labor and Capital: A Study in International Investment and Labor Flows.* Cambridge: Cambridge University Press.

———. 1995. "Immigration and Local Labor Markets." In *The Economic Sociology of Immigration: Essays on Networks, Ethnicity, and Entrepreneurship,* ed. Alejandro Portes, 87–127. New York: Russell Sage Foundation.

Sassen, Saskia, and Robert C. Smith. 1992. "Post-Industrial Growth and Economic Reorganization: Their Impact on Immigrant Employment." In *U.S.-Mexico*

Relations: Labor Market Independence, ed. Jorge A. Bustamante, Clark W. Reynolds and Raúl A. Hinojosa-Ojeda, 372–93. Stanford, CA: Stanford University Press.

Sassen-Koob, Saskia. 1981. "Toward a Conceptualization of Immigrant Labor." *Social Problems* 29(1):65–85.

Soja, Edward W. 1991. "Economic Restructuring and the Internationalization of the Los Angeles Region." In *The Capitalist City: Global Restructuring and Community Policies*, ed. Michael Peter Smith and Joe R. Feagin, 178–98. Cambridge, MA: Basil Blackwell.

Stoddard, Ellwyn R. 1976. "Illegal Mexican Labor in the Borderlands." *Pacific Sociological Review* 19(2):175–210.

Thomas, Robert J. 1982. "Citizenship and Gender in Work Organization: Some Considerations for Theories of the Labor Process." *American Journal of Sociology* (Supplement: Marxist Inquiries: Studies of Labor, Class and States) 88:S86–S112.

Uzzell, Douglas. 1976. *Ethnography of Migration: Breaking Out of the Bipolar Myth.* Houston, TX: Rice University, Program of Development Studies.

Waldinger, Roger. 1985. "Immigration and Industrial Change in the New York City Apparel Industry." In *Hispanics in the U.S. Economy*, ed. George J. Borjas and Marta Tienda, 323–49. New York: Academic Press.

———. 1994. "The Making of an Immigrant Niche." *International Migration Review* 28(1):3–31.

———. 1995. "The 'Other Side' of Embeddedness: A Case Study of the Interplay of Economy and Ethnicity." *Ethnic and Racial Studies* 18(3):555–80.

Wilson, Tamar Diana. 1992. Vamos para Buscar la Vida: A Comparison of Patterns of Outmigration from a Rancho in Jalisco and Inmigration to a Mexicali Squatter Settlement. PhD diss., University of California, Los Angeles.

———. 1993. "We Seek Work Where We Can: A Comparison of Patterns of Outmigration from a Rancho in Jalisco and Internal Migration into a Mexicali Squatter Settlement." *Journal of Borderlands Studies* 8(3):33–58.

———. 1994. "What Determines Where Migrants Go? Modifications in Migration Theories." *Human Organization* 53(3):269–78.

———. 1998a. "Weak Ties, Strong Ties: Network Principles in Mexican Migration." *Human Organization* 57(4):394–403.

———. 1998b. "Micro-, Meso- and Macropatterns of Women's Migration to Colonia Popular, Mexicali, Baja California." *Journal of Borderlands Studies* 13(2):63–82.

Zabin, Carol. 2000. "Organizing Latino Workers in the Los Angeles Manufacturing Sector: The Case of American Racing Equipment." In *Organizing Immigrants: The Challenge for Unions in Contemporary California*, ed. Ruth Milkman, 150–68. Ithaca, NY: Cornell University Press.

Zabin, Carol, and Sallie Hughes. 1995. "Economic Integration and Labor Flows: Stage Migration in Farm Labor Markets in Mexico and the United States." *International Migration Review* 29(2):397–422.

Zavella, Patricia. 1987. *Women's Work and Chicano Families: Cannery Workers of the Santa Clara Valley.* Ithaca, NY: Cornell University Press.

14

Volunteer Labor: "Adding Value" to Local Culture

Barbara J. Dilly

Volunteer labor is distinguished from market-value labor in a democratic capitalist society in terms of assessing its economic value. The productive and consumptive activities of volunteer labor further differ from those of wage labor in the public organizations that mediate its exchange of goods and services. Within the civic sphere of a capitalist "market" system, particular market niches emerge for goods of deemed social value by both volunteers and recipients (Brown 1999). Charles E. Zech argues that volunteer activities are a form of demand articulation (1982). While the economic value of public goods may be defined in terms of their "market" value, Eleanor Brown notes that it is also necessary to recognize that niche market volunteer goods and services often identify consumers who do not have the ability to pay for the goods and services provided (1999). The value of volunteer labor production in such a "market" is mediated by a civic organization that brings together people who can be friends and neighbors in the production and consumption of goods and services that combine both self-interest and a commitment to the public good (Brown 1999, 5, 13).

Historically, volunteer labor in America came under use as a concept to distinguish the obligations of mutual aid in a cooperative economy from the nonwage labor activity within the civic sphere (Brown 1999). Volunteerism reflected the great value Americans placed on maintaining friendliness and egalitarianism (Lamont 1992, 5). David S. Adams argues that in "the culture of American volunteerism," Americans perceive an obligation to contribute voluntarily to the social good of their community, but he further asserts that little research explains volunteer activities within the contexts of social structure and cultural values (1990).

P. B. Clark and J. Q. Wilson (1961) identify the social and material incentive systems that define the complementarity of the social rewards of member participation with the purposive goods and services produced and consumed. The value of volunteer activities from the perspective of this model is a context-specific measure. The emphasis on interpersonal ties and relationship networks within a context-specific symbolic realm of social solidarity also informs the cost/benefit calculations of volunteering proposed by Matthew J. Chinman and Abraham Wandersman (1999).

The value of volunteering is defined by the symbolic integration of the community in which the costs and benefits of volunteering have both moral and personal rewards. Volunteer labor is assigned symbolic social value in which volunteers exchange their labor for symbols of approval or prestige. In their empirical study of volunteer labor, Kathleen M. Day and Rose Anne Devlin demonstrated that volunteering has a direct "market" value as well (1998). Volunteers gain marketable skills and social contacts as a result of their activities. Volunteer labor must be examined, then, in terms of its formal and informal sector contributions.

Economists expand formal economic cost/benefit principles to measure volunteer labor by identifying nonmarket-driven motivations of volunteers to maximize personal benefits in the production of public goods. The value of the labor and the goods produced is the sum of all benefits to recipients and volunteers (Brown 1999, 6). This model assumes that volunteer labor produces public goods for which there is a demand (Zech 1982). The combination of motivation to gain personal experiences on the part of volunteers in the production of goods and services that meets the needs of other people is termed "joint production" by economists (Brown 1999, 6).

Public policy analysts and sociologists focus on volunteer labor in terms of social capital, which they identify as social networks and their ability to organize community resources for the public good. Social capital studies identify the individual actor's position in a social structure or system of integrated and embedded networks (Borgatti, Jones, and Everett 1998; Wellman 1988). Economic anthropology draws on both cost/benefit and social capital network analyses, but operationalizes these concepts as local cultural dynamics.

In this study, I hypothesize that the motivations of volunteers to maximize individual experience, the quantity and quality of social networks to organize public good, and the demand articulation of public goods for "joint consumption" are related and understood in local contexts as cultural processes that reproduce local culture.

I argue that the cultural value of the goods and services produced by volunteer labor in small communities is a better measure of the value of volunteer labor contributions than is the motivation of individual obligations to do one's part or the sum of social networks to organize resources. Beyond the model of "joint production" defined by economists, I argue for a model of "joint consumption" in which the volunteers who produce public goods are also consumers of cultural goods and services.

LOCAL CULTURAL CONTEXT

An ethnographic study of volunteer labor in Shelter Rock, a small rural community in northeast Iowa, illustrates the issues raised here. It examines how local culture values and encourages volunteer labor, generates volunteer social networks through "joint production," and adds value to "joint consumption" of public goods in the reproduction of culture. I argue that an informal economy generated from these cultural dynamics effectively resists the neoliberal market forces that erode local community economic viability. Further, participation in a volunteer labor force—as reproduction of culture at the local level—counters the alienation from self, production, product, and community so frequently experienced by wage and semiprofessional laborers in rural communities.

Shelter Rock and other small rural communities in northeast Iowa suffered steady economic decline beginning in the mid-1960s. A new state highway bypassed the business district and the high school was consolidated into a larger nearby community system. As the farm economy suffered, wage labor in nonfarm industrial employment provided inadequate income opportunities for the region. Several recessions and weakened labor unions dimmed hopes for industrial sector growth. Other sectors are slow to expand in rural regions peripheral to large metropolitan centers. And while discount chain stores penetrate the region with cheap consumer goods, the predominantly working-class and lower-middle-class residents of small rural communities like Shelter Rock experience sporadic unemployment and family incomes well below national averages.

In the 1960s, many residents of small towns migrated to nearby urban centers for economic opportunities but found that their wages did not afford them the quality of life enjoyed in small towns. In the 1970s and 1980s, many of these rural residents moved back to small towns, becoming commuters, sometimes to distances of up to two hours. In the midst of economic uncertainty, extended family and neighborhood social networks provide child care and other forms of mutual aid realized as economic resources. Small-town real estate investments also made sound economic sense. Prices were lower, but stable, and so were the taxes.

Regular social interaction in stable noncompetitive settings where mutual aid is a long-standing tradition provides a measure of social security in meeting basic economic needs of food, shelter, and child care. Mutual aid traditions also provide the motivation and opportunity for cooperative volunteer endeavors that define an informal economy of public goods production that enhances and reproduces the quality of rural community life.

THEORETICAL DISCUSSION
Volunteer labor has long been the mainstay of rural social and economic life. Historically termed "mutual aid," the nonwage, noncompulsory, freely extended labor of individuals and groups was essential to the survival and development of frontier community life. The system of mutual aid in America reflected culturally constructed pragmatic institutions of moral obligation to persons who shared a geographic community (Simpson 1999; Adams 1990), a sense of religious duty (Adams 1990), and symbolic boundaries of friendliness, conflict avoidance, and cultural egalitarianism (Lamont 1992, 5).

It is important to this study, and to the studies of volunteer labor in comparative cultural contexts, to recognize a theoretical difference between rural and urban conceptions of volunteer labor. The volunteer labor concept appears to have emerged separately from the mutual-aid ethic as a byproduct of urbanization. Economist Eleanor Brown argues that volunteering is a measure of the American ethic of mutual aid, but must be distinguished from it (1999). Brown asserts that volunteering in the civic sphere implies a greater level of commitment to the public good than the personal responsibility that motivated the mutual-aid ethic (1999, 13). I argue that the line drawn here between the moral obligation of individuals to cooperate in mutual-aid projects within bounded communities and the impersonal public orientation that motivates participation in volunteer projects can be understood as an urban/rural distinction.

Volunteer labor in urban settings is rationalized by social networks, consumer needs, and definitions of public goods that transcend moral obligations and cultural dynamics. The urban model attempts to identify benefits for volunteers and consumers as values that can be quantified independently from each other in an equation that produces the sum of all benefits. The urban model obscures the cultural dynamics of rural communities where volunteer labor not only produces a private and public good but also is the means by which individual self-worth is enhanced in the reproduction of rural culture.

RURAL LOCAL CULTURE MODEL OF VOLUNTEER LABOR

The rural local culture model does not attempt to measure the market values of volunteer labor, or to identify specific social networks. Rather, it explains the cultural meanings and the cultural characteristics of volunteer relationships that add value to volunteer labor production and the reproduction of social and cultural processes. The rural local culture volunteer labor model defined in Shelter Rock balances the goals of individuals who seek to maximize their own opportunities for status and self-satisfaction with the goals of mutual aid and community purpose to reproduce a valued way of life. Volunteerism is a means by which individuals can make contributions to the good of the community and by which they validate their membership. Volunteers also experience the freedom to express themselves in ways that affirm their individuality and sense of self-worth when wage-labor opportunities outside of the community do not provide these benefits.

Rural social networks of kin, neighbors, and group membership enable individuals to maximize their volunteer labor contributions. Self-worth and prestige through recognition of contributions is enhanced when volunteers generate relationship networks that are both embedded inside the community and extended to outsiders. Valued is added by both.[1] The more opportunities are generated for volunteer participation, the more value is added to the local culture.[2] The more people jointly produce the goods and jointly consume the goods, the greater the value of the goods and the volunteer labor.[3] These cultural processes reproduce Shelter Rock's culture.

Structures of interaction and symbols of shared meaning are connected through institutions of friendliness, inclusion, individual investment in the symbols, feelings of belonging, pride in accomplishment of met goals, mutual experiences, emotional drama, geographic proximity and convenience, sense of obligation to others, shared history, and solidarity.

Despite the egalitarian values of volunteering in rural community, volunteer opportunities are structured around demographic characteristics typical of rural society. Couples have the most opportunities to make valued contributions, as most volunteer activities and groups are organized around social relationship networks. While single men and women are not intentionally excluded, they are traditionally not included in social groups. The highest status volunteer labor assignments are typically given to men who are "in charge" of events. But wives of volunteer "big men" can also become "big women" in the coordination of events. Single women and men attain high status volunteer positions only if they build the social network connections necessary to coordinate volunteer labor.

While volunteer roles are often prescribed by the local social structure, individual volunteers in rural communities can and do enhance the development of their personal identities as volunteers over their life-cycle. Persons of goodwill with integrity can certainly extend traditional boundaries. In addition, the development of creative skills and leadership abilities through education, training, and practice adds social status for individuals and extends their social networks. These skills and abilities also contribute substantial value to the community and the local culture. For example, volunteer firemen and ambulance personnel engage in regular training to update their certifications. The status of EMT (emergency medical technician) is of great value to rural communities and adds significant status to the individual who sacrificed many hours of personal time in training. Perhaps less dramatic, but certainly no less significant, is the development of musical talent skills. Individuals take singing and dancing lessons to further their ability to make contributions to the spring variety show. In addition to their personal talent training investment, local "stars" sacrifice several nights a week for three to four months of rehearsals to guarantee the delight of spectators. Retirement offers additional opportunities to develop one's skills and abilities. The more introverted individuals donate labors of love, created from many hours, in the form of highly skilled crafts to church bazaars and other fund-raisers. Gardeners donate sweat-of-the-brow labors to the annual community garden club fund-raiser.

Individuals whose volunteer labor makes monetary contributions to the community are most likely to develop the greatest networks of cooperation and support for their ideas. This is particularly significant in rural communities where economic activities have direct consequences on social structures (Nash 1968). However, it is also more likely in rural communities that individuals with limited wage-labor skills and/or opportunities can contribute to locally valued social goods. In fact, unemployment or underemployment for some individuals actually contributes to greater volunteer labor contributions. This is particularly true if their basic economic needs are met by other household members or kin and their social networks are well established. In rural communities, the informal sector provides a viable arena for productive and socially valued labor contributions that generate status comparable to, or even exceeding, that earned by individuals with high wage-labor status.

DISCUSSION OF VOLUNTEER LABOR ACTIVITIES IN LOCAL CONTEXT

My participant observation of volunteer labor in Shelter Rock over the last six years was conducted serendipitously. Despite its economic woes, I decided to build a home for my retirement in Shelter Rock because of the reputation of the community for its rich rural folk life. Since the 1960s, the community has expanded its volunteer productions each year, gradually incorporating more local and regional residents into folk events that reproduce local culture. One successful event, a spring variety show, now produces self-satisfaction for nearly two hundred volunteers, over $20,000 in profits each year for community projects, and a demand for more public goods. Approximately 4,500 people from surrounding areas can be counted on to purchase $6.00 tickets for one of twelve performances each spring, not just because the volunteers are talented, although they exhibit a remarkable range of musical talents. Knowledge that profits go toward community mutual-aid projects adds greater value to the experience of consuming the "goods," usually material.

The spring variety show does not, however, absorb all of the volunteers in the community. The commitment in time is nearly four months of rehearsals and not everyone can sing and dance or play musical instruments, create stage sets, or make costumes. The even more fantastic Fourth of July event incorporates a wider range of talents with less commitment in time. Nearly every able-bodied citizen in town is involved in some volunteer labor capacity producing goods and services for over ten thousand consumers. Over the last twenty years, the four-day spectacle, which includes a parade, fireworks, carnival, street dance, raffles, fund-raising dinners, bake sales, and a beer tent has become the major folk event for the region.

Symbolic integration of local cultural values is easily observed in the Fourth of July parade. Anyone can participate. There is no preregistration. For over two hours, the material culture evidence of a once self-sufficient agricultural regional economy, now under siege, winds through the streets lined with cheering crowds. Following the national and state flags is an elaborate local banner, crafted by a resident artisan, bearing the words "Shelter Rock." Following are the remnants of Shelter Rock's economic heydays: antique tractors, draft horses, cows, goats, chickens, and every form of agricultural implement ever used that can be pushed, pulled, or self-propelled. The parade also includes antique automobiles and semitrailers with "live" square dancers, polka bands, and the variety show performers. There are church floats on hay wagons and agricultural queens in classic convertibles. Civic organizations and local businesses promote their interests in the community. The most volunteer fire department equipment ever found in a single parade can probably be seen in Shelter Rock. This parade symbolically integrates the many people who maintain Shelter Rock's viable rural community culture. It is the display of rural folk-life values and a statement of rural community social structures that maintain an informal self-sufficient economy capable of reproducing culture.

The Fourth of July event volunteers and consumers are further symbolically integrated in the consumption of baked goods and beer. Baked goods and beer are unifying symbols of a culture that values domestic production and public consumption of food and drink in solidarity rituals. While the gendering of volunteer economics in Shelter Rock is most clearly seen in the production of baked goods and beer, the consumption of these goods mediates gender differences and class differences. They are symbols of "authentic" community.

Women are most likely to volunteer in the production and sale of baked goods, largely through civic organizations and churches. Men are most likely associated with the production of the beer tent activities, which are coordinated by the volunteer fire department. Both events require social networks that integrate the entire community. The gendered division of labor does not result in a lowered status for female volunteers, nor is the gendered division of labor a rigid pattern. Women recently joined the volunteer fire department and ambulance crew. Women also sell beer tickets and men clear tables and wash dishes in the church basements.

APPLICATION OF THE LOCAL CULTURE MODEL OF VOLUNTEER LABOR

Joint consumption of baked goods and beer adds value to the goods, as does the labor, through several transactions. The regional consumption patterns reflect a strong appreciation for the value of such products there. While market forces indicate a fair price for baked goods and beer, the social context of their distribution and consumption defines their value, not their market prices.

The greatest value for a piece of pie is generated when someone bakes a pie at home and donates it to the fire department's new pumper fund-raiser. The pie is then purchased by another community member who is required to donate a homemade pie for the church supper but doesn't have time to bake one. In fact, the person who baked the pie delivered it to the home of the church member who paid the fire department for a pie she never saw. At the church supper, pieces of the pie are sold to individuals. Profits go toward the fellowship hall renovation. And finally, a church member purchases one piece of pie and delivers it to the nursing home for another elderly member as an obligation to the mutual ministry committee. Value is added in four separate volunteer labor relationships.

Value is also added in the consumption of beer in the beer tent. Throughout the year, community members save cans and bottles that are redeemed for thousands of dollars. This money is used to lease a tent for the beer, hire bands for the street dance, and contract a carnival with rides for the kids. Committees are required to coordinate each of these activities, which adds more social value to the beer consumption. The profits from the beer tent are spent entirely each year on the fireworks display, which attracts huge crowds. The fireworks add more social value to the beer, which is consumed in even greater quantities after the fireworks. Value is added through production and consumption of public goods at each level.

The economic principles that guide volunteer production in Shelter Rock reflect little attention to market forces. Profit may appear to be the motive for fund-raisers, but efficiency is not always evident and profit is not necessary. Compared to the spring variety extravaganza and the Fourth of July spectacle, most other events are not economically profitable. Events that coordinate large numbers of resources and volunteer hours over a several-month period of time may result in only $200.00 worth of profit but can continue for years, as long as consumption adds value to the volunteer experience and reproduces culture. The production will end only if some members of the group decide that one or more others in the group gain prestige by exploiting others' volunteer labor.

The most successful volunteer labor exploits the motives of both insiders and outsiders in joint production and consumption of cultural goods and services. Embedded networks are often necessary for the production of new events, but these networks need to be rapidly expanded to avoid alienation of the group from the larger community. This was evidenced in the highly successful volunteer activities of a group consisting of former mayors and other business professionals who possessed experience, good ideas, and organizational skills. When the publicity for the activities generated higher levels of status and prestige for this group and its members than any other group in the community, the group fell under criticism. It was argued that they sought prestige through community consumption of goods for which value was not added through joint production. In order to maintain the value of its contributions, the group refocused its agenda to include more members in the production of public goods. They also resolved not to put their pictures in the paper for a period of time.

Another problem in cultural reproduction identifies individuals who are asked to volunteer in activities in which they are not recognized as equals with those who coordinate the events. While individuals do not seek private recognition, they will rarely contribute their labor to projects where others are recognized at their expense. Nor can new members in the community achieve status through volunteer labor apart from building social networks. This is particularly true if a professional moves into town with experience, ideas, and material resources at his or her disposal. Such individuals are advised to first volunteer in egalitarian activities like washing dishes after a waffle breakfast. If they seek to coordinate large events without first adding value to their volunteer labor through social networks, they are accused of exploiting the social capital for their own gain and undermining the volunteer labor-status hierarchy already in place. Social forces, not market forces, add or diminish value to volunteer labor.

Volunteer events are considered successful if all the volunteers have fun, supplies are donated or obtained at cost through some one's personal or professional networks, more volunteers and networks for resources are generated, and if there is a demand for the joint consumption of public goods. The interaction between individuals within groups and with broader social networks is essential to the value-added concept. Whenever a new obligation or commitment to the community is created, or a new network for reciprocity is defined, value is added to volunteer labor. The goal is not to produce valued goods and services, as is the case with most volunteer labor, but to use these means toward a greater end of integrating volunteers into the membership of a community where everyone's contributions are essential.[4]

NOTES

1. Studies of social capital argue that the more social networks an individual demonstrates, the greater the social capital, which is generated (Borgatti, Jones, and Everett 1998).

2. The benefits of volunteering are greatest, argue Chinman and Wandersman, when volunteer activity is within a group (1999, 55). They argue that persons who do not participate in group activities experience more interpersonal conflicts, and that while volunteering in a group may not guarantee greater benefits; it does reduces costs (1999, 58).

3. Volunteer groups are more effective when individual members are linked to other groups. The greatest social capital is generated by groups who are well connected to other groups through members who work with others in multiple settings (Borgatti, Jones, and Everett 1998).

4. Shelter Rock illustrates "the mutual emergence of individuality and solidarity in a plurality of activities fostered in a genuine public sphere" (Bellah et al. 1992, 95).

REFERENCES

Adams, David S. 1990. Issues and Ideas in the Culture of American Volunteerism. American Sociological Association Paper, Ohio State University, Lima.

Bellah, Robert, Richard Madsen, William M. Sullivan, Ann Swidler, and Steven M. Tipton. 1992. *The Good Society*. New York: Vintage Books.

Borgatti, Stephen P., Candace Jones, and Martin G. Everett. 1998. "Network Measures of Social Capital." *Connections* 21(2):1–36.

Brown, Eleanor. 1999. "Assessing the Value of Volunteer Activity." *Nonprofit and Voluntary Sector Quarterly* 28(1):3–17.

Chinman, Matthew J., and Abraham Wandersman. 1999. "The Benefits and Costs of Volunteering in Community Organizations: Review and Implications." *Nonprofit and Voluntary Sector Quarterly* 8(1):46–64.

Clark, P. B., and J. Q. Wilson. 1961. "Incentive Systems: A Theory of Organizations." *Administrative Science Quarterly* 6:129–66

Day, Kathleen M., and Rose Anne Devlin. 1998. "The Payoff to Work without Pay: Volunteer Work as an Investment in Human Capital." *Canadian Journal of Economics* 31(5):1179–91.

Lamont, Michele. 1992. *Money, Morals, and Manners: The Culture of the French and the American Upper Middle Class.* Chicago: University of Chicago Press.

Nash, Manning. 1968. "The Social Context of Economic Choice in a Small Society." In *Economic Anthropology: Readings in Theory and Analysis*, ed. Edward E. LeClair Jr. and Harold Schneider, 311–22. New York: Holt, Rinehart and Winston.

Simpson, Charles R. 1999. Fraternity of Danger: Volunteer Fire Companies and the Contradiction of Modernization. American Sociological Association Paper, State University of New York, Plattsburg.

Wellman, B. 1988. "Structural Analysis: From Metaphor to Theory and Substance." In *Social Structures: A Network Approach*, ed. B. Wellman and S. D. Berkovitz, 19–61. New York: Cambridge University Press.

Zech, Charles E. 1982. "Citizen Willingness to Assist as Volunteers in the Provision of Local Public Goods: A Case Study of Volunteer Firemen in 70 West German Cities." *American Journal of Economics and Sociology* 41(3):303–14.

Index

Careyan model, 223, 232–34
Chiang Mai Valley, Thailand. *See*
Thailand, northern: Chiang Mai Valley
chiefdom: Icelandic, Viking Age, 217,
224, 226–27, 231; pre-Hispanic
Philippine, 71
citrus. *See* agriculture: lemon
civil disobedience, 140, 142, 149
class, 4–8, 10–13, 15–16, 19; employing,
21–22; middle, 7, 11, 16, 22; ruling,
20, 21, 297; social, 19–23; working,
21, 22, 28–30, 35, 41, 59, 177, 265,
274, 277–78, 309. *See also*
stratification: class
coal production, 138–39, 144
coffee. *See* agriculture: coffee
cognition. *See* agency: and cognition
Colombia. *See* agriculture: coffee
commerce, 92, 97, 99
community, 89, 92, 103–4, 138–44,
148–51, 158, 165, 197, 198, 206–7,
211, 269, 276, 286, 293, 296, 308–17;
fishing, 68–71, 75, 78
computer: operator, 178–80, 182;
programmer, 182
cooperatives, 37; Seikatsu Club
Consumer Cooperative (SCCC), 157,
159, 161–62; volunteer, 310
corn. *See* maize
corvée labor. *See* labor: corvée
crafts, 93, 97, 248; specialization, 203–7.
See also handicraft
cultural reproduction, 316

daughter communities, 283, 294
Debs, Eugene V., 33, 36
debt, 56, 58, 66–67, 71–73, 75–80, 101,
223–24, 233. *See also* slavery: debt

dependency, 18; of wives, 166
diminishing returns, 217–19

economics: neoclassical, 8, 10, 65, 193;
theory, 81, 219, 222, 267, 275, 278
economy: formal, 138, 274, 276;
gendered, 138–42; global, 18, 21, 279,
283; informal, 112, 147–49, 266,
271–74, 278, 309–10; new, 194, 265;
planned, 47; political, 13–14, 46–52,
59, 140, 193, 217, 221, 233, 246
elder-junior relationship, 56
elephants, 249
elites, 10, 73, 184, 218, 222, 224
engineers, 249–50, 253
Equal Employment Opportunity Law,
157, 164, 166–67
ethnic diversity, 90, 256–57, 259
ethnicity, 257; Zapotec, 90, 99–103. *See
also* identity: ethnic
excavations. *See* chiefdom: Icelandic,
Viking Age; Oaxaca, Mexico: ancient
extended family. *See* household:
extended family

famines, 14, 255–57
farmworker, 285, 287, 289, 294–95
fishing enterprises, 66–68, 80
folklife, rural, 313–14

gender, 1, 4–5, 13–14, 97, 151, 275, 314;
and division of labor, 100, 142, 146,
149; equality, 137; exploitation, 249;
ideology, 8; inequality, 97; and
masculinity, 73–79; roles, 167. *See
also* economy: gendered; housewives;
women's labor
globalization, 3, 9–13, 45, 55

About the Contributors

Katherine A. Bowie (PhD, University of Chicago, 1988) is professor of anthropology and has served as director of the Center for Southeast Asian Studies at the University of Wisconsin-Madison. She was selected as an Eisenhower Fellow to Thailand and first traveled to Thailand in 1974. She lived over eight years in Thailand, and her primary interest is in Thai agrarian politics and history. Her publications include *Voices from the Thai Countryside: The Necklace and Other Short Stories of Samruam Singh* and *Rituals of National Loyalty: An Anthropology of the State and the Village Scout Movement in Thailand.* Her articles have appeared in *American Anthropologist, American Ethnologist,* and *Journal of Asian Studies.*

Barbara J. Dilly is assistant professor of anthropology at Creighton University in Omaha, Nebraska. Her applied research interests focus on rural social and economic development in Latin America and the American Midwest. Her current projects include comparative and longitudinal studies of rural communities in Iowa undergoing social and economic transformations. She published "Ecotourism and Cultural Preservation in the Guyanese Rain Forest" in *Globalization and the Rural Poor in Latin America.* Her forthcoming study on the development of river recreation tourism in a small rural community in northeast Iowa examines the social and cultural conflicts that accompany economic transitions in agricultural communities.

E. Paul Durrenberger is professor of anthropology at Penn State. He is principal investigator for the NSF project "A Comparison of Union Consciousness in Centralized and Participatory Unions." He has published numerous articles and books on unions (many coauthored with Suzan Erem, most recently *Class Acts: An Anthology of Urban Service Workers and Their Union*), Iceland (*Icelandic Essays*, and with Gísli Pálsson, *Images of Contemporary Iceland* and *The Anthropology of Iceland*), Mississippi (*Mississippi Soundings*), Alabama (*It's All Politics*), Iowa (with Kendall Thu, *Pigs, Profits and Rural Communities*), farming among tribal and peasant people of Thailand, medieval Iceland (*The Dynamics of Medieval Iceland*), and recently collaborated with John Steinberg on the archaeology of medieval Iceland. He is a founding member and past president of the Society for Economic Anthropology.

Gary M. Feinman was one of the participants in the earliest meetings of the Society for Economic Anthropology (along with Linda Nicholas and Steve Kowalewski). He is well known for his contributions on craft specialization in Mesoamerica. His excavations and surveys in Oaxaca are reported in numerous issues of *Latin American Antiquity*. Currently he is involved in fieldwork in Oaxaca and China, as well as serving as chair of the Anthropology Department at the Field Museum of Natural History in Chicago.

Verenice Y. Heredia Espinoza received her PhD in anthropology in 2005 from Purdue University, where she studied with Richard Blanton. Heredia has published on Classic Maya craft specialization and on settlement patterns in the Mixteca Alta, Oaxaca. Her PhD research, funded by FAMSI and Purdue University, involved detailed new studies of ancient towns in the Mixteca, including the spectacular Peñasco at San Mateo. Heredia's research sheds light on the relatively "collective" social and political structure of the Late Formative and Early Classic state.

Dolores Koenig is professor of anthropology at American University in Washington, DC. She has worked on various aspects of the anthropology of development in French-speaking West Africa, with special emphasis on the ways in which household labor allocation responds to the changing political economy. With Tiéman Diarra and Moussa Sow, she has authored *Innovation and Individuality in African Development: Changing Production Strategies in Rural Mali*. Recent articles have appeared in *Journal of Political Ecology*, *Urban Anthropology and Studies of Cultural Systems and World Economic Development,* and the *Women and International Development Annual.*

Stephen A. Kowalewski is professor of anthropology, University of Georgia. He has studied change and continuity in Oaxaca since 1970. With Laura Finsten he published "The Economic Systems of Ancient Oaxaca: A Regional Perspective" (*Current Anthropology*). Most recently Kowalewski has been studying settlement patterns in the Mixteca Alta region of Oaxaca (a summary article appears in the *Journal of Field Archaeology,* 2000).

Robert C. Marshall is professor of anthropology in the Department of Anthropology at Western Washington University. He has been studying Japan's worker cooperatives since 1991 and was in Japan during 2002 as a Fellow of the Japan Foundation to investigate "senior cooperatives," the new consumer-worker hybrid cooperatives of, by, and for the elderly in Japan. His article "The Culture of Cooperation in Three Japanese Worker Cooperatives" appeared in *Economic and Industrial Democracy.*

Judith Martí is professor of anthropology at California State University, Northridge. She coedited with Mari Womack *The Other Fifty Percent: Multicultural Perspectives on Gender Relations* and has published chapters in several edited volumes, including "Nineteenth-Century Views of Women's Participation in Mexico's Markets," in *Mediating Identities, Marketing Wares.* Her research includes archival (nineteenth- and twentieth-century Mexico) and oral histories (Transnational Migration in Los Angeles, United Farm Workers of America). She is on the board of directors for the Institute of Gender, Globalization, and Democracy and is the secretary/treasurer of the Society for Economic Anthropology.

Linda M. Nicholas has mapped more residential terraces than any other archaeologist, and is now involved in excavations of residential terraces representing different social statuses at El Palmillo, in Oaxaca. She has over twenty-five years of experience working (alongside Gary Feinman) in Oaxaca. Nicholas has numerous publications on the Southwest, Mesoamerica, and China, including a chapter on human-land relationships in SEA vol. 10, *Understanding Economic Process.*

Sutti Ortiz is professor emerita at Boston University. She is author of *Uncertainties in Peasant Farming* and numerous articles on peasant decision making. She was the editor of the first conference volume of the association, *Economic Anthropology: Topics and Theories*, and coeditor of the decennial conference volume, *Understanding Economic Process*. Her recent research has been on the topic of rural labor market in Colombia and northern Argentina. It has appeared as a book, *Harvesting Coffee, Bargaining Wages*. She is the author of an article on labor for the *Annual Review of Anthropology*, 2002.

John R. Pulskamp holds an MA in anthropology from California State University, Northridge (CSUN) and is a Fellow in the Society for Applied Anthropology. He has presented papers for the American Anthropological Association, the Society for Applied Anthropology, the Society for Economic Anthropology, the Southwest Labor Studies Association, and others. He has taught anthropology at CSUN, and at East Los Angeles College. He writes not only from a basis of scholarly research but also from personal experience. For many years he was an active member and officer of a union representing over 8,000 technical and professional civil servants.

Martha Woodson Rees is head and associate professor of anthropology at the University of Cincinnati specializing in economic anthropology and Mexico (women's work, migration, households, and community). Having worked and lived in Mexico for over ten years, she has experience throughout Mexico and in Mexican anthropology institutions. In addition, she has worked with Latino migrants in Atlanta, Georgia, and in Cincinnati, Ohio. Her work uses survey and ethnographic methods to understand regional systems and communities, as well as individual and household interactions with those systems. Other publications are on indigenous technologies, migrants to Oaxaca City, and Atlanta Latinos.

Karaleah S. Reichart (PhD, Northwestern University) holds a joint appointment as adjunct assistant professor of anthropology, University of North Carolina, Chapel Hill, and lecturer, University of North Carolina, Greensboro. Professor Reichart specializes in the study of gender and industrial conflict and has presented her ethnographic research at invited and refereed talks, including the Institute for Work and Employment, Massachusetts Institute of

Technology; authored several peer-reviewed articles; and received grants and awards, including Best Dissertation prize from the Industrial Relations Research Association. She is currently writing a book, *Engendering Alliances.*

Susan D. Russell is a professor of cultural anthropology and director of the Center for Southeast Asian Studies at Northern Illinois University. She is interested in labor relations in fishing and maritime societies in the Philippines, as well as patterns of economic development and ritual change. She has edited three books, including *Structuralism's Transformations: Order and Revision in Indonesian and Malaysian Societies,* coedited with Lorraine Aragon, Arizona University Press. Her articles have appeared in the *Journal of Anthropological Research, Human Organization,* and other regional journals.

John M. Steinberg is a research associate at the Cotsen Institute of Archaeology at UCLA. He is an adjunct lecturer in anthropology at UCLA and California State University, Northridge. He was educated at the University of Chicago (BA), the University of Oxford (MSt), and UCLA (MA, PhD). His dissertation concerned stone tool production in Neolithic and Bronze Age Thy, Denmark. He is currently investigating Viking Age settlement patterns in Skagafjordur, Northern Iceland.

Tamar Diana Wilson is a research affiliate with the Department of Anthropology, University of Missouri, St. Louis. She has published articles on Mexican immigration in *Human Organization, Anthropology & Humanism Quarterly, Critique of Anthropology, Latin American Perspectives, Review of Radical Political Economics, Journal of Borderlands Studies,* and *Urban Anthropology.* She also does research on the informal sector in Mexico and has a forthcoming book, *Subsidizing Capitalism: Brickmakers on the U.S.-Mexico Border.*

Frank P. Zeidler, a resident of Milwaukee, Wisconsin, since 1912, was educated in the Milwaukee Public Schools and took correspondence courses from the University of Wisconsin. He did farmwork and had a land surveying business. He joined the Socialist Party in 1932 and has been its candidate for public offices on twelve occasions. He was elected mayor of Milwaukee in 1948 and reelected in 1952 and 1956. He was the Socialist candidate for president in 1976. He worked for the Ford Foundation and taught at colleges and universities. Currently he is an arbitrator and mediator. He has five honorary doctorates.

Christian Zlolniski is an assistant professor of anthropology and Mexican American studies at the University of Texas in Arlington. His research interests include labor, economic restructuring, and migration, particularly in the case of Mexican immigration to the United States. Currently he is participating in a collaborative research project about the impact of export-oriented agriculture on patterns of work and migration in Baja California, Mexico. He has published several articles in academic journals in the United States and Mexico, including *Human Organization* and *Revista Mexicana de Sociología.*